Environment, Climate Change and Migration in South Asia

Climate change has been fueling migration, and, according to some policy reports, there could more than one billion climate migrants/refugees across the world by 2050. In South Asia, disasters, environmental degradation, and climate change are increasing the number of migrants every year. In South Asia, like other parts of the world, migrants and displaced people mainly move within their respective countries, but some cross the porous border. At most places, the migrants and displaced people face hostile situation as they are not welcome by their local host population.

The chapters in the book highlight the challenges and inadequacies of governments and communities in protecting the environment as well as the disproportionate effect that climate change has on the poor and marginalized groups. The book also discusses the gendered experiences of climate-related migrations and policy measures which need to be implemented to counter forced displacements and environment degradation along with the legal and institutional resources which could help mitigate climate change and protect climate refugees.

This book will be of interest to students and researchers of development studies, ecology and environment, migration, sociology, law and governance, human ecology, climate change and economics.

Amit Ranjan is Research Fellow at the Institute of South Asian Studies, National University of Singapore. His latest book is *Urban Development and Environmental History in Modern South Asia* (edited with Ian Talbot). His papers, review essays and book reviews have been widely published in many journals.

Rajesh Kharat is Founder Director of the School of International Relations and Strategic Studies, and Dean, Humanities, University of Mumbai. He is Professor and former Chairperson at the Centre for South Asian Studies, School of International Studies at Jawaharlal Nehru University, New Delhi. He has published several books and research papers on contemporary issues of South Asia.

Pallavi Deka is a researcher on ecological politics and society in/of North East of India. She teaches political science at Department of Political Science, Handique Girl's College, Kamrup, Assam, India.

Migrations in South Asia

Series Editors: Pushpendra and Manish K Jha, Tata Institute of Social Sciences, India

This Series interrogates contemporary forms of migrations in the region shaped by colonial pasts of several South Asian countries and present global economic and political forces. The volumes in the Series intersect with various dimensions of migration such as gender, economic disparity, cross-border movements, citizenship, nativism, conflicts, identity, and religion. They engage with labour processes, urbanisation, agrarian relations, climate change, displacement, neoliberal developmentalism, and state policies. Using transdisciplinary perspectives, the Series intervenes in the socio-economic and cultural aspects of migration, histories, networks, linkages, disruptions, social movements, mutations in social relations, new technologies of migrants' enumeration and surveillance, and changing paradigm of government and politics in the countries of South Asia. The Series also aims to study the dynamics of international migration in and out of the region.

The Series will provide a platform for scholars in the South Asia region working on Migration Studies to share their work and create a vibrant research collective, thereby enriching and diversifying the field. The books in the series will be of interest to those in migration and refugee studies, development studies, social work, political economy, political studies, sociology and social anthropology, gender studies, contemporary history, South Asian Studies and Global South studies.

Home, Belonging and Memory in Migration
Leaving and Living
Edited by Sadan and Pushpendra

Environment, Climate Change and Migration in South Asia
Edited by Amit Ranjan, Rajesh Kharat, Pallavi Deka

For more information about this Series, please visit: www.routledge.com/Migrations-in-South-Asia/book-series/MIGSA

Environment, Climate Change and Migration in South Asia

Edited by Amit Ranjan, Rajesh Kharat and Pallavi Deka

Routledge
Taylor & Francis Group
LONDON AND NEW YORK

First published 2023
by Routledge
4 Park Square, Milton Park, Abingdon, Oxon OX14 4RN

and by Routledge
605 Third Avenue, New York, NY 10158

Routledge is an imprint of the Taylor & Francis Group, an informa business

British Library Cataloguing-in-Publication Data
A catalogue record for this book is available from the British Library

ISBN: 978-1-032-34428-7 (hbk)
ISBN: 978-1-032-43536-7 (pbk)
ISBN: 978-1-003-36780-2 (ebk)

DOI: 10.4324/9781003367802

Typeset in Sabon
by Apex CoVantage, LLC

To Shanaya

Contents

Figures

Tables

Contributors

Amit Ranjan is a research fellow at the Institute of South Asian Studies, National University of Singapore. His latest books include: (with Ian Talbot) *Urban Development and Environmental History in Modern South Asia* (Routledge, London, 2023) and *Contested Waters: India's Transboundary River Water Disputes in South Asia* (Routledge, London and New Delhi, 2020). He is also the author of *India-Bangladesh Border Disputes: History and Post-LBA Dynamics* (Springer, Singapore, 2018). Amit has edited the following books: *India in South Asia Challenges and Management* (Springer, Singapore, 2019), *Partition of India: Postcolonial Legacies* (Routledge, London and New Delhi, 2019) and *Water Issues in Himalayan South Asia: Internal Challenges, Disputes and Transboundary Tensions* (Singapore, 2019). His papers, review essays and book reviews have been widely published in journals, including Asian Survey, Asian Affairs, Asian Ethnicity, Asian Journal of Comparative Politics, Economic & Political Weekly, India Review, Indian Journal of Public Administration, India Quarterly, Journal of Migration Affairs, Journal of the Indian Ocean Region, Roundtable: The Commonwealth Journal of International Affairs, Social Change, Studies in Indian Politics, Society and Culture in South Asia, South Asia Research, Journal of Asian Security and International Affairs, Water History and World Water.

Bharati Torane has been teaching political science since 1994 at undergraduate level and working at Annasaheb Vartak College of Arts, Vasai Road, Palghar, Maharashtra, India. She has an MA in Political Science and her M.Phil. is on "Role of Maldives in SAARC", awarded from the Department of Civics and Politics, University of Mumbai, Mumbai. Recently, she has also submitted her doctoral thesis on "Foreign Policy of Maldives" at the same department of University of Mumbai.

Chetna Sharma is an associate professor at Delhi University's Kamala Nehru College. She is co-editor of Comparative Government and Politics (SAGE,

2019). She holds a Ph.D. in political science from the University of Delhi. Her research interests include minority rights, multiculturalism and citizenship.

Daisy Das completed her Ph.D. in Economics from IIT Guwahati, India and postdoctoral research from Sam Houston University, Texas, USA. At present, she has been working as an associate professor in Cotton University, India. Das has 20 years of teaching experience at both undergraduate and graduate level. Her field of interest is development and environmental economics. She has successfully completed several research projects. Besides presenting and delivering in different national and international conferences, Das has also published a large number of research papers in journals as well.

Dennis Mombauer has over a decade of experience working in research, management, administration and coordination in the private sector and the development sector. His key areas of work include coordination of knowledge management, communications and research activities across various projects, covering thematic areas related to climate change, adaptation and resilience, loss & damage, human mobility, climate finance, risk management, just transition, sustainable development, ecosystem conservation and others. Dennis is a member of several international technical expert groups and a regular contributor to national and international media outlets and scientific publications on climate risk management, adaptation, loss & damage, human mobility and related topics. He holds a master's degree in education, English studies and philosophy from the University of Cologne.

Dimpal Dekaraja is currently an assistant professor in the Department of Economics, Nawgaon College, Assam, India. Dekaraja's field of interest is human migration and development economics. She has authored and presented many papers in national seminars and conferences.

Emma Johnson is a climate communicator and journalist. She was a Pulitzer Center on Crisis Reporting fellow in Bhutan in 2019, reporting on the effect of climate change on the country's hydropower development. She also spent a year in Bhutan working for the School for Field Studies.

Farooq Sulehria teaches at Beaconhouse National University (BNU), Lahore. Author of *Media Imperialism in India and Pakistan* (Routledge), he holds a Ph.D. in Development Studies (SOAS). He has also co-edited *From Terrorism to Television: Dynamics of Media, State, and Society in Pakistan* (Routledge).

Fazlullah Akhtar is a senior researcher and postdoc fellow (AvH) at the Center for Development Research (ZEF), University of Bonn, Germany.

During his Ph.D. research at the University of Bonn, he analysed water availability and demand in the Kabul River Basin of Afghanistan. He is also a member of the peer reviewers' group of various international scientific journals in the fields of hydrology, water management, climate change, remote sensing and agriculture and so forth. Besides his academic efforts, Dr Akhtar has considerable experience working with UNFAO, Deutsche Welthungerhilfe, USAID and some prestigious governmental entities including the Ministry of Higher Education and the Presidential Palace (ARG) of Afghanistan.

Kaveri is a doctoral candidate at the *School of Social Work, Tata Institute of Social Sciences (TISS), Mumbai, India*. Before joining TISS, she worked with the *UNHCR-BOSCO* Project as a child protection officer. The nature of her work involved working with refugee children and unaccompanied minors. Her interests and research focus on statelessness, refugee and forced migration studies, human rights, citizenship, and human security. Her articles have been published in journals like Peace Review: Journal for Social Justice (University of San Francisco-Routledge) and Frontiers in Human Dynamics.She can be reached at: kaveri.urmil@yahoo.com

Pallavi Deka is an assistant professor of Political Science at Gauhati University's Handique Girls' College, Guwahati. She holds a Ph.D. from Jawaharlal Nehru University, Delhi. Her research interest lies in migration studies, public policy and north east India.

Pushpa Singh is an associate professor in the Department of Political Science, Miranda House, University of Delhi. She has done her doctoral research in gender and agroecology and has co-edited a book *Comparative Government and Politics* (SAGE India, 2019). Pushpa Singh has published her articles in many peer-reviewed journals such as *Studies in Indian Politics*, *Indian Journal of Public Administration* and *Contribution to Indian Sociology*. She has also contributed to many reference volumes published Thomson Reuters (London), World Scientific (Singapore), Academic Press, Elsevier (USA), Orient Blackswan (India) and Pierson (India). Besides, she has several online publications as a part of e-content generation by ILLL, DU and has been engaged with international and national projects in her research area sponsored by IDS Sussex, ICSSR and DU. She has been actively involved with curriculum development of University of Delhi and IGNOU and has audited the Kings College of London Summer School (2013).

Rajesh Kharat is Founder Director of School of International Relations and Strategic Studies, and Dean, Humanities, University of Mumbai (on deputation). He is a professor and former chairperson at the Centre for South

Asian Studies, School of International Studies and former Chief Advisor EOO at JNU, New Delhi. He has published several books and over 30 research papers on contemporary issues of South Asia. He has started Online Interdisciplinary Research Journals of University of Mumbai, *Sambhasan* (English), *Shodhavari* (Hindi) and *Sambhashit* (Marathi).

Ratul Mahanta is currently a professor in the Economics Department of University of Gauhati, Assam, India. Mahanta's field of interests include environmental economics, natural resources economics and health economics. He has authored a number of articles and presented papers in both national international conferences. Mahanta has published many papers in Elsevier and Springer.

Rishi Gupta is a research fellow at the New York-based Asia Society Policy Institute's India centre. He is a visiting fellow at the Asian Institute of Diplomacy and International Affairs (AIDIA), Kathmandu, Nepal. He was previously associated with the Vivekananda International Foundation, Center for Air Power Studies and Pondicherry University. He holds a Ph.D. from the School of International Studies, Jawaharlal Nehru University (JNU). He was a visiting fellow at the Institute of South Asian Studies, Sichuan University, Chengdu, China. His areas of research interest include the Indo-Pacific, South Asian Regional Security, Himalayan Politics and India's National Security.

Sumallya Mukhopadhyay is Assistant Professor at the Department of English, Faculty of Media Studies and Humanities, Manav Rachna University, Delhi-NCR. He has been awarded the International Oral History Association Scholarship (2020), TATA Trusts – Partition Archive Research Grant (2021) and South Asia Speaks Fellowship (2022). His articles have been published in journals like Narrative Culture (Wayne State University Press) and Studies in People's History (SAGE).

Usman Shah is a graduate of Monash University, Australia. He conducted his M.A. research on the local impacts of integrated water resource management interventions amongst communities in the Kunduzand Takhar provinces of Afghanistan. He continues to contribute to research on development issues related to natural resources, conflict, migration and security.

Vositha Wijenayake is a researcher and an attorney-at-law specializing in international environmental law and public international law. She has over a decade of experience in working on climate change at national and international level with a special focus on climate change adaptation; climate-induced loss and damage; human mobility; inclusive and participatory climate resilience-building; gender; youth; stakeholder engagement and technology transfer. Vositha is a member of the National Expert

Committee on Climate Change Adaptation of the Ministry of Environment of Sri Lanka and a negotiator for the government of Sri Lanka for the UNFCCC negotiations since 2016. Vositha has an LLM in public international law and an LLB from University of London and a BA (Special Degree) in Humanities from University of Kelaniya, Sri Lanka. Her publications focus on topics related to climate change and sustainable development; resilience building; addressing vulnerabilities and risk management; stakeholder engagement, youth and good governance; gender; climate-induced migration and climate and disaster risk finance.

Preface

This edited book is a collection of papers submitted by the contributors for the Tata Institute of Social Sciences, Routledge series on Migrations in South Asia. Chapters in this edited book discuss the environmental situation in respective South Asian countries, the impact of climate change, and how natural disasters are causing migration and internal displacement in the region. In addition to eight South Asian countries – India, Pakistan, Afghanistan, Sri Lanka, Bangladesh, Nepal, Bhutan, and the Maldives – Myanmar, a part of South East Asia, has been included in this study because of its proximity, and environmental and political spillover effects on South Asia.

Acknowledgements

The editors have been assisted by friends and colleagues too numerous to acknowledge. We are thankful to series editors – Professor Pushpendra and Manish K. Jha – for providing us an opportunity to edit this book as a part of the Tata Institute of Social Sciences, Routledge series. We are grateful to our contributors who submitted their research papers to us within the deadline. Reports from anonymous reviewers helped us improve the book's initial draft. We acknowledge them. Finally, we thank Antara, Shloka and others from Routledge for their support.

Amit Ranjan, Rajesh Kharat and Pallavi Deka

Introduction

Amit Ranjan, Rajesh Kharat and Pallavi Deka

According to the United Nations Department of Economic and Social Affairs study, in 2022 , the two most populous regions of the world were in Asia: Eastern and South-Eastern Asia with 2.3 billion people (29 per cent of the global population), and Central and Southern Asia with 2.1 billion (26 per cent).[1] Population of South Asia, as estimated in various studies, is around 24.89 percent of the total world population.[2] The South Asia region stretches from the high Himalayan peaks to the fertile delta of some of the important river systems of the world to the Indian Ocean. Such a vast geographic expansion means that the region does not have a single climate condition. Like other parts of the world, the different climate regions of South Asia are also witnessing serious environmental problems due to climate change.[3] The environmental consequences of climate change are even forcing some people to migrate from their place of living.[4] According to a policy note, published by the World Bank, if effective steps are not taken to arrest the global rise in temperature, by 2050, the number of "internal climate migrants" in South Asia could be more than 40 million. The report also observes that the share of "climate migrants" in the total internal migrants could reach to 25 percent.[5]

It is evident that since ancient times, people across the world and in South Asia have been moving from one place to another due to reasons associated with environmental deterioration and climate change.[6] Environmental factors were also highly referred as an important factor in the first systematic studies on migration. In his work, German-English geographer Ernst Georg Ravenstein (1834–1913) talked about "unattractive climate" that produce currents of migration. Another geographer, Ellen Churchill Semple (1863–1932), talked about how better environmental conditions attract people and make many to move from their original habitat.[7]

However, it is only in the past 30 years or so that the international community has eventually recognised a close linkage between climate change, environment degradation and human mobility.[8] To cut down the effects of climate change, until the early second decade of 2000, international community has largely focused on mitigation by setting emissions targets for developed and developing countries and efforts were made to bring in new

DOI:10.4324/9781003367802-1

members to a post-Kyoto 2012 framework.[9] Migration has turned into an important point of discussion only when countries began to pay larger attention to adaptation.[10]

In 1990, the first United Nations (UN) intergovernmental panel's report on climate change stated that "the gravest effects of climate change may be those on human migration as millions will be displaced".[11] Also discussed in Chapter 1 of the book, the use of the term "climate migrants" has become popular as a subcategory of "environment migrants" to signify the recent trends of migration pattern in reference to changes in the climate.[12] The terms such as "environmental migrants" or "climate refugees" have raised controversies. The juxtaposition of the terms "environment" or "climate" with "migrants" or "refugees" has been criticised for implying a mono-causal relationship between environmental factors and human mobility.[13] It is argued by many scholars that harsh decision such as leaving one's place has always been a decision of the last resort that is a combination of many factors that pushes people to take such extreme steps. So only limiting the blame to climatic factors may undermine the socio-economic and political aspects of such decisions.[14]

In South Asia, people are living through a "new climate normal".[15] More than half of all people living in South Asia, or 750 million people in the eight countries – Afghanistan, Bangladesh, Bhutan, India, Maldives, Nepal, Pakistan, and Sri Lanka – have been affected by one or more climate-related disasters in the last two decades.[16] According to Internal Displacement Monitoring Centre (IDMC) report 2019, in South Asia, as the countries struggle to manage weather-related extremes, more than 3.3 million people were newly displaced in 2018.[17]

In India, 2.8 million people across its 15 states were displaced because of weather-related hazards. Years of successive dry spells and below average rainfall in Afghanistan caused drought that forced about 371,000 new displacements in 2018. In Sri Lanka, around 75,000 new displacements were recorded in the second half of May 2018. Then riverine floods in Bangladesh triggered 12,000 new displacements in Moulvibazar district and riverbank erosion around 44,000 in Shariatpur, mainly in September 2018.[18] Focusing on the displacements during the monsoon season, the IDMC report of 2021 titled "Internal Displacement in a Changing Climate" stated Cyclone Amphan of May 2020 caused around 2.5 million new displacements in Bangladesh, mostly in the form of pre-emptive evacuations.[19] The cyclone also led to evacuation of more than 2.4 million people in India, particularly in the eastern states of India, West Bengal and Odisha. Then, two weeks later, Cyclone Nisarga prompted another 170,000 evacuations in the western states of Maharashtra and Gujarat. The 2020 south-west monsoon in India triggered about 763,000 displacement between early June and late October.[20] In 2020, the monsoon flood caused displacement of around 1.9 million people in Bangladesh. In 2020, three-month-long monsoon affected the entire Pakistan, particularly Sindh province. The Sindh province accounted for almost all the 810,000 new disaster displacements recorded in Pakistan in 2020.[21] The monsoon in Nepal triggered 48,000 new displacements between June and September 2020.[22] Several such hotspots of climate in- and out-migration are in transboundary areas and that internal migration does not necessarily stop short at borders. They include parts of Nepal, as well as parts of western Bangladesh, along the border with India.[23]

More number of people from the region are expected to face displacement due to weather-related factors, as mentioned earlier. The devastating consequences of the rise in global temperature have been widely discussed in many international, regional and governmental reports. One such comprehensive report on impact of rising global temperature is prepared by the Intergovernmental Panel on Climate Change (IPCC) since its establishment in 1988. IPCC prepared its First Assessment Report in 1990. In August, the IPCC released the first of four reports of its sixth assessment report of Working Group 1 titled "Climate Change 2021: The Physical Science Basis," which finds that if the global warming does not limit to 1.5 degree centigrade or even 2 degree centigrade, its consequences will be beyond reach.[24] The report holds human activities responsible for approximately 1.1 degree centigrade of global warming since 1850 till 1900. The report observes that for 1.5 degree centigrade of global warming, there will be an increase in heatwaves, longer summers and shorter cold seasons. At 2 degree centigrade of global warming, heat extremes would reach at "critical tolerance thresholds for agriculture and health."[25]

About the Indian subcontinent, the IPCC's 2021 report says that there may be an increase in heatwaves and droughts, and more rainfall and cyclones.[26] Expressing his concerns on climate change and related impact, Indian Meteorological Department director, Mrutunjay Mohapatra, said that globally, there is a rise in temperatures by about 1.2 degree Celsius compared to 100 years ago. This has an impact on extreme weather events like heavy rainfall and moderate to light rainfall. He predicts that if this scenario continues then temperature can rise as high as 4 to 5 degrees Celsius by the end of this century that will lead to more frequent and intense extreme events like heatwave, rainstorm, floods in increased area and duration.[27]

It has been claimed that climate change is anticipated to take the heaviest toll on the Pacific, South Asia, and Southeast Asia. Eight of the 10 countries with the greatest number of people living in low-elevation coastal zones are located in these regions. The 2011 Vulnerability Index, assembled by the risk advisory firm Maplecroft, showed that Asian and Pacific countries represent 6 out of the 10 most vulnerable countries worldwide, all ranked as countries at extreme risk. Bangladesh tops the list, followed by India (2nd), Nepal (4th), the Philippines (6th), Afghanistan (8th), and Myanmar (10th).[28] In another revelation, the "Environmental Risk Outlook 2021" report by the same organisation, it has been confirmed yet again that amongst world's 576 largest urban centres on their exposure to a range of environmental and climate-related threats, 99 of the world's 100 riskiest cities are in Asia, including 37 in China and 43 in India.[29]

In a research paper published in *Nature Communications*, Scott A. Kulp and Benjamin H. Strauss (2019)[30] from *Climate Central* argue that the projected rise in sea levels by 2050 would be higher enough to threaten land which are currently home to about 150 million people to a permanently below the high-tide line. The worst-affected Asian countries from the sea rise would be the Maldives, China, Bangladesh, India, Vietnam, Indonesia, Thailand, the Philippines and Japan. The picture used by the authors to show the affected areas from the sea flooding includes Mumbai and few other coastal cities of India.[31] Bangladesh, Sri Lanka and the Maldives are the other three South Asian countries with significant coastal line. On threat from climate change and linking with internal displacement in her country, Bangladesh's Prime Minister Sheikh Hasina has told the United Nations that one-metre rise in sea level – a plausible scenario – this century would submerge a fifth of the country and turn 30 million people into climate migrants.[32]

Not only floods, the South Asian countries are also likely to experience droughts in many parts, which may lead to more out-migration of the poor people. It is already happening in some parts of India, as an earlier report by the Centre for Development Alternatives shows.[33]

Unlike other South Asian countries, Bhutan is a small landlocked but ecologically rich country located in the north-east end of the region. It is facing climate change challenges due to uneven development and dispersed geography. Despite being a water-rich country, some parts of Bhutan are expected to face water stress by 2030.[34] Bhutan is also among the Vulnerable 20 Group (V20) members, a forum of 20 countries of climate vulnerability launched in 2015.[35] Nepal and Afghanistan are the other two landlocked countries from the region. In 2016, that a village in upper Mustang in Nepal had to be relocated gives a glimpse of the impact and case for human mobility.[36] According to the United Nations Environment Programme, 80% of the conflicts in Afghanistan are related to land, water and food insecurity, which are immediate consequences of global warming.[37]

According to the Global Climate Risk index 2021, Pakistan is one among the most vulnerable to the impacts of weather-related events in the world when it comes to the effects of climate change over the past two decades.[38] Arid region of Baluchistan is one of the most vulnerable to water scarcity situation. This province has faced many severe droughts in the past, that is, 1967–1969, 1971, 1973–1975, 1994 and 1998–2002, which had a drastic impact on livelihoods and its economy.[39] Then, the Karachi heatwave of June 2015 created havoc and killed more than 1,200 people.[40] Not only summer heat, Pakistan has also witnessed a number of flooding seasons. One of the most severe flood occurred in 2010 in which around 1600 people died, 38, 600 square kilometers of area inundated and a damage worth around US$10 billion happened.[41] The floods of 2022 were more severe than the one occurred in 2010. According to the Pakistani media reports 33 million people were affected and more than eight million displaced.[42]

More serious than the other South Asian countries, the Maldives faces existential threat due to climate change. According to multiple reports published by the National Aeronautics and Space Administration and the U.S. Geological Survey, almost 80% of the Maldives could become uninhabitable by 2050. At present, 80 per cent of the total islands of the Maldives are just a metre above sea level, making them vulnerable to rising sea waters.[43] To deal with the situation, in 2008 the then President-designate Mohamed Nasheed and now speaker of the Maldivian parliament, said,

> We can do nothing to stop climate change on our own and so we have to buy land elsewhere. It's an insurance policy for the worst possible outcome. After all, the Israelis [began by buying] land in [the] Palestine . . . We do not want to leave the Maldives, but we also do not want to be climate refugees living in tents for decades.[44]

He also said that Sri Lanka and India were possible options as they have similar culture, cuisine and climate. Australia was also considered due to the availability of large tracts of unoccupied land.[45]

Even though Myanmar is not a part of the contemporary political South Asia, migration from the country affects politics, economics and social fabric of the region. More than a million Rohingya Muslims from Myanmar have taken refuge in the South Asian countries, primarily in Bangladesh and India. Moreover, climate-related happenings in Myanmar affect South Asia and vice versa. For instance, on May 1, 2008, tropical Cyclone Nargis devastated an unprepared Myanmar. The cyclone led to the deaths of over 138,000 people and destroyed lands along Myanmar's coastline and Irrawaddy delta, making it among the 10 most destructive cyclones in recorded history. Coastal lands were flooded, and tidal surges inundated low-lying areas including the nation's most populous city, Yangon.[46] Nargis also landed in South Asia. Then, in 2020, as mentioned earlier, Cyclone Amphan has devastating impact on Myanmar, Bangladesh and India.

As the climate change is affecting all aspects of human life, several literatures have been published looking at it from various dimensions. One such dimension is migration and displacement of people. In this book, an effort has been made to investigate links between weather hazards, climate change, environment disaster and migration in South Asia. This edited book has eleven chapters apart from introduction. It has studied eight South Asian countries and Myanmar because of aforementioned reasons. Three broad objectives, which have also worked as the basic framework for each chapter of the book, are identified as follows:

1 Look at the scenarios of migration due to environmental reasons.
2 The policy responses of the countries in South Asia are examined in order to find out their effectiveness.

3 As the weaker sections of population within the respective South Asian countries are most vulnerable to the impacts of climate change, an attempt is being made to mainly discuss the issue from their perspective.

This edited book starts with a chapter by Amit Ranjan titled "Climate Change, Environmental Migration and Population Displacement". The author, primarily, argues that unlike other forms of migration, environmental migrants move to other place to protect their lives and for livelihood. This chapter begins with a theoretical explanation to the question as to why people migrate. Referring extensively to the global organizations reports and documents and critical literatures on the theme, this chapter shows that the impact of the climate change is going to worsen in the coming days.

The second chapter "The Spectre of Climate Change-Induced Migration in Afghanistan" by Fazlullah Akhtar and Usman Shah investigates a detailed relation climate change has with life condition in Afghanistan. The impacts of climate change are expected to be amplified in future by more rapid spring snowmelt combined with the downstream effects such as land degradation, vegetative cover loss, land mismanagement, decrease in crop productivity; changes in livelihood; fall in the amount of exports; financial losses as well forced migration.[47] This chapter argues that climate change has served to exacerbate existing livelihood vulnerabilities and create the tipping point motivating once-resilient populations to eventually migrate.

Bringing into the uniqueness of the location and magnitude of the problem, the third chapter of the book by Pallavi Deka. "Changing Climate and New Migration Crisis in Bangladesh" is an attempt to cover the situation where Bangladesh is placed when the climate change effects are becoming rapid. It also looks into the role of the governmental mechanisms in this situation. This chapter depicts the effects of flood, drought, cyclone and erosion and the coping strategy of the people. The sections on climate change's impact in the Char areas and sea coast look at the struggle of the people to survive due to changing climate.

The fourth chapter "Climate Change and Refugees in Bhutan: The Future Impacts" by Emma Johnson explores the variety of ways that climate change will affect ecosystem, people, politics, economics and culture in Bhutan and also tries to highlight the possible future pathways for handling this crisis and potential cases of climate refugees.

In fifth chapter "Climate Change and Displacement in India: A Gendered Perspective", Pushpa Singh and Chetna Sharma bring in the argument that climate change impacts countries and people differently. In South Asia, the intersectionality of gender and poverty makes women particularly susceptible. This chapter discusses the climate change-induced displacements, particularly during droughts and floods from a gendered lens and proposes that government policies must be structured in ways that are mindful of all these critical aspects of vulnerability and marginality.

The sixth chapter by Daisy Das, Dimpal Dekaraja, and Ratul Mahanta "The Dynamics of Deforestation, Riverbank Erosion and Migration in India With Special Reference to Assam" is a study on the extent of deforestation in India and its relation with migration. In this chapter, the authors have focused on the Indian state of Assam which shows that the extent of migration is related with crop land eroded area. This study shows that distressed people mostly migrate to other areas to compensate the income loss caused by erosion and resulting land degradation. Some people do not migrate and use coping strategies in the less erosion prone areas. But severely affected people are left with no other options than to migrate. The entire discourse reveals that India needs afforestation measures and stringent actions for environmental conservation. Climate is changing mainly because of anthropogenic activities and carbon emission due to energy use has been identified as the devil and afforestation will definitely help to combat climate change.

The seventh chapter "Climate Change-Induced Internally Displaced Persons of the Maldives" by Bharati discusses the factors responsible for the climate change-induced internal migration in the Maldives. It also tries to see how Small Island Developing States (SIDSs) like the Maldives have raised the issues of small island countries' vulnerabilities, namely, the erosion of coastal areas and beaches which are impacting the Maldivian livelihood besides submergence of coastal flooding due to climate change. The chapter highlights the policies adopted by Maldives to deal with the situation. It also looks into the role of non-state actors to mitigate the challenges posed by the climate change in Maldives.

The eighth chapter "Understanding Climate Change and Its Impact on Myanmar: Perspectives on Migration, Migrants and Legal Framework" by Kaveri and Sumallya highlights that while those who possess resources and social capital somehow manage to assimilate to the new surroundings, the vulnerability of those from marginalised sections comes to the forefront as they are mainly employed in the informal sectors. Following this, the chapter probes into the various strategies taken by the Myanmar government to harness community resilience against climate change. The chapter foregrounds that introducing an adequate legal framework will bring forth innovative strategies to mitigate and adapt to climate change. The chapter looks at the strategies taken by the government in Myanmar to harness community resilience against climate change. It also highlights the various complications that migrants, as well as countries, come across due to the lack of any governing legal framework to protect climate-induced migrants.

Ninth chapter of this book by Rajesh Kharat and Rishi Gupta looks at the issue of climate change-induced migration and challenges faced by Nepal. Being landlocked and vulnerable to the topography and constant natural disasters, Nepal has always been facing the implications of climate change. The structural developments initiated by the Government of Nepal have also exposed Nepal's helplessness to cope up with the inadequacies of limited institutional capacity, low-income level and limited irrigations facilities despite the abundance hydrological resources. Additionally, due to low-income level, the large proportions of marginal farmers with small landholding are dependent on natural resources which increase the degree of vulnerabilities of climate change. As a result, the effects of climate change for instance, higher flood risks, enhanced soil erosion and diversions of river flows, natural disasters like landslides, eruption of volcanoes, epidemic diseases compel local people to displace from one place to other. Particularly, during the floods, landslides and earthquakes there is tremendous mobility of those people who are inhabited around these locations.

In his chapter, "Pakistan's Climate Migrants Beyond Mediatized Fictions", Farooq Sulehria examines Pakistan's burgeoning environmental challenge in order to foreground the link between climate change and patterns of human migration. Empirical evidence suggests an alarming situation whereby, on the one hand, the country ranks atop the global Climate Risk indices, on the other, climate changes and recurring natural catastrophe are displacing millions in the country. Meantime, the state in Pakistan is ill-prepared to deal with either the climate change or climate-induced migration. Though some policy measures and concrete actions in the past two decades have been initiated – offering some reason for optimism – yet an overall balance sheet is unconvincing to say the least.

Chapter 11, "Climate-Induced Migration in Sri Lanka: Vulnerability, Mobility, and Resilience" by Dennis Mombauer and Vositha Wijenayake, outlines the nexus of migration and climate change impacts, especially prolonged droughts, soil degradation, and changing precipitation patterns, and provides an overview of the socio-economic characteristics of vulnerable households, existing protection systems, gender-specific impacts, the impacts on youth and children, and aspects of equity and social justice.

The three editors would like to thank the series editors, Professor Pushpendra and Professor Manish Kumar Jha, for their encouragement in completing this book. This book could not be completed without cooperation from the contributors. The editors are thankful to all contributors for their contributions. Finally, we are thankful to Antara Raychaudhury and her team from Routledge, Taylor and Francis.

Notes

1 United Nations Department of Economic and Social Affairs, Population Division (2022), World Population Prospects 2022, Summary of Results, accessed from https://population,un.org/wpp/ on 5th January 2023.

2. Population of Southern Asia" accessed from http://www.worldmeters.info on 2nd March 2022.

3 Asian Development Bank (2010), "Climate change in South Asia", accessed from www.adb.org/sites/default/files/publication/27475/climate-change-sa.pdf on 5th May 2019.

4 Asian Development Bank, "Addressing climate change and migration in Asia and Pacific", 3–4, accessed from www.adb.org/sites/default/files/publication/29662/addressing-climate-change-migration.pdf on 9th April 2020.
5 World Bank Group, Groundswell, Preparing for Internal Climate Migration, Internal Climate Migration in South Asia, Policy Note 2, accessed from https://openknowledge.worldbank.org/bitstream/handle/10986/29461/GroundswellPN2.pdf?sequence=7&isAllowed=y.
6 Bahadur Kotlia, et al. (2021), "Last 5ka in South Asia: Climate and civilization, quaternary international", July, Vol. 599–600, 1–3, accessed from www.sciencedirect.com/science/article/abs/pii/S1040618221003840?via%3Dihub on 3rd February 2022.
7 E. G. Ravenstein (1885), "The laws of migration", *Journal of the Royal Statistical Society*, 52(2), 167–235, accessed from www.jstor.org/stable/2979181 on 10th October 2019.
8 Frank Laczko and Christine Aghazarm (ed.) (2009), *Migration, environment and climate change: Assessing the evidence*. International Organization of Migration, 13, accessed from https://publications.iom.int/system/files/pdf/migration_and_environment.pdf on 3rd March 2020.
9 Post Kyoto Framework is about further negotiations amongst signatories of Kyoto Protocol to come up with roadmap to meet with the expectations of both developed and developing countries which have not not been able to reduce absolute emission of Carbon dioxide at global level. See A. Ghezloun, A. Saidane, N. Oucher, and S. Chergui " The Post-Kyoto" *Energy Procedia* 36(2013), 1–8.
10 Oli Brown (2008), *Migration and climate change*. Geneva: International Organization for Migration, p. 36, accessed from https://publications.iom.int/books/world-migration-report-2022 on 31st December 2021.
11 Cited in Etienne Piguet, Antoine Pécoud and Paul de Guchteneire (2011), "Migration and climate change: An overview", *Refugee Survey Quarterly*, 33(3), 5, accessed from https://doc.rero.ch/record/208657/files/Piguet_Etienne_-_Migration_and_Climate_Change_An_Overview_20131112.pdf on 12th November 2021.
12 Marie McAulife and Anna Triandafyllidou (eds.) (2021), *World migration report 2022*. Geneva: International Organization for Migration, 379, accessed from https://publications.iom.int/books/world-migration-report-2022 on 2nd May 2022.
13 Etienne Piguet, Antoine Pécoud and Paul de Guchteneire (2011), "Migration and climate change: An overview", *Refugee Survey Quarterly*, 33(3), 16, accessed from https://doc.rero.ch/record/208657/files/Piguet_Etienne_-_Migration_and_Climate_Change_An_Overview_20131112.pdf on 12th November 2021.
14 Oli Brown (2008), *Migration and climate change*. Geneva: International Organization for Migration, accessed from www.ipcc.ch/apps/njlite/srex/njlite_download.php?id=5866 on 25th April 2020.
15 World Bank Group (2021), "Climate change action plan 2021–2025: South Asia roadmap", accessed from https://openknowledge.worldbank.org/handle/10986/36321?locale-attribute=es on 2nd April 2022.
16 Van Bernice Bronkhorst (2012), *Disaster risk management in South Asia: Regional overview (English)*. Washington, DC: World Bank Group, accessed from http://documents.worldbank.org/curated/en/648281468170977802/Disaster-risk-management-in-South-Asia-regionaloverview on 23rd May 2020.
17 Internal Displacement Monitoring Centre (2019), "Global report on internal displacement report", 34, accessed from www.internal-displacement.org/global-report/grid2019/ on 19th August 2020.

18 Internal Displacement Monitoring Centre (2019), "Global report on internal displacement report", 35, accessed from www.internal-displacement.org/global-report/grid2019/ on 19th August 2020.
19 GRID (2021), "Internal displacement in a changing climate", 52, accessed from www.internal-displacement.org/publications/2021-global-report-on-internal-displacement on 19th January 2022.
20 Ibid., 53.
21 Ibid., 56.
22 Ibid.
23 World Bank Group, Groundswell, Preparing for Internal Climate Migration, Internal Climate Migration in South Asia, Policy Note 2.
24 IPCC (2021), "Climate change widespread, rapid, and intensifying", *IPCC*, accessed from www.ipcc.ch/2021/08/09/ar6-wg1-20210809-pr/ on 19th August 2021.
25 Ibid.
26 IPCC (2021), "Climate change 2021: The physical science basis", 41, accessed from www.ipcc.ch/report/ar6/wg1/downloads/report/IPCC_AR6_WGI_Full_Report.pdf on 19th December 2021. And Esha Roy and Amitabh Sinha (2021, 10 August), "India may see more heat waves, droughts, cyclones: IPCC report", *The Indian Express*, accessed from https://indianexpress.com/article/india/ipcc-report-india-asia-climate-change-heat-waves-cyclones-7445511/ on 18th July 2019.
27 Express News Service (2021, 5 August), "Dr. Mohapatra: Extreme weather events will become more frequent and more intense", *The Indian Express*, accessed from https://indianexpress.com/article/explained/extreme-weather-events-will-become-more-frequent-and-more-intense-7438842/ on 5th August 2021.
28 Asian Development Bank (2012), "Addressing climate change and migration in Asia and the Pacific", accessed from www.adb.org/sites/default/files/publication/29662/addressing-climate-change-migration.pdf on 11th May 2020.
29 Will Nichols (2021), "Asian cities in eye of environmental Storm-global ranking, environmental risk outlook", accessed from www.maplecroft.com/insights/analysis/asian-cities-in-eye-of-environmental-storm-global-ranking/ on 1st June 2021.
30 Scott A. Kulp and Benjamin H. Strauss (2019, 12 December), "New elevation data triple estimates of global vulnerability to sea level rise and coastal flooding", *Nature Communication*, accessed from www.nature.com/articles/s41467-019-12808-z on 6th December 2019.
31 Ibid.
32 United Nations (2014, 27 September), "The 69th session of UNGA, address by HE Sheikh Hasina, Honourable Prime Minister, Government of People's Republic of Bangladesh", accessed from www.un.org/en/ga/69/meetings/gadebate/pdf/BD_en.pdf on 17th March 2019.
33 Anil Kr. Roy and Indira Hirway (2007), "Multiple impacts of droughts and assessment of drought policy in major drought prone states in India, Centre for Development Alternatives and Planning Commission of India", accessed from https://niti.gov.in/planningcommission.gov.in/docs/reports/sereport/ser/stdy_droght.pdf on 7th July 2019.
34 Amit Ranjan (2018), "India-Bhutan hydropower projects: Cooperation and concerns", *ISAS Insights*, accessed from www.isas.nus.edu.sg/papers/309-india-bhutan-hydropower-projects-cooperation-and-concerns/ on 18th June 2019.
35 Emily Wikinson, Lisa Schipper and Catherine Simonet (2016), *Climate change, migration and the 2030 agenda for sustainable development*. Overseas Development Institution, Swiss Agency for Development and Cooperation, accessed from

https://odi.org/en/publications/climate-change-migration-and-the-2030-agenda-for-sustainable-development/ on 1st August 2021.
36 Relief Web (2017), "Nepal: Climate change and human mobility", accessed from https://reliefweb.int/report/nepal/nepal-climate-change-and-human-mobility on 1st November 2019.
37 Sune Engel Rasmussen (2017, 28 August), "How climate change is a death sentence in Afghanistan highland", *The Guardian*, accessed from www.theguardian.com/world/2017/aug/28/how-climate-change-is-death-sentence-afghanistan-highlands-global-warming on 19th November 2020.
38 D. Eckstein, V. Kunzel and L. Schafer (2021), "Global climate risk index 2021", Briefing paper, *Germanwatch*, accessed from www.germanwatch.org/en/19777 on 2nd November 2022.
39 Falak Naz, G. H. Dars, K. Ansari, S. Jamro and N. Y. Krakauer (2020, 10 February), "Drought trends in Balochistan", *Water*, 12, 470, accessed from www.mdpi.com/journal/water on 2nd August 2020.
40 Q. Z. Chaudhry, G. Rasul, A. Kamal, M. Mangrio and S. Mahmood (2015), *Karachi heat wave event June 2015*. Islamabad: Technical Report for the Ministry of Climate Change Pakistan, accessed from http://mocc.gov.pk/SiteImage/Misc/files/Final%20Heat%20Wave%20Report%203%20August%202015.pdf on 22nd May 2020.
41 A. Ali (2013), *Indusbasin floods: Mechanism, impacts and management*. Manila: ADB, 40, accessed from www.adb.org/sites/default/files/publication/30431/indus-basin-floods.pdf on 7th June 2020.
42 "UN sees looming crisis for flood victims in winter", *Dawn*, 11 December 2022, accessed from https://www.dawn.com/news/1725707 on 17th December 2022.
43 Daniel Manzo, Ginger Zee, Sohel Uddin and Dragana Jovanovic (2021, 3 November), "Facing dire sea level rise threat, Maldives turns to climate change solutions to survive", *ABCNEWS*, accessed from https://abcnews.go.com/International/facing-dire-sea-level-rise-threat-maldives-turns/story?id=80929487 on 1st December 2021.
44 Randeep Ramesh (2008, 10 November), "Paradise almost lost: Maldives seeks to buy new homeland", *The Guardian*, accessed from www.theguardian.com/environment/2008/nov/10/maldives-climate-change on 1st December 2021.
45 Ibid.
46 Chew-Hung Chang (2011, March), "Preparedness and storm hazards in a global warming world: Lessons from Southeast Asia", *Natural Hazards*, 56, 677, https://doi.org/10.1007/s11069-010-9581
47 M. Savage, B. Dougherty, M. Hamza, R. Butterfield and S. Bharwani (2009), *Socio-economic impacts of climate change in Afghanistan*. Oxford: Stockholm Environment Institute, accessed from www.weadapt.org/sites/weadapt.org/files/legacy-new/placemarks/files/5345354491559sei-dfid-afghanistan-report-1-.pdf on 28th August 2019.

Chapter 1

Climate Change, Environmental Migration and Population Displacement

Amit Ranjan

Migration of people from one place to the other has been going on since ancient time. People migrate for different reasons, and one of them is impact on environment due to climate change. In recent years, climate change happens because of an increase in the emission of the greenhouse gases (GHG) which raises the temperature of the earth. In its first of four reports of its sixth assessment report of Working Group 1, published in August 2021 and titled *Climate Change 2021: The Physical Science Basis*, the Intergovernmental Panel on Climate Change (IPCC) finds that if the global warming does not limit to 1.5 degree centigrade or even 2 degree centigrade, its consequences will be beyond reach.[1] The report holds human activities responsible for rise in approximately 1.1 degree centigrade of global warming since 1850–1900. The report observes that at 1.5 degree centigrade of global warming, there will be an increase in heatwaves, longer summers and shorter cold seasons. At 2 degree centigrade of global warming, heat extremes would reach at "critical tolerance thresholds for agriculture and health".[2] As weather is expected to turn more unpredictable and erratic, many people are likely to be affected and migrate and displace from their current location.

Unlike the normal patterns of migration, environment-related migration is mainly for survival. Before moving ahead, it is better to clear some globally used terms and phrases for people who move out from their homes due to environmental reasons. First, environmental migrants are those who, "predominantly for reasons of sudden or progressive changes in the environment that adversely affect their lives or living conditions, are obliged to leave their habitual homes, or choose to do so, either temporarily or permanently, and who move within their country or abroad".[3] There is no international consensus on appropriate terminology, the International Organisation for Migration (IOM) has provided working definition for environmental migrants.[4] Second, environmentally displaced persons are those "who are displaced within their country of habitual residence or who have crossed an international border and for whom environmental degradation, deterioration or destruction is a major cause of their displacement, although not necessarily the sole one."[5] The term "environmentally displaced person" is used as a less controversial alternative to environmental refugee or climate refugee

DOI:10.4324/9781003367802-2

that have no legal basis or raison d'être in international law, "to refer to a category of environmental migrants whose movement is of a clearly forced nature".[6] Nevertheless, some of the scholars use the term "climate refugees" and "climate migrants". Third, migration influenced by environmental change is a situation "where environmental change can be identified as affecting the drivers of migration, and thus is a factor in the decision to migrate".[7] Besides defining various terms used for environment related migrations and displacements, it is essential to underline a difference between migration and displacement. Someone is regarded as a migrant if he/she remains away from his/her original home for at least three months. Migration can be within or outside the country. Displacement is a form of migration in which individuals are forced to migrate from their place of living.[8]

In this chapter, the author chiefly argues that people migrate due to various reasons and environment is one of the important factors in many cases. However, in a last few decades climate change related environmental disasters have displaced millions of people across the globe. This chapter has used published reports and data by different government and international organizations. The chapter also uses critically studied secondary sources and news reports to build arguments. In this chapter, both environmental migrants and environmental displacement have been used because, in some cases, environment may not be a sole factor for migration but in a few it is.

Why Do People Migrate?

A detailed discussion on why people migrate is essential to understand the debate related with migration. It will also help us to understand major factors that make people migrate from their location.

There are three major theories on migration: Neo-classical, Historical-Structural, and New Economics of Labour Migration (NELM). At the macro-level, Neo-classical economic theory explains migration in terms of geographical differences in the supply and demand for labour. Difference in wages cause workers to move from low-wage, labour-surplus regions to high-wage, labour-scarce regions. While at the micro-level, neo-classical migration theory views migrants as individual, rational actors, who decide to move on the basis of a cost-benefit calculation.[9] For neoclassical school theorists, people migrate from the underdeveloped to developed regions such as from rural to urban areas to make investment of their labour and reap its benefits. One of the criticisms of this theory is that it is, largely, Euro-centric. It believes that the migration from the rural to industrial areas facilitates "modernisation" of developing countries, as it did in nineteenth- and twentieth-century Europe.[10] However, the structural conditions under which contemporary migration in and from developing countries takes place are rather different.

Historical-structural theory on migration has its structural roots in Marxist political economy and in the world systems theory. The proponents of this theory postulate that economic and political power are unequally distributed among developed and underdeveloped countries, that people have unequal access to resources and that capitalist expansion has the tendency to reinforce these inequalities. The dependency school which developed in 1960s and 1970s views migration not just as detrimental to the economies of underdeveloped countries but also as one of the very *causes* of underdevelopment, rather than as a path towards development.[11] One of the early leading scholars of dependency school was Raul Prebisch, who worked at the United Nations Economic Commission for Latin America. Prebisch along with others found that the stronger countries (core) trade on terms that allowed surplus value to flow from the weaker countries (the periphery) to the core. This is unequal exchange. Looking at the basics of economic relations between core and periphery Andre Gunder Frank coined the phrase "the development of underdevelopment".[12] Karl Polanyi insisted on the distinction between three forms of economic organization which he called reciprocal (a sort of direct give and take), redistributive (in which goods went from the bottom of the social ladder to the top to be then returned in part to the bottom) and market (in which exchange occurred in monetary forms in a public arena).[13] The proponents of this school are of view that migration ruins stable peasant societies, undermines their economies and uproots their populations.

Immanuel Wallerstein's world-systems theory distinguished between the capitalist "core" states and semiperipheral and peripheral areas.[14] There is also an "external" area, Wallerstein maintained, which was not (yet) included in the capitalist system. The division is not merely functional but also geographical.[15] The Marxist criticism of the world system is that while discussing core-peripheral axis of the division of labour, it is being circulationist and neglects the productionist base of surplus-value and the class struggle between bourgeoisie and the proletariat as the central explanatory variable of social change. Secondly, the state autonomists argue that the world-systems analysis makes the political sphere into a zone whose realities are derived from, determined by, the economic base.[16]

Perceptively analysing the structural change in migration in the developing and underdeveloped countries in early 1950s, Arthur Lewis came out with his model of a dualistic economy. He was a pioneer of development economics. For Lewis, "the central problem in the theory of economic development is to understand the process by which a community which was previously saving and investing 4 or 5 per cent of its national income or less, converts itself into an economy where voluntary saving is running at about 12 to 15 per cent of national income or more".[17]

Lewis finds that the capitalist sector develops by drawing a large number of labours from the non-capitalist subsistence sector.[18] The surplus labour in the subsistence sector ensures that wages remain constant because of the exceeding supply. The surplus of output over wages gives profits to the capitalists. The profits help in rise of national income that are further directed towards investment.[19] This sort of migration mainly from rural to industrial cities or from subsistence sector to capitalist sector has helped in development of capitalism in many parts of the world. However, when the reservoir of surplus labour in the 'subsistence' sector is exhausted, and wages in the subsistence sector begin to rise, profits reduce. Hence, both wages and profits are determined by marginal productivity.[20] Lewis model, further, finds that the wages in the modern capitalist sector are primarily determined by opportunity cost and not productivity of labour. Expansion of industries increases employment opportunity and output increases and so the share of profits (savings) in national income rises. Lewis's model shows that low wages and poverty in a labour surplus economy will persist as long as the opportunity cost of labour to the capitalist sector remains low. This model served as an argument for many government-led industrialization programmes in the 1950s and 1960s.[21]

The central postulate of the Lewis's model that the "subsistence sector in developing countries contains an abundance of labour, ensuring that the conventional 'wage' in the subsistence sector rules over the entire economy" faced criticism.[22] There was also criticism made of the "assumed process of labour migration from the 'subsistence' sector to wage employment in the 'capitalist' sector, especially in the light of rising urban unemployment observed in developing countries".[23] Lewis also thought that the speed of integration of the rural workforce into the more productive urban sector would be too slow.[24]

In 1950s, Gunnar Myrdal came out with his theory of cumulative causation that was further elaborated by Douglas Massey in 1990s.[25] Talking about Circular and Cumulative Causation, Myrdal observed that circular relationship between less poverty, more food, improved health and higher working capacity would sustain a cumulative process upwards instead downwards. But if the cumulative process is not regulated, it will increase inequalities.[26] Looking at the problems of the American Negroes and Whites, Myrdal maintained that the low Negro plane of living and white prejudice needs to be studied intensively with reference to other variables such as region, social class, age and sex.[27] Explaining the problem of Negroes in *An American Dilemma: The Negro Problem and Modern Democracy* that white prejudice reduced the standard of living for blacks while the blacks' low standard of living increased white prejudice. He predicted that this vicious circle would end with exogenous forces impelling a decline in white prejudice against blacks, which would increase blacks' standard of living, further reducing white prejudice.[28]

Myrdal talked about how expansion in one locality has centripetal "backwash effects" in the other.[29] For him, migration, capital movement and trade are media through which the cumulative process evolves upwards in the lucky regions and downwards in the unlucky ones. Localities and regions where economic activities expand attract immigration from different parts. The cheap and often docile labour of underdeveloped regions does not usually attract industry.[30] Against this "backwash effects" is centrifugal "Spread

Effects". By it, Myrdal means expansion of economic activities from centres to the other regions where favourable conditions exist for producing raw materials for the growing industries in the centres. If a sufficient number of workers become employed in these other localities, even consumer goods industries will be given spur there.[31]

Elaborating Myrdal's theory of cumulative causation to explain the continuous rise in the magnitude of Mexican immigration to the United States, Massey highlighted seven factors that act in a circular way to cause additional migration: (1) expansion of networks, (2) distribution of income, (3) distribution of land, (4) organization of farm production, (5) culture of migration, (6) distribution of human capital and (7) social labelling.[32]

In the 1980s and 1990s, the main contribution to thinking on migration and development came from the NELM scholars. It was developed by Oded Stark in the 1980s, in cooperation with David Bloom, Eliakim Katz, David Levhari, Robert Lucas, Mark Rosenzweig, and J. Edward Taylor.[33] The new economics of labour migration theory rejects neo-classical models, which were evaluated as too individualistic and rigid to deal with the complex and diverse realities of the migration and development interactions. The NELM framework finds that the decision to migrate is taken by the family. The family does not migrate but sends a member to better place who takes care of the household. NELM is only theory which explicitly links remittances with migration.[34] NELM has gradually turned out to be a viable alternative to not only neo-classical but also structuralist approaches, gaining increasing acceptance throughout the 1990s.[35]

Proposed by Everett S. Lee (1966) the push-pull model says that migration is based on various factors such as one associated with a place of birth, destination, obstacles and individual's decisions.[36] The push-pull model has gained enormous popularity in the migration literature.[37] Two main forces are typically distinguished to create the pushes and pulls: (1) rural population growth causing a Malthusian pressure on natural and agricultural resources, and pushing people out of marginal rural areas, and (2) relatively higher wages luring people into cities and industrialized countries.[38]

In brief, the NELM theory posits that migration is driven by economic factors and happens to increase income. The structural functionalist approach highlights the role of socio-economic structure in which individual action is embedded. Rational choice theories and methodological individualist approach emphasizes on income-maximising factors.[39]

People adopt both legal and illegal ways to migrate.[40] All such migrations were never welcomed in past and are not welcomed by a number of locals in present. The local population looks at the migrants as burden on local resources and finds them as a reason for their unemployment and relatively low wage or salary than expected. The burden on resources hypothesis creates tension between the host and migrant population. Situation can become worse when both – hosts and migrants – depend on common non-renewable resources whose scarcity, as Thomas Homer-Dixon suggests, could lead to conflict between the communities[41] and so between the host and migrant population.

Contrary to the debates that migrants are burden on local economy, Abhijit V. Banerjee and Esther Duflo (2019) argue that the influx of low-skilled workers shifts the demand curve.[42] The newcomers spend money in various ways such as they go to restaurants, get haircut and do shopping. All such activities create jobs which are mainly taken by the local population. The immigrants do not really compete with the local workers as most of them convincingly get ready to work or perform the task that the native labour is hesitant or not willing to do.[43] In case the enterprising individuals migrate, they make investment in the local economy and create jobs for the native workers.[44]

Different from all forms and reasons for migration, as widely discussed earlier, the research on relations between environment and migration is still at early stage. Whatever little work done on this theme supports the argument that change in environment affects people's livelihood and, in turn, has played a role in their migration from one place to the other.[45] Barnett and Webber (2009) exposed the seriousness of the available literature on relations between climate change and migration by saying:

> The literature on climate change and migration is generally very pessimistic about mobility arising from climate change. This creates a starting point bias in thinking about policy responses, eschewing the development of policies that seek to harness migration as a strategy to promote adaptation to climate change.[46]

Migration theories and frameworks have been categorised into maximalist and minimalist approaches towards the environment-induced migration. Maximalists posit that environmental degradation is a direct cause for large-scale displacement. Minimalists, on the other hand, emphasise that migration is not a monocausal phenomenon and that environment change contributes besides other general reasons for migration.[47] Since ancient time, environment has pushed people out of their place. The next section discusses the history of environmental migration.

Environmental Migration and Environmental Displacement in Past

It is better to use the term "Environmental Displacement" than "Environmental Migration" to study the past mainly because in many literatures and documents, environment had not been formally recorded and recognised as sole factor for migration; even though, in some cases, environmental factors predominantly "forced" people to migrate and displaced many; also in some cases, environmental factors forced people to move away from their original home. Some of the recent writings on migration in past do have evidence showing how environment was the most important factor for migration.

The Indus Valley Civilization (3300 BCE–1300 BCE) matured and declined on the banks of river Indus. During and after the Indus Valley Civilization, the climate change played a significant role in migration of people. A study by Anindya Sarkar et al. (2020) shows that climate change moved the people from west to east.[48] About the decline of the Indus Valley Civilization, there are social theories such as invasion of Indo-Aryans, but Nishant Malik (2020) in his study argues that the shifting patterns of monsoon due to climate change caused demise to the Indus Valley Civilization.[49]

Environment was one of the causes for the fall and decline of all-powerful Roman Empire (27 BCE to 476 AD), as the study by Werner Marx et al. (2018) shows. The city of Rome had about one million inhabitants and was well connected with all provinces and Roman centres outside Italy. The decline of the Roman Empire has been discussed among the scholars, but no consensus has emerged. More than 200 different causes for the end of Rome have been proposed, but no one historical discourse is convincing. Some study points at climate change as a major exogenous triggering factor for weakening the power of Rome and for provoking the migration which eventually caused the downfall of the Western Roman Empire.[50] Around AD 370, Huns arrived in the Danube area and sparked massive external pressure on the borders of the Roman Empire. The first phase of migration was followed by successive waves of migration of Alans, Alemani, Franks and Vandals, who increasingly destroyed the Roman hegemony in the West.[51] The loss of North Africa as the Roman "breadbasket" additionally reduced the economic power of the Empire. In 1917, Ellsworth Huntington (1876–1947) published an article in the *Quarterly Journal of Economics*, titled "Climatic change and agricultural exhaustion as elements in the fall of Rome".[52] He believes that climate change contributed much to the fall of the Roman Empire. The Roman Empire reached its maximum peak during a phase of warm, wet and stable climate, fostered by high, stable solar activity and weak volcanic activity. According to Harper, the Roman Climate Optimum (BC 200–AD 150) moved smoothly into the Roman Transition Period (AD 150–450), which was a period of climate disorganization, followed by the Late Antique Little Ice Age (AD 450– 700).[53] Werner Marx et al. have mentioned many other literatures which talk about the probable role of climate change in the decline of Roman Empire.[54]

In the medieval world, religion, culture and people migrated from East to West, from Mesopotamia, Egypt or Troy to Europe.[55] The United Kingdom has never been an insular place; migrants had arrived throughout the Middle Ages and were influencing its language, culture and the country's identity.[56] Economic migrants arrived in England in medieval times in small boats. Danes, Norse, Irish, Frisians, Lombards, Flemings, Francs and Normans came to find work, to trade goods or to be with relatives who had moved to the island. Migrants consistently arrived in England throughout the "medieval millennium", which covers the period from sixth century to the end of the fifteenth century. An early group which arrived in England were the Romans, Vikings and Normans.[57]

Medieval Warm Period (900–1300 AD) is one of the most contentious periods in terms of climate change as IPCC reports and carbon dioxide alarmists claim that it did not happen and things began to change only after 1950 when CO_2 level increased.[58] However, D. J. Easterbrook (2016) finds that there was some climate amelioration around 985 AD which was taken advantage by the Vikings who colonised southern Greenland. Erik the Red explored Greenland and gave it a name. The settlements in Greenland lasted about 500 years before the region cooled down again and about 620 farms have been excavated.[59] The Medieval Warm Period had also impact on the movement of people in the North American Arctic region.[60]

Environment migration has escalated in the modern times. However, unlike past, environmental factors have also been formally recognised as a reason for migration of people. The next section discusses environmental migration in contemporary times.

Environmental Migration and Displacement in Contemporary Times

The First World Migration report of 2000 highlighted the fact that "despite being an 'age-old phenomenon', migration was accelerating as part of broader globalization transformations of economic and trade processes, which were enabling greater movement of labour as well as goods and capital".[61] Globalization and the related developments such as industrialisation and growth in demand for cheap skilled labour for new economy and workers for infrastructure development have seen rise in migration especially from developing to the developed countries. This migration has also helped the developing countries to receive much-needed remittances to improve their economy.[62]

Statistically, according to the 2020 World Migration Report, the total estimated number of international migrants was 150 million in 2000, which has increased to 272 million according to the 2020 report. This has given rise in the remittances. In 2000, the total global remittances was US$126 billion which increased to US$689 billion according to the 2020 report.[63] The development in the age of globalisation has also increased the number of internally displaced persons (IDPs) and stateless people. Globally, the number of IDPs in 2000 was 21 million which increased to 41.3 million in the 2020 report. The number of stateless people in 2020 report has been recorded to 3.9 million.[64]

Besides the reasons which pull and push the migrants, migration is also caused by the environmental factors such as cyclones, floods and wildfires which destroy people's home and force them to move to the other place. Other factors such as rise in sea level, changes in rainfall patterns and droughts also make people to migrate, as this leads to loss of their livelihood.[65] In 2018, the World Bank report estimated that Latin America, Sub-Saharan Africa and Southeast Asia will generate around 143 million more climate migrants by 2050.[66] According to Internal Displacement Monitoring Centre report 2019, in 2018, 28 million people were newly displaced due to conflicts and weather-related hazards disasters. Of the total, 10.8 million displaced due to conflicts, while 17.2 million because of weather-related hazards particularly storms. The Philippines, China and India accounted for 60 percent of the 17.2 million.[67] Many others have to relocate away from their ancestral land, and planned relocation of communities because of coastal erosion and sea-level rise, for instance, is a new reality due to phenomenon of climate change, notably for many Pacific small island developing States.[68] But some people are simply unable to move due to lack of means. They are trapped in places where the adverse impacts of climate change represent a threat to their wellbeing.[69] It is estimated that by 2050, somewhere between 25 million and 1 billion people will be environmental migrants and environmentally displaced.[70]

As mentioned in the introduction of this book, in their paper on sea floods published in *Nature Communications*, Scott A. Kulp and Benjamin H. Strauss[71] have warned that rise in sea level between 20 and 30 centimetres by 2050 will increase the chances of floods and threaten the land which is currently home to about 150 (between 140 and 170) million people to a future permanently below the high tide line. Another about 50 million people (between 20 and 90) million will be exposed to such a rise in sea level by the end of the century. This means around a total of 360 (between 310 and 420) million people are on land threatened by annual flood events by 2100.[72] This is a case when the global warming touches 2 degree centigrade. The most affected countries would be in Asia such as China, Bangladesh, India, Vietnam, Indonesia, Thailand, the Philippines and Japan. Outside of Asia, excluding the Netherlands where an extensive flood control network was not captured by any of the elevation models studied, 19 other countries that were studied are expected to see land currently home to about 10 per cent or more of their population fall below end-of-century high tide lines.[73] Except for Djibouti and Guyana, all of these are island nations, and 13 are classified by the United Nations as Small Island Developing States (SIDS).[74] Such threat to people will make them migrate at relatively safer place. The timing of their migration would be determined by the factors such as understanding of the threat, economic position of the people and the individual state's response to meet the impending danger.

Excessive rainfall leads to availability of more than the quantity of water that can be managed and causes floods. Often heavy floods destroy houses of people and displace many of them. For instance, in the deltaic Bangladesh heavy flood is almost an annual event. Every year many people lose their homes and are displaced from their place due to such heavy floods. Many of such displaced people move to the capital city of Dhaka crowding the already-crowded slums. It is estimated that between 2009 and 2019, nearly 700,000 Bangladeshis were displaced on an average each year due to natural disaster.[75] It is expected that by 2050, about 13.3 million people will be displaced due to varied impact of climate change. Life is really tough for many of the climate migrants arriving in Dhaka's slum which do not have basic facilities and required hygienic conditions. The migrants also need jobs to give rent and fill their and dependents' stomach. For most of the Dhaka residents, the climate migrants are burden on the city's infrastructure.[76]

Simultaneously, there are an increasing number of droughts due to impact of climate change. United Nations Human Development Report of 2006 and United Nations World Water Report of 2020 have given umpteen examples of decline in precipitation and rise in the areas facing water shortages and droughts.[77] For example, in India, water table in many parts of the country has steeply declined. The imminent water stress has been highlighted in June 2018 report by the National Institution for Transforming India (NITI Aayog). The report says:

> 600 million Indians face high to extreme water stress about two lakh (200,000) people die every year due to inadequate access to safe water. The crisis is only going to get worse. By 2030, the country's water demand is projected to be twice the available supply, implying severe water scarcity for hundreds of millions of people and an eventual 6% loss in the country's GDP.[78]

Such a decline in economy is visible in parts of the world such as in India. For example, one of the most developed states in India, Maharashtra, which contributes around 14.4 per cent in Indian economy, every year suffers from drought. In 2018–19, due to agrarian distress, Maharashtra's economic growth remained stagnant at 7.5 per cent.[79] To conserve water and replenish groundwater in December 2014, the Maharashtra government launched the project called "Jalyukt Shivar Abhiyaan" whose objective was to make the state drought-free by 2019. Under it many programmes such as deepening and widening of streams, construction of cement and earthen stop dams, work on nullahs and digging of farm ponds were planned. Through all such constructions, the project aimed to make 5000 villages free of water scarcity every year.[80] However, after five years, the state again faced drought situation. In 2019, the Maharashtra government declared drought in 20,000 villages across 26 districts of the state. Of 26, eight districts of Marathwada region were among the worst affected. About 90 percent of the villages – 7,765 of 8,534 – of the region were affected from the drought.[81] There is no concrete data available showing migration from the region owing to drought.

However, there are evidences from other parts of world about people migrating due to drought, especially where agriculture activities largely depend on rains or rain-fed rivers. For example, according to the United Nations, prolonged droughts are driving a large number of rural families in parts of Central America from their homes to seek better opportunities in the neighbouring countries or in the United States. Five years of recurring droughts have destroyed crops such as maize and bean harvests.[82] A large number of people in a Dry Corridor developed in the Central America that runs through Guatemala, El Salvador, Honduras and Nicaragua are struggling to feed their families. According to 2018 survey carried by the United Nations World Food Program (WFP), 8 percent of the total families interviewed in the Dry Corridor, mostly small-scale farmers, said they plan to migrate because they lack food.[83] It is estimated that about 1.4 million people living in the Dry Corridor need food aid. Germany announced $1.1 million to the WFP in emergency food aid to support the thousands of families in Honduras affected by the drought.[84]

In Africa, the western Sahel region is expected to experience strongest drying with a significant increase in the maximum length of dry spells. West Africa has been identified by the IPCC as a climate-change hot spot with climate change likely to lessen crop yields and production. Southern Africa will also be affected. If the change in global temperature is 1.5 degree centigrade, it means less rainfall over the Limpopo basin and areas of the Zambezi basin in Zambia, as well as parts of Western Cape in South Africa.[85] If it is 2 degree centigrade, Southern Africa is projected to face a decrease in precipitation of about 20 percent and increases in the number of consecutive dry days in Namibia, Botswana, northern Zimbabwe and southern Zambia. West and Central Africa will also face the heat of the global warming.[86] However, none would experience as bad situation as Sahel where population is increasing while natural resources, including land and water resources, are shrinking. Sahel is hit by droughts and floods which devastate people of the region. Climate change along with armed conflict, violence and military operations has caused displacement of around 4.9 million people in 2019.[87]

Climate change is not only fatal but also brings loss to global economy. It is estimated that between 1999 and 2018, about 495,000 people died worldwide and losses of US$3.54 trillion (in PPP) were incurred as a direct result of more than 12,000 extreme weather events.[88] As such weather incidents are likely to increase in future by 2030 and 2050, the world will witness more such deaths and also economic losses.[89]

Environmental migration is not, particularly, about choices but due to fear and for survival. The 2020 World Migration Report mentions about three main framings of environmental migration and human mobility which have emerged in the context of climate change in academia, the media and in policy circles: (a) irregular migration related to environmental change and resource shortages as a border security issue, particularly for areas of destination; (b) protection of environmental migrants; and (c) environmental migration as a form of adaptation and climate risk management reflecting the political sensitivities of migration.[90]

The first framing tends to emphasise on environmental migrants as a part of a wider "threat multiplier", as they cross into the other region or borders of other country. They are looked as a threat to security of the host region and also on their resources. The second framing tends to represent environmental migration as a phenomenon associated with vulnerable people who move to other areas in adverse circumstances and need protection.[91] Largely, this approach shares commonalities with approaches that highlight human rights related to rights to work, education, health care, food and water, and other rights that environmental shocks can disrupt. Both first and second framing approaches – securitization and protection – have been critiqued as they have not sufficiently acknowledged the agency of the people affected by environmental change and emphasise on threats without fully acknowledging opportunities that may also play a role in environmental migration.[92] The third framing views human mobility ranging from migration, displacement and planned relocation as a set of possible adaptive responses to climate impacts and risks. It recognizes the possibility of reducing exposure and vulnerability to physical disruptions associated with climate and other environmental stressors. This framing also emphasizes on the pursuit of approaches to avert, minimize and address displacement related to the adverse effects of climate change.[93]

As mentioned earlier, one of the most vulnerable regions of the world due to climate change is the SIDS. Many of them are likely to lose a large land area due to rise in sea waters. To meet such challenges, they are taking measures but their future, largely, depends on how much the other developed and developing countries control emission. The SIDS leaders have coined the term "migration with dignity" to envisage a situation in which people have control over whether, when, where and how they can move or stay if that is their wish. The idea centres on boosting education standards so that the migrants can compete in the international labour markets and on strengthening networks with the diaspora in the region to create new opportunities and support new arrivals.[94] In the absence of the global frameworks, the region and the individual states are introducing measures to deal with the situation. For example, countries in South America have introduced a non-binding agreement on the protection of people displaced by disasters from the other side of the borders and migrants within the countries.[95] Also, states such as Fiji has come out with Planned Relocation Guidelines which states that "after all other feasible adaptation options have been explored relocation would be the last resort". The guidelines describe the steps needed to be taken such as consultations with all affected stakeholders including people moving, host communities and those who do not choose to move.[96]

A study by Guy J. Abel et al. (2019) finds that climatic conditions, especially severe droughts and the likelihood of armed conflict, played a significant role as an explanatory factor for asylum seeking in the period 2011–2015.[97] The impact of climate change and weather hazards on the conflict is particularly relevant for West Asian countries in the period between 2010 and 2012 when many countries were undergoing political transformation. For example, in Syria, growing water scarcity and frequent droughts coupled with poor water management led to multiyear crop failures and economic deterioration and consequently forced people to migrate to urban areas putting a lot of pressure on cities. This had also led to an increase in unemployment and inequality which caused political unrest followed by conflicts.[98] Guy J Abel et al. have explored bilateral refugee flows data for the years 2006–2015 for 157 countries, and employed sample selection methods for gravity-type models first to estimate the impact of climate on conflict and, second, to know how conflict influences forced migration. Their study unpacks conflict as a causal mediator between climate change on the one hand and asylum migration on the other.[99]

The climate change and conflicts make a large number of people across the world insecure by forcing them to sleep hungry. This has been mentioned in the 2018 United Nations report on hunger which says "driven by climate disasters and conflict, levels of acute hunger surged in 2017, leaving some 124 million people across 51 countries facing hunger crises-11 million more than previous year".[100]

To the national security-obsessed leaders and population, effects of climate change and the related migration are "threat". About four and half decades back in mid-1980s, El-Hinnawi and others wrote about climate refugees, pointing that there are security-related challenges due to climate-induced migrations.[101] The statists gave a logic and still gives that the climate migrants, like some others, will be culturally different, put burden on economy, and may pose criminal or terrorist threat because of different political orientation and ideology.[102] Following such concerns, the political leadership across the world has announced policies to halt climate-induced migration like the other migrations, as mentioned earlier.

After National Security Strategy of 2015 was released in which climate change and its associated impacts were considered as threat to the national security, in 2016's Memorandum for the Heads of Executive Departments and Agencies on subject "Climate Change and National Security" the then US President Barak Obama directed the federal departments and agencies to "perform certain functions to ensure that climate change-related impacts are fully considered in the development of national security doctrine, policies, and plans".[103] To meet such threats, the memorandum enumerated Presidential directives and policies and interagency coordination group was formed to coordinate "the development of a strategic approach to identify, assess, and share information on current and projected climate-related impacts on national security interests and to inform the development of national security doctrine, policies, and plans".[104] The USA is not alone but other countries also have formulated and executed policies to deal with security-related threats due to climate change and environmental migrants.

Conclusion

As discussed in this chapter, change in local climate conditions had moved people or in some situations forced them to leave their home. In recent decades, IPCC report of 1990 gave boost to many studies linking environment with migration. The report warned that climate change could lead to large-scale migration in future.[105] Taking the debate about climate-induced migration further, two years later, in 1992, International Organization for Migration together with the Refugee Policy Group published a report on "Migration and Environment" in which it is stated:

> Large numbers of people are moving as a result of environmental degradation that has increased dramatically in recent years. The number of such migrants could rise substantially as larger areas of the earth become uninhabitable as a result of climate change.[106]

Subsequently, many other studies have been carried out linking environment degradation, climate change and migration. On the ground, like past, change in weather and the associated impacts are palpable in some regions. For example, in India, the unpredictable weather due to climate change has severe impact on the farmers. This is also forcing many farmers to move to the cities for earning their livelihood.[107]

Human history is not only a story of migration[108]; it is also a story of conflicts between the migrants and host population. In past, cheap migrant workers were welcomed by citizens from the developed countries to do "dirty and dangerous" jobs. In past, the skilled migrant workers provided cheap labour to many western economies and catapult economic growth. However, at the present stage of globalization, the migrant workers are largely not welcomed and regarded as a threat to local population's job prospect. Rise of right-wing politics around the world has also made local conditions tough for migrants. Unlike the skilled and ready to do "dangerous and dirty" jobs migrant workers, environmental migrants may not be appropriately skilled to contribute in any way to their host territory. Not only across the border, even within their own country the environmental migrants moving into developed parts and cities are mostly considered unwanted citizens burdening the local infrastructure.

Notes

1 IPCC (2021), "Climate change widespread, rapid, and intensifying", *IPCC*, accessed from www.ipcc.ch/2021/08/09/ar6-wg1-20210809-pr/ on 19th August 2021.
2 Ibid.
3 International Organization for Migration (2014), "Migration, environment, and climate change: Evidence for policy glossary", 13, accessed from https://publications.iom.int/system/files/pdf/meclep_glossary_en.pdf?language=en on 19th June 2019.
4 Md Shamsuddoha, S.M. Munjurul Hannan Khan, Sajid Raihan, Tanjir Hossain (2012), *Displacement and Migration from Climate Hot-spots in Bangladesh: Causes and Consequences*. ActionAid, Bangladesh, p. 18, accessed from https://unfccc.int/files/adaptation/groups_committees/loss_and_damage_executive_committee/application/pdf/displacement_and_migration_in_bangladesh.pdf
5 International Organization for Migration (2014), "Migration, environment, and climate change: Evidence for policy glossary", 13, accessed from https://publications.iom.int/system/files/pdf/meclep_glossary_en.pdf?language=en on 19th June 2019
6 Ibid.
7 Ibid.
8 Md Shamsuddoha, S.M. Munjurul Hannan Khan, Sajid Raihan, Tanjir Hossain (2012), *Displacement and Migration from Climate Hot-spots in Bangladesh: Causes and Consequences*. ActionAid, Bangladesh, p. 18, accessed from https://unfccc.int/files/adaptation/groups_committees/loss_and_damage_executive_committee/application/pdf/displacement_and_migration_in_bangladesh.pdf.
9 Hein De Haas (2008), *Migration and development: A theoretical perspective*. International Migration Institute, James Martin 21st Century School, University of Oxford. Working Paper 9. accessed from www.migrationinstitute.org on 18th June 2020. Also See Hein De Haas (2010), "Migration and development: A theoretical perspective", *International Migration Review*, 44(1), 227–264, accessed from https://doi.org/10.1111/j.1747-7379.2009.00804.x on 20th June 2020.
10 Ibid.
11 Ibid.
12 Immanuel Wallerstein (2004), *World system analysis: An introduction*. Durham and London: Duke University Press, 12.
13 Ibid., 17.
14 Immanuel Wallerstein (2011), *Capitalist agriculture and the origins of the European world economy in the sixteenth century*. Berkeley, Los Angeles and London: University of California Press, 349.
15 Ibid.
16 Immanuel Wallerstein (2004), *World system analysis: An introduction*. Durham and London: Duke University Press, 20.
17 Cited in Colin Kirkpatrick and Armando Barrientos, "The Lewis model after fifty years", Institute for Development Policy and Management University of Manchester, 4, accessed from https://hummedia.manchester.ac.uk/institutes/gdi/publications/workingpapers/depp/depp_wp09.pdf The Manchester School Vol 72 No. 6 December 2004 1463–6786 679–690, 681.
18 Ibid.
19 Ibid.
20 Ibid.

21 Kari Polanyi Levitt, "W. Arthur Lewis: Pioneer of development economics", accessed from www.un.org/en/chronicle/article/w-arthur-lewis-pioneer-development-economics on 12th November 2020.
22 Colin Kirkpatrick and Armando Barrientos, "The Lewis model after fifty years", Paper no. 9, Institute for Development Policy and Management University of Manchester, accessed from https://hummedia.manchester.ac.uk/institutes/gdi/publications/workingpapers/depp/depp_wp09.pdf
23 Ibid.
24 Abhijit V. Banerjee and Eshter Duflo (2019), *Good economics for hard times*. New Delhi: Juggernaut.
25 David M. Heer (2002), "When cumulative causation conflicts with relative economic opportunity: Recent change in the Hispanic population of the United States", *Migraciones Internacionales*, 1(3), accessed from www.scielo.org.mx/scielo.php?script=sci_arttext&pid=S1665-89062002000200002 on 18th July 2020.
26 Gunnar Myrdal (1962), *Economic theory and under-developed regions*. London: Gerald Duckworth & Co. Ltd, 12.
27 Ibid., 18.
28 Ibid and David M. Heer (2002), "When cumulative causation conflicts with relative economic opportunity: Recent change in the Hispanic population of the United States", *Migraciones Internacionales*, 1(3), accessed from www.scielo.org.mx/scielo.php?script=sci_arttext&pid=S1665-89062002000200002 on 18th July 2020.
29 Gunnar Myrdal (1962), *Economic theory and under-developed regions*. London: Gerald Duckworth & Co. Ltd, 27.
30 Ibid., 31.
31 Ibid.
32 David. M. Heer, "When cumulative causation conflicts with relative economic opportunity".
33 Jessica Hagen-Zanker (2008), "Why do people migrate: A review of the theoretical literature", accessed from https://mpra.ub.uni-muenchen.de/28197/1/2008WP002 on 15th May 2021.
34 Ibid.
35 Ibid. Also see De Haas, *Migration and development*. Also See De Haas, "Migration and development".
36 Everett S. Lee (1966), "A theory of migration", *Demography*, 3(1), 47–57, https://doi.org/10.2307/2060063
37 Ibid. Also see De Haas, *Migration and development*. Also See De Haas, "Migration and development".
38 Ibid.
39 Katharine Vincent, Ricardo Safra de Campos, Attila N. Lazar and Anwara Begum (2021), "Gender, migration and environmental change in the Ganges-Brahmaputra-Meghna delta in Bangladesh", in Asha Hans, Nitya Rao, Anjal Prakash and Amrita Patel (eds.) *Engendering climate change: Learning from South Asia*. New Delhi: Routledge, 152–171, 154.
40 Amit Ranjan (2016), "Migration from Bangladesh: Impulses, risks and exploitations", *The Roundtable: The Commonwealth Journal of International Affairs*, 105(3), 311–319.
41 Thomas Homer-Dixon (1994), "Environmental scarcities and violent conflict: Evidence from cases", *International Security*, 19(I), 5–40.
42 Abhijit V. Banerjee and Eshter Duflo (2019), *Good economics for hard times*. New Delhi: Juggernaut, 24.

43 Ibid., 25.
44 Ibid.
45 Lori M. Hunter and Raphel Nawrotzki (2016), "Migration and the environment", in Michael J. White (ed.) *Handbook of migration and population distribution*. Springer, 465–484, accessed from www.researchgate.net/publication/294891660_Migration_and_the_Environment on 12th June 2020.
46 Cited in Frank Laczko and Christine Aghazarm (2009), *Migration, environment and climate change: Assessing the evidence*. Geneva: International Organization for Migration, 10, accessed from https://publications.iom.int/system/files/pdf/migration_and_environment.pdf on 23rd March 2020.
47 Hunter and Nawrotzki, "Migration and the environment".
48 Anindya Sarkar et al. (2020), "*New evidence of early iron age to medieval settlements from the southern fringe of Thar Desert (western Great Rann of Kachchh)*. India: Implications to Climate Culture Co-evolution". *Science Direct*, 21, accessed from www.sciencedirect.com/science/article/pii/S2352226719300364 on 29th June 2020.
49 Nishant Malik (2020, 3 September), "New mathematical method shows how climate change led to fall of ancient civilization", *Science Daily*, accessed from www.sciencedaily.com/releases/2020/09/200903105605.htm on 14th September 2020.
50 Werner Marx et al. (2018), "Climate and the decline and fall of the western Roman empire: A bibliometric view on an interdisciplinary approach to answer a most classic historical question", *MDPI*, accessed from www.mdpi.com/2225-1154/6/4/90 on 14th June 2020.
51 Ibid.
52 Referred in Ibid.
53 Ibid.
54 Ibid.
55 Bernd Schneidmuller and Ruprecht-Karls, "Fitting medieval Europe into the world patterns of integration, migration, and uniqueness", accessed from https://heiup.uni-heidelberg.de/journals/index.php/transcultural/article/view/17446/11347 on 12th September 2020.
56 Donna Ferguson (2020, 16 August), "Economic migrants central to shaping medieval England, says new book", *The Guardian*, accessed from www.theguardian.com/world/2020/aug/16/first-migrants-arrived-in-england-before-england-even-existed on 17th September 2020.
57 Ibid.
58 *Science Direct*, "Medieval warm period", www.sciencedirect.com/topics/earth-and-planetary-sciences/medieval-warm-period on 15th June 2020.
59 "Temperature fluctuations in Greenland and the Arctic", *Science Direct*, accessed from www.sciencedirect.com/topics/earth-and-planetary-sciences/medieval-warm-period on 12th May 2020.
60 M. Friesen and S. A. Finkelstein, "Medieval warm period and little ice age impacts on prehistoric human migrations in the Eastern North American Arctic". American Geophysical Union, Fall Meeting 2014. For Abstract See: https://ui.adsabs.harvard.edu/abs/2014AGUFMGC11A0545F/abstract on 24th January 2020.
61 World Migration Report (2020), "IOM UN migration", 9, accessed from www.iom.int/wmr/
62 Ibid.
63 Ibid., 10.
64 Ibid.
65 Ibid., 253.

66 John Podesta (2019, 25 July), "The climate crisis, migration, and refugees", *Brookings*, accessed from www.brookings.edu/research/the-climate-crisis-migration-and-refugees/ on 19th July 2021.
67 Internal Displacement Monitoring Centre (2019), "Global report on internal displacement report", 34, accessed from www.internal-displacement.org/global-report/grid2019/ on 19th August 2020.
68 Climate Change and Migration in Vulnerable: A snapshot of least developed countries, landlocked developing countries and small island developing States (2019): International Organization for Migration and the United Nations Office of the High Representative for the Least Developed Countries, Landlocked Developing Countries and Small Island Developing States. Geneva. 1.
69 Ibid.
70 Oli Brown (2008), *Migration and climate change*. Geneva: International Organization for Migration, 13.
71 Scott A. Kulp and Benjamin H. Strauss (2019), "New elevation data triple estimates of global vulnerability to sea-level rise and coastal flooding", *Nature Communications*, 10, Article No. 4844. Open Access, accessed from www.nature.com/articles/s41467-019-12808-z
72 Ibid.
73 Ibid.
74 Ibid.
75 Tim Mcdonnell (2019, 24 January), "Climate change creates a new migration crisis for Bangladesh", *National Geographic*, accessed from www.nationalgeographic.com/environment/article/climate-change-drives-migration-crisis-in-bangladesh-from-dhaka-sundabans on 12th July 2020.
76 Ibid.
77 See The United Nations World Water Development Report (2020), "Water and climate change", accessed from https://unesdoc.unesco.org/ark:/48223/pf0000372882
78 National Institution for Transforming India, Government of India (2018), "Composite water management index: A tool for water management", 15, accessed from http://niti.gov.in/writereaddata/files/document_publication/2018-05-18-Water-Index-Report_vS8-compressed.pdf on 18th July 2020.
79 Sandeep Ashar (2019, 18 June), "Drought casts spell on Maharashtra economy, growth stagnant at 7.5%", *The Indian Express*, accessed from https://indianexpress.com/article/cities/mumbai/drought-casts-spell-on-maharshtra-economy-growth-stagnant-at-7-5-5785633/ on 12th July 2019.
80 Government of Maharashtra, "Jalyukt Shivar", accessed from http://mrsac.maharashtra.gov.in/jalyukt/ on 12th September 2019.
81 Surendra P. Gangan (2019, 2 April), "90% drought in Marathwada, 100% apathy, claim villagers", *Hindustan Times*, accessed from www.hindustantimes.com/mumbai-news/90-drought-in-marathwada-100-apathy-claim-villagers/story-dMTmZERpB3ryjlV1qU4cUM.html on 25th April 2019.
82 Anastasia Moloney (2019, 15 August), "Hunger driving migration in drought-hit Central America: U.N.", *Reuters*, accessed from www.reuters.com/article/us-central-america-drought-migration/hunger-driving-migration-in-drought-hit-central-america-un-idUSKCN1V423J on 28th June 2020.
83 Ibid.
84 Ibid.
85 Dan Shepard, "Global warming: Severe consequences for Africa", *Africa Renewal*, accessed from www.un.org/africarenewal/magazine/december-2018-march-2019/global-warming-severe-consequences-africa on 28th May 2020.

86 Ibid.
87 Ibid.
88 David Eckstein, Vera Künzel, Laura Schäfer and Maik Winges, “Global climate risk index 2020: Who suffers most from extreme weather events? Weather-related loss events in 2018 and 1999 to 2018”, *Germanwatch*, accessed from https://germanwatch.org/sites/germanwatch.org/files/20-2-01e%20Global%20Climate%20Risk%20Index%202020_10.pdf on 14th September 2020.
89 Ibid.
90 World Migration Report (2020), “IOM UN migration”, 254, accessed from www.iom.int/wmr/
91 Ibid.
92 Ibid.
93 Ibid.
94 Ibid., 263.
95 Ibid.
96 ibid
97 Guy J. Abel, et al. (2019), “Climate, conflict and forced migration”, *Global Environmental Change*, 54, 239–249, accessed from www.sciencedirect.com/science/article/pii/S0959378018301596 on 12th September 2020.
98 Ibid.
99 Ibid.
100 “Drought and conflict leave millions more hungry in 2017 – UN-backed report”, *UN News*, accessed from https://news.un.org/en/story/2018/03/1005621 on 12th June 2020.
101 Greogry White (2011), *Climate change and migration: Security and borders in a warming world*. Oxford: Oxford Scholarship Online, accessed from https://oxford-universitypressscholarship-com.libproxy1.nus.edu.sg/view/10.1093/acprof:oso/9780199794829.001.0001/acprof-9780199794829-chapter-3 on 21st March 2021.
102 Ibid.
103 The White House, Office of the Press Secretary, “Presidential memorandum on climate change and national security”, accessed from https://obamawhitehouse.archives.gov/the-press-office/2016/09/21/presidential-memorandum-climate-change-and-national-security on 21st March 2021.
104 Ibid.
105 J. T. Houghton, et al. (1990) *Climate change: The IPCC scientific assessment*. Cambridge: Cambridge University Press, accessed from https://archive.ipcc.ch/publications_and_data/publications_ipcc_first_assessment_1990_wg1.shtml on 21st July 2020.
106 Cited in Frank Laczko and Christine Aghazarm (2009), *Migration, environment and climate change: Assessing the evidence*. Geneva: International Organization for Migration, 13, accessed from https://publications.iom.int/system/files/pdf/migration_and_environment.pdf on 23rd March 2020.
107 “Climate Change forcing farmers into cities”, *DW*, 27 February 2020, accessed from www.dw.com/en/climate-change-forcing-farmers-into-cities/av-52553231 on 12th September 2020.
108 Amit Ranjan (2018), *India-Bangladesh border disputes: Post-LBA dynamics*. Singapore: Springer.

Chapter 2

The Spectre of Climate Change-Induced Migration in Afghanistan

Fazlullah Akhtar and Usman Shah

Introduction

Landlocked and mountainous Afghanistan will be spared from the impacts of climate change-induced sea level rises which are projected to affect most of its other South Asian neighbors. However, a warming planet and shifting climatic patterns will have myriad other impacts on the country's already-vulnerable environment and population. Indeed, despite the average Afghan producing 0.2 metric tons of CO_2 per year compared to 16 metric tons produced by an average American, they are disproportionately vulnerable to the impacts of changing global climate and Afghanistan is therefore ranked the 10th most vulnerable country in the world.[1,2]

This chapter relies largely on secondary research to outline the emerging and projected impacts of climate change on Afghanistan and contextualizes this in terms of the wider human development outlook of the country. This chapter then discusses how these factors, combined with a growing population and ongoing insecurity, are serving to compound the factors of vulnerability that create the conditions for exacerbating the already-problematic levels of internal displacement and outward migration from Afghanistan. It then discusses some suggestions for how policymakers and other stakeholders may be able to mitigate the negative effects of climate change in Afghanistan.

Discourse on climate change has become increasingly focused on migration as a symptom of negative effects and of societies' lack of capacity to mitigate against them.[3] Many of the earlier studies focused on low-lying island nations and the expected exodus of their populations as future sea levels rise.[4] Indeed, it has been increasingly recognized that the nature and intensity of environment-induced migration have evolved radically in recent years and that this will be an increasing challenge in the coming century.[5]

Some studies suggest that the least developed countries, such as Afghanistan, will likely experience more climate change-induced migration and conflicts compared to the developed countries due to the fact of dependency of these nations on limited and scarce natural resources which are risked to be

DOI:10.4324/9781003367802-3

not able to feed the growing population of the world. However, the political fallout may extend beyond the least developed countries which have increasingly manifested in the form of populations traversing the globe in order to seek asylum and more secure lives in the developed world. As borders become more fortified, the inevitable hostile sentiments may foster a fertile atmosphere for global terrorism recruitment, which may already be underway and for which countries such as Afghanistan are already paying a high price.[6] The least-developed countries such as Afghanistan are expected to suffer more due to intensifying competition over land, water and other resources. This, in turn, is already fueling tensions between herders and the farming community, compounding socioeconomic exclusion and raising the chances of youth being absorbed into the violent groups or otherwise forced to migrate.[7] According to Klare,[8] (2013), the scarcity of vital natural resources, including energy, water, land, food and critical minerals and climate change, is going to produce a global explosion in the following decades and it is likely to produce a tidal wave of unrest, rebellion, competition and conflict among the local population and may produce tensions at the international level too.

A 2012 study released key judgments and analyzed seven major river basins of the world, from a security point of view, for their relevant issues and challenges; all the selected river basins are transboundary with two or more countries.[9] Among these river basins, Afghanistan shares its geographical area and contributes to the overall streamflow with the Indus River basin system as well as the Amu Darya River basin. Both river basins have significant tributary shares within Afghanistan. The key issues associated with these two river basins identified were (1) poor internal and transboundary water management; (2) inefficient agricultural practices; (3) soil salinization; (4) inadequate infrastructure; (5) greater variability in water availability; (6) water pollution; (7) inadequate water agreements; (8) and degradation of water quality and disruption of flows.

Some analysts and researchers in the region consider the current violence, insecurity and political imbalance along Afghanistan's borders with Pakistan and Iran to be a pretext for the predicted transboundary antagonisms over natural resources, especially water, between the neighboring states.[10] Any further issues such as climate change will multiply the existing complications which may trigger not only violence but also loss of infrastructure and humans as well as force the local dwellers to migrate. In this regard, Afghanistan provides something of an extreme case due to multiple intersecting factors: its overall status as one of the least developed countries, the ongoing context of violent conflict and instability across the country, the projected population increase for the country, and the projected impacts of climate change on the country's ability to sustain its population. Given that Afghanistan has proven to be a significant source country for migrants as a result of protracted conflict and lack of economic opportunity, any future negative impacts of climate change will only serve to exacerbate these dynamics.

Climate Change Projections for Afghanistan

Variation in Temperature

Since 1950, Afghanistan's mean annual temperature has increased by 1.8°C.[11] In the period between 1951 and 2010, a strong warming trend was experienced in major parts of the country. The warming trend has been stronger in the southwest which was around 2.4°C; In the Central Highlands and the North, the mean annual temperature rise was 1.6°C and 1.7°C, respectively, while in the Hindukush region, the warming was around 1°C; in the East, the warming is still significant, but with 0.6°C, which is lower than that in the rest of the country.[12] In some sub-regions of the Eastern part of the country, there was also little or no warming or even a slight decrease in temperature; this area is part of the Kabul River basin's downstream region which discharges eventually into the Indus River in Pakistan.[13]

Variation in Precipitation

There has been no major shift in precipitation across the country, however, a partial increase (i.e. up to 85%)[14] in the mean annual precipitation in the Wakhan corridor and partly in most southern part of the country (most likely due to the result of a more active Indian Ocean monsoon), while a decrease has been observed in the Southwestern part of the country. A thorough analysis of spring and winter precipitation shows that the spring precipitation has significantly decreased by almost a third while the winter precipitation has slightly increased. The decrease in precipitation in the spring season (March-May) is very much relevant for agriculture and farming practices across the country.[15] The fact that spring crops are typically rain-fed and dependent on considerable rainfall during this period; therefore, there is a high risk of drought and consequent negative effects on agricultural productivity. This may severely affect the livelihood of the population, especially the rural communities dependent on subsistence agriculture.

Studies conducted by Afghanistan's National Environmental Protection Agency and the United Nations have found that the East, Central Highlands and Northern regions of the country have experienced significant agricultural land experience decreases in the spring precipitation.[16] The largest decrease was observed in the Central Highlands, i.e. 40% from 1950 until 2010.[17] While in the Hindukush and South regions, the decrease in precipitation was less pronounced during these months; there was even a slight increase in the Wakhan and the far South. On the other hand, winter precipitation across the country has been increased in general but in a few parts, a partial decrease has been observed.

Furthermore, increased temperatures are expected to cause more rapid and earlier spring snowmelt, this will, in turn, exacerbate the intensity of flash flooding and other relevant disasters. Meanwhile, decreased precipitation in some parts of the country may lead to drought conditions which may exacerbate the impact of heavy precipitation by hardening the soil layers caused by evaporation from the soil surface and reduced permeability, which can cause flash floods or landslides.[18]

Glacial Retreat and Change in the Snow Cover Extent

An Afghan proverb exhorts: (کابل دې بې زرو وي خو بې واورې نه) "*may Kabul be without gold but not without snow*"; it underscores the crucial place that snow cover has for life and economy, being the key source of water in the key consuming sectors of Afghanistan. Most of Afghanistan's rivers are fed by snowmelt, which commences with increasing temperatures from February onwards. It is estimated that around 98% of the surface water supply is diverted for agriculture (e.g. irrigation and livestock),[19] while the remaining water is used for groundwater recharge and municipal and industrial consumption across the country.

However, the patterns that have governed snowmelt in Afghanistan are shifting. According to the latest climate projections of the World Bank Group for Afghanistan, the mean annual temperature is projected to increase between 1.4°C and 4.0°C by the 2060s, and between 2.0°C and 6.2°C by the 2090s.[20] The spring and summer seasons are projected to observe the fastest rate of warming with pretty even warming across the entire country.

Amid this global warming, the decline in snow cover in the Himalayas has been one of the major fallouts but a new study challenges these predictions through records of actual measurements over the past decade. This analysis reveals that snow cover has increased in some regions of the Himalayan belt. The temporal coverage of this study carried out between 2000 and 2010 demonstrates that the snow-covered extent of the Himalayas has increased in some regions in contrast to the decline reported in the previous decade. The detailed analysis in this study shows that the snow cover area in the western and eastern regions of Hindukush Himalaya has an increasing trend, while the central region shows a declining trend in this decade. Increased snow cover in Afghanistan's mountains, especially from summer, precipitation is understood to be caused by increased marine evaporation caused by climatic warming and monsoonal enhancement in the Indian Ocean.[21] However, the researchers report a declining trend across the region during the springtime.[22] In short, rainwater runoff in Afghanistan's mountain catchments will increase at the expense of glacier runoff.[23]

A study in the Swiss alps by[24] found that a seasonal increase of 3°C to 5°C mean temperature reduces the depth of snow cover and period by more than a month. Snow melts two months earlier in the rock habitat zone, which also typically represents the case of Afghanistan. The impacts of climate change are expected to be amplified in the future by more rapid spring snowmelt combined with the downstream effects such as land degradation, vegetative cover loss, land mismanagement, decrease in crop productivity, changes in livelihood, fall in the number of exports, financial losses as well forced migration. The pasture loss has already severely affected the nomadic population and has caused mass migration into Mazar and Herat provinces.[25] A further change in temperature and precipitation is likely to increase labor migration and food insecurity in Afghanistan in the decades ahead.[26]

In 2018, Afghanistan's Ministry of Energy and Water (MEW) launched its first database of glaciers. The study found that between 1990 and 2015, the country lost 406 km^2 of its glacier area, constituting 13.8% of the total area.[27] A study of aerial images found that the Kuh-e Myana Glacier in the north-eastern Badakhshan Province has followed the overall pattern of melting as seen in other high mountain areas of Central Asia and the Himalayas by retreating as many as 250 meters between 2002 and 2014, with the rate of retreat increasing markedly in the years since 2004.[28]

Natural Disasters and Increasingly Vulnerable Populations

Such phenomena are observable in earlier and reduced snowmelts (i.e. avalanches), flash floods, earthquakes, mudflows and landslides in the mountainous regions of the country. Although very little specific research has been carried out in Afghanistan to assess the impacts of climate change on the environment, health (e.g. air and water quality) and water availability but frequent environmental shocks as mentioned earlier have been some of the key contributing factors to poor water quality, biodiversity loss, health issues, erosion of the soil fertile layers and migration of the local birds and relocation of human beings.

In 2019, natural disasters resulting from flash floods, avalanches and heavy snow and rainfall affected around 295,900 people across the country (Figure 2.1). Afghanistan's western region (especially Badghis, Farah and Herat provinces) was severely affected by extreme precipitation, which affected at least 42,151 and 57,302 individuals in Badghis and Farah provinces, respectively. The second most affected region has been the Southern region of the country (i.e. Kandahar and Helmand provinces). The projected increase in winter precipitation and mean annual temperature are expected to accelerate the flash flood events and eventually maximize the number of individuals affected; this shift of climate might force the most vulnerable communities to migrate and relocate to safer places instead.

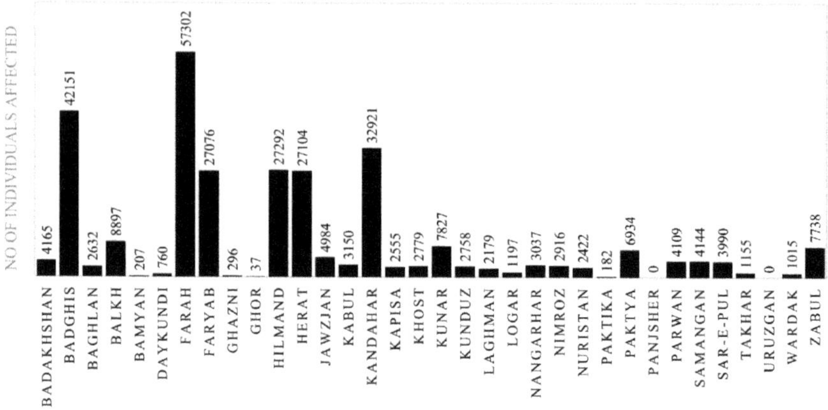

Figure 2.1 Impact of the natural disasters (e.g. flash floods, avalanches, snowfall and rainfall) across the provinces of Afghanistan

Source: HDX. (2020). *re3data.org: Humanitarian Data Exchange; Editing Status 2021-11-16*. re3data.org – Registry of Research Data Repositories. http://doi.org/10.17616/R31NJMO9. Retrieved 03 November, 2022 from United Nations Office for theCoordination of Humanitarian Affairs

Graph developed by: Akhtar and Shah

Food Insecurity in a Changing Climate

Afghanistan remains a largely agrarian society, and agriculture continues to be viewed as central to the country's economy. This is reflected in the programming of international development donors as well as in national policy, including the National Agricultural Development Framework of 2009, which states: "When the Afghan economy is overwhelmingly agricultural, agriculture is the dominant factor in the economy, in food security, livelihoods, sustainable natural resources and national security. Agriculture will determine whether Afghanistan will succeed or fail".[29]

Most of the largely rural population of Afghanistan is dependent on subsistence farming on already marginal lands; they are the most vulnerable communities to the impacts of climate change because of their main dependency on irrigated crops.[30] Across most of the country, the vegetable farming and orchard seasons begin in the months of February and March and grow until July–August; this season mainly brings cash returns to the farmers. While the projected scenarios of climate change foresee a decrease in spring precipitation (March-May); as the most demanding period of moisture supply to the crops and orchards, any decrease in precipitation will have negative consequences for the rural communities in terms of crop-water and land productivity across the whole country.

Likewise, Afghanistan's pastoralists are also facing the flow-on impacts of climatic shifts and their impacts on food production. Herders in Afghanistan are dealing with negative changes in vegetation composition as a result of decreased and erratic snow and rainfall patterns, which are also causing livestock deaths due to heavy snowfall and water scarcity in traditional water sources along migration routes.[31] Herding communities such as the transhumant Kuchis are facing coalescing climatic and social forces, which mean not only reduced pasture, as a result of excess grazing pressure, recurrent droughts and lack of accessible water for livestock,[32] but also competition over contested land which has seen the conversion of former rangeland into farmland.[33]

Analysis of FEWSNET (2022) shows that by June 2021, Ghor, Bamyan, Maidan Wardak, Daikundi, Uruzgan, Kandahar, Ghazni, Nuristan and Badakhshan provinces have been specifically in extreme crises in terms of food security. This was understood to have been caused by pandemic-induced sluggishness in the economy, reduced income-earning opportunities, below-average remittances and higher staple food prices.[34]

As regards nutrition, the key sources of carbohydrates and proteins in the diet of most Afghans include cereals, legumes, potatoes and sugar which come mainly from the limited irrigated land while a huge amount of these cereals is imported. The consequent decrease in the production of these products as a result of changes in precipitation amount and pattern will further worsen the already import-dependent agriculture sector of Afghanistan, while the fact is that after the fall of the country to the Taliban, between March and May 2022, 19.7 million Afghans suffer from an all-time high level of acute food insecurity, categorized as a Crisis or Emergency by IPCC.[35] Without immediate plans for mitigating food insecurity at a time when foreign donations are limited and the challenges of population growth, groundwater depletion, insecurity, and poverty are dominating, there are risks of internal displacement and migration that will increase over time.

It has been argued that structurally, there has been a failure of creating a productive agricultural economy because the modernization of farming arrived in Afghanistan is too late and this has not been reflected in policy. As a result, there have been limited development interventions at both the village and national levels in terms of state support and investment in infrastructure.[36]

The Impacts of Climate Change on Migration in Afghanistan

Afghanistan presently suffers from the world's most acute internal displacement crises due to protracted conflict, ongoing insecurity and natural disasters, such as droughts, floods, storms and earthquakes. The prevailing situation has been further exacerbated by high unemployment, poverty (an estimated 40% of the population living below the poverty line despite two decades of international development interventions),[37] insecure public services and climate shocks at times when the country is already isolated under the Taliban's regime.[38] In such conditions, mobility seems to have emerged as a key survival strategy for many Afghans and, in some cases, an inevitable part of life for at least the past two generations, and will likely continue to be so in the future.[39] Given the current and projected climate scenario of the country, all of these factors mean an even more acute displacement as multiple forces begin to coalesce with greater intensity and rapidity. It is felt that climate shocks and "headwinds" will have cumulative impacts on people's livelihoods, including worsened poverty, increased competition over ever-scarce resources, weakened governance and exacerbated instability, and in turn, contribute to increased displacement.[40]

In a case study of Afghanistan and climate change-induced migration,[41] point to the number of terms used to define the term – climate refugee, environmental refugee, environmentally displaced person, forced migrant due to environmental change and so forth – to underscore the complexity of the underlying dynamics at play.[42] Furthermore, analysis of dynamics in countries such as Afghanistan has led some to argue against the notion of "climate refugees," instead of calling for the use of the term "migrants" for different reasons, including that migration has remained largely internal, is not necessarily forced, because isolating the environmental or climatic push factors is difficult, and because climate migration discussions might then lose their focus on preventive measures.[43]

The IOM estimates that since 2010, at least one-third of Afghanistan's population has been displaced.[44] This is a consequence not only of protracted localized violent conflict but also of environmental forces such as drought.[45] This is also further compounded by the fact that over the past decade, refugees once hosted in Iran and Pakistan have returned to Afghanistan which is already experiencing high levels of displacement, such that it is estimated that half of the returnees have not been able to settle in their place of origin.[46] Other IDPs choose to settle in informal urban settlements due to short-term security concerns[47] or with a longer-term vision of accessing public services and livelihood opportunities. The outskirts of each of the country's major cities are characterized by displaced person camps, and international aid support for which is ebbing away.[48] Despite this, Afghanistan is believed to have one of the fastest rates of urbanization – 5% per annum – and roughly 70% of the population resides in informal neighborhoods.[49] Thousands of Afghan households reside on land for which they have unclear or contested tenure, often because the public or private land has been occupied without formal permission, as a result of which they often face forced evictions.[50]

Important to note is that the rapid internal migration trend of movement from rural to urban areas, in one of the poorest countries on earth, has caused a parallel shift from rural poverty to urban poverty across Afghanistan.[51] Large-scale migration from rural areas to the country's urban centers appears to be a trend that will continue not only to access better economic opportunities[52] but also due to conflict and increasingly, environmental shocks.[53] While urban and more educated segments of the population are more able to migrate to industrialized countries, the poorest make up the greater proportion of IDPs in Afghanistan.[54] According to the Internal Displacement Monitoring Centre, while the total number of displacements only in 2021 due to conflict and violence in Afghanistan was 723,000, the total of displacements due to natural disasters was 25,000.[55] Several hundred more displacements occurred as a result of floods in May 2020 in the districts of Argo and Baharak in Badakhshan province as well as Parun (Nuristan), as well as heavy rains in Paktia province.[56] Therefore, although the attention of the international humanitarian community has tended to focus on violent conflict as a driver of migration and displacement, environmental shocks form a significant proportion of overall displacements currently affecting the country's population. Given the projected increase in such shocks as avalanches, flash floods and landslides, these trends will likely continue. Discussions regarding the potential impacts of climate change on migration in Afghanistan are further compounded by the wider context of ongoing violence and instability.

One of the key driving factors for migration is the destabilizing effect of long-term conflict and prevailing insecurity on economies. For example, conflicts affecting rural livelihoods have pushed migration to bigger cities and sometimes neighboring countries. The urban and educated groups tend to migrate to developed countries while the poorest make up a large part of internally displaced people. Besides, growing demographic pressure with an increasing youth population across the country and their search for economic opportunities is also one of the main reasons for migration.[57]

Studies of migration dynamics of Afghan migrants arriving in countries such as Greece have demonstrated that while earlier trends were dominated by Afghan refugees to neighboring countries such as Iran and Pakistan,[58] there has been an increasing trend towards irregular migration directly out of Afghanistan.[59] This shift points to multiple forces impacting human security in Afghanistan, which are likely to intensify in the future amidst changing climatic conditions.[60]

In terms of the nexus between conflict and migration,[61] analysis of the cumulative effects of conflict and climate change divides projected dynamics into several scenarios, including conflicts associated with restricted access to vital services such as health facilities.

They also discuss conflict resulting from a lack of regional cooperation and management over shared water resources which has been exacerbated by increased competition in upstream Afghanistan as refugees and displaced communities attempt to return to their former lands. Lastly,[62] discuss conflict associated with growing urbanization which has occurred as a result of sudden and slow-onset disasters and conflict and most often without basic services meaning that the factors of vulnerability to future displacement are heightened.

Although analysis has often pointed to the significance of Afghan resilience to social, political and environmental shocks, it is clear that eventually the critical mass of a growing and vulnerable population, when faced by too many, multifarious external forces, will be left with few choices with which to locally secure lives and livelihoods and they will therefore seek them elsewhere within the region and beyond. To this end, some have called for a greater focus on treating migration as an adaptation strategy for dealing with the consequences of a changing climate.[63]

Conclusion

It is clear that Afghanistan, already struggling with the challenges of weak and contested governance, poverty and conflict, will not be ideally placed to deal with the increasing and cumulative effects of a changing global climate. As a consequence, migration, both within the country, as a result of localized displacement, and out of the country as an economic response to climate-driven forces, will become an increasingly problematic issue. As discussed earlier, there are some pathways to mitigation that policymakers and international development actors can engage in, such as awareness-raising, establishing early warning systems, and national policy dealing with internal displacement. Lastly, while it has been acknowledged that migration itself is an adaptation to climate change, it is undeniable that the prevailing global governance paradigm places importance on citizenship and the policing of borders, and therefore some shifts in thinking will be needed in order to provide just solutions to a global problem that will have uneven reverberations at the local level.

Afghanistan, one of the top 6 most affected countries in the world due to climate change,[64] is prone to natural disasters such as droughts and flash floods amidst global warming and climate change; flash floods were observed in August 2020 in Logar, Wardak, Kapisa, Parwan, Kabul, Nuristan, Kunar, Laghman and Nangarhar provinces; and the flash floods and intensive rainfall destroyed around 2049 houses and washed agricultural lands and public infrastructure as well as caused loss to human lives.[65] According to estimates, 3398 houses were destroyed in August 2022 as a result of flash floods, which also claimed the lives of 63 people and seriously injured another 115. Flash floods are believed to have killed 256 people so far this year, 118 of whom have died since August 1. This represents a 75% increase over the 147 fatalities caused by floods in 2021.[66] In order to avoid and mitigate the projected increase in dangers to human lives, agriculture, health and infrastructure sectors, the government, with the support of specialized international agencies, is required to urgently highlight and identify the areas which are most prone to the impacts of climate change. It is important to prioritize those areas for intervention that are at stake, increase the presence of fact-finding resources, data centers (i.e. ground-based hydrometeorological observation units) and assess the impact through modern techniques supported by various scientific models compounded by satellite observations, whereas the current relevant institutes are not used to or are not trained to make use of those facilities.

In addition to physical data stations, capacity-building programs are required at the national and subnational levels in order to create awareness about climate change and its projected future impacts on natural resources, health and infrastructure. Civil society organizations across the country need to be trained and supported to raise public awareness of and encourage the launching of eco-friendly technologies and lessen dependency on fossil fuels and other sources of greenhouse gas emissions; there is also a need to include public-private partnerships, which has so far been kept aside to touch upon climate-friendly initiatives across the country.

The present curriculum of higher education institutes barely addresses the issues of climate change, mitigation and adaptation; therefore, it is strongly recommended to incorporate subjects and materials into the curricula to streamline the local practices keeping in view the local climate, topographic features, energy resources and its utilization means in the light of the science and technology-based adaptable measures. It is extremely important to explore each sector individually and to identify their key needs in terms of adaptation and mitigation. Besides these measures, political will at all levels is vital for the synchronization of the activities and efforts aimed at climate change mitigation and adaptation for lasting and durable results.

Perhaps pertinent to the case of Afghanistan is the importance of shifting paradigms when attempting to deal with the issue of climate change-induced migration. There has been a shift from referring to "environmental migrants" toward terms such as "human mobility." This encompasses more broadly a wider range of phenomena that occur in the context of climate change including irregular migration related to environmental change and resource shortages as a border security issue, particularly for areas of destination; protection of environmental migrants; and environmental migration as a form of adaptation and climate risk management, reflecting the political sensitivities of migration.[67] Beyond this, there have been increased calls to focus on environmental migration through the prism of human security, and in doing so, place the most vulnerable populations at the center of concern.[68] Such understandings are based on the idea of migrants as having both agency and adaptive capacity and that human mobility can be one of a spectrum of responses to climate impacts and risks.[69]

Another arena in which shifting dynamics might spurn change concerns Afghanistan's reliance on international development aid. Since 2014, there has been a marked reduction in international aid commitments to Afghanistan. This has had economic reverberations throughout the Afghan economy and society as major sources of revenue and employment have been lost.[70] That said, international aid accounts for roughly 77% of the government's budget and despite some optimism regarding the country's ability to benefit from its as yet largely untapped extractive industries potential and flow-on industrialization, the necessary substantial capital investment has not materialized.[71] It has been argued that even if the ongoing peace talks are successful, Afghanistan will continue to be dependent on billions of dollars of aid. In order to place the country on the path to self-reliance, the government and donors will need to foster broader and more equitable economic participation with a greater focus on export-led growth, diversification of trade, and mobilization of tax revenues.[72] There have also been calls for more targeted reformulations of international intervention taking into account Afghanistan's specific vulnerabilities to climate change by, for instance, including climate security into the UN mandate in Afghanistan.[73]

Furthermore, raising awareness of the projected climate change scenarios for Afghanistan is important not only for public policymakers but also for communities. If communities are better informed about climatic shifts at the global and regional scales, then they will be better equipped to mitigate their vulnerability to climate-induced shocks, and consequently may not need to turn to migration as a survival strategy. To this end, there is evidence of international development interventions aimed at improving the information on climate risk and appropriate response measures for staff of agriculture and irrigation departments as farmers and pastoralists.[74]

Another clear issue impacting stakeholders' ability to tackle the issues at hand is the lack of sufficient data. The Government of Afghanistan has conceded that a lack of data makes it difficult to develop effective climate projections.[75] Even in contexts where increasingly reliable figures for new internal displacements are being produced, it has been acknowledged that it is difficult to compute reliable estimates for the number of people moving in anticipation of or response to slow-onset processes such as desertification.[76] In order to address this, investment in capacity building in Afghanistan's ability to gather and monitor data is required.[77] There are some examples of such systems that provide the basis for effective monitoring and early warning systems if provided with ongoing external support. For instance, the World Bank-steered Global Facility for Disaster Reduction and Recovery has been developing a road map for the establishment of early warning systems in Afghanistan.[78] Another example is the USAID-funded famine early warning system, which analyses food insecurity in terms of commodity prices and the wider economic outlook.[79] As a result, the impacts of such extreme shifts in climate and weather patterns may be mitigated. These systems are aimed at not only ensuring the protection of human populations but delivering specialized agricultural advisory services such as drought and flood monitoring and other hydrological information for integrated water resource management. In order for them to continue to be effective, and in light of the reduced international development commitment to Afghanistan, there must be ongoing technical support to Afghan stakeholders, with a long-term view to building national capacity to steward data management and monitoring systems.

One of the pillars of understanding climate change adaptation is ensuring more diversified livelihood opportunities, something that is being supported via various international development interventions.[80] However, it appears that there is a need for more nuanced understandings. For instance, remittance-recipient households can often display a less adaptive capacity to environmental and climatic stressors.[81] Given that Afghanistan's future outlook is likely to be further defined by water scarcity, one identified issue has been the need to adapt to more frequent and intense droughts by improving water security through irrigation infrastructure improvements. For its part, the Government of Afghanistan has identified seven priorities for adaptation to climate change. These are (a) enhancing adaptive capacity and resilience and disaster risk reduction; (b) integrating climate change into national planning processes; (c) promoting economic development through the sustainable management of environmental resources and increased access to modern forms of efficient and sustainable energy; (d) building technical capacity in governmental institutions; (e) having adaptive and integrated land and water management; (f) improving water access in rural communities; and (g) Raising public awareness in Afghanistan.[82] The Afghan government has estimated that its adaptation plans would cost $10.785 billion between 2020 and 2030.[83]

Another important matter impacting Afghanistan's ability to respond to the challenges at hand concerns the lack of a coherent national policy on internal displacement which speaks directly to the climate change-induced push factors causing communities to leave their homes. Research has demonstrated that the majority of new displacements across the globe in recent years have occurred in "environments characterized by a high-risk exposure to natural and human-made hazards, high levels of socioeconomic vulnerability, and low coping capacity of both institutions and infrastructure".[84] It is expected that this will become more protracted as governments with a weak coping capacity struggle to respond to the multiple, varied and complex needs of IDPs. As a result, IDPs' vulnerability could persist and worsen over time. In this context, it is only natural that displacement will intensify in the future and be further exacerbated by cross-cutting issues such as weak governance and violent conflict. To date, the Government of Afghanistan has not enacted any policy specifically focused on internal displacement. Doing so would serve to mitigate some of the flow-on effects of climate change if attention is paid to issues such as securing land tenure, protection of human rights, protection of women and children, health care and education of IDPs.

Lastly, another important matter for Afghanistan concerning climate change-induced migration concerns the lack of regional cooperation around shared resources and increasingly shared issues arising from their management. Scarcer water and arable land is set to increase already-widespread community-level and inter-ethnic conflict at the local scale, while at the regional scale, reductions in transboundary water resources may escalate regional tensions.[85] For these reasons, Afghanistan will benefit from greater cooperation and clarity around shared water resources, including through joint river basin management, which will encourage better overall water resource management.

Notes

1 Afghanaid. (2021). *Afghanistan and COP26*. Retrieved November 2, 2022, from https://www.afghanaid.org.uk/news/countdown-to-cop-26

2 NEPA. (2017). *Afghanistan's Second National Communication (SNC) under the UNFCCC (2015–2016)*. National Environmental Protection Agency (NEPA). Retrieved September 10, 2021, from https://www.unep.org/resources/report/afghanistans-second-national-communication-snc-under-unfccc-2015-2016

3 Savage, M., Dougherty, B., Hamza, M., Butterfield, R., & Bharwani, S. (2009). *Socio-economic impacts of climate change in Afghanistan*. Stockholm Environment Institute.

4 Mortreux, C., & Barnett, J. (2009). Climate change, migration and adaptation in Funafuti, Tuvalu. *Global Environmental Change*, *19*(1), 105–112.

5 Přívara, A., & Přívarová, M. (2019). Nexus between climate change, displacement and conflict: Afghanistan case. *Sustainability*, *11*(20), 5586.

6 Reuveny, R. (2007). Climate change-induced migration and violent conflict. *Political Geography*, *26*(6), 656–673.

7 United Nations. (2019). *Massive displacement, greater competition for scarce resources cited as major risks in security council debate on climate-related threats*. Retrieved July 27, 2020, from https://press.un.org/en/2019/sc13677.doc.htm

8 Klare, M. T. (2013). *How resource scarcity and climate change could produce a global explosion*. Retrieved November 3, 2022, from https://www.thenation.com/article/archive/how-resource-scarcity-and-climate-change-couldproduce-global-explosion/

9 Intelligence Community. (2012, February 2). *Global water security (Intelligence Community Assessment), ICA 2012–08*. Retrieved August 25, 2020, from https://www.dni.gov/files/documents/Special%20Report_ICA%20Global%20Water%20Security.pdf

10 Sadat, S. H., & Sayed, N. (2019). Afghanistan: Water management for peace. *The Interpreter*. Retrieved September 10, 2022, from https://www.lowyinstitute.org/the-interpreter/afghanistan-water-management-peace

11 NEPA & UN Environment. (2016). *Afghanistan: Climate change science perspectives*. National Environmental Protection Agency & UN Environment. Retrieved September 10, 2021, from https://postconflict.unep.ch/publications/Afghanistan/UNEP_AFG_CC_Science_perspectives.pdf
12 Ibid.
13 Ibid.
14 Ibid.
15 Ibid.
16 Ibid.
17 Ibid.
18 Ibid.
19 FAO. (2012). *Country profile – Afghanistan*. AQUASTAT – FAO's Global Information System on Water and Agriculture. Retrieved October 10, 2021, from https://www.fao.org/aquastat/en/countries-and-basins/country-profiles/country/AFG
20 World Bank. (2020). *Climate change knowledge portal, Afghanistan*. World Bank Group. Retrieved August 25, 2022, from https://climateknowledgeportal.worldbank.org/country/afghanistan/climate-data-projections
21 Haritashya, U. K., Bishop, M. P., Shroder, J. F., Bush, A. B., & Bulley, H. N. (2009). Space-based assessment of glacier fluctuations in the Wakhan Pamir, Afghanistan. *Climatic Change*, *94*(1), 5–18.
22 Bhatta, A. (2011). *Increasing Himalayan snow cover challenges warming theory*. Nature India.
23 Immerzeel, W. W., Van Beek, L., Konz, M., Shrestha, A., & Bierkens, M. (2012). Hydrological response to climate change in a glacierized catchment in the Himalayas. *Climatic Change*, *110*(3), 721–736.
24 Keller, F., Goyette, S., & Beniston, M. (2005). Sensitivity analysis of snow cover to climate change scenarios and their impact on plant habitats in alpine terrain. *Climatic Change*, *72*(3), 299–319.
25 Savage, M., Dougherty, B., Hamza, M., Butterfield, R., & Bharwani, S. (2009). *Socio-economic impacts of climate change in Afghanistan*. Stockholm Environment Institute.
26 WFP, UNEP, & NEPA. (2016). *Climate change in Afghanistan: What does it mean for rural livelihoods and food security?* UNEP. Retrieved November 15, 2020, from https://www.unep.org/resources/report/climate-change-afghanistan-whatdoes-it-mean-rural-livelihoods-and-food-security
27 ICIMOD. (2018). *Glacier dynamics application for Afghanistan*. Retrieved August 15, 2020, from https://servir.icimod.org/science-applications/glacier-dynamicsapplication-afghanistan/
28 Pelto, M. (2014). *Kuh-E Myana Glacier retreat, Afghanistan*. Retrieved September 1, 2020, from https://blogs.agu.org/fromaglaciersperspective/2014/11/20/kuh-e-myana-glacier-retreat-afghanistan/
29 NADF. (2009). *Umbrella document for the National Agriculture Development Framework*. Ministry of Agriculture, Irrigation and Livestock. Retrieved November 3, 2022, from http://www.ipcinfo.org/fileadmin/user_upload/fsatmis/docs/Umbrella%20Document%20for%20NADF%20V4%2001%20April%202009.pdf
30 UNEP. (2003). *Afghanistan post-conflict environmental assessment*. United Nations Environment Program.
31 Ali, A., & Shaoliang, Y. (2013). Highland rangelands of Afghanistan: Significance, management issues, and strategies. In *High-altitude rangelands and their interfaces in the Hindu Kush Himalayas*, 15.

32 Ghoryar, M. A., & Roggero, P. P. (2019). Assessment of rangeland issues, challenges and options in the western region of Afghanistan. *Academicia: An International Multidisciplinary Research Journal*, *9*(1), 34–48.
33 Ali, A., & Shaoliang, Y. (2013). Highland rangelands of Afghanistan: Significance, management issues, and strategies. In *High-altitude rangelands and their interfaces in the Hindu Kush Himalayas*, 15.
34 FEWSNET. (2022). *FEWS NET data center: Afghanistan food security classification*. FEWSNET. Retrieved October 10, 2022, from https://fews.net/fews-data/333
35 IPCC. (2022). *Afghanistan: Acute food insecurity situation for March–May 2022 and Projection for June–November 2022*. FEWSNET. Retrieved November 3, 2022, from https://www.ipcinfo.org/ipc-country-analysis/details-map/en/c/1155595/?iso3=AFG
36 Pain, A., & Huot, D. (2018). Challenges of late development in Afghanistan: The transformation that did not happen. *Asian Survey*, *58*(6), 1111–1135.
37 World Bank. (2015). *Afghanistan poverty status update: An analysis based on National Risk and Vulnerability Assessment 2007/08 and 2011/12*. World Bank Group. Retrieved October 12, 2020, from https://openknowledge.worldbank.org/handle/10986/22917
38 IDMC. (2022). *Country profile: Afghanistan*. International Displacement Monitoring Center. Retrieved November 3, 2022, from https://www.internal-displacement.org/countries/afghanistan
39 Howard, C., & Madzarevic, J. (2014). Enhancing security of land tenure for IDPs. *Forced Migration Review*, (46), 38–41. https://www.fmreview.org/sites/fmr/files/FMRdownloads/en/afghanistan.pdf
40 Brown, O. (2019). Climate-fragility risk brief: Afghanistan. *Brief, Climate Society Expert Network*, *30*.
41 Přívara, A., & Přívarová, M. (2019). Nexus between climate change, displacement and conflict: Afghanistan case. *Sustainability*, *11*(20), 5586.
42 Ibid.
43 Ionesco, D. (2019). *Let's talk about climate migrants, not climate refugees*. United Nations. Retrieved November 3, 2022, from https://www.un.org/sustainabledevelopment/blog/2019/06/lets-talk-about-climate-migrants-not-climate-refugees/
44 IOM. (2019). *A third of Afghans have migrated or been displaced since 2012: IOM*. International Organization for Migration. Retrieved November 3, 2022, from https://www.iom.int/news/third-afghans-have-migrated-or-been-displaced-2012-iom
45 Ibid.
46 NRC/IDMC. (2017). *Global report on internal displacement – 2017*. Norwegian Refugee Council/Internal Displacement Monitoring Centre (NRC/IDMC). Retrieved November 3, 2022, from https://www.refworld.org/docid/599339934.html
47 Solomon, A., & Stark, C. (2011). *Internal displacement in Afghanistan: Complex challenges to government response*. The Brooking Institution. Retrieved November 3, 2022, from https://www.brookings.edu/wp-content/uploads/2016/06/From-Responsibility-to-Response-Nov-2011_Afghanistan.pdf
48 GIZ. (2017). Internally Displaced Persons (IDPs) in Afghanistan. *GIZ*. Retrieved September 3, 2020, from https://www.giz.de/en/ourservices/55909.html
49 Rao, S., & Turkstra, J. (2014). Enhancing security of land tenure for IDPs. *Forced Migration Review*, (46), 15–18. https://www.fmreview.org/sites/fmr/files/FMRdownloads/en/afghanistan.pdf

50 Howard, C., & Madzarevic, J. (2014). Enhancing security of land tenure for IDPs. *Forced Migration Review*, (46), 38–41. https://www.fmreview.org/sites/fmr/files/FMRdownloads/en/afghanistan.pdf
51 Stigter, E. (2006). Afghan migratory strategies–an assessment of repatriation and sustainable return in response to the convention plus. *Refugee Survey Quarterly*, *25*(2), 109–122.
52 Garrote-Sanchez, D. (2017). *International labor mobility of nationals: Experience and evidence for Afghanistan at macro level*. World Bank. http://hdl.handle.net/10986/30268
53 Lopez-Lucia, E. (2015). Migration and conflict in Afghanistan. *GSDRC Helpdesk Report, 1243*.
54 Ibid.
55 IDMC. (2022). *Country profile: Afghanistan*. International Displacement Monitoring Center. Retrieved November 3, 2022, from https://www.internal-displacement.org/countries/afghanistan
56 IOM. (2020). *World migration report 2020*. United Nations.
57 Lopez-Lucia, E. (2015). Migration and conflict in Afghanistan. *GSDRC Helpdesk Report, 1243*.
58 Dimitriadi, A. (2013). Migration from Afghanistan to third countries and Greece. *IRMA Background Report*, 1–34.
59 Ibid.
60 IOM. (2009). *Compendium of IOM's activities in migration, climate change and the environment*. International Organization for Migration. Retrieved November 3, 2022, from https://www.iom.int/jahia/webdav/shared/shared/mainsite/activities/env_degradation/compendium_climate_change.pdf
61 Přívara, A., & Přívarová, M. (2019). Nexus between climate change, displacement and conflict: Afghanistan case. *Sustainability*, *11*(20), 5586.
62 Ibid.
63 Hunzai, K. (2013). *The role of migration as an adaptation strategy in the Hindu Kush Himalayan Region*. International Organization for Migration. Retrieved November 3, 2022, from https://environmentalmigration.iom.int/blogs/rolemigration-adaptation-strategy-hindu-kush-himalayan-region
64 Eckstein, D., Künzel, V., & Schäfer, L. (2021). *Global Climate Risk Index 2021: Who suffers most extreme weather events? Weather-related loss events in 2019 and 2000–2019*. Germanwatch eV.
65 Floodlist. (2020). Afghanistan – flash floods death toll rises to 145. *Floodlist*. Retrieved August 27, 2020, from https://floodlist.com/asia/afghanistan-flashfloods-update-august-2020
66 OCHA. (2022, August 24). *Afghanistan: Flash flooding in the Central, Eastern, Western and South-Eastern regions – flash update no. 5*. United Nations Office for the Coordination of Humanitarian Affairs. Retrieved November 4, 2022, from https://www.humanitarianresponse.info/en/operations/afghanistan/document/afghanistan-flash-flooding-central-eastern-western-and-south-eastern
67 IOM. (2020). *World migration report 2020*. United Nations.
68 IOM. (2009). *Compendium of IOM's activities in migration, climate change and the environment*. International Organization for Migration. Retrieved November 3, 2022, from https://www.iom.int/jahia/webdav/shared/shared/mainsite/activities/env_degradation/compendium_climate_change.pdf
69 Ionesco, D. (2019). *Let's talk about climate migrants, not climate refugees*. United Nations. Retrieved November 3, 2022, from https://www.un.org/sustainabledevelopment/blog/2019/06/lets-talk-about-climate-migrants-not-climate-refugees/

70 Nasery, J. A. (2014). *The economic shock to Afghanistan caused by aid reduction and troops withdrawal* (No. 202). IEE Working Papers.
71 Sidhu, A. (2020). Trade, aid, and a self-reliant Afghan economy. *Rise to Peace.* Retrieved November 3, 2022, from https://www.risetopeace.org/2020/07/02/afghan-development/asidhu/
72 Ibid.
73 Brown, O. (2019). Climate-fragility risk brief: Afghanistan. *Brief, Climate Society Expert Network, 30.*
74 World Bank. (2018). *Strengthening hydromet and early warning services in Afghanistan: A road map*. World Bank Group.
75 NEPA. (2015, September 21). *Islamic Republic of Afghanistan: Intended nationally determined contribution submission to the United Nations Framework Convention on Climate Change.* Retrieved November 3, 2022, from https://unfccc.int/NDCREG
76 IDMC. (2018). *No matter of choice: Displacement in a changing climate*. International Displacement Monitoring Center. Retrieved November 3, 2022, from https://www.internaldisplacement.org/sites/default/files/publications/documents/20181213-slow-onset-intro.pdf
77 Brown, O. (2019). Climate-fragility risk brief: Afghanistan. *Brief, Climate Society Expert Network, 30.*
78 World Bank. (2018). *Strengthening hydromet and early warning services in Afghanistan: A road map*. World Bank Group.
79 FEWSNET. (2020). Food security outlook update: Second season crops developing normally, while staple wheat prices decline but remain above average. *FEWSNET*. Retrieved August 25, 2020, from https://fews.net/central-asia/afghanistan/food-security-outlook-update/august-2020
80 UNDP. (2014). *Climate Change Adaptation Project (CCAP) strengthening the resilience of rural livelihood options for Afghan communities in Panjshir, Balkh, Uruzgan and Herat Provinces to manage climate change-induced disaster risks.* Global Environmental Facility. Retrieved October 10, 2022, from https://www.thegef.org/projectsoperations/projects/5202
81 IOM. (2020). *World migration report 2020*. United Nations.
82 NEPA. (2017). *Afghanistan's Second National Communication (SNC) under the UNFCCC (2015–2016)*. National Environmental Protection Agency (NEPA). Retrieved September 10, 2021, from https://www.unep.org/resources/report/afghanistans-second-national-communication-snc-under-unfccc-2015-2016
83 NEPA. (2015, September 21). *Islamic Republic of Afghanistan: Intended nationally determined contribution submission to the United Nations Framework Convention on climate change.* Retrieved November 3, 2022, from https://unfccc.int/NDCREG
84 NRC/IDMC. (2017). *Global report on internal displacement – 2017*. Norwegian Refugee Council/Internal Displacement Monitoring Centre (NRC/IDMC). Retrieved November 3, 2022, from https://www.refworld.org/docid/599339934.html
85 Brown, O. (2019). Climate-fragility risk brief: Afghanistan. *Brief, Climate Society Expert Network, 30.*

Chapter 3

Changing Climate and New Migration Crisis in Bangladesh

Pallavi Deka

Introduction

Over the past two decades, discussions on climate change slowly moved out of the seminar rooms to everyday life as the world finally woke up to observable changes in the environment and extreme weather conditions made it impossible to deny it any longer. According to the United Nations Framework Convention on Climate Change (UNFCCC), climate change means "a change of climate which is attributed directly or indirectly to human activity that alters the composition of the global atmosphere and which is in addition to natural climate variability observed over comparable time periods".[1] In one of its report titled "Global Warming of 1.5 Degree Celsius", the Intergovernmental Panel on Climate Change (IPCC), a UN body to specifically monitor climate change, states that the warming of the planet by 1 degree Celsius above pre-industrial level has been already caused by human activity till 2017.[2] In a statement, what UN Secretary-General Antonio Guterres called the IPCC report of 2022 "an atlas of human suffering and a damning indictment of failed climate leadership"[3] has scientifically analysed that global warming of 1.5°C relative to 1850–1900 would be exceeded during the 21st century under the intermediate, high and very high GHG emissions scenarios considered in the recent IPCC report.[4] Extreme weather conditions like increased rainfall in some parts and increased drought in some others, rise in sea level, melting of the permafrost, frequent cyclones, damage to global flora and fauna and heightened risk of vector borne diseases are some of the impacts that are directly associated with it.[5] Because of these, ecosystems that sustain humans are likely to reduce, global net cropped area is likely to shrink or become less productive and activities like fishing are also going to take a hit while displacement, poverty and malnutrition are likely to increase. Many changes in the climate system become larger in direct relation to increasing global warming. They include increases in the frequency and intensity of hot extremes, marine heatwaves, heavy precipitation and, in some regions, agricultural and ecological droughts; an

DOI:10.4324/9781003367802-4

increase in the proportion of intense tropical cyclones; and reductions in Arctic sea ice, snow cover and permafrost.[6]

Like any other country of the world, Bangladesh too is likely to be affected by climate changes, but there are some factors that make it 'the most vulnerable country'. According to Global Climate Risk Index 2021, in terms of long-term Climate Risk Index, Bangladesh has ranked seventh in the period 2000–2019.[7] In this chapter, a detailed discussion on the factors causing such vulnerability will be studied and also their impact on the people and environment of Bangladesh. Along with these the strategies of adaptation people of Bangladesh are resorting to with their impact on migration patterns will be deliberated beside the steps the government is taking.

What Makes Bangladesh Most Vulnerable?

The geographical location of Bangladesh is unique – in the north of the country lie the Himalayas and in the south, it is surrounded by the Bay of Bengal. Three major river systems of South Asia – Ganga (called Padma in Bangladesh), Brahmaputra (Jamuna here) and Meghna pass through the country. But while this increases water resource availability for the country, it also comes with its set of problems. Also as all these rivers originate in neighbouring countries, Bangladesh being a low elevation country has no control over the flow of waters in them.

Every year during the monsoon, these rivers cause seasonal flooding and soil erosion, not just damaging the populations and ecology of the riverine districts in the short term but also causing loss of land in the long term. B.G. Verghese captures this unique predicament of Bangladesh, which faces 'a flood problem of the nature and magnitude that' no other country in the world faces when he says:

> A monsoon flood discharge, draining over 1.5 million square miles in five countries straddling both sides of the Himalayas and containing far and away the highest rainfall density zones in the world, **funnels into the sea through the nozzle of Bangladesh** (*emphasis mine*) comprising barely 7.5 percent of the total basin.[8]

Verghese's comparison, of Bangladesh as the nozzle of a funnel comprising high altitude, heavy rain density zones of India, Nepal, Bhutan, Myanmar and China gives an apt, graphic account of the problem. Further, the swelling flood waves of the tri-river system have to go through the lower Meghna river – a single outlet, before being emptied into the Bay of Bengal.[9] However, the capacity of lower Meghna to dispose these excess waters and silt into the sea decreases whenever tide levels increase in the Bay of Bengal, and when this coincides with peak flows of waters in tri-river system during monsoons, misery in the form of flood spills over most of the country's flood plains.[10] These natural processes have been going on like this since a long time and hence, floods are a part of life in Bangladesh. However, what is new is the increased intensity of the problem, and its compounding by climate change-induced factors like higher occurrence of cyclones, extreme weather conditions like drought, increase in average temperatures and salinity.

What turns Bangladesh into a 'Malthussian basket case' is its increasing population, decreasing resources and environmental degradation.[11] It is the eighth most populous country of the world,[12] with one of the highest population density ratios in the world.

This exacerbates the struggle for meagre resources among a large number of people and as the life expectancy is at the rise, the struggle becomes more acute. In the absence of a vibrant manufacturing sector (except the recent success of textile exports) and services, agriculture and allied sectors become the main employer for majority of the population, but loss of land due to erosion and loss of crops due to floods are causing severe damage; the rest of the damage is done by rising sea levels and cyclones which are becoming regular due to climate change.

Around two-thirds of Bangladesh is only five meters above the sea level and 28 percent of the country's population lives on the coast.[13] Climate experts even predict that by 2050, rising sea level will submerge around 17 percent of the nation's land and will displace about 20 million people[14] turning them into 'environmental refugees'. A resilient government-civil society mechanism to cope up with these challenges, along with the urban infrastructure to absorb people thus displaced, could have mitigated the damage caused by climate change. But Bangladesh lags badly in terms of these requirements. Due to lack of opportunities in other urban areas, its only metro Dhaka becomes the prime destination for people displaced by these climatic conditions.

Scale of the Problem

While disasters like floods, cyclones, storm surges and drought affect most of the population in the affected area, children, women and elderly people are the worst hit. A number of past studies on the effects of natural disasters on populations have highlighted this fact.[15] The immediate impact comes in the form of destruction of houses and trees, crop loss and loss of livelihood, foodstuff, livestock and so on. In the long term, lack of availability of fresh water and healthcare become major issues. Socio-economic impact, health impact and increase in vulnerability are some of the outcomes of post-disaster scenario.

As has been discussed earlier, Bangladesh is a land of rivers and floods. The country that is situated at the end of the catchment area of Ganga-Brahmaputra-Meghna (GBM) river system occupies only about 7 percent

Table 3.1 Primary environmental disasters in Bangladesh[16]

Common environmental disasters	*Geographical spreads*
Sea level rise and Flood	On an average, 1/4th of the total area is annual submerged which increases up to 36% in case of severe cases. Half of Bangladesh's geographical location is 12.5 metre above the mean sea level.
Cyclone	One to three moderate to severe storm hit Bangladesh every year.
Drought	The north-western part of the country is affected by drought, sometimes severe one.
Riverbank erosion	These are common and recurrent in 35 sub-districts of the country.

Source: Mahmuda Khatun (2013), "Climate change and migration in Bangladesh: Golden Bengal to land of disasters", *Bangladesh's E Journal of Sociology*, 10(2), 67, accessed from https://citeseerx.ist.psu.edu/viewdoc/download?doi=10.1.1.682.1886&rep=rep1&type=pdf#page=64 on 25th February 2020

of the combined catchment area. Since a little fraction of the catchment area needs to manage the discharge of more than 92 percent of the water volume, over 80 percent of which is being discharged in about five months alone during the monsoons, flood is most frequent and also causes much havoc in this part.[17]

The trend of the major flood events show that such events are due to flooding that occurred because of extreme rainfall in the catchment areas. This holds true for the three major floods that occurred in 1987, 1988 and 1998 and the flooded areas were 66 percent, 68 percent and 70 percent, respectively, of the total area of Bangladesh. The case also continued for the flood years 2004 and 2008 as well.[18]

The water-related impacts of climate change, particularly riverine and coastal flooding have been listed as the most significant issues for Bangladesh, by the National Adaptation Program of Action (NAPA), Ministry of Environment and Forest of the Government of Bangladesh. In terms of flooding, a report by the Organisation for Economic Co-operation and Development (OECD) states that future changes in precipitation in Bangladesh has four distinct implications:

- Change in timing of occurrence of floods have implications for the seasonality of the hydrological cycle.
- Increased precipitation in the GBM basins may increase the magnitude of floods
- The timing of peaking in the major rivers may also change, which may in turn change the likelihood of synchronization of flood peaks of major rivers
- Increased magnitude, depth, extent and duration of floods will bring a dramatic change in land use patterns in Bangladesh.[19]

It has already been recorded that more than one million people have lost their homes and 70 percent of these people have become landless due to river erosion. River erosion is still high in Bangladesh that is a threat to life and livelihood for many. River erosion has also escalated due to surging monsoon that brings heavy rainfall. Studies have shown that each year over 0.1 percent people become homeless due to river erosion.[20]

Sea level rise has become one of the most critical development of climate change impact that is affecting Bangladesh and other low lying countries of the world. There has already been many effects of sea level rise in the country; this include land erosion, increased salinity in coastal areas, and biodiversity collapse leading to reduction of food production and fisheries in Bangladesh.

While the entire country of Bangladesh is exposed to weather and climate-related stresses, the densely populated coastal region along the Bay of Bengal constitutes a vulnerability "frontline".[21] The population in such vulnerable coastal districts will have no choice but to migrate to other parts of the country as their homes and land are destroyed.[22]

Along with large-scale flooding, drought has become a regular feature of the climatic condition in Bangladesh. The Intergovernmental Panel for Climate Change assessment reports that droughts will affect eight million people in Bangladesh by 2050.[23] Food and Agricultural Organization (2007) reported that the droughts in Bangladesh are products of two related factors: climate change and lack of surface water.[24] Droughts are a threat to the livelihoods, agricultural production, and economy of the affected areas as it leads to with land degradation, low livestock population, unemployment and malnutrition. In these terms even though the droughts caused more devastation than the floods, for some reason droughts received less attention from policy makers and researchers.[25]

Drought-prone area inhabitants took different strategies for their survival. They did not consider migration as an alternative option in the first instance believing droughts do not last forever. However, migration as an obvious response to other rural areas or urban centres cannot be totally ruled out.[26] The vulnerable drought-prone districts are Dhaka, Manikganj, Faridpur, Gazipur, Sirajganj, Tangail, Rajbari, Faridpur, Pirojpur, Patuakhali; and parts of Gaibandha, Sherpur, Chapainawabganj, Rangpur, Dinajpur, Khushtia, Narail, Cumilla, Kishorganj and Bhola.[27] It has also been found that migration decision of the people did not change even after receiving financial assistance and information assistance regarding coping methods with the droughts.[28]

Another major climate hazard that Bangladesh faces are cyclones. Some of the most devastating natural disasters in recorded history with high casualties were tropical cyclones that hit the region now comprising present-day Bangladesh.[30] In a study by IUCN on cyclones that affected Bangladesh from 1960 to 2007, it was found that 56 tropical cyclones hit

Table 3.2 Major droughts, affected area and their impact in Bangladesh[29]

Year	*Affected area and impact*
1973	Northern Bangladesh and it resulted in the 1974 famine.
1975	Affected 47 percent of the country and more than half of the population.
1978–79	One of the most severe ones that reduced the food production affecting 42 percent of the cultivated lands and 44 percent of the population.
1989	Dried up most of the rivers in the north-western part of the country with severe dust-storm.
1994–95	Whole country was affected by severe drought.
2009–15	Drought has become a regular feature in the country hitting the northern, southern western and central region severely.

Source: Food and Agriculture Organization of the United Nations (2007), *Climate variability and change: Adaptation to drought in Bangladesh*. Rome: FAO, p. 15, accessed from http://en.banglapedia.org/index.php?title=Bangladesh on 1st April 2020.

the coast of Bangladesh of which 48.2 percent were categorized as very strong and 17.9 percent as severe cyclonic storms.[31] Cyclone Amphan hit coastal West Bengal and Bangladesh on 20 May 2020. It was the first super cyclone to form in the Bay of Bengal since 1999 and one of the fiercest in the past 100 years. The cyclone intensified from a cyclonic storm (Category 1) to a super cyclone (Category 5) in less than 36 hours.[32] Table 3.3 lists the major cyclones that came during that period and the lives lost due to them.

Table 3.3 Cyclone severity and deaths in Bangladesh 1960–2007,[33] 2013 and 2020[34]

Year	*Number of deaths*	*Wind speed (kmph)*
1960	8,119	210
1965	20,152	210
1970	500,300	223
1974	50	162
1985	11,069	154
1991	138,958	225
1995	172	100
1998	233	112
2007	4,234*	250
2013	17	85
2020	18	85

Source: Ubydul Haque, et al. (2012), "Reduced death rates from cyclones in Bangladesh: What more needs to be done", *Bulletin of the World Health Organization*, 90(2), 152, accessed from www.ncbi.nlm.nih.gov/pmc/articles/PMC3302549/ on 7th May 2020.

"12F major cyclones from the past", *Dhaka Tribune*, accessed from www.dhakatribune.com/bangladesh/environment/2017/05/30/majorcyclonesbangladesh/?fbclid=IwAR06XP8lyCu0X0gBDSWsMYF7geFoR0nH99-gjEcJvpq2agRUAI39OODTyxk on 20th May 2020

The data reveals that with the exception of 2007 when Cyclone Sidr hit Bangladesh, the number of deaths due to cyclones is steadily declining. Table 3.3 covers the cyclones from 2009 to May 2020, and the data in it also confirms that the number of deaths due to cyclones is declining.

However, while the deaths are declining, the impact on populations affected by the cyclones is not. The reason is straightforward – disaster preparedness regarding early warning and evacuation of people in affected areas reduces the number of deaths. But the impact on crops, households, livestock and means of livelihood like agricultural land or fisheries could not be averted. As a result, though structures to save lives during crisis have come in place, there are not sufficient mechanisms to help people cope up with post-disaster situation.

The people thus saved during disasters, return back to their inundated homes to find their houses and crops destroyed, livestock dead and fields unsustainable for agriculture due to post-cyclone salinity. Floods cause a similar impact and lack of clean drinking water in this situation, along with rampant open defecation leads to various health hazards and spread of diseases. River erosion works a bit differently as the process is generally gradual. However, its impact is no less severe as while floods or cyclones only inundate the land temporarily, or make it saline, land thus claimed by river disappears from the map, and sometimes takes couple of decades to re-emerge. In almost all of these cases, family members of the affected people or whole families have to take recourse to migration. The people who migrate under these circumstances are termed 'environmental migrant'.

The terminology and concerns regarding environmental migrations and refugees started gaining traction in development studies in the 1980s after United Nations Environmental Program (UNEP) published a report titled 'Environmental Refugees'. The 2007 definition of UNEP considers as environmental refugees.

> Those people who have been forced to leave their traditional habitat, temporarily or permanently, because of a marked environmental disruption (natural and/or triggered by people) that jeopardized their existence and/or seriously affected the quality of their life. By 'environmental disruption' in this definition is meant any physical, chemical, and/or biological changes in the ecosystem (or resource base) that render it, temporarily or permanently, unsuitable to support human life.[35]

Here, both environmental migrants and refugees are more or less clubbed together, though some scholars say that 'victims of climate events are climate migrants', who are 'forced to migrate' due to displacement by climate change.[36] As they are likely to suffer economic marginalization and hardships at their migration destinations, they should be entitled to some protections under the 1951 UN Refugee Convention but an absence of such arrangement further increases their vulnerability.

It is quite difficult to measure the scale of the problem as the actual number of people affected by climate change who migrate to other areas is not known. The Association for Climate Refugees (ACR) made an attempt to measure this through an innovative procedure. They held workshops in all seven divisions of Bangladesh (Dhaka, Rajshahi, Rangpur, Barisal, Chittagong, Sylhet and Khulna) between March–May, 2010. Each of these divisional workshops were attended by 25–30 community leaders who gave an estimated number of families in their districts and subdistricts that were displaced due to climate-related reasons. Along with this, approximate numbers of affected people were also given by representatives from all 24 coastal and mainland districts from where majority of climate displaced people come. These figures were then taken together to arrive as a number. It is not a full proof method but an attempt was made in this manner to arrive at an approximate number and the results were stunning. ACR concluded after this exercise that around 6 million people have been displaced because of climate hazards in Bangladesh,[37] and the number was expected to grow to 7.5 million by 2010.[38] In a statement issued by World Health Organisation ahead of third edition of Global School on Refugee and Migrant Health in Dhaka, it has been claimed that over 7.1 million Bangladeshis were displaced by climate change in 2022, a number that could reach 13.3.million by 2050.[39] The Government of Bangladesh has acknowledged that by 2050, one in every seven people in Bangladesh will be displaced by climate change.[40]

Another field-based study conducted by Ahsan (2013)[41] as a part of his doctoral thesis pointed to the trend that migration due to climate events has increased since 2006 because of frequent disasters in the coastal belt. A sample survey amongst the climate migrants in Khulna and Dhaka carried out in 2010 by the researcher suggested that the volume of migrant flow is clearly influenced by extreme climatic events. The survey demonstrated that most respondents in Dhaka were displaced by river erosion. But in Khulna cyclones and soil salinity are the main migration drivers.[42]

Another interesting aspect that this study revealed was the case of double-layered migration. In fact most of the cases in the field survey were the second-generation migrants, who originally migrated as a result of climate-driven factors and subsequently migrated again from another city for economic or social reasons;[43] thereby projecting a complex phenomenon of climate migrates being overlooked and mistaken to be ruled by traditional factors of migration.

Climate Change and Char Areas: Migration as a Coping Strategy

It has already been mentioned earlier that due to changing nature of climate, there is a swelling in the flood hazard of Bangladesh. The floods in future will be not only severe but also enormous and more in duration around the globe and Bangladesh as well. It has been claimed that extreme recurrent flood events have already started in Bangladesh and the floods of 1988 and 1998 were the early signs that created havoc and submerged 61 districts totalling approximately 68 percent of the total area.[44] This part of the study will try to assess the impact of such flood havoc and other related consequences due to climate change in Char areas of Bangladesh.

Char areas are such land masses that are created due to the process of riverbank erosion and sedimentation deposited in the main rivers or in the coastal areas over a time of one to two years. In Bangladesh, it is estimated that almost 4–5 percent of the total population lives there. There are 56 big and 226 small chars in the country.[45]

There are roughly 6.5 million people who are living on these river islands *(chars)* with agriculture as the most common livelihood.[46] The literacy rate in these areas is around 25% that is in gap with the national rate of 51% and the poverty rate is roughly 80%.[47] So these vulnerable poor people living in the char areas do not have adequate protective measures and they also lack the capability to cope with the losses of the climate change effects. Most of the char dwellers are farmers and fisherman and they have no permanent asset since the land they dwell is itself temporary.

It has been found in some studies that the needs and concerns of the char people are of low priority for the policy maker's circles and the government offices. Providing basic services in terms of health, education and livelihood needs are difficult due to difficulty in travelling and lack of infrastructure.[48] However, three very large *char*-based projects were launched in the early 2000s. These are the Chars Livelihoods Programme (CLP), the Char Development and Settlement Program (CDSP) and the Social Investment Programme Project (SIPP, later called Nuton Jibon.[49] Each projects is different in approach with the common holistic objective of working for economic, social and institutional needs of the char areas and the impact differ according to the funding pattern and organizational structure.[50]

Though it has been found that living with flood and struggling against it has been an integral part of the lives of char dwellers; these people get displaced at least once in their lifetime. Hence, short- or long-term displacement and migration are the general norms for them. Riverbank erosion is an integral part of the flooding scenarios in the char areas. The impacts of climate change on soil erosion have been studied by the CLASSIC project that took into account the data from 1973 to 1999 for analysis. The study looked at the Brahmaputra-Jamuna basin and predicted that, by 2050, an increased peak discharge of 10 percent may increase erosion by 20 percent.[51] However erosion in one part of the char leads to formation on the other side or formation of new one through accretion. But erosion is almost 6th times faster than accretion and therefore also the loss. It has also been found that there is loss of fertility in the fresh lands that are formed due to accretion.[52]

The International Organization for Migration in one of its reports stated that subsistence activities and their lack are the main connection between climate change and migration.[53] In case of the char dwellers, the reason for lack of subsistence activity is mainly the loss of land and so the scope for cultivation. Therefore, from this point of discussion, migration becomes a way out due to the failure to adapt at a local level. However, migration can be seen and it has been promoted at many levels as a strategy for local people to respond and adapt to changes in the environment.[54] Though, it has also been argued that to consider a decision to migrate, either as an adaptation strategy or as an escape due to lack of adaptation is related to the fact whether the process of migration is voluntary or involuntary.

From the aforementioned discussion on the effect of climate change on the chars, there has been indication of the prevalence of high level of migration in char areas. Other studies conducted in north-western Bangladesh, including both residents of chars and people affected by riverbank erosion, found that almost all households had migrated several times in those areas.[55] It has also been agreed upon that for people to move, whether individually or with family, resource availability (including financial resources), attachment to ancestral land, the presence of relatives and the availability of social networks are the most commonly cited context upon which such decision are made.[56]

Locating the migration pattern and reasons, in context to the classical theories of migration, be it the Push-Pull theory of Ravenstein[57] or its refined version by Lee where push pull factors are linked to age, gender, class, education, social capital and so on, gives a clearer picture to it.[58] So while environmental factors substantiated by climate change that results in enormous and untimely floods as well as erosion in chars is a factor that pushes people outside; there are also other factors that contribute to the push factors like governance issues, corruption, lack of transparency, lack of legal aid and lack of monitoring by the local authorities are the major non governance concerns. Therefore, if the government is claiming for making migration as an adaptation technique against climate change impacts, which it is, it has to ensure the strengthening for governance mechanism in such events.[59]

There are also several 'pull' factors for the char dwellers to take the decision to migrate; amongst them are land availability and its cultivability, cost of living, height of the place of migration, proximity to the previous char and presence of family acquaintance. It is also claimed by some field-based studies that migrant char dwellers give preference to those areas where there is presence of active participation of non-governmental organisations since that increases the chance of better minimum amenities of livelihood.[60]

There are three different categories of migrants (permanent, temporary and cyclical) depending upon the severity of the push factors as well as the strength of the pull factors.[61] Permanent migration in char areas primarily due to changes in climatic conditions take place when there is total loss of the land people live in, due to large scale erosion. In such case, relocation of the whole family occurs and in most cases, they only migrate very short distances, either in the same char or to some nearby chars. This is due to lack of resources to relocate in a better place and the expectation to repossess when the chars re-emerge, despite knowing that the relocated land mass is equally vulnerable.[62] In temporary environmental migration, people migrate to some nearby places temporarily due to hazards like floods, draught, cyclone and other. So once these are over, the migrants revert back to their habitation. Again the cyclical environmental migration is due to loss of economic resources and livelihood loss. So here the people who choose to migrate do not lose the habitation but lose their livelihood due to environmental hazards. Here, it is mainly the male members of the households who take upon the migratory journey. It is because of this reason that it has been found that in char areas and embankments, the female headed households are three times higher than mainland.[63]

In the char areas, people migrate in order to relieve themselves from living in anticipatory risks; higher the risk, higher is the pressure to migrate. Therefore, in order to make migration process voluntary and less-pressure-laden, there are areas where the state needs to play a crucial role. Otherwise the claim of the government describing migration as an adaptation technique to face climate change impacts by the community remains falsified. Here needs the innovative policy interventions where the community feels the strong existence of the system and that can be ensured through infrastructure building (for education, health, economic activities) like houses, schools, clinic, markets and so on which are easily accessible and re-locatable. So floating and mobile hospitals on boat gives the healthcare facilities, floating markets give the people scope to earn without moving outside in pressure.[64]

Therefore, on the whole, the discussion points to the conclusion that people in the char areas in Bangladesh migrate to distance places as an option of last resort and generally they remain near to the land they belong to, even if migration becomes utmost necessity. Hence, the claims that there will be massive displacement of people in to cities[65] and people flocking in Dhaka city due to environmental disasters and climate change impact does not hold much ground here.

Sea Coast and Climate Change Migration

The coastal Bangladesh is one of the most climate stressed areas of the world. It has been projected that in next 120 years, the coastal areas of Bangladesh, presently populated by 1.3 billion people, will be inundated by sea level rise.[66] This will put 40 percent of the productive land in south Bangladesh under severe threat. It has also been found that in Bangladesh, episodic tidal inundation and storm surge are major sea level rise hazard, amplified by increase in soil salinity, riverine flooding caused by cyclones and seasonal monsoons.[67] It is also predicted that since 30 percent of the cultivable land are in coasts, there is to be a rise in food crisis in the country and the climate change impacts in these areas will displace around 200,000 people annually.[68]

The initial studies on climate migration simply estimated the population at risk due to major environmental hazard and assumed that major chunk of population will be displaced.[69] This was too simplistic in explanation without focusing on actual migratory pattern and behaviour that are influenced by socio-economic and political drivers.[70] These people in the coasts, live in poverty, face sudden onset of climate hazards like flooding, storm, erosion as well as slow onset challenges of sea level rise, salinization and soil subsidence.

Fussel et al. argue that it is environmental stress as well as other determinant factors of socio-economic nature that leads to migration decision; however, there is also the cost and other migration obstacles that "trap" population.[71] It is both environmental hazards triggered by climate change and socio-economic reasons that make people take the decision to migrate. But here also two counterviews coexists: one that believes that it is the poorest of the poor who take resort to migration as 'last resort'; the other view opines that more well-off people resort to migrating as they have resources to move.[72] Here it is not alone the push factors, but the factors like economic opportunities and economic disparities between rural and urban areas that work as pull factors. However, most of the migrants are temporary, returning in less than six months to their families. Of the permanent migrants from coastal areas, primarily from rural to urban has increased in the past few decades; in 1984, the rate per decade was 1.2 per thousand, which increased to 22.5 in 2010.[73]

There is again an attempt to draw a line of distinction between "economic migrants" and "Climate migrants". The argument that is cited, that is, the economic migrants respond to both push and pull factors, makes calculative decisions; while climate migrants have no real choices in terms of destination due to the struck of immediate exigencies, but to flee with whatever comes, so they respond to only push factors. So they may be considered to be called a new type of migrant where they become serial, multistage migrants.[74]

Salinization, which is growing in rivers, groundwater and soil, has come out as a slow climate change effect. Around 26 million people living in coastal Bangladesh and Sundarbans are threatened with groundwater salinity.[75] Sea level rise as well as land subsidence are the major player; however, it is further worsened by human interventions. Many scholars point to the diversion of the Ganga at the Farakka Barrage in India, which has reduced the flow of freshwater into the southwest region of Bangladesh as one of the many human led factor of increasing salinity. There is a projection that over the next 50 to 100 years, there may be an increase in the share of moderate to highly saline river area in the southwest as much as 40 percent and create even greater shortages of drinking and useable irrigation water.[76]

Soil salinity in the sea coast areas leads to loss of agricultural resources that ultimately leads to internal migration. It has been found that there is a direct link between the two. At the same time, it is also found in a study that increase of salinity in soil in coastal areas does not lead to long term or international migration. Overall liquidity constraint has been a factor in limiting short distance mobility and since it is the poor household who migrate as a last option, the resources needed for long-distance settlement are limited; therefore, people generally look for alternative arrangements like fish farming or shrimp farming.[77] So like the people in chars, the inhabitants of the coastal areas too first explore the adaptation technique through diversification of economic activities like aquaculture. In fact, there is a minimal migratory pattern to flooding and inundation.[78] Human migration in most cases is found to be linked with soil salinity increase and erosion that have aggravated due to climate change.

Government Response

The aforementioned discussion on the change in the climatic condition and the resultant outcome makes it clear that the biophysical and socio-economic condition of Bangladesh is making the climate change vulnerability of the country more acute. The government therefore not only has the task of locating the physiological variations of different regions of the country but also with this the socio-economic condition of the community therein should be accounted to formulate any plan with regard to climate change. Along with this the target groups based on the criteria like migrants, gender and religion, regional specificity also needs a sharp reflection in the plans and programmes.

In Bangladesh, it is the Ministry of Environment and Forests (MoEF) that functions as the focal ministry for climate change adaptation and mitigation initiatives and led in the development of the various plans and projects like National Adaptation Programme of Action (NAPA), Bangladesh Climate Change Strategy and Action Plan (BCCSAP), and the Climate Change and Gender Action Plan. There is another agency called Bangladesh Climate Change Trust (formerly Climate Change Unit) within the MoEF that coordinates the Climate Change Cells that are placed within relevant ministries.

The NAPA and BCCSAP are the most valuable flagship programme that Bangladesh has developed and pushing hard for implementation. NAPA was developed between 2003 and 2005 with support from GEF, and it was further updated in 2009. The 2009 update identified 38 adaptation measures that need to be adopted due to impact of climate change.[79]

NAPA in its detailed reports assessed the following problems with regard to climate change in Bangladesh: fresh water scarcity, drainage congestion, riverbank erosion, frequent floods, prolonged drought and salinity in the coastal zone. However one aspect of NAPA that needs to be considered is that it treated migration as an undesirable outcome of climate change that leads to crime in places of migrant concentration. In its project no. 11,

NAPA promotes adaptation to coastal crop agriculture to fight salinisation and making it an alternative arrangement for long-term outcomes including community adaptation to flood/tidal surge and sea level rise. And it adds: "Affected community would not migrate to cities for job and livelihood" (p 35); and "social consequences of mass scale migration to cities would to some extent be halted" (p 36). This seems to be a negative portrayal of migration as a potential security issue and also inconsistent with thinking on migration as a potential adaptation method.[80]

In 2008, BCCSAP was adopted with new and bolder initiatives. The BCCSAP upheld 44 short-, medium- and long-term as well as some immediate programmes to mitigate and adapt to climate change, based on the six pillars of food security: social protection and health; comprehensive disaster management; infrastructure; research and knowledge management; mitigation and low carbon development; capacity building and institutional strengthening.[81] There is also a stipulated framework for enactment of the BCCSAP within Bangladesh's Vision 2021 that has been further concretised through its mention in the country's seventh Five-Year Plan.[82] Again the National Planning Commission incorporates climate change into the Annual Development Programme, thereby making the aspect of climate change a matter of serious discussion in planning process of the governmental mechanism.

There are also many other initiatives prioritising climate change adaptation and mitigation that are elaborated in sectors like the Coastal Zone Policy, the Master Plan for Agricultural Development in the Southern Region of Bangladesh, the National Agricultural Policy, the National Water Act, the National Water Management Plan, and the Food Policy's Plan of Action.[83] In most of these plans and programmes, it has been found that the focus area is adaptation.

Adaptation is also a strong component of the National Determined Contribution (NDC), the first report of which has been submitted to United Nations Framework Convention on Climate change (UNFCCC) in 2016. In this report, Bangladesh claimed itself to be highly vulnerable due to climate change that can affect a projected annual loss of 2 percent of GDP by 2050. Therefore, it has committed to be a partner of the Global Action Plan for reduction of Global greenhouse emission though at present it contributes less than 0.35 percent of total global emission. The adaptation part is to be taken forward as part of the National Adaptation Plan process that will help Bangladesh in the implementation of the framework of NDC that involves five thematic areas: governance; mitigation; adaptation; finance; and Measurement, Reporting, and Verification (MRV).[84] The Bangladesh government has invested around 10 billion US dollars from 1980 to 2010 in making the community more climate resilient and less vulnerable.[85]

Again the country also has two national climate change trust funds. One is the Bangladesh Climate Change Trust Fund (BCCTF), created in fiscal year 2009–2010. To this, the government has allocated approximately US$390 million from 2009–10 to 2016–2017 fiscal years supporting 440 projects.[86] The establishment of BCCTF based on revenue from the national budget, within a legal mandate by the Climate Change Trust Act passed in Parliament in 2010, was undertaken after spotting the uncertainties and inadequacies of international adaptation finance. The BCCTF is a "block budgetary allocation" of US$100 million each year for three years (2009–2012, totalling up to US$300 million). According to the Climate Change Act stipulation, 66 percent of this amount can be spent on the implementation of projects prioritised under BCCSAP and the rest can be set as a "fixed deposit" for emergencies.[87]

The second one is the Bangladesh Climate Change Resilience Fund (BCCRF), a multi donor trust fund, established in 2010, as an agency for the development partners to support Bangladesh in implementing the Bangladesh Climate Change Strategy and Action Plan. There are 13 projects funded through BCCRF till 2016 demonstrating a value of US$146.4 million.[88]

BCCRF was first attempted when urgency was expressed by development partners to bring about some financial mechanism in an UK-Bangladesh Climate Conference in Dhaka in April 2008, to assist Bangladesh in combating the impacts of climate change. The Government of Bangladesh created "Multi-Donor Trust Fund" to manage the funding from the partner countries. This Trust Fund evolved into the BCCRF, with contributions from five main donors: the UK, with a contribution of US$94.6 million; Denmark, Sweden, the EU and Switzerland.[89]

To deal with its water-related problems and mitigate the impact of climate change, Bangladesh has prepared the "Bangladesh Delta Plan 2100". It was approved by the National Economic Council in September 2018. It has a vision of 'achieving a safe, climate-change resilient and prosperous delta'. The main objective of this plan to ensure the sustainable use of water resources and prevent natural disasters.[90] Of the total, 35 percent will be spent in flood control, preventing river erosion, river excavation, dredging, river training and navigation. In the first phase, a total of 80 projects have been proposed.[91]

The aforementioned discussion brings out the fact that Bangladesh has pioneered in mainstreaming climate change and its impact in the national resource mechanism. This is visible through the enormous plans, programmes and funding strategies it has adopted till date. However, they are also not devoid of shortfalls. The first sets of issues are associated to the BCCSAP. The plan is clearly termed as a "knowledge strategy"[92] that needs to go a long way to be transformed into an implementation strategy. While it identified six thematic areas, it did not prioritize action on the ground within the background of susceptibility and this action is critical for allocating resources to deal with immediate and urgent needs. It is an exemplary initiative taken by the government through BCCTF, for the use of national revenue to finance climate action, despite other urgent national priorities like poverty reduction. However, this makes the government more accountable in terms of use of public funds more effectively and prioritizes the need of the most vulnerable areas and communities. It is also vital that the decisions of the Trustees, most of whom are minister and elected representatives, are not influenced by partisan politics and political interest. The key challenges with regard to the BCCRF will be upholding country ownership and independence in decision making if differences arise between the government and development partners on the priorities of the Fund in future.

Bangladesh is also playing a vibrant role in global climate negotiation platforms. Amongst the least developed countries (LDCs), Bangladesh has been a leading one in terms of developing scientific expertise as well both government- and non-government-level policies and programmes to face the issue of climate change. The important challenge that remains is to implement policies efficiently and to make certain that lessons are learnt and acted upon. The Current policy frameworks and arrangements require more institutional solidification and working process requires more transparency and accountability. There is a criticism that in terms of allocation of adaptation of investments in both sectorial and geographic senses, a balance is required in context of vulnerability, which is not up-to the mark at present. The same concerns are being labelled regarding selection of projects, programs and monitoring of them.[93]

Conclusion

Often cited as one of the most vulnerable parts of the world due to climate change impacts; Bangladesh's vulnerability is not only due to peculiar biophysical characteristics, which is definitely a factor, but also its socio-economic conditions (like poverty, agriculture dependency, high population density etc.).[94] Within the country, the hotspot of climate change vulnerability varies according to variation in geographical and socio economic scale. Climate stress has been one of the triggers that has been resulting in rising internal migration and the rapid growth of urban population.[95] Due to more recurrent extreme weather events such as flooding, rising sea levels and soil salinity, many people are pushed to migrate out of their communities. Along with the large-scale internal population movements, international migration is also increasing with about 400,000 to 500,000 migrating abroad annually.[96] However, there is also a counter-argument which tries to portray that though climate change is having an impact on the life and livelihood of Bangladeshi people, their choice to move is limited by both lack of resources and also because of their climate resilient lifestyle. Therefore, any decision to migrate due to climate change is a decision of 'last resort' and that too to nearby places where 'return' will be easy. Therefore, flocking of climate migrants to cities like Dhaka do not have a direct link. Here the connection of climate change impact into economic crisis needs to be linked because economic push is still the prominent reason of people migrating rather than due to atypical climatic condition. The government's efforts to make migration an adaptation mechanism to climate change is still a distant dream since migration is still not a choice, but a force with no other option left.

Notes

1 United Nations Framework Convention on Climate Change, United Nations, 1992, page 7, accessed from http://unfccc.int/files/essential_background/background_publications_htmlpdf/application/pdf/conveng.pdf on 12th November 2019.
2 Special report: Global warming of 1.5 degree Celsius, 2018, Intergovernmental Group on Climate Change, 31, accessed from www.ipcc.ch/site/assets/uploads/sites/2/2019/06/SR15_Full_Report_Low_Res.pdf on 1st January 2020.
3 Kelly Levin et al. (2022, 27 February), "Five big findings from the IPCC 2022: Report on climate impact, adaptation and vulnerability", *World Resources Institute*, accessed from www.wri.org/insights/ipcc-report-2022-climate-impacts-adaptation-vulnerability?utm_medium=cpc&utm_source=google&utm_campaign=ipcc2022&gclid=Cj0KCQjw8_qRBhCXARIsAE2AtRayotiet8Awf7Fgd-z52uXRcfcNjiOg3vGmkjCouWlHQhuTXS2lBIfMaAqi7EALw_wcB on 29th March 2022.
4 Working Group I, Technical support Unit, IPCC, 2019, IPCC Special Report: Global Warming of 1.5 degree Celsius, 35, accessed from www.ipcc.ch/site/assets/uploads/sites/2/2019/06/SR15_Full_Report_High_Res.pdf on 6th January 2021.
5 Ibid.
6 Op. cit.
7 David Eckstein, et al. (2021), *Global climate risk index 2021: Who suffers most from extreme weather events? Weather related loss events in 2019 and 2000–2019*. Germanwatch: Bonn, 13, accessed from https://germanwatch.org/sites/germanwatch.org/files/Global%20Climate%20Risk%20Index%202021_1.pdf on 28th March 2022
8 B. G. Verghese (1991), *Waters of hope*. Delhi: IBH, 122.
9 Sanjoy Hazarika (1995), *Strangers of the mist*. Delhi: Penguin, 14.
10 Ibid.
11 Md Niaz Murshed Chowdhury and Md. Mobarak Hossain (2018), "Population Growth and Economic Development in Bangladesh: Revisited Malthus", MRPA paper no. 90826, accessed from https://mpra.ub.uni-muenchen.de/90826/ on 20th June 2021.
12 www.worldometers.info/world-population/bangladesh-population/
13 Environmental Justice Foundation Report (2018), "On the frontlines: Climate change in Bangladesh", 2, accessed from https://ejfoundation.org/resources/downloads/Climate-Displacement-Bangladesh-briefing-2018-v20.pdf on 3rd August 2020.
14 Szczepanski Marcin, Frank Sedlar and Jenny Shalant (2018), "Bangladesh a country underwater, a culture on the move", accessed from www.nrdc.org/onearth/bangladesh-country-underwater-culture-move on 23rd March 2021.
15 R. Kabir, H. T. A. Khan, E. Ball and K. Caldwell (2016), "Climate change impact: The experience of the coastal areas of Bangladesh affected by cyclones Sidr and Aila", *Journal of Environmental and Public Health*, 2016, 1–2.

16 Mahmuda Khatun (2013), "Climate change and migration in Bangladesh: Golden Bengal to land of disasters", *Bangladesh's E Journal of Sociology*, 10(2), 67, accessed from https://citeseerx.ist.psu.edu/viewdoc/download?doi=10.1.1.682.1886&rep=rep1&type=pdf#page=64 on 25th February 2020.
17 Ahsan Uddin Ahmed and M. Monirul Qader Mirza (2000), "Review of causes and dimensions of floods with particular reference to flood' 98: National perspectives", in Qazi Kholiquazzaman Ahmad (ed.) *Perspectives on floods 1998*. Dhaka: University Press Limited, 67.
18 Pallavi Deka (2014–2015), "Floods in Bangladesh and the Indian state of Assam: A systemic study of the politics of relief, 1991–2010", Doctoral Thesis. Delhi: Jawaharlal Nehru University.
19 A. Rahman and M. Alam (2003), "Mainstreaming adaptation to climate change in least developed countries (LDCs): Bangladesh country case study", *IIED Working Paper*, accessed from https://www.iied.org/sites/default/files/pdfs/migrate/10003IIED.pdf on 28th October 2020.
20 Tehera Akter (2009), *Climate change and the flow of environmental displacement in Bangladesh*. Dhaka: Unnayon Onneshan, 8.
21 Saleh Ahmed and Elizabeth Eklund (2021), "Climate change impacts in coastal Bangladesh: Migration, gender and environmental injustice", *Asian Affairs*, 52(1), 155–174, p. 156, https://doi.org/10.1080/03068374.2021.1880213, accessed from www.tandfonline.com/doi/abs/10.1080/03068374.2021.1880213 on 16th November 2021.
22 Dr. S. M. Reazul Ahsan (2014), "Climate induced migration: Lessons from Bangladesh", *The International Journal of Climate Change: Impacts and Responses*, 5, 7, accessed from www.researchgate.net/publication/281549970_Climate_Induced_Migration_Lessons_from_Bangladesh on 7th March 2019.
23 Saleemul Huq (2011), "Lessons of climate change, stories of solution Bangladesh: Adaptation", *Bulletin of Atomic Scientists*, 67(1), 56–59, accessed from https://journals.sagepub.com/doi/full/10.1177/0096340210393925 on 2nd October 2019.
24 Selvaraju Ramamasy and Stephan Bass (2007), "Climate variability and change: Adaptation to drought in Bangladesh", FAO of UN and Asian Disaster Preparedness Centre, accessed from https://www.fao.org/3/a1247e/pdf on 25th September 2020.
25 Shamsuddin Shahid and Houshang Behrawan (2008), "Drought risk assessment in the western part of Bangladesh", *Natural Hazards*, 46, 391–413, p. 392.
26 Bimal Kanti Paul (1998), "Coping mechanisms practiced by drought victims (1994/95) in North Bengal, Bangladesh", *Applied Geography*, 18(4), 366.
27 M. A. Aziz, A. B. M. Zahid Hossain, Md. Moniruzzaman, Rokib Ahmed, Taslima Zahan, Saiful Azim, Md. Abdul Qayum, Md. Abdullah Al Mamun, Md. Abdul Kader and Niaz Md. Farhat Rahman (2021), "Mapping of agricultural drought in Bangladesh using geographic information system (GIS)", *Earth Systems and Environment*, 4, https://doi.org/10.1007/s41748-021-00231-8
28 International Organization for Migration (2010), *Assessing the evidence: Environment, climate change and migration in Bangladesh*. Dhaka: Regional Office for South Asia, 46–47.
29 Food and Agriculture Organization of the United Nations (2007), *Climate variability and change: Adaptation to drought in Bangladesh*. Rome: FAO, p. 15, accessed from http://en.banglapedia.org/index.php?title=Bangladesh on 1st April 2020.
30 Irin Hossain and A. Rahman Mullick (2020), "Cyclone and Bangladesh: A historical and environmental overview from 1582 to 2020", *International Medical Journal*, 25(6), 2595–2614, p. 2595.

31 Abdul Qadir, Iqbal Dewan and Md. Anwar, "Tropical cyclones: Impacts on coastal livelihoods", 2, accessed from https://portals.iucn.org/library/sites/library/files/documents/2008-067.pdf on 13th June 2019.
32 IPCC (Intergovernmental Panel on Climate Change) (2022), "Climate change 2022: Impacts, adaptation and vulnerability, the Working Group II contribution to the sixth assessment report of the Intergovernmental Panel on Climate Change (IPCC)", 4–47, accessed from https://report.ipcc.ch/ar6wg2/pdf/IPCC_AR6_WGII_FinalDraft_FullReport.pdf
33 Ubydul Haque, et al. (2012), "Reduced death rates from cyclones in Bangladesh: What more needs to be done", *Bulletin of the World Health Organization*, 90(2), 152, accessed from www.ncbi.nlm.nih.gov/pmc/articles/PMC3302549/ on 7th May 2020.
34 "12F major cyclones from the past", *Dhaka Tribune*, accessed from www.dhakatribune.com/bangladesh/environment/2017/05/30/majorcyclonesbangladesh/?fbclid=IwAR06XP8IyCu0X0gBDSWsMYF7geFoR0nH99-gjEcJvpq2agRUAI39OODTyxk on 20th May 2020.
35 United Nations Environment Programme (2007), *Global environment outlook GEO4*. Washington, DC: UNEP, 312.
36 Reazul Ahsan, Sadasivan Karuppannan and Jon Kellett (2016), "Climate migration and urban changes in Bangladesh", in Rajib Shaw et al. (eds.) *Urban disasters and resilience in Asia*. Butterworth-Heinemann, 297.
37 "Climate displacement in Bangladesh: The need for urgent housing, land and property (HLP) rights solutions", *Displacement Solutions*, 2012, 4, accessed from https://unfccc.int/files/adaptation/groups_committees/loss_and_damage_executive_committee/application/pdf/ds_bangladesh_report.pdf on 14th March 2020.
38 "Latest news on climate displacement in Bangladesh" (2010, 10 June), accessed from https://displacementsolutions.org/latest-news-on-climate-displacement-in-bangladesh/ on 2nd February 2019.
39 UNB, Dhaka (2022), Over 7.1m Bangladeshis displaced by climate change in 2022: WHO accessed from https://www.thedailystar.net/environment/climate-change/news/over-71m-bangladeshis-displaced-climate-change-2022-who-3181851?amp on November 28, 2022.
40 "Displacement solution", Bangladesh, accessed from https://displacementsolutions.org/ds-initiatives/climate-change-and-displacement-initiative/bangladesh-climate-displacement/ on 21st June 2021.
41 Reazul Ahsan (2013), "Climate migration and urban changes: A study of adaptation in Bangladesh", PhD Dissertation. Australia: School of Natural and Built Environments, University of South Australia.
42 ibid, 295.
43 Ibid, 296.
44 K. S. Rasheed (2008), *Bangladesh: Resource and environmental profile*. Dhaka: AH Development Publishing House.
45 Babul Hossain, Md. Salman Sohel and Crispin Magige Ryakitimbo (2020), "Climate change induced extreme flood disaster in Bangladesh: Implications on people's livelihoods in the Char Village and their coping mechanisms", *Progress in Disaster Science*, 2, accessed from www.sciencedirect.com/science/article/pii/S2590061720300168 on 12th November 2021.
46 M.A. Rahman and M.A. Siddik (2018), "Livelihood analysis of the Char Dwellers using Capital Asset Framework", *Journal of Environmental Science and Natural Resources*, 11(1&2): 27–36, accessed from https://wwwbanglajol.info/index.php/JESNR/article/view/43362/31979 on 5th November 2021.

47 Ibid, 200 and 224. Pranab Kumar Pandey (2015), "Livelihood options, essential services and social protection mechanisms in the chars of Bangladesh: Governance issues and challenges", in Asif Imran Khan et al. (eds.) *First National Char Convention*. Dhaka: Unnayan Shamannay, Secretariat. Distributed by: Ireland and UK: Concern Worldwide, 195, accessed from http://cdrc-rda.org/assets/backend/files/uploads/3.%20National%20Char%20Convention-%20Let%20the%20light%20of%20the%20development%20spread%20over%20the%20Chars.pdf on 15th August 2020.

48 Aminuzzaman (2001), *Local governance and charland: An overview*. Dhaka: University of Dhaka, Department of Public Administration, 52, accessed from http://gsdrc.org/docs/open/pf11.pdf on 21st July 2020

49 Shireen Akhter (2019, 13 March), "Land beneficiaries in Char Development and Settlement Project (CDSP)", Presentation at 63rd Annual Meeting, United Nations Commission on the Status of Women. International Women's Anthropology Conference (IWAC).

50 Suzanne Hanchett and Mustafa Alam (1993), "Riverain Sandbars (Chars) of Bangladesh: Constraints and potential in socio-economic development". Paper presented to the joint meeting of the International Studies Association (ISA), Western Region, and Asian Studies on the Pacific Coast (ASPAC), Monterey, CA.

51 Maminul Haque Sarkar (2010), CEGIS (undated), Impact of climate change in water and agriculture in Bangladesh, 4, accessed from https://edepot.wur.nl/319635 on 15th June 2020.

52 Environment and GIS Support Project for Water Sector Planning (EGIS) (2000), *Riverine chars in Bangladesh environmental dynamics and management issues*. Dhaka: University Press Limited.

53 The International Organization for Migration (IOM) (2008), "World migration report 2008: Regional overviews", 399, accessed from https://worldmigrationreport.iom.int/2008 on 6th January 2020.

54 Ibid, 399 and 400.

55 M. N. Islam (2012), "Riverbank erosion induced migration by the Char Dwellers in Bangladesh: Towards a better strategy", *Asian Journal of Environment and Disaster Management*, 4(3), 243–267, p. 249, https://doi.org/10.3850/S1793924012001435

56 C. E. Haque and M. Q. Zaman (1989), "Coping with riverbank erosion hazard and displacement in Bangladesh: Survival strategies and adjustments", *Disasters*, 13, 310, accessed from https://pubmed.ncbi.nlm.nih.gov/20958684/ on 27th February 2020.

57 E. G. Ravestein (1885), "The laws of migration", *Journal of the Statistical Society*, Part II, XLVIII, 167–200.

58 E. S. Lee (1966), "A theory of migration", *Demography*, 3, 47–57.

59 Rabab Fatima and Adnan Ahmed Sirajee (2009, 16 November), "Climate change and displacement in Bangladesh", *International Organization for Migration*, accessed from https://reliefweb.int/report/bangladesh/climate-change-and-displacement-bangladesh-silent-crisis on 22nd December 2019.

60 Marie-Pierre Arseneault, Mohammed Nurul Azam and Sate Ahmad (2015), "Riverbank erosion and migration in Bangladesh's Char lands", in Bishawjit Mallick and Benjamin Etzold (eds.) *Environment, migration and adaptation evidence and politics of climate change in Bangladesh*. Dhaka: AHDPH, 48.

61 K. Kartiki (2011), "Climate change and migration: A case study from rural Bangladesh", *Gender & Development*, 19, 29 & 30, accessed from www.tandfonline.com/doi/abs/10.1080/13552074.2011.554017 on 11th September 2019.

62 C. E. Haque and M. Q. Zaman (1989), "Coping with riverbank erosion hazard and displacement in Bangladesh: Survival strategies and adjustments", *Disasters*, 13, 307 and 308, accessed from https://onlinelibrary.wiley.com/doi/10.1111/j.1467-7717.1989.tb00724.x on 11th September 2019.

63 K. M. Elahi, K. S. Ahmed and M. Mafizuddin (eds.) (1991), *Riverbank erosion, flood and population displacement in Bangladesh*. Dhaka: Riverbank Erosion Impact Study (REIS), Jahangirnagar University.

64 Marie-Pierre Arseneault, Mohammed Nurul Azam and Sate Ahmad (2015), "Riverbank erosion and migration in Bangladesh's Char Lands", in Bishawjit Mallick and Benjamin Etzold (eds.) *Environment, migration and adaptation evidence and politics of climate change in Bangladesh*. Dhaka: AHDPH, 58.

65 E. Penning-Rowsell, P. Sultana and P. Thompson (2013), "The last resort: Migration and global environmental change: CS4-population movement in response to climate related hazards in Bangladesh", *Environmental Science and Policy*, 7(Supplement 1), S.56, accessed from www.sciencedirect.com/science/article/abs/pii/S1462901112000470?via%3Dihub on 22nd August 2020.

66 U. C. Peter, D. S. Jeremy, A. M. Shaun, C. M. Alan, E. Michael, K. Scott, L. Anders, A. M. Gkenn, L. P. Patrik, D. S. Benjamin, P. S. Daniel, S. Susan, F. S. Thomas, H. S. Benjamin, J. W. Andrew, W. Ricarda, A. David, B. Edouard, G. Aaron, L. Kurt, T. P. Raymond and K. P. Gian (2016), "Consequences of twenty-first-century policy for multi-millennial climate and sea-level change", *Nature Climate Change*, 6, 6, of online publication, accessed from https://doi.org/10.1038/nclimate2923 on 1st June 2020.

67 X. Lu, et al. (2016), "Unveiling hidden migration and mobility patterns in climate stressed regions: A longitudinal study of six million anonymous mobile phone users in Bangladesh", *Global Environmental Change*, 38, 1–7.

68 J. Chen and V. Mueller (2018), "Coastal climate change, soil salinity and human migration in Bangladesh", *Nature Climate Change*, 8(16), accessed from www.nature.com/natureclimatechange on 30th April 2019.

69 International Organization of Migration (2010), *Assessing the evidence: Environment, climate change and migration in Bangladesh*. Geneva: IOM.

70 E. Fussell, L. M. Hunter and C. L. Gray (2014), "Measuring the environmental dimensions of human migration", *Global Environmental Change*, 28, 182, accessed from www.sciencedirect.com/science/article/abs/pii/S0959378014001277?via%3Dihub on 25th December 2019.

71 Ibid., 183.

72 Koko Warner and Tamer Afifi (2014), "Where the rain falls: Evidence from 8 countries on how vulnerable households use migration to manage the risk of rainfall variability and food insecurity", *Climate and Development*, 6(1), 1–17, https://doi.org/10.1080/17565529.2013.835707

73 Amelie Bernzen, J. Jenkins and Boris Braun (2019), "Climate change-induced migration in coastal Bangladesh? A critical assessment of migration drivers in rural households under economic and environmental stress", *Geosciences*, 9(1), 51, p. 2, https://doi.org/10.3390/geosciences9010051

74 Rezaul Ahsan, Jon Kellet and Sadasivam Karuppannan (2014), "Climate induced migration: Lessons from Bangladesh", *International Journal of Climate Change: Impacts and Responses*, 5, 4, accessed from www.researchgate.net/profile/Dr-S-M-Reazul-Ahsan/publication/281549970_Climate_Induced_Migration_Lessons_from_Bangladesh/links/55ed527a08ae3e121847ff82/Climate-Induced-Migration-Lessons-from-Bangladesh.pdf on 7th August 2019.

75 Working Group II to AR6 (2022), "Climate change 2022: Impacts, adaptation and vulnerability-summary for policy makers", Intergovernmental Panel on Climate Change, February, 4–38.

76 Sharifuzzaman Choudhury, Susmita Dasgupta, Farhana Akhter Kamal, Zahirul Huque Khan and Ainun Nishat (2014), "River salinity and climate change: Evidence from coastal Bangladesh (English)", Policy Research working paper no. WPS 6817, 32. Washington: World Bank Group, accessed from http://documents.worldbank.org/curated/en/522091468209055387/River-salinity-and-climate-change-evidence-from-coastal-Bangladesh on 7th August 2019.
77 J. J. Chen and V. Mueller (2018), "Coastal climate change, soil salinity and human migration in Bangladesh", *Nature Climate Change*, 8(16), accessed from https://doi.org/10.1038/s41558–018–0313–8 on 3rd October 2019.
78 M. Call, C. Gray, M. Yunus and M. Emch (2017), "Disruption, not displacement: Environmental variability and temporary migration in Bangladesh", *Global Environmental Change*, 46, 161, accessed from www.sciencedirect.com/science/article/abs/pii/S0959378016302758 on 7th September 2020.
79 S. Nakhooda, M. Norman, S. Barnard, C. Watson, R. Greenhill, A. Caravani, N. Canales Trujillo, M. Hedger and S. Whitley (2014), "Climate finance: Is it making a difference?", *ODI*, 48 and 50, accessed from www.odi.org/sites/odi.org.uk/files/odi-assets/publications-opinion-files/9359.pdf, and http://www.climatechangecell.org.bd/Documents/NAPA%20october%20 2009.pdf on 7th August 2019.
80 Maxmillan Martin, Yi Hyun Kang, Motasim Billah, Tasneem Siddiqui, Richard Black and Dominic Kniveton (2017, October), "Climate-influenced migration in Bangladesh: The need for a policy realignment", *Development Policy Review*, 35, 372, accessed from https://ssrn.com/abstract=3049099 or http://dx.doi.org/10.1111/dpr.12260
81 General Economic Division, Planning Commission, Government of the People's Republic of Bangladesh, Seventh Five Year Plan, FY 2016-FY 2020: Accelerating Growth, Empowering Citizens, 402, accessed from www.unicef.org/bangladesh/sites/unicef.org.bangladesh/files/2018-10/7th_FYP_18_02_2016.pdf on 25th September 2019.
82 Ministry of Foreign Affairs of the Netherlands (2018), "Climate change profile: Bangladesh", 10, accessed from www.government.nl › binaries › on 11th February 2019.
83 J. Ayers, S. Huq, H. Wright, A. M. Faisal and S. T. Hussain (2014), "Mainstreaming climate change adaptation into development in Bangladesh", *Climate and Development*, 6(4), 293–305, p. 300, http://dx.doi.org/10.1080/17565529.2014.977761
84 Ricardo Energy and Environment and Nature Conservation Management (2016), "Supporting the Government of Bangladesh to implement its Nationally Determined Contribution", 1, accessed from https://cdkn.org/wp-content/uploads/2016/06/Flyer-Bangladesh-NDC-project.pdf on 15th August 2019.
85 C. C. Ventom and S. Majumder (2013), "The economics of early response and resilience: Lessons from Bangladesh", 15, accessed from https://assets.publishing.service.gov.uk/media/57a08a0ced915d3cfd000570/61114_Bangladesh_Report.pdf on 19th July 2019.
86 accessed from www.bcct.gov.bd/index.php/trust-fund on 10th March 2019.
87 S. M. Munjurul Hannan Khan, Saleemul Huq and Md Shamsuddoha (2018), "The Bangladesh national climate funds: A brief history and description of the Bangladesh Climate Change Trust Fund and the Bangladesh Climate Change Resilience Fund", LDC paper published by International Institute for Environment and Development, funded by DfID, UK, 5, accessed from www.ldc-climate.org/wp-content/uploads/2018/02/LDC-paper-series-18.pdf on 23rd August 2020.

88 Bangladesh Climate Change Resilience Fund, Annual Report, 2015, 34, accessed from https://documents1.worldbank.org/curated/en/451431498049314242/text/116487-AR-BCCRF-AR-2015-PUBLIC.txt on 30th October 2019.
89 S. M. Munjurul Hannan Khan, Saleemul Huq and Md Shamsuddoha, 8, op. cited.
90 Amit Ranjan (2020), "Water issues in Bangladesh: Growing pollution and mismanagement", *Asian Affairs*, 51(2), 331, accessed from www.tandfonline.com/doi/abs/10.1080/03068374.2020.1749456 on 20th February 2022.
91 Ministry of Finance Government of the People's Republic of Bangladesh, "Bangladesh on a Pathway to Prosperity Time Is Ours, Time for Bangladesh Budget Speech 2019–20", p. 44, accessed from http://nbr.gov.bd/uploads/budget/Budget_Speech_2019-20_ English_Final_Print.pdf on 31st December 2020.
92 Bangladesh climate Change Strategy and Action Plan (2009), "Government of the People's Republic of Bangladesh", accessed from http://nda.erd.gov.bd/en/c/publication/bangladesh-climate-change-strategy-action-plan-bccsap-2009 on 30th October 2019.
93 S. Huq and G. Rabbani (2011), "Climate change and Bangladesh: Policy and institutional development to reduce vulnerability", *Journal of Bangladesh Studies*, 13, 16.
94 J. Ayers, S. Huq, H. Wright, A. M. Faisal and S. T. Hussain (2014), "Mainstreaming climate change adaptation into development in Bangladesh", *Climate and Development*, 6(4), 298. accessed from http://dx.doi.org/10.1080/17565529.2014.97776 on 30th June 2020.
95 M. Martin, Y. Kang, M. Billah, T. Siddiqui, R. Black and D. Kniveton (2013), "Policy analysis: Climate change and migration Bangladesh", Working paper no. 4., Refugee and Migratory Movements Research Unit (RMMRU), University of Dhaka, and Sussex Centre for Migration Research (SCMR), University of Sussex, 9. accessed from http://migratingoutofpoverty.dfid.gov.uk/files/file.php?name=wp4-ccrm-b-policy.pdf&site=354 on 1st May 2019.
96 Ibid, 16.

Chapter 4

Climate Change and Refugees in Bhutan

The Future Impacts

Emma Johnson

Environment, Culture, and Politics of Bhutan

Bhutan is a country in South Asia, on the eastern ridge of the Himalayan mountains. The kingdom is bordered to the south by India and to the north by Tibet. Although a small country of only about 40,000 square kilometers, the climate is extremely diverse and changes rapidly with elevation, which ranges from 160 meters in the southern foothills to 7,541 meters in the Himalayan mountains.[1] This 7,000-meter change in elevation happens over only 175 kilometers, which is the length of Bhutan from north to south.[2] This creates pockets of drastically different climate zones throughout the country. There are three primary climate regions: the tropical plans and foothills along the southern border, the temperate middle belt of the Lesser Himalayas, and the northern alpine region of the Great Himalayas.[3] While often known for its mountains, the geography in Bhutan is also defined by the rivers that run between them. The many river networks that run through Bhutan's valleys form critical agriculture and development sites. A total of 56 rivers flow from Bhutan, many originating in the glacial lakes in the high Himalayas, to the eastern state of Assam in India to join the Brahmaputra River, which sustains millions of people.[4]

Bhutan is a primarily Buddhist country, although a large portion of the southern part of the country that is of Nepali descent practices Hinduism. Until 2008, the country was an absolute monarchy. Today, there is both a King – currently King Jigme Khesar Namgyel Wangchuck, the Fifth King of the Wangchuck dynasty – as well as a parliamentary democracy. There are three main ethnic groups in the country: the Ngalop, who are descendants from Tibetan peoples, and primarily in the north, west, and central parts of the country; the Sharchop, who are thought to be the earliest inhabitants of Bhutan and related to the hill tribes in Assam and Arunachal Pradesh in India and live in the east of Bhutan; and the Lhotsampa, the Nepalese ethnic group that live in southern and southwestern Bhutan.[5] There have been historical and current internal political tensions between the Ngalop and Lhotsampa that included the driving out of about 95,000 Lhotsampa

DOI:10.4324/9781003367802-5

in the 1990s.[6] Some of these internal tensions are reflected in Bhutanese society today.

Worldwide, Bhutan is known for its strong national environmental protections that have contributed to some of the most intact ecosystems in South Asia. The Bhutanese Constitution, adopted in 2008, has numerous provisions within it that address environmental protection within the country. Article 5 of the Constitution reads as follows[7]:

> *Every Bhutanese is a trustee of the Kingdom of Bhutan's natural resources and the environment for the advantage and benefit of the present and the future generations, and it is the fundamental duty of every citizen to contribute to the protection and conservation of the rich biodiversity and natural environment of Bhutan and prevention of all forms of ecological degradation including noise, visual and physical pollution through the adoption and support of environment-friendly practices and policies.*

As part of this constitution, the natural environment is protected as an inalienable part of Bhutan's policies. Further pieces of this section in the constitution describe how no generation has the right to destroy this legacy of a protected environment for future generations.[8] While this article makes considerable strides in determining actions by the government and individuals across the country, it only discusses the internal protection of the natural world and not specifically the effects of climate change or other disasters. This means that there is no legislative framework within the Bhutanese constitution that discusses climate displacement or government responses to climate change, which could have implications for any future climate refugees that may be seeking protection or support.[9]

One key tenet of Bhutanese society is the developmental policy of "Gross National Happiness", a term that was coined by the Fourth King in 1979. The premise of Gross National Happiness is that any development should be about not only increasing wealth but also increasing a person's happiness.[10] In order to measure this indicator, the Government of Bhutan has developed a Gross National Happiness Index, which is composed of nine domains: psychological wellbeing, health, education, time use, cultural diversity and resilience, good governance, community vitality, ecological diversity and resilience, and living standards.[11] The inclusion of the natural environment within Gross National Happiness principles is interesting because it can foster greater interest in environmental issues across the country as well as provide greater insight into relationships between people and the environment in Gross National Happiness reports. In the latest survey that was conducted in 2015, the surveyors asked respondents how affected they were by different environmental issues. 43 percent of the 8,871 people surveyed said that wild animals were the biggest issue, likely affecting farmers whose livelihoods are hurt by wild animals. Issues related to climate change, such as forest fires and floods, were at the bottom of the list, with only 0.58 and 0.56 percent of people surveyed, respectively, being affected by these issues. This is important information to note, as it suggests climate-related challenges had not yet been dramatically impacting the well-being of the Bhutanese, or at least not as directly or immediately as some of the other environmental issues. Continuing to ask these questions and adding more specifics about other climate-related environmental challenges, in future, Gross National Happiness surveys could illuminate if climate change has any lasting impacts on people's health and well-being.

Migration, driven by a variety of reasons, is a common practice within Bhutan. Article 7 of the Constitution states that "a Bhutanese citizen shall have the right to freedom of movement and residence within Bhutan", which indicates that Bhutanese have the right and protection to engage in internal and external migration, although does not explicitly touch on environmental motives.[12] As cities in the country grow and more youth seek jobs in industries other than agriculture in their home village, Bhutan has seen an increase in the trends of rural to urban migration. It is the most common form of migration within the country, accounting for 32.7 percent of all internal migrants.[13] The most cited reasons for migration as listed in the 2017 Population and Housing Census were family move, employment, and education.[14] This migration pattern is majorly from the east and central regions to western Bhutan, where the primary urban centers are located, including Thimphu, the capital; Phuentsholing, the town on the border with India; and Paro, a growing city with the only international airport. These three urban centers attracted 41.1 percent of all recent internal migrants.[15] Emphasizing this pattern is the finding that two-thirds of the towns of central and eastern Bhutan experienced net population loss due to internal migration.[16] Most of these internal migrants are young people, and it is a common story within Bhutan for children to be born in rural areas and then seek the urban centers later in their lives for better education and job opportunities.

It is difficult to determine in the census report the extent to which climate change plays a role in people's reasons for migrating. In 2017, 0.1 percent of the Bhutanese population – or 556 people – listed "Natural Calamities" as the reason for migrating, which could indicate a move because of an extreme weather event such as flooding or drought, events that are becoming stronger with climate change.[17] This percentage was reported as 0.2 in 2005.[18] As climate change encompasses many different environmental shifts that are occurring over an extended period of time, it can be difficult to pin down or ask about these reasons directly in a census questionnaire. The current census data likely does not completely encapsulate why people are migrating now or why they will be migrating in the future. Some studies suggest that certain sectors of the population, such as those individuals working in agriculture, are already experiencing challenges related to a changing climate and have migrated to urban areas in order to pursue a different occupation.[19]

Current and Future Effects of Climate Change in Bhutan

As a country in the Himalayas, even though it is landlocked, Bhutan is still extremely vulnerable to many of the effects of climate change. The Himalayan region has warmed faster than the global average over the past 10 years, and this warming is expected to occur more rapidly in the future in mountainous regions in the coming decades.[20] While long-term data collected from Bhutanese weather stations does not exist, temperature data from global satellites can show general, country-wide trends of temperature change. The data from these global datasets indicates a clear upward trend in temperatures over the last 100 years in Bhutan.[21] Since 1997, average temperatures in the country have not dropped below the mean temperatures recorded since 1901.[22] Temperatures are expected to keep rising in the coming decades in conjunction with the rise in temperature globally. A report from the National Environment Commission in Bhutan that was published in coordination with the United Nations concluded that, consistent with climate modeling for all of South Asia, Bhutan can expect to see a median increase in temperature of 2.3 degrees Celsius by 2100, and the greatest amount of this warming will occur at higher elevations.[23] As a country that depends on many of the resources and systems that originate in or depend on the Himalayas, this prediction has wide-ranging implications not only for the people and climate in Bhutan but also for all of the other countries in South Asia. After the Intergovernmental Panel on Climate Change (IPCC) released its Sixth Assessment Working Group I report on the physical science of climate change in August 2021, Sonam Wangdi, Bhutan's National Environment Commission Secretary and Least Developed Countries (LDCs) chairperson, emphasized that climate change was hurting communities in LDCs first and worst and urgent action is needed to reduce these impacts.[24]

The warming that will occur in the high-elevation locations within Bhutan will lead to extensive melting of the glaciers and permafrost, which are crucial systems for feeding the water supply of the country as well as the many larger rivers of South Asia, such as the Brahmaputra.[25] Bhutan, as a Himalayan country, contains many glaciers and glacial lakes that are currently at risk because of climate change. Despite the country's small size, there are 983 glaciers and 2,794 glacial lakes.[26] Glaciers across the Himalayas are at risk from climate change, but the ones in Bhutan have been less well-studied than glaciers in other countries. Studies using satellite data to map changes in area have illuminated the extent of change in glacial area over the past few decades. From 1980 to 2010, researchers found that there was an overall decrease of about 23 percent in glacial area within Bhutan.[27] The United Nations Development Program has reported that based on current warming trends, the glaciers in Bhutan are receding at a rate of about 30 to 60 meters per decade.[28] While there has been increase in the number of glaciers over those 30 years, that combined with the decrease in glacier size displays a similar trend to other countries in the Himalayas, where glaciers are shrinking and fragmenting. This result shows that even though there are more glaciers being recorded, they are taking up less area than before.[29] The continued melting of glaciers will have enormous consequences for water storage, agriculture, and water availability throughout the country.

As the glaciers melt and retreat at faster and faster rates, there will also be increasingly greater strains put on the glacial lakes that form at the foot of the glaciers. Under growing pressure from the larger volumes of water now present because of glacial melt, the natural dams that hold the glaciers in place are more likely to burst, sending a dangerous flood of water cascading down the river. Glacial lake outburst floods can be devastating events, and past occurrences in Bhutan's history have wiped out towns, important cultural and religious structures, and killed numerous people. The most notable of these events in recent history was the Lugge Tsho glacial lake outburst flood in 1994, which destroyed most of the Punakha Dzong, or fortress, which serves as an important religious and administrative center, and killed 20 people.[30] In addition, the 1994 flood damaged 816 acres of dry land and 965 acres of pastures and washed away five water mills and about 16 tons of food grains.[31] Especially as many of Bhutan's populated areas are built in river valleys, for the ease of cultivating crops and building homes, these areas will only become more at risk from these glacial lake outburst floods as temperatures rise and melting speeds increase.[32] While there are alarm systems currently in place and government agencies within Bhutan have monitoring systems set up to alert officials in the case of a moraine dam burst, there is still a great risk to the people who live in those flood zones. People who do not hear the warning or are unable to move out in time will face great risk to their possessions, home, livelihoods, and even their lives.

The communities in the northern regions of Bhutan are located in extremely remote regions and are nearly completely dependent on the natural environment to survive. A traditional livelihood for northern Bhutanese is yak herding, and many of the livelihoods of these yak herders depend on having suitable areas to move the yak to in the changing seasons, a process that is becoming harder and harder as less snow falls and temperatures rise in the high elevation areas.[33] Other changes to the climate that some yak herders of northern Bhutan have noted include an increase in the frequency of landslides and flash floods, drying water sources, a decline in soil fertility, and an increase in droughts.[34] Because of the challenging environmental conditions that restrict people to certain livelihoods, these northern communities in Bhutan are both especially vulnerable to climate change and may not easily be able to adapt to new economic and cultural systems.[35] While a study on yak herders in Bhutan found that a majority of the respondents felt that climate change was not contributing to the rural to urban migration of yak herders,[36] that may change in the future as climate change accelerates in the high Himalayas.

Climate change is also shifting seasonal rainfall patterns within Bhutan, which can have some potentially serious long-term consequences. Overall, average precipitation in Bhutan is predicted to increase in the coming decades.[37] However, this precipitation will not be distributed evenly throughout the year – the summers, which are already the rainy, monsoon season, will be likely to become wetter, while the winters, which are already the dry season, will be likely to become drier. Experts predict that precipitation during the dry season will decline by 5 percent by 2100, and in the rest of the year, precipitation will increase by a median of 11 percent.[38] Already, the summer monsoon generates approximately 70 percent of the annual rainfall in Bhutan.[39] Along with the increased glacier melting, there is more danger of flash floods and landslides as the monsoons that come up from the Indian Ocean are striking Bhutan more erratically and intensely. Farmers have reported anecdotally that the monsoon has been coming later in the season over the past few years, and that instead of dropping steady rain throughout the entire summer, has provided driving rainstorms in short bursts. This means that in the summer, there is an excess of water, often causing flooding, landslides, and other damage to cities and towns within Bhutan. In the winter, the periods of drought have become longer, which puts much of the Bhutanese landscape at risk from devastating wildfires. And although Bhutan is currently a carbon-negative country and is committed to permanently remaining carbon-neutral, large wildfires have the potential to upend this pledge if these large tracts of forests are burned and the trees release their stored carbon back into the atmosphere.[40] Combatting this increasingly polarized seasonality in Bhutan will be a key challenge for any climate mitigation or adaptation plans.

Rising temperatures and shifting water availability can also have a cascading effect for other environmental problems. Especially in the winter months, Bhutanese farmers may not have the water to sustain certain crop types if the drought season continues to lengthen. Generally, people report that there is increasing water scarcity across the country, even as there is greater precipitation in the summer months and there is more glacial melt with increasing temperatures.[41] This is most common in scattered, remote communities that live on mountain slopes high above rivers, where the primary source of water is instead from small streams and springs.[42] As rainfall becomes more erratic, these small streams and springs may not be reliable sources of water for these villages. In addition, with the increasing risk of landslides and erosion from more intense rain and flash floods, these small streams and springs also have a higher chance of becoming polluted and unsafe for human consumption. While Bhutan is generally thought of to be a very water-rich country, especially when compared to its neighbor, India, so little is known about the state of Bhutan's water sources, which means that it is difficult to make predictions about what shifts climate change will cause.[43]

There are considerable concerns about how climate change will affect agriculture activities within Bhutan. One challenge is that as climate zones shift northwards as average temperatures rise, areas that are currently suitable for a certain type of crop may in the future no longer be able to support it, which could affect the livelihoods for thousands of farmers. Especially as about 60 percent of the Bhutanese workforce currently works in the agricultural sector, these changes could have devastating impacts for the local population.[44] With changing temperature and precipitation patterns, there also could be increased threat from crop pests and diseases that previously would not have been able to survive in the Bhutanese climate.[45] There is already some previous evidence of pests devastating local rice and maize crops, which indicate that this problem could be scaled up within the country with the added pressures coming from climate change events.[46]

Finally, as the tropical southern zone in Bhutan potentially extends northward with warming temperatures, the climate may be more suitable for mosquitos and other disease-carrying insects to come in that currently occupy only more tropical locations. If the range of the mosquito expands further into Bhutan, this may also increase the spread of the diseases that these mosquitos carry, putting additional strain on the Bhutanese healthcare system. One example of how this is already being recorded is in the increasing reports of dengue in Bhutan. Dengue was first recorded in the country in 2004, and now comes close to a crisis during every monsoon season, which are hot, humid, and rainy times.[47] This has especially become a problem in southern Bhutan in border towns. Other mosquito-borne diseases like malaria and Japanese encephalitis are also concerns as the range and season of mosquitos continues to expand within Bhutan. Currently, Thimphu, which is the capital and the most populated urban area in the country, does not lie within the range of areas at risk from malaria and other mosquito-borne diseases. However, informal reports have noted that mosquitos have become more common in Thimphu in recent years, and this could mean that threats of diseases are not far behind as the climate continues to warm and the range of the mosquito spreads northward.

While it has been fairly well-established in the literature the many climate risks that Bhutan faces in general terms, there is little available data to back up specific trends and provide concrete information at a detailed scale. Data collected from Bhutanese weather stations only extends back to the 1990s, so there is only just now getting to be enough data that scientists can begin looking at climate rather than weather trends within different locations in the country.[48] Especially for a country as mountainous as Bhutan, there is an incredible amount of geographic and spatial variability in climate, with each valley and peak forming their own microclimates that are extremely difficult to discern while using global-level data. There is some work being done now to address this, including setting up weather stations in locations across the country and releasing consistent data, but it will take time for a sufficient amount of enough data to accumulate to analyze it for climate trends. Programs that involve schools around the country, where the students take part in setting up the weather station and monitoring the data that it collects, can play an important part not only in the data collection but also in the climate education of Bhutanese children.[49] More granular climate data will be critically important in informing climate policies within Bhutan as well as simply establishing with a greater level of understanding what areas of the country will be affected most and what timeline the country needs to be acting on to combat climate change.

In addition to a lack of specific, granular climate data, there is also very little adaptative capacity within the country.[50] There is little money to implement new technologies that can help create more adaptive, resilient communities and many government departments do not have the resources to execute advanced climate resiliency projects. Because of this, the Bhutanese Minister of Agriculture and Forest Yeshey Penjor appealed to the wealthier, developed countries at the United Nations Framework Convention on Climate Change Conference, COP26, to follow through with the US$100 billion climate finance commitment to support climate adaptation efforts.[51] Furthermore, a significant portion of the country's revenue comes from hydropower electricity sales to India, operations that could be threatened in the future by climate change.[52] As the monsoon season becomes more erratic, glaciers melt faster, and winters become drier, the conditions that the hydropower plants were built in may not be efficient or productive enough a few decades from now. And once the plants are built, it is impossible for them to be restructured to accommodate the changing climactic conditions. Other than the revenue that comes from hydropower, Bhutan is also dependent on money from development organizations such as the United Nations Development Program to fund projects and provide expertise, which are not always consistent sources of support and may not be able to fund and see through the necessary long-term climate resilience projects. As hydropower is seen as a renewable resource in Bhutan, there also has been little investment in other forms of renewable energy generation that could supplement for hydroelectricity if something in that system failed. Solar panels are mostly used in communities that are not connected to the national grid and have not been implemented in a larger-scale plan. There are a few wind turbines but the twisting, mountainous geography throughout Bhutan makes large-scale adaptation of both solar and wind energy challenging, leaving Bhutan to forge ahead with hydropower even with its uncertain future.

Climate Refugees in Bhutan

There are only a few studies that examine how Bhutanese will migrate in response to climate change. The ones that are published mainly focus on communities that are the most vulnerable to the impacts of climate change, such as nomadic communities of yak herders in the mountainous north[53] or full-time farmers in remote, rural areas.[54] There are no studies, as far as could be determined, that consider climate migration in Bhutan on a large scale or raise concerns about the future possibility of Bhutanese climate refugees. While government census reports and other documents highlight climate change as a present and growing threat, there is little direct connection stated between climate change and human migration. Far more research needs to be done into what will likely be a critical issue in the future.

As described in the introductory section, the reports detailing internal migration showed that in surveys, people listed family, employment, and education as the primary reasons for internal migrations. Furthermore, the Bhutanese who were interviewed as part of this census were moving to settle in a new city or town and would not be labeled as a "refugee" because they were not forced out of their homes, or it was not recorded to be as such as part of the survey. It is also possible that some people have been forced to move because of a climate event but did not record it so in the government census because it was not a factor explicitly asked about. There are also many other factors that Bhutanese people could be considering before they move, even if they otherwise would have moved because of a climate event, such as economic status, occupation, and property ownership. It will be valuable to continue monitoring the census reports to see if there is any documented change in Bhutanese responses to reasons for migrating in the future. The government is mandated to conduct the census every 10 years, which means that the next census is expected to be conducted in 2025.

One academic study in particular, conducted by Ngawang Chhogyel et al. in the *International Journal of Environmental Science and Technology*, does clearly link climate change to migration among a subset of Bhutanese farmers.[55] Six districts were chosen, with 40 farmers randomly sampled in each district, for a total of 240 farmers surveyed. The majority of farmers perceived a number of different ways that climate change is affecting their lives, including erratic patterns of rainfall, shorter winters, reduced snowfall, unpredictable weather patterns, and drying of irrigation sources. The study also found that 71.7 percent of the farmers surveyed listed climate change effects as a reason to be migrating to urban areas. In addition, 63 percent of the respondents see migration as a possible adaptation strategy to cope with the challenges of a changing climate, especially as they relate to crop failure. If farming continues to become more uneconomical because of the difficult climate conditions, more farmers might leave their lands fallow and migrate to urban areas, which could have large consequences for the entire agricultural sector in Bhutan. More studies like this one are needed to more accurately determine how climate change is influencing migration among vulnerable populations in Bhutan and what can be done to address these challenges.

While large populations of climate refugees do not currently exist in Bhutan, this does not mean that this will not occur in the future. For individuals living in glacial lake outburst flood zones, such as in villages or cities along the river downstream of glaciers and glacial lakes, the increasing frequency of flooding or the increased risk of a calamitous outburst could force people in those areas to flee suddenly and their homes could be destroyed in the process. This scenario could be envisioned for some other climate-driven environmental disasters in the country, such as larger, more intense wildfires, monsoon-driven flooding, or extreme drought. It is likely that none of these events would occur within the next few decades based on current climate projections, although due to the lack of granular climate data for Bhutan, it is also difficult to accurately predict any future environmental disasters.

In addition, there may be some climate events that occur within Bhutan but that force people to become climate refugees in neighboring areas outside of the country. For example, many famers in the Indian state of Assam, which lies to the southeast of Bhutan, are vulnerable to changes that occur on the river that runs from Bhutan to them. In 2016, there were flash floods in a district in southern Bhutan called Sarpang that had catastrophic downstream consequences to farmers in two districts in Assam. The large amounts of silt flushed into the river from the flash flood washed onto the shores in Assam and turned large farmland areas into desert, enough so that even a few years later some farmers are unable to cultivate rice in some areas.[56] Events like this one, where environmental catastrophes cross political borders, could contribute to forcing from people from their homes. An example of how this could manifest itself occurred in 2017, when the Sarpang River flooded again and the floodwaters washed away some parts of a town on the Bhutan side of the border, leaving 52 families without a home.[57] There were likely families on the Indian side who were also affected by that flood. It was not reported what happened to those families. This will be a difficult situation to navigate in terms of political relationships, as climate change–driven events that may start in Bhutan could have long-lasting and devastating implications for people outside of the country as well.

Furthermore, Bhutan has direct ties between climate change and its national security, which could have implications for the safety of its citizens in the face of extreme weather events. As discussed previously, hydropower is a dominant sector within the country and is also extremely vulnerable to climate change through changing water flows, landslides, and glacial lake outburst floods. Since Bhutan is completely dependent on India for the trade in hydroelectric power, disruptions to the hydropower system due to an outburst flood or landslide could place many Bhutanese's livelihoods in jeopardy.[58] There is also the potential that the increased risk from climate-driven events causes disruptions in other crucial systems, such as flooding key trade roadways or power grids, all of which might leave people stranded without necessary supplies or equipment. Along Bhutan's other border, which it shares to the north with Tibet, a warming climate means that this previously inaccessible stretch of border might be more passible by people.[59] If this becomes the case, there will likely be increased political disputes between communities in these Himalayan regions, which could force northern Bhutanese communities to relocate and may serve to continue escalating already high tensions between India and China. There are many interconnected factors with climate change, politics, economics, and culture that will influence how people move within Bhutan in the coming decades.

Many gaps in knowledge around the topic of climate change, climate refugees, and migration exist in Bhutan. From the specific effects that climate change will have in the country to how environmental shifts will impact the people living in those areas, much of this information remains a mystery. There is widespread acknowledgment from other researchers that better monitoring is needed of both climate and migration trends in order to better inform any future policy solutions.[60] All of this is further complicated by Bhutan's development goals: the country hopes to graduate from the United Nations' category of LDC by 2023, an ambition that will require them to continue increasing their hydropower production and commissioning new, large dam projects that will have profound consequences for river flows and local environmental degradation. Bhutan's political location in Asia, sandwiched between its large, power- and land-hungry neighbors of India and China, will also affect any decision that Bhutan makes regarding national policies.

Finally, Bhutan's response to any future Bhutanese who are forced to become climate refugees will be influenced by the country's culture, including its Buddhist traditions, its influence of the much-loved and respected Wangchuck Dynasty, and its signature development policy of Gross National Happiness. On the policy front, Bhutan has been active in addressing climate change at multiple levels of governance. The country is a signatory on many international climate agreements, including the United Nations Framework Convention on Climate Change in 1995 and the Kyoto Protocol in 2002.[61] At a regional level, Bhutan is an active member advocating for climate work among the South Asian Association for Regional Cooperation, and at the national level, includes climate actions across disciplines in its Five-Year Plan.[62] The current Five-Year Plan, which is the 12th, lists maintaining a carbon neutral development path and building climate resilience to environmental disasters as important key results areas to focus on before the Plan ends in 2023.[63] While migration and the potential to be addressing large movements of people moving due to climate events is not explicitly described in the Plan, many of the themes are intertwined. The government's desire to strengthen resiliency to climate disasters will help communities protect the areas where they live so they will not be forced to flee if a disaster occurs. It is likely that the government will need to address climate change migration more directly in the coming years as the climate crisis continues to worsen around the globe.

There are many unknowns regarding climate change and the possibility of climate events leading to climate refugees in Bhutan. This is due to the fact that the formalized collection of weather data that can then be used to model climate change trends has only occurred relatively recently. Furthermore, many of the worst predicted effects of climate change in Bhutan have yet to come, and likely will not occur within the next few decades based on current projections from global-level data. As many of the other Himalayan countries actively struggle with rising sea levels, crippling droughts, and massive flooding, all of which, combined with political instability and other cultural factors, are forcing people to become climate refugees, Bhutan is not actively facing these challenges. With its secure borders, small population and small population density, stable government, and trust in the King, Bhutan will likely approach the possible challenge of climate refugees in a way very different from its neighboring countries and will likely be able to handle them effectively.[64] What is crucial for the country now is actively investing in community resilience and adaption strategies that will enable its vulnerable communities to adapt to the inevitable extreme weather events that will be coming so that the people can continue to have a place to live and a way to earn a living. With a flexible system that addresses the nuanced needs of various Bhutanese communities, thoughtful climate policies, and empathetic leadership, Bhutan may find that it can respond to its internal climate struggles without perpetuating undo harm to its citizens.

Notes

1 Fakhruddin, B. (2015, 14 May), "Development of flood forecasting system for the Wangchhu River Basin in Bhutan", *Journal of Geography and Geology*, 7, https://doi.org/10.5539/jgg.v7n2P70
2 Bisht, M. (2013, 1 December), "Bhutan and climate change: Identifying strategic implications", *Contemporary South Asia*, 21(4), 398–412, https://doi.org/10.1080/09584935.2013.859658
3 Katel, O. (2016, June), "Addressing climate change concerns in Bhutan Himalaya", *Governance Today*, 3.
4 Yashwant, S. (2018, 27 August), "Villagers in Bhutan and India come together to share river", *The Third Pole* (blog), accessed from www.thethirdpole.net/2018/08/27/villagers-in-bhutan-and-india-come-together-to-share-river/
5 Rizal, D. (2004, 1 June), "The unknown refugee crisis: Expulsion of the ethnic Lhotsampa from Bhutan", *Asian Ethnicity*, 5(2), 151–177, https://doi.org/10.1080/1463136042000221861
6 Ibid.

7 Jolly, S., Ahmad, N. (2018), *Climate refugees in South Asia: Protection under international legal standards and state practices in South Asia*. Singapore: Springer Nature.
8 Ibid.
9 Ibid.
10 Zurick, D. (2006), "Gross national happiness and environmental status in Bhutan", *Geographical Review*, 96(4), 657–681.
11 Centre for Bhutan Studies & GNH Research (2016). *A Compass towards a just and harmonious society: 2015 GNH Survey Report*. Retrieved from: https://www.bhutanstudies.org.bt/publicationFiles/2015-Survey-Results.pdf
12 Poissonnier-Lescuras, M., Gemenne, F. (2013) Bhutan. "Case study in the framework of the project", *The Institute for Sustainable Development and International Relations*, 31.
13 Tshering, C. (2018), *Rural-urban migration and urbanization in Bhutan*. Bhutan: National Statistics Bureau. Retrieved from: https://bhutan.unfpa.org/sites/default/files/pub-pdf/rural%20urban%20migration%20and%20urbanization.pdf
14 Wangmo, K. (eds.) (2018), *2017 population & housing census of Bhutan: National report = Brug Gi Mi Rlobs Dang Khyim Gyi Grangs Rtsis 2017*. Thimphu: National Statistics Bureau, Royal Government of Bhutan.
15 Tshering, *Rural-urban migration and urbanization in Bhutan.*
16 Ibid.
17 Wangmo and Bhutan, *2017 Population & Housing Census of Bhutan.*
18 Ibid.
19 Chhogyel, N., Kumar, L., Bajgai, Y., Hasan, M. K. (2020, 1 August), "Perception of farmers on climate change and its impacts on agriculture across various altitudinal zones of Bhutan Himalayas", *International Journal of Environmental Science and Technology*, 17(8), 3607–3620, https://doi.org/10.1007/s13762-020-02662-8
20 Hoy, A., Katel, O., Thapa, P., Dendup, N., Matschullat, J. (2016), "Climatic changes and their impact on socio-economic sectors in the Bhutan Himalayas: An implementation strategy", *Regional Environmental Change; Dordrecht*, 16(5), 1401–1415, http://dx.doi.org/10.1007/s10113-015-0868-0
21 Ibid.
22 Ibid.
23 Zangmo, T., Namgyel, T., Sinha, S. (2009), *Strategizing climate change for Bhutan*. Bhutan: National Environment Commission.
24 Bhutan's Daily Newspaper, "Bhutan joins LDCs calling for more support following IPCC report", *Kuensel Online*, accessed from https://kuenselonline.com/bhutan-joins-ldcs-calling-for-more-support-following-ipcc-report/ on 2nd April 2022.
25 Johnson, F. A., Hutton, C. W. (2014, 1 November), "Dependence on agriculture and ecosystem services for livelihood in Northeast India and Bhutan: Vulnerability to climate change in the tropical river basins of the upper Brahmaputra", *Climatic Change*, 127(1), 107–121, https://doi.org/10.1007/s10584-012-0573-7
26 Meenawat, H., Sovacool, B. K. (2011, 1 June), "Improving adaptive capacity and resilience in Bhutan", *Mitigation and Adaptation Strategies for Global Change*, 16(5), 515–533, https://doi.org/10.1007/s11027-010-9277-3
27 Bajracharya, S. R., Maharjan, S. B., Shrestha, F. (2014), "The status and decadal change of glaciers in Bhutan from the 1980s to 2010 based on satellite data", *Annals of Glaciology*, 55(66), 159–166, https://doi.org/10.3189/2014AoG66A125

28 Islam, F., Hove, H., Parry, J. (2011), "Bhutan | UNDP climate change adaptation", accessed from www.adaptation-undp.org/explore/bhutan
29 Bajracharya, S., Maharjan, S., & Shrestha, F. (2014). The status and decadal change of glaciers in Bhutan from the 1980s to 2010 based on satellite data. *Annals of Glaciology, 55*(66), 159-166. doi:10.3189/2014AoG66A125
30 Singh, S. M. (2009). *The cost of climate change: The story of Thorthormi glacial lake in Bhutan*. Bhutan: World Wildlife Fund.
31 Poissonnier-Lescuras and Gemenne, "Case study in the framework of the project".
32 Meenawat and Sovacool, "Improving adaptive capacity and resilience in Bhutan".
33 Wangchuk, K., Wangdi, J. (2018), "Signs of climate warming through the eyes of yak Herders in Northern Bhutan", *Mountain Research and Development*, 38(1), 45–52.
34 Ibid.
35 Amoako Johnson and Hutton, "Dependence on agriculture and ecosystem services for livelihood in Northeast India and Bhutan".
36 Wangchuk and Wangdi, "Signs of climate warming through the eyes of yak Herders in Northern Bhutan".
37 Tenzin, Y. (2016, May), *State of climate change report for the RNR sector*. Bhutan: Ministry of Agriculture and Forests.
38 Zangmo et al., "Strategizing climate change for Bhutan".
39 Islam et al., "Bhutan | UNDP climate change adaptation".
40 Johnson, E. (2019, 12 August), "Rethinking a conservation narrative from one of the world's only carbon-negative countries", *Pulitzer Center*, accessed from https://pulitzercenter.org/reporting/rethinking-conservation-narrative-one-worlds-only-carbon-negative-countries
41 Wangchuk and Wangdi, "Signs of climate warming through the eyes of yak Herders in Northern Bhutan".
42 Gyelmo, D. (2016, 21 April), "Bhutan struggles with local water supply shortages", *The Third Pole* (blog), accessed from www.thethirdpole.net/2016/04/21/bhutan-water-shortages/ on 23rd June 2020.
43 Ibid.
44 Chhogyel, N., Kumar, L. (2018, 1 November), "Climate change and potential impacts on agriculture in Bhutan: A discussion of pertinent issues", *Agriculture & Food Security*, 7(1), 79, https://doi.org/10.1186/s40066-018-0229-6
45 Bisht, "Bhutan and climate change".
46 Ibid.
47 UNDP, "The climate shifts. Bhutan responds – Bhutan", *ReliefWeb*, accessed from https://reliefweb.int/report/bhutan/climate-shifts-bhutan-responds on 23rd June 2020.
48 Hoy et al., "Climatic changes and their impact on socio-economic sectors in the Bhutan Himalayas".
49 "Institute for conservation and environmental research", *HEROES*, accessed from www.heroes.gov.bt/web/index.php on 8 July 2020.
50 Meenawat and Sovacool, "Improving adaptive capacity and resilience in Bhutan".
51 Penjor, Y. (2021, 9 November), "Statement by his excellency Mr. Yeshey Penjor at the high level segment of COP26" (UNFCCC COP26, Glasgow, Scotland), accessed from https://unfccc.int/sites/default/files/resource/BHUTAN_cop26cmp16cma3_HLS_EN.pdf

52 Johnson, E. (2019, 28 October), "Unstoppable rivers: Bhutan's quest for energy security and development in a changing climate", *Pulitzer Center*, accessed from https://pulitzercenter.org/reporting/unstoppable-rivers-bhutans-quest-energy-security-and-development-changing-climate
53 Wangchuk and Wangdi, "Signs of climate warming through the eyes of yak Herders in Northern Bhutan".
54 Chhogyel et al., "Perception of farmers on climate change and its impacts on agriculture across various altitudinal zones of Bhutan Himalayas".
55 Ibid.
56 Yashwant, "Villagers in Bhutan and India come together to share river".
57 Ibid.
58 Bisht, "Bhutan and climate change".
59 Ibid.
60 Poissonnier-Lescuras and Gemenne, "Case study in the framework of the project".
61 Bisht, "Bhutan and climate change".
62 Ibid.
63 Tobgay, T. (2017), *12th five year plan*. Thimphu: The Royal Government of Bhutan.
64 Poissonnier-Lescuras and Gemenne, "Case study in the framework of the project".

Chapter 5

Climate Change and Displacement in India

A Gendered Perspective

Pushpa Singh and Chetna Sharma

Introduction

Climate change has emerged as one of the major concerns of contemporary times. It causes rapid and irreversible changes in the environment, inducing natural disasters and diminishing natural resource, making survival very difficult. The disruption of the ecology, biodiversity and natural resources poses an existential threat to human beings as they are immensely dependent on the environment for their life and livelihood. Climate change is often associated with the massive movement of human population for adaptation; in search of safety, survival, improvement of quality of life and diversification of income. In the past, environment often has directly or indirectly induced migration; climate change is likely to amplify this dramatically with numbers never seen in written history.[1] This displacement and relocation of the human populace would disrupt geopolitical stability increasing the conflict for resources, especially in politically and geographically fragile states. It may trigger a conflict between and within nations, as resources become sparse, and disasters collapse livelihoods, increasing the number of migrants and refugees.[2] The countries of South Asia are particularly vulnerable to climate change due to their location in the tropics, which is a high-risk area. By virtue of demography, topography and geography, India is ground zero for climate change.[3] These consequences have already started affecting livelihoods, security and welfare in Global South.[4] This chapter focuses on climate change-induced migration mainly caused by floods, droughts and displacement in India from a gendered perspective.

Climate change is manifested in various forms: surging global temperature, unpredictable weather patterns leading to droughts, floods, desertification, rise in sea level and temperature that are steadily diminishing biodiversity and natural resources. With the aggravating extreme climate event, natural disasters, heat and cold waves, erratic and extreme weather conditions, climate change is posing a formidable threat to food production, water availability and secure habitat, the very foundations of human survival. These impacts will be most severely experienced in areas where a vast

DOI:10.4324/9781003367802-6

majority of the population is dependent on climate-sensitive resources like local water and food supply, as highlighted by the Intergovernmental Panel on Climate Change (IPCC).[5] As a consequence, to mitigate and adapt to these adversities, population migrate to safe and resourceful places particularly cities. However, these urban spaces are already overpopulated and lack adequate infrastructure. Though, here also the migrants are most likely to end huddled up in crowded shelters without proper access to drinking water or health care facilities. The inflow of migrants generates a complex set of problems in these cities. Competition over the finite resources is amplified, creating acrimony against migrants.

Climate Change, Women and Migration in India

Climate change-induced consequences impact all countries and people; however, its impact tends to be skewed towards the developing nations and marginalised communities, amplifying the existing inequalities. It disproportionately affects those who lack access to sufficient financial and material resources and technical and institutional capacity to cope or adapt. Climate change impacts men and women differently due to their socially structured gender-differentiated role that defines their access to economic, political and social decision making. Women's fragility is accentuated by illiteracy, low socioeconomic skills or employment, inadequate access to assets and lack of access to early warning to be prepared for impending danger.[6] On the one hand, women lack the resources necessary for disaster preparedness, mitigation, rehabilitation and on the other adaptive capacities such as swimming and climbing trees are culturally not encouraged for them. Because of these reasons, women and children are more likely to die than men during a calamity. More than three decades back, one of the significant research and advocacy organisation of India, the Centre for Science and Environment (CSE), argued in their *The State of India's Environment Report* (1985) that no other group is more affected by environmental destruction than poor village women.[7] They could well be reaching their limits of physical endurance with its rapid ecological deterioration. Resonating with this is the report on gender and climate change by Women's Environment and Development Organisation which states that its impact will be the most severe for world's poor, and those below the poverty line, 70% of whom happen to be women.[8]

Women inhabit a deeply patriarchal society, constrained by gendered-cultural norms and political and socioeconomic barriers in most countries of South Asia. Within the household, they share the unequal burden of domestic responsibilities for being primary caregivers of their families. They are responsible for procuring drinking water, fuel, managing livestock, medicinal plants, and other goods of sustenance. Hence, a decline in the availability of any of these due to climate change magnifies their troubles. They remain at the lower rung of social hierarchy in developing countries and have little capacity to adapt or to mitigate the adversities created by calamities. Women are often overrepresented in agriculture and informal sector and are also more prone to disasters. Climate change worsens women's pre-existing vulnerabilities like existing conditions of inequality, lower income, lack of access to resources and information and reduces their resilience to the shocks.[9]

A host of international institutions are increasingly recognising the gendered implications of climate change. IPCC acknowledges the increased vulnerability of the poor and vulnerable sections due to their lack of resources and capacity to fight its ill effects and on average women tends to be poorer.[10] United Nations Framework Convention on Climate Change (UNFCCC) underscores the gendered aspects of climate change, in response to which it created Lima Work Programme on Gender in 2014 for promoting gender justice in climate change policies.[11] India also reiterated the unequal burden of climate change consequences for men and women and emphasised the need for systematic integration of gender-sensitive and participatory education, training, public awareness in this regard.[12] India's National Action Plan on Climate Change (NAPCC) remarks:

> The impacts of climate change could prove particularly harsh for women, due to increasing scarcity of water, reductions in yields of biomass, and increased risks to human health with children, women and the elderly in a household becoming the most vulnerable . . . and would add to the deprivation that women already encounter.[13]

Though, unfortunately, this acknowledgement has not translated into NAPCC's policy mechanism, as gender-specific measures remain a far cry.

Climate change does not impact all women in uniform ways. Instead, the extent of vulnerability is variegated depending upon their class, caste, ethnicity, education, employment and location of physical settlement, to name a few. These social stratifiers intersect with gender identity and may amplify the vulnerability of women. The most common adaptation strategy to cope with climate change is migration. As the environmental deterioration will worsen in the coming times; the associated displacement and migration will rise regionally as well as globally. According to the estimation by the International Organization for Migration (IOM), around 200 million people could permanent or temporary migrate due to climatic factors by 2050.[14] These people are called climate migrants or refugees.

Climate Change, Droughts and Food Security

For millions of Indians, farming has been the traditional livelihood and sources of sustenance. Agriculture in India employs 85% of the rural women.[15] As agriculture is highly climate-sensitive, the climatic alterations would have huge ramifications across the country. In India and South-East Asia, the contraction in GDP due to climate change is estimated at between 9% and 13% by 2100 compared with a situation without climate change.[16] The IPCC Second Working Group Report (2001) emphasised a gradual decline in crop yields leading to a severe food security crisis in most countries lying in tropical and subtropical regions.[17] Food security refers to the assurance of access to adequate and nutritious food for health and productive lives.[18] In a 700-page report "The Stern Review on the Economics of Climate Change", economist Professor Nicholas Stern predicted an alarming drop in crop yields, agricultural output causing the severe challenge to food security.[19] Based on his empirical study of developing countries, Mendelsohn summarises that agriculture in countries like India and Brazil are sensitive to even modest warming, though there will be the heterogeneous impact on different zones within the countries.[20]

Climate change has disrupted the hydro-climatic patterns resulting in unpredictable precipitation, intense heatwaves, catastrophic floods, hailstorms and untimely snowfall, causing colossal damage to the crops. With monsoons becoming erratic, short periods of intensive rainfall causes flooding in the fields and eroding the soil. Hectares of fertile agricultural land is degrading into a wasteland due to sand deposition in eco-fragile and flood-prone states like Assam, Bihar and West Bengal. On the other hand, prolonged dry spells and scarce rain hit rain-fed agriculture systems the hardest, which constitutes 65% of India's agriculture.[21] Temperature variations and hot and humid conditions give rise to new pests which increase the infestations and damage the crops. Delayed monsoons shift the sowing season of Kharif crops leaving no sufficient time for maturity for long-duration paddy crops. While the yield is on a constant decline, there is a considerable increase in the input costs in agriculture arising from higher demand for irrigation and agrochemicals like pesticides, fertilisers.

The dwindling agricultural productivity will result in food scarcity, leading to increased food prices, affecting not just the farming household but all the low to medium-income households. It will exacerbate the impoverishment, nutrition deficiency and diseases having a debilitating impact on health and wellbeing. In regions with higher impact, the recurring scarcity of rain leads to draughts and famine-like conditions. For example, in 2017, Tamil Nadu state received 62% less rainfall causing worst draughts in the state in the past 110 years, resulting in the declaration of state-wide drought in 2017.[22] This distress resulted in the loss of life of almost 200 farmers between 2016 and 2017.[23] Decreased rainfall has also resulted in crucial shrinking of water in Narmada dam and other state reservoirs in Gujarat, due to which the state prohibited use of this water for irrigation.[24] Even Himachal Pradesh reported water shortage 56% below average due to poor rainfall in 2018, calling upon the state to address this shortage.[25] The emerging water shortage would impact the food production and availability, resulting in further increase in food prices.

Across South Asia, women are predominantly employed in agriculture. Climate change-induced outmigration of men from rural areas is on the increase, resulting in the greater feminisation of agriculture in India.[26] Incurring considerable losses in agriculture, more men forsake farming in search of works in the cities, where they mostly end up as construction labourers. Men generally stay for preparation of the field before sowing and then migrate seasonally to the nearby towns in order to augment the income from farming. Some of them abandon farming altogether for another occupation. In the absence of men, the entire responsibility of farming falls on women's shoulder in addition to the caretaking of livestock and household works.[27] Migration of men also leads to a shortage in local labour-supply. In most of rural India, farming is also interlinked with various non-farm income-earning activities. Less rainfall means less water and fodder for the cattle and livestock. Along with agriculture, the consequences of climate change destroy even the relevant off-farm avenues, escalating the food insecurity. Any impact in the farming sector is bound to have an immense and immediate effect on women and other marginal communities residing in rural areas.

In India, most vulnerable sections, including women, are primarily engaged in traditional livelihood like agriculture, fishery and sericulture, cotton and tea plantations. These livelihoods are dependent on climate-sensitive resources and hence are at the highest risk of being destroyed by consequences of alterations in environment and ecology. Climatic variability diminishes critical ecological resources like water and forest, which provides sustenance to women, tribal, fisherfolk and peasants. These adversities are documented by a report on *Impacts of Climate Change on Marginalised Women: An Exploratory Study across 6 Districts in Assam* (2012).[28] It illustrates the climatic stress in North-Eastern India, resulting in shifts in livelihood in rural areas with collapsing social security, health and education of the girl child. Production in tea plantations that primarily employed women in this region has fallen, making most of them unemployed. According to the temperature and rainfall data of Indian Metrological Department, there has been an increase of temperature by nearly 0.6 degree centigrade, and annual rainfall has decreased by 2.96 mm per year between 1951 and 2010 in Assam.[29] Increased temperature and humidity have resulted in reduced production of Muga silk, used for women wear.[30] The declining household income makes young girls drop the school to supplement the family income and make them vulnerable to trafficking for jobs and flesh trade.

These findings resonate with conclusions of studies on the environmentally fragile region of the Hindukush Himalayas by the International Centre for Integrated Mountain Development (ICIMOD). Its report "Status of Gender, Vulnerabilities, Adaptation to Climate Change in the Hindu Kush Himalaya" (2017) illustrates how due to differential impacts, poor people are likely to suffer disproportionately.[31] Climate change has compounded the environmental challenges of the hill by intensifying floods, droughts, soil erosion in recent decades. The hill households employ labour-intensive activities, predominantly performed by women. Men's migration increases their drudgery, with additional agricultural and pastoral work. Draughts and famines add to their hardships. Recurrent floods ravage all the states falling in the Himalayan belt, a fallout of climate change. Erratic and extreme weather consequences like flash floods are resulting in the displacement of many people from Uttarakhand who migrate to plain in search of safety and survival. The migration has created many ghost villages in Uttarakhand as shown by the Census 2011; out of 16,793 villages, more than a thousand villages have been completely abandoned, while almost ten villages have less than ten residents. The acuteness of this problem was acknowledged by the then state Chief Minister Harish Rawat in 2016 and Uttarakhand Rural Development and Migration Commission Chairman S.S. Negi while sharing the Commission's Report on Status of Migration in the state with media in 2018.[32] Nevertheless, the rescue and rehabilitation remain tardy in the absence of effective policies and adaptation programmes.[33]

Another research project delineating similar concerns arising from the gendered impact of climate change is by Ahmed and Fazber in which, they have studied three villages in coastal districts of Gujarat.[34] They demonstrate that climate change has aggravated the strength and intensity of cyclones, devastating the crops, farms, buildings, and other infrastructure. While all women are feeling the heat, those belonging to lower castes and tribal groups are gripped in huge pressure. Dalit women in these villages reside in outskirts of villages which are flood-prone. Most of these women work in rain-fed, small agricultural farms, therefore failing precipitation adds to their misery. Given that in a family's hierarchy of needs, women always stand last, decreased resources in the family tend to further reduce their wellbeing.

Climate change has magnified the crisis of water with the depletion of groundwater, drying of water bodies, and scarce rainfall. According to the Ministry of Water Resources, Government of India "the amount of water available per person in India is decreasing steadily from 3450 cm in 1951 to 1250 cm in 1999. It is expected to decline further to 760 cm per person in 2050".[35] India River Studies 2017 emphasise the loss of river to dams, pollution, encroachment, mining and climate change illustrated in SANDRP Reports 2017.[36] Himalayan rivers are drying out, whereas perennial streams remain at the threshold of flooding due to temperature rise causing rapid melting of glaciers. At the same time, the surging temperature would increase evapotranspiration dramatically increasing the amount of rainfall in some river basins such as that of the Godavari, Cauvery and Mahanadi, further intensifying flooding conditions.[37] The hydrological imbalance would have a natural spill over interrupting the complex web of interconnected ecology.

For example, the delicate balance between the amount of rain received and the evaporation taking place (precipitation effectiveness index) is crucial for many species of plants and trees and its disruption may threaten the biodiversity of the region.[38]

Climate Change, Floods, Displacement and Women

Flood and other water-induced migration is another major cause of concern in India. Rising sea level is inundating coastal regions, threatening habitat as well as the livelihood of millions of people. The entering of saline water in the freshwater disrupts the fragile coastal ecosystem, impacting fishing there. The cyclones and severe sea conditions caused by climate change result in higher deaths of fisherwomen than fishermen because of women's inability to swim back and their lesser physical strength to cope.[39] Fishing is bound to become a zone of increased conflict as increasing sea temperature is making the fishes, crabs and lobsters migrate to the colder water. This will result in a reduced supply of seafood; more so for fisherwomen as they do not go in the deep sea like fishermen with well-equipped boats.[40] Climate scientists report that even for fishermen, these developments will add to their struggle in trade conflicts concerning fishing, resulting in a diminished supply of food, profit and employment.[41] Global warming is likely to fuel fishing wars as countries will clash for exclusive economic rights to the fish beyond their waters due to fishes' migration to the deeper sea.[42] Flooding frequently causes internal displacement in India, making people move to other places to avert these threats.

According to national disaster management authority over 40 million hectares, that is 12% of India's land is prone to floods and river erosion. States like Assam experience flood almost every monsoon with major floods at least every four years that has eroded approximately 7.4 per cent of total landmass since 1950.[43] Total 74% of the area of north Biharis affected by the devastating and frequently occurring floods.[44] Coastal regions of Andhra Pradesh, Odisha, West Bengal and Southern Gujarat are other flood-prone areas of India. Worldwide, floods were responsible for 84% of all disaster-related deaths between 2000 and 2005, and 65% of disaster-related economic losses between 1992 and 2001.[45] One estimate based on data from 1980 to 2017 mentioned 278 floods affected more than 750 million people in total.[46] According to studies, by 2040, twenty-five million Indians would be at risk of severe floods, and, as per this trend, it would be a sixfold increase from 3.7 million facing a threat between 1971 and 2004.[47] Finance Commission of India introduced the concept Disaster Risk Index in 2020. On the scale of 100 concerning different parameters of disaster, Odisha has scored 90 points, Bihar 80 and Assam and Arunachal Pradesh 70 each.[48]

Floods are one of the most common natural catastrophes faced by human civilisation. However, the strategies of adaptation varied with reference to cultural and social factors. Water and river-centric culture and flood-plain dwelling, coupled with their traditional knowledge, has helped certain indigenous communities to adapt well to the movements of rivers by enduring in that environment or migrating temporarily. This indigenous wisdom included being able to interpret signs about the occurrence of rains and floods, practice of traditional medicine and healing systems; knowledge and skills in swimming and in making rafts and boats; house building; fishing; and crop cultivation.[49] Although the communities have lived and coped with floods for years using their traditional knowledge and skills, their coping practices and mechanisms are failing because of the highly erratic nature of floods in terms of both frequency and intensity.[50]

Climate change is likely to have an extremely adverse effect on flooding and erosion in South Asia. With the increase in precipitation, rapid melting of snow due to global warming, the volume of river water will increase, causing overflowing of rivers. Hence, the frequency of floods and the destruction would increase in the near future. The United States Department of Defence has characterised climate change as a "threat multiplier", stating that existing vulnerabilities will accentuate and new security risks will emerge.[51]

The impact of climate change and related destructions will be felt by almost all nations and communities, but it will be more devastating for the most vulnerable, which includes women.[52] In one of its report, WHO while discussing the vulnerabilities of women stated, "There is a pattern of gender differentiation and exclusion at all level of disaster process, i.e. exposure to risk, risk perception, preparedness, response, physical impact, psychological impact and recovery".[53] The vulnerability of women is further entrenched because it crosscut race, class, caste and significantly influenced by the social and cultural norms.

The physical, mental and cultural attributes play a significant role in coping up with the crisis. For instance, the tribal women (Missing, Deori, Sonowal Kacharis) of Majuli the largest river island located in the Brahmaputra river are comfortable in the water. They can swim, manage boats and rafts, and live in traditional houses (Chang Ghars) on stilts that are appropriate for the flood-prone area. The harvesting of paddy is carried out by women in the fields submerged in water. In the case of early floods, the water level is quite high, but, women paddle through the water and stay immersed for long hours. However, women from other communities are not trained to live and survive in this kind of environment. Several women have been married into the villages from areas that are not flood affected or not as acutely flood-affected as their in-laws' village, and they are not equipped to cope in highly flood-prone areas. It is difficult for them to manage in a situation and against the impacts which are new for them and, hence, they find themselves more vulnerable than others. Living in houses with the temporarily raised platforms they survive the floods by staying confined to their houses, sometimes standing on the raised platforms for weeks, and starting from the beginning again afresh after the floods recede.[54]

Britton noted, "Disaster is a social product; vulnerability is contingent on social preconditions".[55] For instance, in Chars (river islands) of Assam people live in a world that is "vague, diffuse or unspecific, slippery, ephemeral, elusive or indistinct." *Chars* the sandbars or small sandy islands are formed by the Brahmaputra and account for about 5% of the total area of Assam. Suspended particles and the bed load combine during floods create these almond-shaped formations. Flood and associated erosion determine the fate of their inhabitants regularly because they have to move at least once every six to seven years when the braided river channels changed that configuration.[56] Living the life of unpredictability and uncertainty, which requires constant adjustments people are forced to develop their livelihoods to cope with the river's moods, which Kunthala Dutta-Lahiri and Gopa Samanta calls "Dancing with the rivers".[57] Poverty, illiteracy, inequality, vulnerable livelihoods, changing social aspirations and land erosion in the context of the recurring nature of flood meant disasters have become a part of the lived reality of its inhabitants. The life of uncertainty involves personal loss due to floods and erosion, coping, recovering and preparing for the future, and losing everything again to the river.[58]

With a population of 25 lakh (as per socio economic survey 2002–2003) which is twice the population density of the rest of Assam, char dwellers are neither visible to nor considered a priority for, the policymakers.[59] There are only two essential surveys conducted by the Government of Assam that provide some relevant data of these areas. The life that depends on land and changing moods of the river makes the struggle for existence tougher because with repeated floods, and cultivable erosion land has declined from 70 per cent to 67.13 per cent during 1992–93 to 2002–03. There has been a simultaneous decline in the per capita availability of cultivable land as well.[60] The transitory nature of chars muddles the ownership right over land, further complicated by confusing policies and states apathy. In the absence of clarity when a new char emerges or an old eroded char reappears, the locally powerful dewanis and matabbars try to get control over it creating armed conflicts among different groups under them. In case of a newly emerged char, peasants rush to occupy the lands that also lead to land conflicts.[61] Land, an essential resource of survival, is a significant cause of conflict after floods because a large mass of land got submerged in water and identification and demarcation of landowners in the absence of proper documentation emerge as a challenge.

Access to health, education, sanitation, drinking water and livelihood remains a challenge in post-flood situations, thus people are forced to drink contaminated water, take contaminated food and spend most of the time in an unclean and unhygienic environment in the char areas. Amidst the daily struggle of survival, women endure additional burden both from the society within and from the state since various programmes and initiatives for their empowerment, health, nutrition, education and financial reliance do not reach these areas. Globally, women and girls are responsible for collecting water in eight out of ten households.[62] Women and children collectively spend an estimated 200 million hours per day collecting water.[63] In Chars of Assam where 91% of the population does not have access to safe drinking water, the burden of arranging water for the family falls on women. Increasing resource scarcity results in less time for school, work or other activities, and it can also put women and girls in danger as they travel greater distances to collect resources.[64] Data shows that three-fifth of the 115 million children worldwide that do not go to school are girls.[65] The number of girl school dropouts increases after the disaster for various reasons that include migration, poverty and social norms that put an additional burden of household responsibilities on women.

The scarcity of clean water during flood further compromises hygiene and health for women and girls, primarily due to the sanitation needs particular to pregnancy and menstruation. Women often experience considerable stress, even health complications arising from social anathemas around mensuration and modesty norms which prevent them from attending their requirements. For instance, in Chars of Assam, only 1.4% has access to proper toilet facilities.[66] The limited access to health care, limited knowledge of risk and social and cultural hierarchy where women are already at the last paddle increase women's vulnerability. In a report published by Orissa (now Odisha) State Disaster Mitigation Authority, the number of sick and injured women during cyclones and floods in coastal areas was far more than men.[67] A study by ADB found that in societies where the socio-economic status of women is low, natural disaster kills more women than men both directly and indirectly through related post-disaster events.[68] According to the WHO study 2014 globally, disasters such as flood tend to kill women at a younger age. The WHO in its studies repeatedly raised concerns related to the accessibility of safe water because many infections and disease like chronic gastrointestinal illness spread due to its unavailability.[69]

The access to various livelihood resources is shaped by gender-based social relations reflected in sexist norms, values, roles and responsibilities. Women in India lack access to assets, and this thereby hinders the capability to adapt and reduce their vulnerabilities.[70] Land as an essential source of livelihood provides security and status to its beholder, but across Asia, the land owned by women on average is about 10%.[71] A study by Landesa and Oxfam in two districts (Madhepura and Supaul) of Bihar found that only 7 % of women own land while at the national level, around 12% of women have land ownership.[72] In a situation of disasters like flood with limited access to credit, information and relief services, women have fewer resources to rely upon. The formal financial institutions like banks show their reluctance to help disadvantaged and self-help groups are also of not much benefit in the vulnerable terrains to get financial services.[73] Thus, to survive in the difficult times, women often go to the local money-lenders for loans in cash or kind, at a very high-interest rate. This is the trap of indebtedness which forces the people into the vicious cycle of poverty. The post-disaster cramped living conditions in relief camps, lack of privacy can escalate sexual violence and abuse of female survivors. Sometimes poor women to receive aid or help or to fulfil the needs of family fall in the trap of sexually gratifying men.[74] Psychological trauma, hardships, poverty and the lack of job opportunities put them at increased risk of falling victim to human trafficking.[75] The National Crime Record Bureau has reported the high prevalence of women trafficking from Bihar to other parts of India. As per the report, nearly 20,000 women from flood-affected 12 districts have been reported missing during the 2007–11 period. However, the actual number of missing women may be many times greater than these reported numbers as claimed by different non-governmental organisations (NGOs).[76]

The livelihood strategies of poor and vulnerable are linked with the ability to diversify income and assets. The poor always attempt to spread their 'livelihood basket' to survive the whims of seasons. Thus, in an attempt to find greener pastures, men prefer to migrate to big cities and towns in search of income. This form of migration adds to the pre-disaster vulnerability of women and brings with it new challenges. The patriarchal structure, local culture and practices define women's role in a manner that restrict their activities in the domestic realm without financial independence. In many communities, social conditions for women include a lack of rights to property or access to legal or financial assets.[77] In the absence of a regular source of income, their situation worsens post-flood because women are left to normalise the non-functional house along with the other household chores and care burdens. During and after floods, women face considerable difficulty in keeping the household functioning, for example, maintaining or dismantling the house as appropriate, cooking and finding drinking water. In peak floods, moving cattle to higher land such as an embankment is a problem, while storage of fodder and shortage of funds necessitates the sale of a valuable asset. Women with their limited personal assets bear the burden of household recovery by finding work as a labourer and selling or mortgaging assets, including jewellery. Women are mostly confined to their homes and hardly ever go out of the villages. Thus, their choices are limited. The intersectionality of gender with class and caste further increases the vulnerability of poorer and lower-caste women during and after such disasters.[78]

In post-flood situations, relief efforts slowly decrease following the retreat of the monsoon. Most of the time relief funds also reduce because donors work with a perception that flood-affected populations returned to their homes as the flood recedes. The displacement which is supposed to be temporary in reality turn out to be permanent because most families have nothing to return to as the lands are still submerged. The decision to move back to their places is often determined by the probability of getting back their land which in most of the cases is a remote possibility. TISS assessment report of 2008 mentions that the flooding of Kosi has submerged 1.1 lakh hectares of farmland.[79] The river has shifted over 120 km eastwards, going back to the course it had abandoned more than 200 years ago and washed away hundreds of villages. "Gender distinctions in vulnerabilities determine not only who migrates but also for whom it is easier to return and restore their lives".[80] In post-flood situations as well, women have fewer options to recover.[81]

Climate change has been cited as one of the growth drivers of migration across the world.[82] With the acceleration of out-migration as one of the strategies to cope with disaster new issues nationally as well as internationally would be faced by humanity. Migrations in the wake of natural disasters like a flood are characterised by a lack of choice and agency for victims. The decision determined by the need for immediate survival is not migration but can best be described as displacement. The human development report of 2014 also declared that climate change has limited the choice of an individual and would further erode "human freedoms".[83] This also implies that those that are most vulnerable to the effects of climate change are often the least equipped to take an independent, informed decision. In cases where the landless and the poorest migrate, they did so more because they were compelled and less out of choice. Thus, circumstances push them to migrate, and the people who have the agency and resources move away from the river. But the most vulnerable among them the poorest of the poor or women stay back by the river to face increasing uncertainties that come with it.

The decision of migration, both voluntary and forced, is a gendered and socially embedded process.[84] Mechanic A. Abebe argues, "Migration as a coping strategy is gendered because it requires not only physical mobility but also economical and physical capacities that are not equally available to women".[85] Even in the process of migration, women encounter specific security issues. They are susceptible to sexual and gender-based violence, and thus rarely decide as an independent agent.[86] The social structure also determines the common choice mechanism that restricts women's decision making power. The decision to migrate, which in most of the situations is taken by men comes with psychological and emotional trauma for women because the burden of survival in a fragile environment offering few resources falls on women. The experience of women migrating from Bangladesh to chars (river islands) of India amplifies this. Kuntala Lahiri Dutt and Gopa Samantha in their work on Chars (River Island) mentioned women during interviews discussed that they were better off in Bangladesh, where family and support networks were more extensive.[87] In case of Chars, women need to reinvent to settle in changed circumstances that involve negotiating with their uprooted status, fluid nature of chars, uncertainties of life and livelihood and the most crucial citizenship status. There are complex and interlinked outcomes of people's illegal immigration to India and their indirect exposure to floods and river erosion. Located between belonging and non-belonging, women are also forced to negotiate their difference with the state, which denies space of disagreements based on either ethnicity or gender.[88]

The massive displacement of population post-floods may cause conflict in states receiving migrants.[89] Conflicts linked to food security of the hosting state is one probability, as discussed by scholars.[90] Increased competition for job opportunities and resources would also lead to ethnic tensions, thus threatening political stability and lead to an increase in armed conflict around the world.[91] In countries like India and Bangladesh, there are many instances of migration leading to ethnic tension and conflicts. For example, in Assam, the presence of people coming from central India and Bihar has caused ethnic tensions and violence in the past. Similarly, the perceived threat that people from Bangladesh will immigrate to the northeastern part of India has raised threats of ethnic clashes and violence in the region. Roughly once every ten years one-third of Bangladesh is severely affected by floods, while the catastrophic floods of 1988, 1998, 2004 and 2007 caused inundation of more than 60% of the country's area.[92] Legal and illegal immigration in the northeast, especially Assam, has entangled the citizenship issue and has led to ethnic tensions and conflicts.[93]

Policy Challenges

Given the scale of climate change-induced problem, India's response to climate migration has been far from adequate. The omission of climate migration as a problem issue in India's policy agenda is justified by highlighting immediate challenges like poverty alleviation, population growth and urbanisation by policymakers. UN Security Council in its debate on climate change in 2011 have stressed on activities combating climate change, however, what is evident from India's stance is that it does not see climate change as a threat to national or international security.[94] This is a deliberate gesture on the part of India as the country does not want to trade-off its ongoing projects and pursuits which would be affected by the austerity measures. Additionally, India aspires to be acknowledged as a significant global player and does not want to be portrayed as a victim in the narrative of climate-security. Also, the broader debate on climate change is already couched in the polarised understanding between the developed world versus the developing world.

It is because of these reasons that even in NAPCC, climate migration has not been identified as the prime concern. Though in the past, institutional focus has been more on scientific climate change trends like varying precipitation patterns, temperature rise and so on, in recent times socioeconomic concerns also occupy sufficient coverup in the adaption policies regarding climate-induced migration.[95] Effective management of climate change migration would minimise the humanitarian crisis, avoid conflict and provide opportunities to people, thereby expanding the social limits of adaptation.[96] Besides, the country policy formulation and decision-making mechanism should incorporate women in crucial roles. Women have been absent from the tables on climate change negotiations, and nor have been there any effort to bring gender aspects in the deliberations, in the domestic as well as international forums. However, the participation of women and accommodating their voices are crucial.

Informal institutional reforms, whereby individuals at the community level become agents of change, need to be incorporated in the policy agenda for enhancing the ability of the poor and vulnerable to adapt to climate change. For instance, in Bihar, an informal institution called "Chakroya Vikas Pranali" was formed to negotiate a set of rules to govern the use of local land and water resources.[97] Community-level efforts would help in minimising climate change impacts. However, to incorporate women and their experiences, it is crucial that local and informal institutional arrangements are shaped by the specific and often different needs, roles and responsibilities of men and women.

While there are many frameworks, conventions and norms related to migration that may have some relevance to climate migrants, there are significant gaps in international law on this issue with very less attention paid to women climate migrants.[98] However, this mostly uncharted terrain of international law requires essential deliberations in the interest of humanity. The 2018 UN Global Compact for Migration, signed by 164 countries, made a start by including a section on climate change in its effort to define a common approach to migration. Though, the nonbinding nature of the agreement reduces its effectivity. In recent times, some literature discuss the importance of gendered factors in the migration process and decisions. Still, they need to incorporate women's perspectives into the security conversation at the local, national and international levels.

As with post-conflict settings, climate-related migration may result in the upheaval of social norms surrounding women's roles and social capital, creating opportunities for advancement as well as a retrenchment of patriarchal structures and behaviours.[99] Chindarkar argues, "On one hand [migration outcomes] may seem to be empowering women, while on the other they may exacerbate their socioeconomic status and make them worse off."

The river impacts the lives of people who are commonly "voiceless" or do not have the agency to articulate their perspectives in relevant forums. The connection between those who govern water and those that are governed needs to be incorporated in policy structures. It is nevertheless essential to recognise that if the perspectives of the "governed", that is, the people whose lives revolve around these rivers, are not incorporated in formulating policies, it would be impossible to ensure environmentally just and sustainable processes.[100]

Conclusion

In contemporary times of increasing climate migrants, there is a need for change in approach and orientation of city planning and administration. Urban spaces must gear up to the inflow of dislocated people who should not be seen as a burden; instead, if creatively accommodated, they could add to labour supply in the local economy. Central and state government could think of suitable provisions such as low-cost housing, alternative employment schemes and skill development programmes for migrants to enable them livelihood opportunities. The Special Report on climate change and land by IPCC has come up with some crucial suggestions like shift from meat to plant-based diet and shift to sustainably produced animal-sourced food, curb on deforestation of Amazonian forest, to preserve and restore forests in all parts of the world.[101] In resonance with the objectives laid by IPCC and Paris Agreement in 2015, India announced an ambitious plan to climate actions by emphasising massive scale-up of renewable energy.[102] Under this plan, five key areas are highlighted: to increase renewable energy, e-mobility solution to reduce use of crude oil, Jal Shakti Abhiyan (water mission) for conservation and rejuvenation of water bodies, building coalitions with other countries like France for International Solar Alliance and developing low carbon pathways for net-zero emissions in steel and cement industries.

In 2019, India developed new projects in partnership with UNDP to boost climate resilience in three coastal states with the help of Green Climate Funds established under UNFCCC.[103] Under this six-year project, the states of Andhra Pradesh, Maharashtra and Odisha will benefit from improved shoreline protection and safeguarding of vulnerable ecosystems. This project is expected to help 1.7 million people in an effort towards climate change adaptation. One of the significant aspects of this project is that it is expected to benefit marginal sections including women and female-headed households. Likewise, all the policies have to be gender-sensitive and gender-responsive to address the women-specific depravations and adversities caused by climate change, as discussed in the chapter. All adaptation and support policies must incorporate a nuanced and gendered understanding of the issue.

Notes

1 Benoît Mayer (2012), "Governing international climate change-induced migration", in S. Lorraine Elliott (ed.), *Climate change, migration and human security in Southeast Asia*. Singapore: Rajaratnam School of International Studies, RSIS monograph No. 24, 28.

2 Dankelman, Irene, Khurshid Alam, Wahida Bashar Ahmed, Yacine Diagne Gueye, Naureen Fatema, and Rose Mensah-Kutin. (2008), *Gender, Climate Change and Human Security: Lessons from Bangladesh, Ghana and Senegal.* New York: Women's Environment and Development Organization.
3 Niel Padukone (2010), "Climate change in India: Forgotten threats, forgotten opportunities", *Economic & Political Weekly*, xlv(22), 47.
4 World Bank Report (2013), "India: Climate change impacts", accessed from www.worldbank.org/en/news/feature/2013/06/19/india-climate-change-impacts on 15th August 2018.
5 Intergovernmental Panel on Climate Change (IPCC) (2007), *Summary for policymakers. Climate change 2007: Impacts, adaptation and vulnerability*. Contribution of Working Group II to the Fourth Assessment Report of the IPCC, New York: Cambridge University Press, p. 9.
6 A. Brody, J. Demetriades and E. Esplen (2008), *Draft-gender and climate change: Mapping the linkages. A scoping study on knowledge and gaps*. Brighton: BRIDGE Institute of Development Studies, accessed from http://www.bridge.ids.ac.uk/sites/bridge.ids.ac.uk/files/reports/Climate_Change_DF ID_draft.pdf; These aspects of vulnerability of women have been highlighted by many studies such as by (Ahmad & Fajber, 2009; Archer, 2003; UNISDR, 2008; Neumayer & Plumper, 2007)
7 A. Agarwal and S. Narain (1985), *The state of India's environment report*. New Delhi: The Centre for Science and Environment (CSE), p. 172.
8 Irene Dankelman, Khurshid Alam, Wahida Bashar Ahmed, et al. (2008), "Gender, climate change and human security lessons from Bangladesh, Ghana and Senegal", *Women's Environment and Development Organisation*, accessed from http://gdnonline.org/resources/WEDO_Gender_CC_Human_Security on 22nd June 2020.
9 Briana Mawby and Anna Applebaum (2020), "Addressing future fragility: Women, climate change and migration", in Soumita Basu, Paul Kirby and Laura J. Shepherd (eds.) *New directions in women, peace and security*. Bristol: Bristol University Press, 208.
10 Intergovernmental Panel on Climate Change (IPCC) (2014), *AR5 synthesis report: Climate change 2014*. Geneva: IPCC, accessed from www.ipcc.ch/report/ar5/syr/ on 23rd June 2020.
11 "The Enhanced Lima Work Programme on Gender", *United Nations Climate Change*, accessed from https://unfccc.int/topics/gender/workstreams/the-enhanced-lima-work-programme-on-gender
12 *Submission by India on SBI Agenda item 20: Gender and Climate Change*, Government of India, accessed from https://www4.unfccc.int/sites/SubmissionsStaging/Documents/201804051550---India%20Gender%20submission.pdf on 22nd June 2020.
13 Prime Minister's Council on Climate Change: National Action Plan on Climate Change, Government of India, 2009, 14, accessed from https://archivepmo.nic.in/drmanmohansingh/climate_change_english.pdf on 20th October 2020.
14 Brown Oli (2008), *Migration and climate change*, no. 31, IOM Migration Research Series, Geneva: International Organization for Migration.
15 Oxfam (2018), "Move over 'Sons of the soil': Why you need to know the female farmers that are revolutionizing agriculture in India", accessed from www.oxfamindia.org/women-empowerment-india-farmers on 22nd April 2021.
16 Alassane Drabo and Linguère Mously Mbaye (2011), "Climate change, natural disasters and migration: An empirical analysis in developing countries, The Institute for the Study of Labor (IZA) in Bonn, IZA, Discussion Paper No. 5927, 10.

17 IPPC Second Working Group Report (IPPC) (2001), *Climate change impacts, adaptations and vulnerability, contribution of Working Group I to the third assessment report of the Intergovernmental Panel on Climate Change*. London and New York: Cambridge University Press.
18 FAO (1996), *The state of food and agriculture*. Rome: FAO.
19 Nicholas Stern (2007), *"The economics of climate change": The Stern review*. Cambridge: Cambridge University Press.
20 R. Mendelsohn (2009), "The impact of climate change on agriculture in developing countries", *Journal of Natural Resources Policy Research*, 1(1), https://doi.org/10.1080/19390450802495882
21 Planning Commission, GOI (2008), "Eleventh five year plan (2007–2012) agriculture, rural development, industry, services and physical infrastructure", accessed from https://niti.gov.in/planningcommission.gov.in/docs/plans/planrel/fiveyr/11th/11_v3/11th_vol3.pdf on 14th August 2022.
22 Chauhan Chetan (2017), "States stare at drought as 59% of India get deficit rainfall, food output at the lowest", *Hindustan Times*, accessed from www.hindustantimes.com/india-news/states-stare-at-drought-as-59-of-india-get-deficit-rainfall-food-output-at-the-lowest/story-L754PYi3N6HCoCVQ2lGXHJ.html
23 Chandran Rina (2017), "Feature: Heat and drought drive south India's farmers from fields to cities', *Reuters*, accessed from www.reuters.com/article/us-heatwave-india-migration/feature-heat-and-drought-drive-south-indias-farmers-from-fields-to-cities-idUSKCN1BV015
24 Langa Mahesh (2018), "Summer of discontent: Water crisis looms in Gujarat", *The Hindu*, accessed from www.thehindu.com/news/national/other-states/summer-of-discontent-water-crisis-looms-in-gujarat/article23357979.ece on 24th June 2020.
25 Himachal CM calls meeting to discuss looming water crisis (2018), *Times of India*, accessed from http://timesofindia.indiatimes.com/articleshow/62610650.cms?utm_source=contentofinterest&utm_medium=text&utm_campaign=cppst on 25th June 2020.
26 Itishree Pattnaik, Kuntala Lahiri-Dutt, Stewart Lockie& Bill Pritchard (2018), "The feminization of agriculture or the feminiazation of agrarian distress? Tracking the trajectory of women in agriculture in India", *Journal of the Asia Pacific Economy*, 23:1, 138–155, DOI: 10.1080/13547860.2017.1394569
27 This was reported in the field study of Nayagarh district in Odisha where more than 50 women farmers interviewed highlighted their increased responsibility in agriculture due to seasonal and permanent migration of male members. Source: Pushpa Singh (2020), "Politics of knowledge in development: Seed sovereignty and gender", Unpublished PhD Thesis. Delhi: University of Delhi.
28 *Impacts of Climate Change on Marginalised Women: An Exploratory Study across 6 Districts in Assam* (2012), Centre for Environment, Social and Policy Research (CESPR), and Rashtriya Gramin Vikas Nidhi (RGVN) in collaboration with Indian Network on Ethics and Climate Change (INECC), accessed from http://ced.org.in/docs/inecc/publications/Impact%20of%20Climate%20Change%20on%20Marginalized%20Women.pdf on 24th February 2020.
29 Ibid, 8.
30 Ibid, 36.
31 Chanda Gurung Goodrich (2017), *Status of gender, vulnerabilities and adaptation to climate change in the Hindu Kush Himalaya*, ICIMOD Working Paper 2017/3, accessed from www.gdnonline.org/resources/icimodWP3-017.pdf on 25th June 2020.
32 Over 700 Uttarakhand villages deserted in 10 years: Report (2018), *The Economic Times*, accessed from https://economictimes.indiatimes.com/news/politics-

and-nation/over-700-uttarakhand-villages-deserted-in-10-yearsreport/articleshow/64044151.cms?utm_source=contentofinterest&utm_medium=text&utm_campaign=cppst on 25th April 2020.
33 Lal Neeta (2016), "Climate migrants lead mass migration to India's cities", *Reliefweb*, accessed from https://reliefweb.int/report/india/climate-migrants-lead-mass-migration-india-s-cities on 25th April 2020.
34 Sara Ahmed and Elizabeth Fajber (2009), "Engendering adaptation to climate variability in Gujarat, India", *Gender and Development*, 17(1), 34.
35 Gupta Vijaya (2005), "Climate change and domestic mitigation efforts", *Economic and Political Weekly*, 40(10), 982.
36 *India Rivers Studies 2017: Rivers Succumbing to Dams, Pollution & Climate Change*, (Report) 2017, South Asia Network on Dams, Rivers and People (SANDRP), accessed from https://sandrp.in/2018/03/13/india-rivers-studies-2017-rivers-succumbing-to-dams-pollution-climate-change/ on 20th October 2010.
37 Ibid.
38 Gupta Vijaya (2005), "Climate change and domestic mitigation efforts", *Economic and Political Weekly*, 40(10), 983.
39 Parekh Jyoti (2007), *Gender and climate change: Framework for analysis, policy and action, integrated research and action for development*, UNDP India, accessed from www.undp.org/content/dam/india/docs/gnder_cc.pdf on 20th October 2020.
40 Ibid.
41 Shepherd Marshall (2018), "Climate change may be creating a seafood trade war, too", *Forbes*, accessed from www.google.co.in/amp/s/www.forbes.com/sites/marshells hephard/2018/06/15/climate-change-may-be-creating-a-seafood-tradewar-too/amp/ on 25th June 2020.
42 Wright Pam (2018), "Fishing wars will increase as climate change drives fish to cooler but exclusive waters", accessed from https://weather.com/science/environment/news/2018-06-15-fishing-wars-climate-change-fish on 25th June 2020.
43 For further details refer to Assam government, Flood and Erosion problems, accessed from https://waterresources.assam.gov.in/portlets/flood-erosion-problems on 6th July 2020.
44 Government of Bihar, Bihar State Disaster Management Authority, accessed from http://bsdma.org/Know-Your-Risk.aspx?id=3 on 6th July 2020.
45 Ali Akhtar (2013), "Indus basin floods mechanisms, impacts, and management", *Asian Development Bank*, accessed from www.adb.org/sites/default/files/publication/30431/indus-basin-floods.pdf on 4th July 2020.
46 The international disasters Database EM, DAT, 2018.
47 India Spend Team (2019, 27 December), "Five charts show how India fared on climate change, unemployment and women's safety in 2019", *Scroll*, https://scroll.in/article/947946/five-charts-show-how-india-fared-on-climate-change-unemployment-and-womens-safety-in-2019.
48 Chaki Bijay (2020, 4 February), "Odisha most vulnerable to natural calamities", *The New Indian Express*, accessed from https://www.newindianexpress.com/cities/bhubaneswar/2020/feb/04/odisha-most-vulnerable-to-natural-calamities-2098735.html on 29th October 2022.
49 Alassane Drabo and Linguère Mously Mbaye (2011), "Climate change, natural disasters and migration: An empirical analysis in developing countries", Discussion Paper No. 5927 IZA, Germany, accessed from https://docs.iza.org/dp5927.pdf on 29th October 2022.

50 United Nations Environment Programme (2019), "How climate change is making record-breaking floods the new normal", accessed from www.unep.org/news-and-stories/story/how-climate-change-making-record-breaking-floods-new-normal on 21st April 2021.
51 Sarah E. Light (2014), "Valuing national security: Climate change, the military, and society", *UCLA Law Review*, 61, 1772–1812, p. 1799.
52 Gopal Dutt Bhatta, Aggarwal Pramod Kumar, Poudel Santosh and Belgrave Anne Debbie (2015), "Climate-induced migration in South Asia: Migration decisions and the gender dimensions of adverse climatic events", *The Journal of Rural and Community Development*, 10(4), 1–23. M. R. Islam and M. Shamsuddoha (2017), "Socioeconomic consequences of climate induced human displacement and migration in Bangladesh", *International Sociology*, 32(3), 277–298.
53 WHO (2002), *Gender and health in disaster*. Geneva: WHO. Accessed from https://apps.who.int/iris/bitstream/handle/10665/68886/a85575.pdf?sequence=1 on 6th July 2020.
54 Sen Sucharita With Arundhati Deka, Farzia Yashmeen, Tsheten Dorji, ATM Zakir Hossain, Suparana Katyaini, Mirza Rahman and Ranju Dodum (2018) "Genderscape of the Brahmaputra River An Exploratory Exposition Saci WATERs South Asia Consortium for Interdisciplinary Water Resources Studies Hyderabad, India May, 2018 Report 2/2018 South Asia Consortium for Interdisciplinary Water Resources Studies Hyderabad, India", accessed from www.saciwaters.org/brahmaputradialogue/assets/downloads/Gender%20Narratives%20by%20S%20Sen.pdf on 20th October 2020.
55 Neil R. Britton (1986), "Developing an understanding of disaster", *Journal of Sociology*, 22(2), 254–271, p. 254.
56 Gorky Chakraborty (2012), *Roots and ramifications of a colonial 'construct': The wastelands in Assam*, Occasional Paper, 39. Kolkata: Institute of Development Studies, 21. According to government records 6, 03, 754 bighas of char areas in 9 districts of Assam were encroached upon in the last several years. For details see The Staff Reporter, (2017) 6, 03, 754 bighas of char land grabbed in Assam, *The Sentinel*, 20 February.
57 Kuntala Dutta-Lahiri and Samanta Gopa, (2013) *Dancing with the river People and Life on the Chars of South Asia*. New Haven and London: Yale University Press, 18–19.
58 For details see Dutta-Lahiri and Gopa, *Dancing with the river people*.
59 Directorate of Char area development, accessed from https://dircad.assam.gov.in/about-us/history-0 on 28th October 2020, (2002–2003 is the only survey organized by government agencies available for char areas).
60 Chakraborty, "Roots and ramifications of a colonial 'construct' ", 23.
61 M. Q. Zaman (1991), "Social structure and process in Char land settlement in the Brahmaputra-Jamuna floodplain", *Man, New Series*, 26, 673–690.
62 World Health Organization and United Nations Children's Fund (2017), *Progress on drinking water, sanitation, and hygiene: 2017, update and SDG baselines*. Geneva: World Health Organization and United Nations Children's Fund, 11, accessed from www.unicef.org/publications/files/Progress_on_Drinking_Water_Sanitation_and_Hygiene_2017.pdf on 3rd July 2020.
63 UNICEF (2016), "UNICEF: Collecting water is often a colossal waste of time for women and girls", accessed from www.unicef.org/press-releases/unicef-collecting-water-often-colossal-waste-time-women-and-girls on 6th July 2020.
64 I. Dankelman (2009), "Human security, climate change and women", *UN Chronicle*, XLVI, 3 and 4.

65 Madhuri (2016), "The impact of flooding in Bihar, India on women: A qualitative study", *Asian Women*, 32(1), 31–52.
66 Aishwarya Tripathi and Gaurav Vivek Bhatnagar (2019, 27 November), "Minorities in Assam's char, dropouts in Telangana: Tracking India's most excluded. The India Exclusion Report 2019 also talks about waste pickers and migrant labourers", *The Wire*, accessed from https://thewire.in/rights/minorities-in-assams-chars-dropouts-in-telangana-tracking-indias-most-excluded on 29th October 2022.
67 Aurobindo Behera, Prafulla Mishra and Sneha Mishra (2002), *Voicing silence: Experience of women with disasters in Orissa*. Orissa: Orissa State Disaster Mitigation Authority, accessed from https://tnsdma.tn.gov.in/app/webroot/img/document/library/59-Voicing-Silence.pdf on 29th October 2022.
68 ADB, UNESCAP and UNDP (2013), "Asia-Pacific aspirations: Perspectives for a post-2015 development agenda, Asia-Pacific Regional MDGs report 2012/13", accessed from www.adb.org/sites/default/files/publication/30414/asia-pacific-regional-mdgs-report.pdf on 5th July 2020.
69 WHO (2002), "The world health report: Reducing risks, promoting healthy life", accessed from https://www.who.int/publications/i/item/9241562072 on 31st October 2022; WHO (2005), "Gender, climate change and health", accessed from http://apps.who.int/iris/bitstream/handle/10665/144781/9789241508186_eng.pdf;jsessionid=8211E8E214F1CC5E2C5BD8C9B2903CE4?sequence=1 on 31st October 2022.
70 Marlene Roy and Henry David Venema (2002), "Reducing risk and vulnerability to climate change in India: The capability approach", *Gender Development*, 10, 78–83.
71 Rao Nitya (2011), "Women's access to land: An Asian perspective", Expert group meeting enabling rural women's economic empowerment: Institutions, Opportunities and Participation, UN Women/FAO, IFAD and WFD, Accra, 20–23 September. Parnita B. Udas and Chand A. Goodrich (2018), "Gendered vulnerabilities in Diaras struggling with floods in the Gandak river basin", *Economic and Political Weekly*, LIII(17), 46–56.
72 Golder Shakti (2017), *Development in Bihar: Some policy prescriptions from a gender lens* (Policy Belief, No. 24). New Delhi: Oxfam, accessed from https://www.oxfamindia.org/knowledgehub/policybrief/development-bihar-gender-related-policy-recommendations on 31st October 2022.
73 Shahjahan Ali Sheikh and Kanchan Dutta (2019), "Poverty and microfinance in Char areas of Dhubri district in Assam", in Das Ramesh Chandra (ed.) *Handbook of research on microfinancial impacts on women empowerment, poverty and inequality*. Hershey, USA: IGI Global, 386–401.
74 Thomson Reuters Foundation (2013), "Women in disasters", accessed from https://news.trust.org//spotlight/Women-the-poorer-half-of-the-world/%3ftab%3dbriefing on 31st October 2022.
75 U. Niaz (2009), "Women and disasters", in P. S. Chandra, H. Herman, J. Fisher, M. Kastrup, U. Niaz, M. B. Rondon and A. Okasha (eds.) *Contemporary topics in women's mental health: Global perspectives in a changing society*. West Sussex: John Wiley and Sons, 369–386.
76 Thomas Reuter Foundation (2016), "Floods, disasters 'raise risk' of women, children being sold into slavery", accessed from https://news.trust.org/item/20160826153515-2b3lk/ on 31st October 2022.
77 E. Neumayer and T. Plümper (2007), "The gendered nature of natural disasters: The impact of catastrophic events on the gender gap in life expectancy, 1981–2002", *Annals of the Association of American Geographers*, 97(3), 551–566.

78 Ibid.
79 Manish K. Jha and Vijay Raghavan (2008), *Disaster in Bihar: A report from the TISS assessment team*. Mumbai: TISS.
80 Namrata Chindarkar (2012), "Gender and climate change-induced migration: Proposing a framework for analysis", *Environmental Research Letters*, 7(2), 1–7.
81 UN Women (2016), *Women and sustainable development goals*. Nairobi: Un Women Eastern and Southern Africa Regional Office, 22.
82 ADB (2012), *Addressing climate change and migration in Asia and the Pacific*. Philippines: Asian Development Bank.
83 UNDP (2007), *Human development report: Fighting climate change: Human solidarity in a divided world*. New York: Palgrave Macmillan, accessed from http://hdr.undp.org/sites/default/files/reports/268/hdr_20072008_en_complete.pdf on 6th July 2020.
84 Chindarkar, "Gender and climate change-induced migration".
85 M. A. Abebe (2014–2015), "Climate change, gender inequality and migration in East Africa", *Washington Journal of Environmental Law and Policy*, 4(1), 104–140.
86 Srilakshmi Gururaja (2000), "Gender dimensions of displacement", *Forced Migration Review*, 9, 13–16.
87 Lahiri Dutta Kuntala and Gopa Samanta (2013), *Dancing with the river people and life on the Chars of South Asia*. New Haven and London: Yale University Press, 131.
88 Ibid, 132.
89 Jon Barnett and W. Neil Adger (2007), "Climate change, human security and violent conflict", *Political Geography*, 26(6), 639–655.
90 JoAnn McGregor (1994), "Climate change and involuntary migration: Implications for food security", *Food Policy*, 19(2), 120–132.
91 Kurt M. Campbell, Jay Gulledge, J. R. McNeill, John Podesta, Peter Ogden, Leon Fuerth, R. James Woolsey, Alexander T. J. Lennon, Julianne Smith, Richard Weitz and Derek Mix (2007), *The age of consequences: The foreign policy and national security implications of global climate change*. Washington: Center for Strategic and International Studies.
92 Abul Kalam Azad, Mokaddem Khonodoker Hossain and Mahbuba Nasreen (2013), "Flood induced vulnerabilities and problems encountered by women in northern Bangladesh", *International Journal of Disaster Risk Science*, 4(4), 190–199.
93 For details see Sharma Chetna (2019), "Citizenship Amendment Bill 2016: Continuities and contestations with special reference to politics of Assam, India", *Asian Ethnicity*, 20(4), 522–540.
94 Ingrid Boas (2012), "Climate change migration (India)", in Ray Anderson et al. (eds.) *The encyclopedia of sustainability: China, India, and East and Southeast Asia: Assessing sustainability*. Berkshire: Berkshire Publishing Group, p. 63.
95 For example, India received huge grant from Green Climate Fund, UNDP for projects to generate climate-resilient livelihoods for 1.7 million people in Andhra Pradesh, Maharashtra and Odisha. For details, refer to www.adaptation-undp.org/india-gets-usd-43-million-green-climate-fund-boost-climate-resilience-3-coastal- on 21st April 2021.
96 Douglas K. Bardsley and Graeme J. Hugo (2010), "Migration and climate change: Examining thresholds of change to guide effective adaptation decision-making", *Population and Environment*, 32(2/3), 240.

97 Marlene Roy and Henry David Venema (2002), "Reducing risk and vulnerability to climate change in India: The capabilities approach", *Gender and Development*, 10(2), 78–83, B. Agarwal (1997), "The gender and environment debate: Lessons from India", in N. Visvanathan et al. (eds.) *The women, gender and development reader*. London: Zed Books.

98 Joseph Kweku Assan and Therese Rosenfeld (2012), "Environmentally induced migration, vulnerability and human security: Consensus, controversies and conceptual gaps for policy analysis", *Journal of International Development*, 24(8), 1046–1057.

99 Houria Djoudi, Maria Brockhaus and Bruno Locatelli (2013), "Once there was a lake: Vulnerability to environmental changes to northern Mali", *Regional Environmental Change*, 13(3), 493–508.

100 Sucharita Sen and SaciWaters (2018, January), "Genderscape of the Brahmaputra River an exploratory exposition", in *South Asia consortium for interdisciplinary water resources studies*. Hyderabad: The Asian Foundation, p. iii.

101 Special report, Climate Change and Land: An IPCC Special Report on climate change, desertification, land degradation, sustainable land management, food security, and greenhouse gas fluxes in terrestrial ecosystems, IPCC, available at www.ipcc.ch/srccl/ on 21st April 2021.

102 Anjali Jaiswal and Sameer Kwatra (2019), "India announces stronger climate action", accessed from www.nrdc.org/experts/sameer-kwatra/india-announces-stronger-climate-action on 21st April 2021.

103 India gets USD43 million from Green Climate Fund to boost climate resilience in 3 coastal states PTI (2019), "India gets USD 43 million from Green Climate Fund to boost climate resilience in 3 coastal states", www.indiatoday.in/india/story/green-climate-fund-to-boost-climate-resilience-india-1618650-2019-11-13 on 21st April 2021.

Chapter 6

The Dynamics of Deforestation, Riverbank Erosion and Migration in India With Special Reference to Assam

Daisy Das, Dimpal Dekaraja and Ratul Mahanta

Introduction

Deforestation, clearance for agriculture and pastures, degradation and fragmentation of forests are some of the important causes of land use land cover changes.[1] Deforestation has always remained a major cause of environmental degradation and subsequent migration in many parts of the world. Among the tropical countries, between 1880 and 1930, the annual rate of deforestation in India (1.0–3.0 Mha per year) was higher than many other tropical countries like Indonesia, Mexico, Bolivia, Sudan and Peru.[2,3,4] Considering the harmful effects of deforestation increasing forests cover has remained a priority for Ministry of Environment and Forests of the Indian government. In India, although the first forest policy was adopted in 1894 by the Imperial ruler to maintain adequate forests cover, but the actual motive of this forest policy was to maximize revenue. The policies during colonial rule did not serve the purpose of maintaining adequate forest cover and as a result deforestation did not come to a halt. Considering the importance of forest cover, Government of India introduced various initiatives in the post-independence period in order to increase forest cover. It started with the National Forest Policy (NFP) of 1952, which recommended that 33 percent of the total land area should be under forest cover in plains while mountains and hills should have a minimum of 60 percent forest cover. For the first time, this policy emphasized that there should be a minimum prescribed area under forest.[5] Subsequently, four classifications of forests namely protected forests, national forests, village forests and tree lands were made during this policy in order to protect forest land in a more systematic way. Out of the four classifications, the concept of protected and national forests supported the growth of many national parks and wild life sanctuary in India.

The NFP of 1952 was preceded by Social Forestry Program (SFP) of 1976. The aim of SFP was to increase the plantation of trees by the people of the country to combat adverse climate and ensure regular supply of firewood, fodder, minor timber for housing and raw materials for local forest based

DOI:10.4324/9781003367802-7

industries. However, the program could not be so successful owing to failure of management. Soon a need was felt for a comprehensive policy to conserve ecology and genetic biodiversity and accordingly the Forest (Conservation) Act of 1980 and Forest Policy of 1988 were introduced. The forest policy of 1988 re-insisted that there should be 33 percent forest cover in the plains and 60 percent in the hills. This policy emphasized large scale afforestation and SFP for restoration of ecological balance and conservation of forests.

A new dimension under the influence of the experience in the western world emerged in the management practices of Indian forest policies. The idea was to involve local people in the expansion of forests area and allow people to use forests produce for their benefits. To fulfill the objective, the Indian government introduced the Joint Forest Management Act, 1990. This was the first institutional measure to involve local people in the management of forests. As a result, almost 1.5 million hectares of forest land have been protected by about 10,000 formal and informal community institutions in India by 1992.[6] However, against the success story, if we look at the overall Indian forestry situation, we can see poor performance of community forest management. Joint Forest Management could cover only 2 percent of Indian forests till 1993. Due to imbalance in the rights and unequal opportunities between state (Forest Department) and local communities, the community forest management started with the slogan of managing forests "with the people" has failed to fulfill its commitment.[7]

During the decades of 1985, 1995 and 2005, there has been a significant decrease of forest cover (between 22.18 percent to 23.25 percent) in India.[8] In this period, there has been a continuous decrease in land cover in the form of forests with concomitant increase in cropland and built-up area. Although the rate of deforestation in India was lower (–0.43 percent) than global average (–0.60 percent) during 2009–11, deforestation has remained a major challenge for the policy makers ever since the inception of the first forest policy in 1894. Different initiatives have resulted in the increase of forests but it still falls short of targeted 33 percent forest cover area of total geographical area. Unfortunately, during 2011–19 in the north-eastern region of India excluding Assam, the forest cover decreased by 18 percent (Ministry of Environment and Forest, 2019). Roy et al.[9] confirmed a steady decrease in forest area in both central India and parts of northeast India between 1985 and 2005.

Deforestation causes environmental degradation and it leads to outmigration.[10,11] Deforestation-induced environmental degradation leads to scarcity of common property resources and people not having enough resources migrate to other places in search of livelihood.[12,13,14,15] It happens because poor people are heavily dependent on nature and its resources. Deforestation causes scarcity of fertile land that pushes the farmers to adopt intensive cultivation. This process robs the soil of nutrients and loss of productivity. Farmers are impoverished and tend to move to other areas for diversification of livelihood.[16] Thus, environmental change affects migration both directly and indirectly. It is also associated with conflict over resources and public policy debate along with economic consequences like changing livelihoods, agricultural productivity and location of industry.[17,18,19,20]

The foregoing discussion clearly shows that land degradation is one form of environmental degradation caused by deforestation. The relation between deforestation and land degradation has been established in Indian context too by several authors.[21,22,23,24] Researchers have also addressed the causes and cost of land degradation in India.[25] Similarly, the linkage between environmental degradation and migration have also been examined by various authors under different themes like dry land degradation and migration,[26] common property resources degradation and migration[27] riverbank erosion and migration.[28]

Our study enriches the literature by focusing on the dynamics of deforestation as well as land degradation and its relation to human migration. Both secondary and primary information have been used for the study. The information on migration across states has been collected from 64th round of National Sample Survey Organisation (NSSO) report of Government of India. The information on statewise deforestation has been gathered from Ministry of Environment and Forest (MoEF), Government of India. Similarly, information on land degradation has been collected from various government sources such as Water Resource and Revenue Department of Assam, Census of Assam and some non-government sources. Besides collecting secondary information, a primary survey has also been incorporated to substantiate the issue. We find that environmental degradation leads to forced migration and causes a vicious cycle of environmental destruction.

This chapter has been divided into three sections excluding introduction and conclusion. First section deals with the nexus between deforestation, land degradation and human migration. Dynamics of deforestation, land degradation and migration in India has been described in the second section. This is followed by a case study in the third section.

Nexus Among Deforestation, Land Degradation and Human Migration

The history of deforestation is very old on the earth. Many prominent civilizations like Harappa in the ancient time have been destroyed by the impact of deforestation and the rate of deforestation has become faster in the last century.[29] Different factors are responsible for deforestation but human encroachment for agriculture and shifting cultivation have been considered two major causes of deforestation in many parts of the world.[30,31] Shifting cultivation is practiced by almost 250 million people across South America, Central and West Africa and South Asia. Zhang et al.[32] confirm that continuation of shifting cultivation along with rural population growth will convert 94 percent of primary forest land into cropland, fallow and secondary forests by 2050 in Central Africa. In Indian north-eastern states, a huge amount of wood biomass was removed between 1984 and 1994, which is fair enough to cause forest cover loss.[33] Similarly, Starkel and Singh[34] have stated shifting cultivation as the major cause of deforestation which causes soil degradation in the Cherapunji region of Meghalaya, a north eastern state of India. A study by Roy et al.[35] has shown that the decrease in forest cover types in Assam valley and Garo hills of Meghalaya are due to felling of trees and shifting cultivation.

Deforestation causing landslide and erosion is a major cause of land degradation.[36] Land degradation poses a considerable challenge in achieving the goal of sustainable development and poverty reduction. As a result, human outmigration often takes place.[37,38,39,40,41] Increasing level of human out migration amongst forest users affects the management of community forestry.[42,43] The common-pool resource theorist argue that community-based natural management cannot sustain if there is human outmigration on large scale.[44,45] The responsibility of forest management often falls on adult members of society and outmigration of adult members makes forest management institutions vulnerable to failure.[46,47] Forest management by community is more effective because they work in group in which close coordination and cost minimization is possible. But community forests have suffered in Nepal due to migration of adult members and persistence of traditional practices.[48] Moreover, due to human out migration from hill areas, population pressure increases in other areas and leads to decline in vegetation cover. These people tend to encroach fertile and arable land closer to riverbank.[49] Ives and Messerli[50] argued that deforestation by the country's hill farmers was the main cause of flooding in the plains of Nepal. It has also been argued that shortage of labor due to human out migration leads to change in agricultural cropping pattern.[51]

It is clear from the foregoing discussion that migration induced by environmental degradation is harmful for the environment itself. To prevent human out migration, there are attempts to implement sustainable land management (SLM) and sustainable livelihood for providing opportunities to people affected by change in land cover and land use. Contrary to it, a study finds that outmigration is not a consequence of environmental degradation but rather a cause. Migrant farmers arrive on the internal frontier region of forest and cleared land for their agricultural expansions. Forests have been cleared further for expansion of agricultural practices for commercialization. This leads to land scarcity which compels migrant farmers to increase the intensity of farming that results reduction of soil fertility. The land scarcity again forces farmers to migrate to external frontier forests.[52] However, a study by Sundarlin and Resosudarmo[53] argues that deforestation does take place not only because of population factors but also for non-population push factors such as conversion of agricultural land as well as technological change and pull factors like road construction, the infrastructural benefits offered through the formal transmigration program and certain forms of attractive rural program.

Among different forms of environmental degradation, riverbank erosion is a risky and severe one.[54] The issue lies in the domain of geology and refers to reduction in riverbank area or growth in channel length and width owing to geomorphologic process. The main cause of riverbank erosion is flood which itself is a climate change induced phenomenon.[55] When there is deforestation, it causes an imbalance in the complex relationship between biology, landscape and water. River networks are often disturbed by deforestation induced erosion.[56] In India, 64 percent of total land degradation is because of water erosion.[57] Around the world, millions of people migrate to cope with degradation of environment and flood.[58] Flood and riverbank erosion is a common problem in some parts of India too.[59] Such erosion causes other problems like loss of cropland, loss of homestead area, household properties, loss of livelihood, erosion induced education and transportation problems, and environmental problems.[60,61,62] These lead the existing poverty situation worse among the landless and marginal farmers as they lost their sources of livelihood.[63] This forces the landless families to send either their adult members or the whole family to migrate.[64] However, availability of coping mechanisms in the flood- and erosion-affected areas may prevent people from migrating and help victims cope with adverse economic condition.[65,66,67,68]

Dynamics of Deforestation, Land Degradation and Migration in India

In India, conservation of forests was never a priority of the government neither during the colonial period nor in the post-colonial period. The colonial policies mainly tried to prevent indigenous people from forest extraction so that the state could use these resources for commercial purposes. Most of the policies initiated during colonial period was motivated by the custodial attitude of the state and importance was given on forests protection for their own benefit[69] which causes huge deforestation either due to international demand or for preparation of slippers for railways.[70] However, for the first time, the Forest Policy introduced in 1855 took into consideration the long-term environmental, economic and climatic effects of unplanned logging. The Indian Forest Act, 1865 converted the indigenous decentralized forest management system into a centralized body, Forest Department to exercise state's power over forests. In order to expand state's control over forests, British administration redefined forests by including wastelands through the Forest Act 1878 and tried to regulate local people's rights over forests by dividing forests into three categories-protected forests, reserved forests and village forests. Further, National Forest Policy of 1894 and Indian Forest Act of 1927 made state's control over forests stronger and tried to eliminate the people's right to forest use. The forests were divided into four classes and the third class (low-quality timber, fuel wood and fodder) and fourth class (pastures and grazing lands) land were meant for meeting local people's demand with restrictions on use of those resources.

The post-colonial forest policies implemented after independence were also mere duplication of the imperial policies. In order to meet the growing demand for timber and firewood, in 1972, National Commission on Agriculture was set up. The Commission advocated the setup of social forestry in community and private lands. In order to control over forests, Government of India with the 42nd amendment of constitution brought the forest under central concurrent list and it was enacted through the Forest (Conservation) Act in 1980. Serious conservationist policies such as Forest Conservation Act 1980, Indian Forest Policy 1988 followed by Joint Forest Management Programme 1990 started from 1974 onwards. But even after the implementation of various forest policies and a separate department, Indian government could not succeed in achieving the target of 33 percent forest cover of total land. It was felt that due to restriction laid down by various forest policies on use of forest products by the forest dwellers, forest-dependent people were not interested in the protection of forest. It was the Forest Policy, 1988 that gave emphasis on local people in forest conservation and subsequently the government adopted community-based forest management strategy in 1990.

After the Forest Policy introduced in 1988, the Government of India introduced Scheduled Tribes and Other Traditional Forest Dwellers (Recognition of Forest Rights) Act, (FRA) 2006 to protect the land rights of forest dwellers and compensate the deprivation of tribal people from forest land. This bill created a lot of expectations in the minds of forest dwellers. But its implementation has not been effective and the rate of claims and its outcome is not even across different states of India.[71] The implementation of this bill has been affected by local political interest and ecological condition. Recently, the draft report of New Forest Policy, 2019 has been published in which climate change, pollution and forest dwellers land rights have been highlighted.

The extent of forest gain and loss in India has been presented in Table 6.1 for the period 2005–19. This table shows that northeastern region has the highest forest coverage as percentage of total geographical area. Northeastern region have the maximum forest cover showing highest (78 percent) in Mizoram and lowest in Assam (31 percent). During this period, a huge loss of forests has occurred in Andhra Pradesh followed by Nagaland and Tripura. Among union territories (UT), Dadra and Nagar Haveli experience deforestation. However, West Bengal, Kerala and Bihar have experienced gains in forest cover. Better management and protection measures with the involvement of local people, afforestation activities, tree plantation drives and agro forestry may be the drivers behind the gain in forest cover while shifting cultivation, forest fires, felling of trees, natural calamities, anthropogenic pressures and development activities are some of the reasons behind the loss of forest cover.[72]

Table 6.1 Forest cover in states/UTs of India (area in km)

Administrative area	*2005*	*2019*	*Percentage of forest cover to total geographical area in 2019**	*Percent change (2005–19)*
Andhra Pradesh	44,372	29,137	6	−34.33
Arunachal Pradesh	67,777	66,688	73	−1.61
Assam	27,645	28,327	31	2.47
Bihar	5,579	7,306	2	30.96
Chhattisgarh	55,863	55,611	17	−0.45
Delhi	176	195.44	0	11.05
Goa	2,164	2,237	31	3.37
Gujarat	14,715	14,857	0	0.97
Haryana	1,587	1,602	1	0.95
Himachal Pradesh	14,369	15,434	21	7.41
Jammu and Kashmir	21,273	23,612	8	11.00
Jharkhand	22,591	23,611	4	4.52
Karnataka	35,251	38,575	10	9.43
Kerala	15,593	21,144	59	35.60
Madhya Pradesh	76,013	77,482	3	1.93
Maharashtra	47,476	50,778	3	6.96
Manipur	17,086	16,847	71	−1.40
Meghalaya	16,988	17,119	66	0.77
Mizoram	18,684	18,006	78	−3.63
Nagaland	13,719	12,486	72	−8.99
Odisha	48,374	51,619	12	6.71
Punjab	1,558	1,849	1	18.68
Rajasthan	15,850	16,630	0	4.92
Sikkim	3,262	3,342	36	2.45
Tamil Nadu	23,044	26,364	8	14.41
Tripura	8,155	7,726	50	−5.26
Uttar Pradesh	14,127	14,806	2	4.81
Uttarakhand	24,442	24,303	32	−0.57
West Bengal	12,413	16,902	4	36.16
Andaman & Nicobar	6,629	6,743	88	1.72
Chandigarh	15	22.03	8	46.87
Dadra and Nagar Haveli	221	207	1	−6.33

Table 6.1 (Continued)

Administrative area	*2005*	*2019*	*Percentage of forest cover to total geographical area in 2019**	*Percent change (2005–19)*
Daman and Diu	8	20.49	0	156.13
Lakshadweep	25	27.1	0	8.40
Pondicherry	42	52.41	10	24.79
Total	677,088	712,249	10.60	5.19

*Calculated by authors

Source: Forest Survey of India, Govt. of India, 2005 and 2019, available at www.fsi.nic.in.

Table 6.2 The classification of land degradation in India, by types and regions (in 1,000 ha)

Region	*Water erosion*	*Total degraded area*	*Area*	*Degraded area (percent)*
North	23,449	40,562	101,061	40
North-East	4,136	12,614	26,219	48
Central	17,883	26,210	44,345	59
East	9,249	15,157	41,833	36
West	16,446	21,350	50,743	42
South	22,330	30,565	63,576	48
Union Territories	187	205	825	25
India	93,680 (64 percent)	146,663	328,602	45

Source: Mythili and Goedecke, 2019.

Using remotely sensed MDVI data, Le et al.[73] have shown that 16 percent of total geographical area has been degraded in India during 1982–2006 of which about 26 percent is forest cover area. Water-induced soil erosion is the main cause of land degradation in India and eroded almost 64 percent of total land area. This is followed by shifting cultivation. The land degradation data (Table 6.2) shows that central region (59 percent) is the worst affected area followed by northeastern (48 percent) and southern regions (48 percent).[74] Table 6.2 gives an idea about the extent of land degradation in India.

Nearly 12 percent land in India is prone to riverbank erosion alongside any major river like Brahmaputra, Ganga and Yamuna. In India on an average every year, 75 lakh hectares of land is affected,1600 lives are lost and the damage caused to crops, houses and public utilities is Rs.1,805 crores due to floods during 1996 to 2005.[75] Looking at the severity of riverbank erosion and human displacement, National Sample Survey (NSS) in its 64th round has included migration due to "natural disaster" as one of the factors of forced migration to see the extent of migration reasons. It has been found in the survey that in India on an average 7 out of 1,000 migrants households are prone to the vagaries of natural disaster like flood, drought etc. during 2007–08 (Table 6.3). Natural disaster induced human migration has been found to be higher in rural areas.

In case of individual migrants, 2 people out of 1,000 migrated from both rural and urban areas due to natural disaster during 2007–08 (Table 6.4). There is more migration from rural areas and within rural area, majority of the migrants are male. While in case of urban areas, there are two male migrants against one female migrant. This corroborates earlier results that due to environmental degradation, male member of household migrants more than female for livelihood.[76,77,78]

Table 6.3 Distribution (per 1,000) of migrant households by reason for migration (2007–08)

Reasons for migration	*Present place of residence*		
	Rural	*Urban*	*Anywhere in India*
Employment related reasons	552	665	608
Studies	267	210	238
Forced migration	**24**	**19**	**22**
Natural disaster	**13**	**2**	**7**
Social Political problem	7	2	5
Displacement by development projects	4	15	10
Others	145	106	127
All (including not reported)	1000	1000	1000

Source: NSS 64th round, GOI, available at www.microdata.gov.in.

Table 6.4 Distribution (per 1,000) of migrants by reason for migration (2007–08)

Reasons for migration	*Present place of residence*		
	Rural	*Urban*	*Rural + Urban*
Employment-related reasons	36	228	99
Studies	16	40	24
Forced migration	**8**	**7**	**8**
Natural disaster	**2**	**1**	**2**
Social political problem	5	4	5
Displacement by development projects	1	2	1
Others	935	720	866
All (including not reported)	1000	1000	1000

Source: NSS 64th round, GOI, available at www.microdata.gov.in

While comparing the forced migration situation of northeastern region with rest of India from NSS 64th round report of 2007–08, we find that the incidence of forced migration is more in the northeastern states compared to the national level. Out of north eastern region, Tripura (190) has the highest number of forced migrants followed by Assam and Mizoram. The NSSO report of 64th round reveals that the number of migrants due to natural disaster is more in rural areas. Gender wise there are more forced migrants among male than female. For example, in Tripura, out of 190 migrants considering all the categories (rural, urban, male and female), there are 454 rural male migrants against 126 female rural migrants (National Sample Survey, 64th round, 2007–08). Similarly if we consider rural and urban areas, there are 379 male migrants against 115 female migrants.

Case Study

The foregoing discussion with the help of secondary data drawn for different states has provided evidence in support of a linkage between deforestation, land degradation and migration. We further try to find this nexus with the help of a case study which considers the problem of riverbank erosion and its impact on people's life. Environmental degradation is an important factor in determining migration if the people are dependent on nature for livelihood. People migrate to diversify risks. Some form of environmentally induced migration may be adaptive and others may reflect the fact that people migrate when they fail to cope with a disaster.[79] Flood and riverbank erosion destroy crop and property and creates income shock. Therefore, people migrate to other places in search of livelihood both internally and externally and this phenomenon is recognized as forced migration. People migrating for coping with the vagaries of environment are known as environmental refugees. Environmental refugee of this type is a major problem nowadays in most of the countries in the world.[80]

Riverbank erosion is a recurring but serious phenomenon in Assam which is one of the largest states of northeast India. It causes displacement due to disappearance of arable land. Nearly 17 riverine districts lose its land and villages in riverbank erosion in the state every year. Farmers lose both land crop and home and nearly 30 percent of the people live in penury. The river Brahmaputra alone eroded almost 59.5 million hectare of land during 1971–2009 and displaced 78,000 families.[81]

To mitigate riverbank erosion problem, the government of Assam has initiated various structural and non-structural measures with the help of Flood and Riverbank Erosion Management Agency of Assam (FREMAA). The structural steps include the comprehensive riverbank protection projects started at highly eroded districts and use of new technology of international standard such as use of sand filled Geo-textile bags at apron of the riverbank revetment. The non-structural steps include some scheme like strengthen the ability of vulnerable people to reduce loss from the risk, and strengthen the linkages between communities and local governments. To operationalize these schemes, FREMAA is linked with Water Resource Department, Assam State Disaster management Authority (ASDMA) and other line departments.

Our case study uses primary data collected by a field survey. To conduct the survey, we use multi-stage sampling technique. We choose two districts namely, Dhemaji and Dhubri, which are severely affected by erosion in the first stage. Next, we select one erosion-prone development block from each district. Thus, we have two blocks and in the third stage, from each block, we randomly select six villages depending on the degree of erosion. We also select two non-eroded villages, one for each district, to make a comparison with the eroded villages. Finally, we select 10 percent households randomly from each village. Altogether we have eight villages from which we survey 437 households. To conduct the survey, we apply a semi-structured schedule which comprises questions on demographic information, the extent of riverbank erosion and its effect on the household, mitigation and adaptive measures. Three local educated youths were appointed as data enumerator. We conducted the survey in the beginning of the year 2016.

The demographic characteristics are almost uniform among households in eroded and non-eroded villages. However, mean income, assets like livestock and size of land holding of people in eroded area differ from that of people in non-eroded area. People in eroded area are economically weaker. They have smaller size of land holdings and the possible cause is loss of land in erosion. Loss caused by erosion causes poverty among households and the vicious circle of poverty comes into force. As a result, these people are economically weaker. We find from the survey that households whose lands have been eroded by floods suffer from different socio-economic problems. It is apparent from Table 6.5 that people in eroded areas suffer more than those in non-eroded areas. Students have to leave studies incomplete or migrate to educational institution of nearby places. Erosion often sweeps away roadways, cultivable land and houses. There is loss of livestock, transportation problems and their livelihood is adversely affected by erosion. Consequently, farmers shift to non-farming occupation and migrate to other areas. It may appear that problems in eroded and non-eroded villages are almost similar. But such problems appear in non-eroded villages during

Table 6.5 Loss of assets and problems faced

Category	*Eroded (overall)*	*Non-eroded*
Loss of livestock income (Rs)	10351.41	0.00
Education problem (0=no, 1=yes)	0.76	0.27
Transportation problem (1=Yes, 0=No)	0.95	0.22
Change in occupation (0=no, 1=yes)	0.74	–

Source: Calculated from primary data by the authors.

rainy season, whereas problems become worse and perennial in eroded villages due to breaches of bridges, embankments and connecting roads.

It has been observed from Table 6.6 that migration in eroded area is higher than non-eroded area. Here, it is worth mentioning that migration occurring in the non-eroded villages is basically long-term migration while migration in eroded villages is mostly short term in nature for coping with erosion. The short-term migrants are those people who go out for a period of 12 months or less and long-term migrants' move permanently or for more than 10 years. People in the study area take migration as a strategy to smoothen their fluctuating income due to climatic and other socio-economic factors in in both short and long runs. In the eroded village, a few people prefer to migrate as a long-term strategy to take advantage of wage differential and employment opportunities in other areas. However, rest of the migrants choose to migrate to cope with income shock created by erosion and resulting loss of livelihood. During distress, people go to urban areas for work and come back after accumulating a sufficient amount of income. In the long term, young adult member mainly male members migrate to different states like Kerala, Karnataka and other southern states. In Dhemaji and Lakhimpur districts of Assam, excessive sand deposition after flood occurs in paddy field makes the paddy cultivation difficult and compels many households either to send their family members outside or to opt off farm activities as livelihood source.

The informal discussion with the people affected by soil erosion shows how erosion disrupts livelihood. One respondent Jadav Chetia (name changed) from Sissirborgaon Development Block of Dhemaji district reported that he had lost all his cultivable land and became penniless. As a result, his sons had to stop their studies and went outside the state for work. Another respondent Tahir Hussain (name changed) from South Salmara development block of Dhubri district reported that he lost his land and earned his living by pulling rickshaw. Ranjit Bora (name changed) of Ujjalpur village of Dhemaji district narrated how erosion took away his cropland of 10 bighas and he had to became a wage earner. This list is not exhaustive and there are

Table 6.6 Level of migration and its impact

Category	*Eroded (overall)*	*Non-eroded*
All migrants (1=Yes, 0=No)	0.60	0.46
Short-term migrants (1= Yes, 0=No)	0.42	0.24
Long-term migrants (1= Yes, 0=No)	0.24	0.13

Source: Calculated from primary data by the authors.

Table 6.7 Coping strategies

Survival strategy	*Percentage of households who adopts*
Cultivation/farming on lease land	19.7
Agricultural labour/MGNREGA worker	20.5
Sale of land/leasing out	16.7
Sale of livestock	24.4
Sale of bamboos/woods	15.3
Others	3.4

Source: Calculated from primary data.

hundreds of people who still stay in those areas and go out during the day time to nearby towns and work as unskilled workers.

There are some people who have preferred to cope with their economic problems caused by soil erosion rather than leaving or sending family members to other places. They try to compensate the damage or loss by sale of properties, livestock and trees and so forth. These people rear livestock and diversify crop diversification for survival. But these people who possess superior coping strategies are from those areas where erosion is moderate. It is apparent from Table 6.7 that sale of livestock is the most preferred option for such people and it can work as insurance strategies against the risk of income loss due to erosion.

It is evident from Table 6.7 that Mahatma Gandhi National Rural Employment Guarantee Act (MGNREGA) has provided people with opportunities to work for cash in rural areas. This is one of the biggest social safety nets which provide income opportunities in the rural areas for 100 days by providing them opportunities to work as wage earners in different infrastructure and environment-related projects like water harvesting and water conservation, fisheries and so on.

Conclusion

This study tries to find the relation between environmental degradation and migration and it has been established that environmental degradation in the form of deforestation leads to the problem of land degradation. It is observed that deforestation is a perennial problem in India and the British government did not take any serious effort on it. Rather, it was the result of organized exploitation during that period. Even after independence also we do not observe any systematic and organized attempts to curb it.

Degradation of land caused by deforestation induces outmigration and other socioeconomic problems. Although outmigration is a coping strategy for the destitute where a member of the family or the entire family shifts to a different place temporarily or permanently, it may prove detrimental because pressure of population caused by migration leads to over exploitation of natural resources in the destination. The case study which we conduct to demonstrate the relation between environmental degradation and migration shows that distressed people mostly migrate to other areas to compensate the income loss caused by erosion and resulting land degradation. Some people do not migrate and use coping strategies in the less erosion-prone areas. Existence of social safety nets could be used as a stay put measures for the erosion affected people to smoothen the income shock caused by erosion This study reflects how deforestation leads to land degradation and how it affects people's life. The whole scenario becomes more complex due to the onset of the impact of climate change. Therefore, mankind needs to devise suitable mitigation and adaptation strategies to cope with the emerging difficulties due to environmental degradation.

*****

Notes

1 R. K. Manhas, J. D. S. Negi, R. Kumar and P. S. Chauhan (2006), "Temporal assessment of growing stock, biomass and carbon stock of Indian forests", *Climatic Change*, 74, 191–221.

2 R. A. Houghton (1996), "Land-use changes and terrestrial carbon: The temporal record", in M. J. Apps and D. T. Price (eds.) *Forest ecosystems, forest management and the global carbon cycle* (NATO ASI Series, Vol. I). Berlin, Heidelberg: Springer-Verlag.

3 D. A. Posey (1993), "Indigenous knowledge in the conservation and use of world forests", in K. Ramakrishna and G. M. Woodwell (eds.) *World forests for the future: Their use and conservation*. Binghamton: Yale University Press.

4 Manhas et al. (2006), "Temporal assessment of growing stock, biomass and carbon stock of Indian forests".

5 A. K. Joshi, P. Pant, P. Kumar, A. Giriraj and P. K. Joshi (2011), "National forest policy in India: Critique of targets and implementation", *Small-Scale Forestry*, 10, 83–96.

6 M. Sarin (1995), "Joint Forest management in India: Achievement and unaddressed challenges", *Unasylva*, 46, 30–36.

7 D. Sarker (2009, 24 January), "Joint forest management: Critical issues", *Economic and Political Weekly*, 15–17.

8 P. S. Roy, A. Roy, P. K. Joshi, M. P. Kale, V. K. Srivastava, S. K. Srivastava, R. S. Dwevidi, C. Joshi, M. D. Behera, P. Meiyappan, Y. Sharma, A. K. Jain, J. S. Singh, Y. Palchowdhuri, R. M. Ramachandran, B. Pinjarla, V. Chakravarthi, N. Babu, M. S. Gowsalya, P. Thiruvengadam, M. Kotteeswaran, V. Priya, K. M. V. N. Yelishetty, S. Maithani, G. Talukdar, I. Mondal, K. S. Rajan, P. S. Narendra, S. Biswal, A. Chakraborty, H. Padalia, M. Chavan, S. N. Pardeshi, S. A. Chaudhari, A. Anand, A. Vyas, M. K. Reddy, M. Ramalingam, R. Manonmani, P. Behera, P. Das, P. Tripathi, S. Matin, M. L. Khan, O. P. Tripathi, J. Deka, P. Kumar and D. Kushwaha. (2015), "Development of decadal (1985–1995–2005): Land use and land cover database for India", *Remote Sensing*, 7, 2401–2430.

9 Ibid.

10 K. Warner (2010), "Global environmental change and migration: Governance challenges", *Global Environmental Change*, 20, 402–413.
11 É. Piguet (2013), "From 'primitive migration' to 'climate refugees': The curious fate of the natural environment in migration studies", *Annals of the Association of American Geographers*, 103, 148–162.
12 A. M. Findlay (2011), "Migrant destinations in an era of environmental change", *Global Environmental Change*, 21, S50–S58.
13 C. Gray and R. Bilsborrow (2013), "Environmental influences on human migration in rural Ecuador", *Demography*, 50, 1217–1241.
14 L. M. Hunter, S. Murray and F. Riosmena (2013), "Rainfall patterns and US migration from rural Mexico", *International Migration Review*, 47, 874–909.
15 C. Radel, B. D. Jokisch, B. Schmook, L. Carte, M. Aguilar-Støen, K. Hermans, K. Zimmerer and S. Aldrich (2019), "Migration as a feature of land system transitions", *Current Opinion in Environmental Sustainability*, 38, 103–110.
16 D. López-Carr and J. Burgdorfer (2013), "Deforestation drivers: Population, migration, and tropical land use", *Environment: Science and Policy for Sustainable Development*, 55(1), https://doi.org/10.1080/00139157.2013.748385
17 R. Black, W. N. Adger, N. W. Arnell, S. Dercon, A. Geddes and D. S. G. Thomas (2011), "The effect of environmental change on human migration", *Global Environmental Change*, 21S, S3–S11, http://dx.doi.org/10.1016/j.gloenvcha.2011.10.001
18 R. McLeman (2014), *Climate and human migration: Past experiences, future challenges*. New York: Cambridge University Press.
19 E. Piguet, A. Pe´coud and P. de Guchteneire (2010), "Migration and climate change: An overview", Centre on Migration, Policy and Society, Working Paper N. 79, University of Oxford, accessed from www.compas.ox.ac.uk/publications/working-papers/wp-10-79
20 L. Fussell, L. M. Hunter and C. L. Gray (2014), "Measuring the environmental dimensions of human migration: The demographer's toolkit", *Global Environmental Change*, 28, 182–191.
21 Ministry of Environment and Forest (MoEF) (1999), *National forestry action programme of the ministry of environment and forests*. New Delhi: Government of India, 1:79.
22 Ravindranath, N. H., N. Srivastava, I. K. Murthy, S. Malaviya, M. Munsi, and N. Sharma (2012), "Deforestation and forest degradation in India – implications for REDD+". *Current Science*, 102(8), 1117–1125.
23 R. Priya and R. Pani (2015), "Land degradation and deforestation in India: A district level analysis", *Annals, NAGI*, XXXV(1).
24 The Energy and Research Institute (TERI) (2018), "Economics of desertification, land degradation and, drought in India, Vol. I: Macroeconomic assessment of the costs of land degradation in India", accessed from www.teriin.org/sites/default/files/2018-04
25 Mythili, G. and J. Goedecke (2016), Economics of Land Degradation in India. In *Economics of Land Degradation and Improvement – A Global Assessment for Sustainable Development* edited by Nkonya, E., A., Mirzabaev, J.V. Braun, Springer International Publishing, Switzerland, DOI 10.1007/978-3-319-19168-3.
26 A. Shah (2005), "Land degradation and migration in dry land region in India", *SANDEE,* working paper no. 10-05, accessed from www.sandeeonline.org
27 R. Mahanta and D. Das (2012), "Common property resource degradation and migration: A study of Assam", *Journal of Human Ecology*, 38(3), 223–230.

28 M. S. Rana and A. M. Nessa (2017), "Impact of riverbank erosion on population migration and resettlement of Bangladesh", *Science Journal of Applied Mathematics and Statistics*, 5(2), 60–69.
29 S. Babu (2016), "Land degradation: Role of deforestation", accessed from https://eco-intelligent.com/2016/10/29/land-degradation-role-of-deforestation
30 Q. Zhang, O. J. Christopher and V. D. Paul (2002), "Impacts of simulated shifting cultivation on deforestation and the carbon stocks of the forests of Central Africa", *Agriculture, Ecosystems and Environment*, 90, 203–209.
31 L. Starkel and S. Singh (eds.) (2004), *Rainfall, runoff and soil erosion in the globally extreme humid area, Cherrapunji Region, India*. Warszawa: Polska Akademia Nauk, Instytut Geografii i Przestrzennego Zagospodarowania im. Stanisława Leszczyckiego.
32 Zhang et al. (2002), "Impacts of simulated shifting cultivation on deforestation and the carbon stocks of the forests of Central Africa".
33 Manhas et al. (2006), "Temporal assessment of growing stock, biomass and carbon stock of Indian forests".
34 Starkel and Singh (2004), *Rainfall, runoff and soil erosion in the globally extreme humid area, Cherrapunji region, India*.
35 Roy et al. (2015), "Development of decadal (1985–1995–2005)".
36 S. Jaquet, G. Schwilch, F. Hartung-Hofmann, A. Adhikari, K. Sudmeier-Rieux, G. Shrestha, H. P. Liniger and T. Kohler (2015), "Does outmigration lead to land degradation? Labour shortage and land management in a western Nepal watershed", *Applied Geography*, 62, 157–170.
37 Ibid.
38 K. Marquardt, D. Khatri and A. Pain (2016), "REDD+, forest transition, agrarian change and ecosystem services in the hills of Nepal", *Human Ecology*, 44, 229–244.
39 H. R. Ojha, K. K. Shrestha, Y. R. Subedi, R. Shah, I. Nuberg, B. Heyojoo, E. Cedamon, J. Rigg, S. Tamang, K. P. Paudel, Y. Malla and P. McManus (2017), "Agricultural land underutilisation in the hills of Nepal: Investigating socio-environmental pathways of change", *Journal of Rural Studies*, 53, 156–172.
40 D. P. Poudel (2019), "Migration, forest management and traditional institutions: Acceptance of and resistance to community forestry models in Nepal", *Geoforum*, 106, 275–286.
41 Radel et al. (2019), "Migration as a feature of land system transitions".
42 Jaquet et al. (2015), "Does outmigration lead to land degradation?".
43 K. Shrestha and R. Fisher (2018), "Labor migration, the remittance economy and the changing context of community forestry in Nepal", in R. Thwaites, R. Fisher and M. Poudel (eds.) *Community forestry in Nepal: Adapting to changing world*. London: Earthscan, 171–192.
44 E. Ostrom (1990), *Governing the commons: The evolution of institutions and collective action*. Cambridge: The University of Cambridge.
45 A. Agrawal (2001), "Common property institutions and sustainable governance of resources", *World Development*, 29, 1649–1672.
46 Shrestha and Fisher (2018), "Labor migration, the remittance economy and the changing context of community forestry in Nepal".
47 Poudel (2019), "Migration, forest management and traditional institutions".
48 Ibid.
49 S. Jaquet, G. Schwilch, F. Hartung-Hofmann, A. Adhikari, K. Sudmeier-Rieux, G. Shrestha, H.P. Liniger, and T. Kohler (2015), "Does outmigration lead to land degradation?".

50 J. D. Ives and B. Messerli (1989), *The Himalayan dilemma reconciling development and conservation*. London: Routledge.
51 G. Schwilch, A. Adhikari, M. Jaboyedoff, S. Jaquet, R. Kaenzig, H. Liniger, I. M. Penna, K. S. Rieux and B. R. Upreti (2017), "Impacts of outmigration on land management in a Nepali mountain area", in K. Sudmeier-Rieux et al. (eds.) *Identifying emerging issues in disaster risk reduction, migration, climate change and sustainable development*. Cham: Springer International Publishing, https://doi.org/10.1007/978-3-319-33880-4_11
52 López-Carr and Burgdorfer (2013), "Deforestation Drivers: Population, Migration, and Tropical Land Use". *Environment: Science and Policy for Sustainable Development,* 55(1): doi:10.1080/00139157.2013.748385.
53 W. Sunderlin and I. A. P. Resosudarmo (1999), "The effect of population and migration on forest cover in Indonesia", *The Journal of Environment & Development*, 8(2), 152–169.
54 A. F. M. Uddin and J. K. Basak (2012), *Report on effects of riverbank erosion on livelihood*. Bangladesh: Unnayan Onneshan. Centre for Research and Action on Development.
55 D. R. N. Brown, T. J. Brinkman, W. R. Bolton, C. L. Brown, H. S. Cold, T. N. Hollingsworth and D. L. Verbyla (2020), "Implications of climate variability and changing seasonal hydrology for subarctic riverbank erosion", *Climatic Change*, 162, 1–20, accessed from https://doi.org/10.1007/s10584-020-02748-9
56 R. Emberson (2017), "Deforestation: Accelerating riverbank erosion", *Nature Geoscience*, 10, accessed from www.nature.com/naturegeoscience.
57 Mythili, G. and J. Goedecke (2016), Economics of Land Degradation in India. in Economics of Land Degradation and Improvement – A Global Assessment for Sustainable Development edited by Nkonya, E., A., Mirzabaev, J.V. Braun, Springer International Publishing, Switzerland, DOI 10.1007/978-3-319-19168-3.
58 World Migration Report (2010), *International organization for migration*. Geneva, Switzerland: United Nations.
59 T. K. Das, S. K. Halder, I. D. Gupta and S. Sen (2017), "Impact of riverbank erosion: A case study". *Australasian Journal of Disaster and Trauma Studies*, 21(2), 73–81.
60 N. Mili, S. Acharjee and M. Konwar (2013), "Impact of flood and river bank erosion on socio-economy: A case study of Golaghat revenue circle of Golaghat District, Assam", *International Journal of Geology, Earth & Environmental Sciences*, 3(3), 180–185.
61 T. H. Mollah and J. Ferdaush (2015), "Riverbank erosion, population migration and rural vulnerability in Bangladesh (A case study on Kazipur Upazila at Sirajgonj District)", *Environment and Ecology Research*, 3(5), 125–131.
62 Das, T. K, S. K. Halder, I. D. Gupta, and S. Sen (2017), "Impact of Riverbank Erosion: A Case Study". *Australasian Journal of Disaster and Trauma Studies*. 21(2), 73–81.
63 D. K. Nayak and M. Das (Undated), "An assessment of redistribution of population in Majuli Island due to riverbank erosion", 1–10, accessed from http://iussp.org/sites/default/files
64 S. J. Baishya (2013), "A study on river bank erosion by the River Baraliain Melkipara village of Hajo revenue circle, Kamrup District, Assam, India", *International Journal of Scientific and Research Publications*, 3(9), 1–10.
65 F. Islam and B. Rashid (2011), "Riverbank erosion displaces in Bangladesh: Need for institutional response and policy intervention", *Bangladesh Journal of Bioethics*, 2(2), 4–19.

66 M. Ashraf and J. K. Rautray (2013), "Perception and understanding of drought and coping strategies of farming households in north-west Balochistan", *International Journal of Disaster Risk Reduction*, 5, 549–560.
67 A. Bormudoi and M. Nagai (2017), "Perception of risk and coping capacity: A study in Jiadhal Basin, India", *International Journal of Disaster Risk Reduction*, 21, 376–383.
68 S. Dercon (2005), *Insurance against poverty*. Oxford: Oxford University Press.
69 S. Balaji (2002), *Forest policy in India – in retrospect and prospect*. Chennai: IUFRO Science/Policy Interface Task Force regional meeting, M.S. Swaminathan Research Foundation.
70 V. M. R. Kumar (2010), "Green colonialism". *Global Environment: A Journal of History and Natural and Social Sciences*, 5, 101–126.
71 J. I. Lee and S. A. Wolf (2018), "Critical assessment of implementation of the Forest Rights Act of India", *Land Use Policy*, 79, 834–844.
72 India State of Forest Report (2019), accessed from www.fsi.nic.in/forest-report-2019 on 12th September 2020.
73 Q. B. Le, E. Nkonya and A. Mirzabaev (2014), *Biomass productivity-based mapping of global land degradation hotspots*. ZEF Discussion Paper on Development Policy No. 193. Bonn: Centre for Development Research, University of Bonn.
74 Mythili, G. and J. Goedecke (2016), Economics of Land Degradation in India. In *Economics of Land Degradation and Improvement – A Global Assessment for Sustainable Development* edited by Nkonya, E., A., Mirzabaev, J.V. Braun, Springer International Publishing, Switzerland, DOI 10.1007/978-3-319-19168-3.
75 National Disaster Management Authority (NDMA) (2013), *Vulnerability profile of India*. Government of India, accessed from www.ndma.gov.in
76 Ojha, H. R., K. K. Shrestha, Y. R. Subedi, R. Shah, I. Nuberg, B. Heyojoo, E. Cedamon, J. Rigg, S. Tamang, K. P. Paudel, Y. Malla, and P. McManus (2017), "Agricultural Land Underutilisation in the Hills of Nepal: Investigating Socio-Environmental Pathways of Change". *Journal of Rural Studies*, 53, 156–172.
77 Poudel, D. P. (2019), "Migration, Forest Management and Traditional Institutions: Acceptance of and Resistance to Community Forestry Models in Nepa". *Geoforum*, 106, 275–286.
78 Radel, C., B. D. Jokisch, B. Schmook, L. Carte, M. Aguilar-Støen, K. Hermans, K. Zimmerer, and S. Aldrich (2019), "Migration as a Feature of Land System Transitions", *Current Opinion in Environmental Sustainability*, 38, 103–110.
79 Warner, K. (2010), "Global Environmental Change and Migration: Governance Challenges", *Global Environmental Change*, 20, 402–413.
80 World Migration Report, *International organization for migration*. United Nations.
81 Revenue and Disaster Management Department, Govt. of Assam, 2014.

Chapter 7

Climate Change-Induced Internally Displaced Persons of the Maldives

Bharati Torane

Introduction

The Maldives is spread vertically in the Indian Ocean over 800 kilometres north to south and covering 130 kilometres east to west, in the South West of India and Sri Lanka. It is an archipelago of 26 natural atolls consisting of 1,192 tiny islands with sharp coral reefs and has a total area of 90,000 km^2 of which about 298 km^2 is only land and the rest is all water. The entire 'Land mass' is formed by a coral reef and shallow lagoon encircling each island within the atoll's water.

Confusion exists about the total number of Islands in the Maldives as different sources present different numbers. Maldivians themselves talk in terms of 2,000 islands; however, as per the CIA Fact Book (2020), an archipelago of 1,190 coral islands grouped into 26 atolls (200 inhabited islands, plus 80 islands with tourist resorts).[1] This discrepancy in the number of islands is due to the natural phenomena of the creation of new islands and the disappearance of some of the old ones. The Intergovernmental Panel on Climate Change, (IPCC) Report (2014)[2] revealed projected sea level rise throughout the twenty-first century and beyond, coastal regions and low-lying areas would increasingly experience adverse impacts such as submergence, coastal erosion and coastal flooding.

Small Island Developing States (SIDSs) share some common characteristics that help to define their high vulnerability and low adaptation potential to climate change effects.[3]

> Vulnerability assessment typically seeks to achieve three main goals: to identify the degree of future risks induced by climate change and sea-level rise; to identify the key vulnerable sectors and areas within a country; and to provide a sound basis for designing adaptation strategies and their implementation[4]

Therefore, the Maldives being one of the SIDSs may face threats to its survival and existence due to its location in the Indian Ocean. In the past,

DOI:10.4324/9781003367802-8

the reef system helped to defend the islands and was a major security system from any external threat. However, due to its remoteness and isolation, the Maldives' geo-strategic location has insulated it from the influences of its South Asian neighbours. Thus, it could maintain its national identity and preserve its secure peaceful culture.

The Maldives has a population of 549,287 as on 4 June 2021, based on Worldometer elaboration of the latest United Nations data and these numbers are equivalent to 0.01% of the total world population.[5] Moreover, the Maldives ranks number 173 in the list of countries (and dependencies) by population. The population density in the Maldives is 1802 per km^2 (4,667 people per mi^2). The total land area is 300 km^2 (116 $miles^2$) 34.5 % of the population is urban (186,634 people in 2020) and the median age in the Maldives is 29.9 years.[6]

In the Maldives, about 10% of the land is occupied by agricultural/cultivated land, 3% by forested land, and 3% by pastures.[7] The soil is thin and of poor quality, being a maximum of about 20 cm deep and not too fertile, while often containing rock and sand. It is alkaline due to an excess of calcium from coral rock and sand. The Maldives has a tropical climate, with the air temperature generally varying from 23 to 31°C and an annual average temperature of 28°C. The weather is dominated by the two monsoon periods, the southwest monsoon from May to November and the northeast monsoon from January to March. Average annual precipitation varies regionally and increases from north to south, with the northern atolls receiving an average of approximately 1700 mm/year and the southern atolls receiving an average of approximately 2350 mm/year.[8] Precipitation has great inter-annual variability, although the wettest months tend to be May, August, September, and December, with the driest being January to April; overall humidity ranges from 75% to 83%.[9]

Vulnerabilities of Maldivian Island Communities

Socioeconomic Vulnerabilities

Since 1966 onward, the Maldivian government on many occasions reiterated that their primary concern is to improve the living conditions of their people and being one of the smallest Member States in the United Nations, the most serious impediments to their social and economic development are meagre natural resources and the extreme fragmentation of their sprawling clusters of islands, which stretch over an area of approximately 100,000 km^2 in the Indian Ocean.[10] To quote the former president of the Maldives, Abdul Gayoom in the United Nations General Assembly in 1976:

> Almost 90 per cent of our national income had been dependent on the fishing industry. Our efforts to find other sources of revenue have

> resulted in the establishment in recent years of some exchange earning industries, the most promising of which has turned out to be tourism.[11]

On the demographic front, Maldives is unevenly distributed as it has a land area of one-third of the total country's area which is in the centre of the country and is among the most densely populated urban areas in the world. In September 2014, a total of 129,381 persons (38 per cent of the total resident population in the Maldives) were living in Male' on 2 km^2. As the 2014 Census shows 35 per cent of the resident population of the Maldives are youth and the Maldives is ripe for a demographic dividend.[12] In reality, this demographic dividend could not take place due to inadequate infrastructure and the scarcity of opportunities either in employment or in other economic activities like agriculture, fishing, shipping, tourism and trading.

In the Maldives, agricultural activities always remained insignificant, even today; it is very much restricted due to the physical features of the soil such as sand with poor water retaining capacity and alkaline. The economic growth also suffers from environmental hazards and inadequate infrastructure like irrigation, seeds, and new scientific methods. The archipelagic feature of the Maldives limits the smooth internal transportation and communication within the country as 98 per cent of its territory consists of water. Moreover, the Maldives is also constrained by the absence of level-based mineral resources and vulnerability to natural disasters and environmental hazards.[13]

In the 1970s and early 1980s, the Maldivian economy was based on three major industries fishing, tourism and shipping. However, presently, shipping remained the most insignificant sector, whereas fishing and tourism are two dominating industries in the economy as a source of government revenue and foreign exchange earnings. Therefore, in 1985, then President Abdul Gayoom in the United Nations General Assembly said:

> The international community to give greater consideration to the economic damage being done to the small island states, by prevailing financial and trading arrangements. We strongly feel that the vulnerability of small island states and their fragile economies must become high priority area in which adequate measures must be taken urgently to redress the existing grave inequalities.[14]

Thus, the Maldives faces innumerable and formidable economic difficulties and limitations due to its small size and remoteness from the market hub countries, transport and communications constraints, the restricted purchasing power of its people and scarcity of natural resources. These factors further contributed to adverse regional developments in terms of infrastructural facilities and scarcity of employment opportunities. Despite these constraints, the Maldives made significant progress and graduated from the least developed country status in January 2011.[15] For instance, in 1995 prices, per capita GDP increased from around $400 in 1977 to nearly $1,700 in 1997 and more than $2,400 in 2004.[16] Rapid economic growth has largely been due to the success of the tourist industry. During this period, the number of resorts increased from 73 to 86 and the number of annual tourist arrivals from 366,000 to more than 600,000.[17] In other words, the tourism industry flourished in terms of employment and generating income on the islands along with the fisheries industries which have earned income in the exports of marine products. Thus, the Maldives could achieve most of the Millennium Development Goals (MDGs),[18] which was absent in most of the South Asian Countries.

However, basic human development indicators are high in the Maldives. It ranks 101 out of 189 countries in the Human Development Index (HDI) for 2017, the second-highest HDI rank in South Asia. The country's GDP per capita reached $11,890 in 2018, compared to $200 in 1978.[19] In previous years, in terms of employment, these two sectors alone account for more than one-third of total employment. The total labour force of the country is estimated at around 50 per cent of the working-age population, which, coupled with the low level of educated labour, has led to expatriate labour, especially, teachers, doctors and other professionals and also a large number of lower-skilled workers such as domestic helpers and construction workers in the Maldives. This situation is not changed even in recent times. As reported in a World Bank Report on the Maldives,

> The country's exposure to natural hazards and climate variability poses a threat to lives and the economy. The additional challenge of the country's geography leads to a dispersed population across many small islands, which makes service delivery difficult and can limit opportunities for job creation and economic diversification. Compounded with inclusion issues, this has caused relatively elevated levels of youth unemployment at 15.3 percent and low rates of women participating in the workforce.[20]

Furthermore, the development process of the country has been supported by the government, the private sector, nongovernmental organizations (NGOs) and foreign donors. The external donor assistance includes grants, official bilateral and multilateral aid and NGOs' assistance to Maldives constituting about 70 per cent of total development expenditure.[21] Therefore, despite the challenges like adverse geographical features and uneven demographic distribution, Maldives has been able to make economic gains due to its growing tourism, fishing and service sectors. While the government has concentrated on providing basic socio-economic services, the private sector has played a key role in the development of tourism, distribution of trade, transport and fisheries among other activities. In terms of job creation, the tourism sector is an important source of local employment, particularly for women and employs about 13 per cent of the country's total labour force.

Despite this, the growth in the aforementioned sectors is constrained by a shortage of qualified manpower, poor health conditions, the rapidly changing structure of the fishing industry, past neglect of the agriculture sector and severe regional imbalance in the economic development.[22] Moreover, according to the United Nations Development Programme (UNDP), the Maldivian economy also suffers from the shortcomings like subsistence agriculture, pervasive weakness of administration, an acute shortage of trained manpower at all levels, inadequate inter-atoll and intra-atoll transport and communication, narrow industrial base, high population growth rate, poor health and sanitary conditions and traditionally unfavourable balance of trade.[23]

Environmental Vulnerabilities

The Maldives is also vulnerable to the impact of climate change and associated sea level rise. The coastal locations of the Maldives make it more vulnerable to natural disasters like sea level rise and changes in temperatures and rainfall patterns. As mentioned before, climate change will also impact the social and economic development of the Maldives as the entire population and the infrastructure of the country are very close to the sea water level. The rise in sea level would lead to, land loss from beach erosion and inundation and also damage human settlements and vital infrastructure.[24] The Maldives is creating an artificial island named *Hulhumalé* and also plans to build the City of Hope on it. Its making require a sand deposition from surrounding atolls and depositing on the shallow reefs. The highest natural island is only 2.5 metres above sea level, while the fortified walls of the new island are 3 metres above sea level.[25] The creation of artificial islands will surely have repercussions as the coral reefs can grow naturally. Some scientists believe that some atolls and islands of Maldives are growing, based on the images by Google Earth.[26]

The Maldives' vulnerabilities are quite evident when the highest tidal waves seriously damaged the entire archipelago. According to the United Nations Department of Humanitarian Affairs, Report (13 April 1987),

> One third of the capital 'male' was affected by severe flooding which resulted in physical damage to breakwaters, retaining walls, coastal roads, Hulule international airport, access harbour, fuel jetty, radio antennae. A number of houses were destroyed resulting in some 300 people being evacuated and homeless. No loss of life reported.[27]

During this crisis, a certain percentage of reclaimed land has also been lost. Thirteen out of 19 atolls were affected, but the centre of most damage was at Male. Numerous boats were lost.[28] However, the Humanitarian Relief Action groups working in the country helped the Maldivian government to accommodate all the displaced persons in their homes.[29] In addition to these, resettlement and rehabilitation initiatives, the Maldivian government also took a keen interest in providing health assistance to the affected coastal communities. Thus, the Maldives followed proactive policies on the domestic front and used international platforms like the United Nations to sensitize world leaders. In his speech, on 19 October 1987, at the United Nations General Assembly (UNGA), the then President Abdul Gayoom said,

> We in the Maldives have seen and lived through grim experiences which could be indicators of the dire consequences of global environmental change provoked and exacerbated by man. Geographically, the Maldives Islands lie in the equatorial calm of the northern Indian Ocean, away from cyclone paths. The brief annual monsoonal turbulences and the occasional high tidal swells have hardly ever endangered the 190,000 inhabitants of the islands until now. This year the frequency and magnitude of unusual tidal wave action have risen alarmingly. The period from 10 to 12 April recorded the highest sea level evidenced in the country, during which unusual high waves at high tide struck the islands with a ferocity that inflicted extensive and unprecedented damage throughout the country. Male, the capital island, housing one-quarter of the nations' population, suffered the worst of the ordeal. One fourth of the urban land was inundated by salt water and 30 per cent of the land reclaimed during the last seven years was completely washed away.[30]

He also feared that the countries like the Maldives and other low-lying archipelagic nations may have to suffer the most immediate and extreme effects of a global sea level rise; there is a potential danger to a significant portion of the world's population in the near future.[31]

Furthermore, the Maldives has realized its entire population is dependent upon its seas for day-to-day livelihood and any degradation of the maritime ecosystem or any rise in the mean sea level due to the so-called greenhouse effect is a matter of serious concern to them. And moreover, the Maldives has already witnessed the deadly tidal eruption three times in 1987 which damaged its economic and societal infrastructure set-up. Therefore, being SIDS always shared concerns and expressed its solidarity toward the issues of environmental preservation.

Thus, Maldives has been raising its voice and expressing persisting fear of continuing its existence either physically or notionally due to its topographical and atmospheric conditions of climate change. In 2001, the First National Communication of the Republic of Maldives to the United Nations

Framework Convention on Climate Change also identified some of the priority vulnerabilities of the Maldives to climate change. To note,

- Land loss and beach erosion
- Infrastructure damage
- Damage to coral reefs
- Impacts on the economy
- Food security
- Water resources
- Human health.[32]

All the aforementioned vulnerabilities in general apply to most of the SIDSs whether they are from Asia or Europe. Being the most vulnerable SIDS the Maldives took the initiative in addressing the concerns of the impact of climate change. As a result, the Maldivian government introduced the policy document the 'Maldives Climate Change Policy Framework' on 10 August 2015, which intends to be guided by seven principles, namely, climate leadership, intergenerational equitability, mainstreaming climate change, international commitments, multinational partnerships, transfer of technology and climate resiliency.[33]

The basic objective of this policy framework is:

> fostering and guiding a national plan of action against current, short-, medium- and long-term effects of climate change, setting out strategic priorities in responses to climate-change, promoting a coordinated approach among all national stake holders, and building and strengthening current policies, plans and institutional structures and incorporating these into all related sector plans.[34]

This plan covers a 'holistic' set of pragmatic and feasible measures for the resilience of SIDS to the adverse impacts of climate change and prioritizes building a sustainable society in harmony with our fragile ecosystem.'[35] To quote President Solih,

> Initiative focuses on achieving environment-related targets in eleven key areas, including the designation of environmentally protected areas; installation of new technology; establishing inter-island connectivity; safeguarding food and water security; promoting green tourism; ensuring climate-resilient infrastructure; transitioning to renewable energy; and sustainable waste management, among others.[36]

In addition to this, a recent study in the Maldives shows that due to socioeconomic reasons, there is a lukewarm response to the land reclamation for climate adaptation to how projects are done in the country. Because building new land is reshaping nature which impacts coral reefs, tidal flows, marine life and vegetation. In other words, it will push the problem of erosion to new areas rather than solve it. To quote, Sara Naseem from Transparency Maldives:

> We find a lot of projects designed and implemented in a lot of these islands that destroy the natural barriers to climate change. And one of the main issues that we find with it is the fact that people are not consulted in any of these processes . . . Quite often, these projects are designed in a way that it actually makes the islands more vulnerable to climate change. And so, while we raise funds to increase the resilience of the islands, while we raise funds to protect our mangroves and our wetlands, you also find that mangroves are destroyed in another part of the island and coral reefs are destroyed for reclamation projects.[37]

Thus, socio-economic and environmental concerns are the major pitfalls of as far as climate change in Maldives. The aforementioned examples may hold some arguments in present circumstances.

Climate Change-Induced Migration or Displacement?

The Maldives realized the implications of climate change only in the late 1980s when the capital city Male witnessed massive flooding and physical damage and lost the reclaimed land. A rise in sea levels of 88 cm between 1990 and 2100, according to the worst-case scenario, would imply that many islands of Maldives could be either submerged or uninhabitable,[38] but also that many islands are likely to face a severe risk of inundation much before that, as the sea rises. Some experts believe that disaster risk reduction can perhaps delay this prospect by decades.[39] However, all of the aforementioned factors point to a situation in which potentially important levels of internal displacement can be anticipated, as well as a possible need in the future to find alternatives outside the physical territory of the Maldives. Since then, the Maldivian government consistently started raising its voice through regional as well as international forums like United Nations and other similar organizations. However, the perception of the Maldives toward climate change changed when the country faced the severe consequences of the Tsunami of December 2004, which compelled the Maldives to understand the gravity of the situation vis-à-vis the impact of climate change. For instance, Maldivian people had encountered the challenges of storms which resulted in flooding with coastal erosion and alteration of beaches and persistent fear of submergence. Particularly, the coastal settlements in the lowland area have been exposed to hazards such as sea level rise and tropical storms and are vulnerable if they do not rehabilitate or resettle in safety zones in the coming days.

Rehabilitation and Resettlement of IDPs

Being a SIDS, the Maldives was going through the horrific experiences of the consequences of climate change since the late eighties, all of a sudden it faced the Tsunami on 26 December 2004 and the whole system of infrastructure and operational functions of disaster management system crumbled.

> Tsunami swept across Maldives flooding all but nine islands of the archipelago. When the floodwaters receded and emergency operations got underway, it was confirmed that 82 people died, 26 went missing, 1,313 were injured, and over 15,000 lost their homes. One of the most affected islands was Kandholhudhoo, in Raa Atoll; the deadly waves had washed the entire island, extensively damaging houses and buildings, and contaminating groundwater. The more than 3,600 inhabitants of Kandholhudhoo were left homeless and had to evacuate.[40]

During this disaster, many lost their lives and became homeless. The displaced families needed to rebuild their lives on a new and safer island. To rehabilitate the affected people, the government's National Disaster Management Centre, (NDMC) identified the uninhabited island of Dhuvaafaru in its vicinity and found it as the most appropriate location to relocate the affected communities of the Kandholhudhoo. The decision and the process of rehabilitation of these communities were based on 'community preference, location, size, and reef characteristics (which are important in protecting from tidal surges). Due to these geographical and reef characteristics, Dhuvaafaru was considered to be a 'safer island' when compared to Kandholhudhoo', both located in Raa Atoll area.[41]

Moreover, international nongovernmental agencies, like the International Federation, paid particular attention

> to the protection of over 6,000 internally displaced persons (IDPs) by funding the construction of temporary shelters that met internationally-recognized standards. The community of Kandholhudhoo was sheltered in five such IDP camps in sister islands within Raa Atoll; Alifushi, Hulhudhuffaru, Maduvvari, Meedhoo and Ungoofaaru – with the majority in Ungoofaaru.[42]

The work of rehabilitating has started in April 2006 on the 40-hectare coral island which was uninhabited. By 2009, and at a cost of US$35 million, it has been transformed into a thriving community that now boasts 600 new houses, three schools, one mosque, a health centre, and an island administration block complete with an auditorium and sports stadium.[43] While doing so, the Maldivian government had to face the logistic challenges of creating an entire community on a small island in the middle of the Indian Ocean. For instance, a non-interrupted supply of cement, construction materials and machinery all had to be brought in by ship together with the 600-strong labour force, many of whom originate from countries as far as fields as China, Indonesia and the Philippines.[44]

Tsunami also affected another island of Kuramathi, where, as reported no one was killed or injured. Some divers and snorkelers' had difficulties due to strong currents and poor visibility, but everybody returned safely.[45] There were damages but those were not so severe, for instance, some water in a few bungalows and parts of the sandy beaches were eroded by the extremely high water, and soil from the island was washed into the atoll lagoon. The long sandbank at the west end of Kuramathi was practically cut in two by the tsunami. Surprisingly, it did not affect the vegetation like the salt-tolerant vegetation along the supra littoral fringe, including the succulent saltbush (*Scaevola* sp.), the screw pine (*Pandanus* sp.), and the coconut trees (Cocos nucifera).[46]

The post-Tsunami Maldives has observed that the International Federation established and created different field teams to increase awareness and participation among the community to monitor temporary shelters and to evaluate the immediate and future needs of displaced persons.[47] It was a forward-looking policy and strategy to take into consideration that the success of any project is to get the communities involved and participated who are beneficiaries.

> The team established contact and worked in close coordination with the government, other humanitarian actors, respective island offices, atoll offices and IDP committees. As well as managing the physical construction of the settlement, the IFRC has also trained community members to run and maintain the island's utilities.[48]

In addition to this, by December 2008, most of the IDPs of the Maldives were also relocated to Dhuvaafaru, with assistance from the army, coast-guard and police. The island of Dhuvaafaru in North Maalhosmadulu Atoll is being developed with the assistance of the International Federation of Red Cross and Red Crescent to settle the people of Kandholhudhoo whose homes were destroyed in the 2004 tsunami. On 10 December 2008, then President Mohamed Nasheed visited Dhuvaafaru and had meetings with some of the senior members of the Dhuvaafaru Island Developing Committee and other associations of the island, and discussed with them ways of developing the island. The president also opened Dhuvaafaru Health Centre.[49] The move had taken careful planning; IFRC began by bringing all heads of households to Dhuvaafaru to take part in a lottery where they drew numbers that corresponded to their homes and basic amenities and housing are provided to all taking up residence on the island.[50]

Thus, the Maldives experienced managing not only large-scale internal displacement, during the Indian Ocean Tsunami of 2004, but also the devastation of its economic and social infrastructure, which resulted in losses exceeding 62 per cent of gross domestic product (GDP).[51] These losses, which were proportionately much higher than those experienced by other countries, such as India, Sri Lanka and Thailand, which lost less than 3 per cent of their GDP,[52] demonstrate the extreme vulnerability of the Maldives to the impact of such events. The tsunami severely affected the infrastructure of the country and destroyed or damaged thousands of homes, displacing an estimated 12,000 people from their islands, and causing another 8,500 persons to be temporarily relocated to other places within their own islands. According to government authorities, 39 islands were significantly damaged, while 14 islands were completely destroyed and had to be evacuated.[53]

Restoring these houses and getting the displaced back to their homes was a priority for the government, the United Nations and many international stakeholders. However, the World Bank Team also witnessed that 1,600 persons were still living in temporary shelters in very difficult conditions while awaiting the construction of their houses.[54]

> The Maldives is enhancing adaptation and building climate resilience to reduce climate risks. At present, the country spends more than 50 per cent of its national budget on adapting to climate change. It is experimenting with 3-D printed coral structures or a floating city. It is home to the Modular Artificial Reef Structure, a coral-forming project on the Summer Island and will start the construction of a floating island city in 2022.[55]

Domestic and International Responses and Policies

Soon after the Tsunami of December 2004, the United Nations General Assembly came out with a Report under the banner of Human Rights Council Nineteenth Session Agenda Item no 3: 'Promotion and protection of all human rights, civil, political, economic, social and cultural rights, including the right to development Report'. It was prepared by the Special Rapporteur on the Human Rights of Internally Displaced Persons, Chaloka Beyani Addendum – Mission to the Maldives.[56]

This report has carried out a detailed study based on field visits and personal interviews with the affected communities of the tsunami in the

Maldives. As mentioned in the Report, the domestic responses to the Tsunami-induced IDPSs were:

Responses and Policies are summarized here:

- As the Maldives has experienced disaster and displacement first time of such magnitude, the Government of Maldives introduced new assistance programs and institutions for IDPs such as Inter-Ministerial Committee relief operations and the NDMC. Important initiatives were undertaken to develop policy, legislative and institutional frameworks, focusing principally on disaster risk reduction, climate change and environmental sustainability.
- Legislative initiatives have been taken in the form of the Disaster Management Bill, to establish the specific roles and responsibilities of the different levels of the government concerning the effective coordination and management of disasters and related matters. It created NDMC, a Disaster Management Steering Committee and a National Disaster Management Authority to promote an integrated and coordinated system of disaster management, with a special emphasis on risk reduction and mitigation.
- Moreover, the broad responsibilities for disaster prevention, mitigation and response, capacity-building and the allocation of funds are assigned to every ministry, department and provincial-level government authority. Provincial-, atoll- and island-level disaster management committees have been assigned coordination, monitoring, preparedness, response and awareness-raising roles, and can receive claims and appeals emerging from a natural disaster.
- In consultation with key stakeholders, a framework on internal displacement has been put in place in line with international human rights standards and the Guiding Principles on Internal Displacement.
- In June 2011, the Government of Maldives endorsed the Strategic National Action Plan for Disaster Risk Reduction and Climate Change Adaptation 2010–2020 which provides a road map for dealing with natural disasters and climate change. It aims to build the resilience of the nation and island communities to disasters and climate change impacts by consolidating good practices, incorporating risk reduction into decentralization and sustainable development strategies, and identifying a set of specific programmes to be undertaken by the government together with development partners and possible donor assistance.
- It is intended to enhance security and safe spaces for vulnerable communities through safe housing and community infrastructures, coastal protection projects, risk-sensitive use of land and development strategies, and livelihoods and social protection measures. This protection and disaster risk reduction programme will be piloted in five vulnerable islands experiencing severe beach erosion.

- Maldives has endorsed the Maldives Low Emission Climate Resilient Development Programme, which seeks to take a new approach to climate change by narrowing its geographic focus and increasing resilience in one particularly vulnerable area of the country, namely the Laamu atoll. The programme takes a climate-resilient, low-carbon development approach which integrates strategies to address energy security, rising sea levels, water and sanitation, disaster risk reduction, natural resources and sustainable growth. It also seeks to address socioeconomic vulnerabilities by integrating livelihood, food security and health issues, and to build the capacity of local authorities.
- With regard to internal displacement, in particular, the UNDP supported the efforts of the NDMC by providing the services of a consultant to work on lessons learned on the management of IDPs in the Maldives and to develop a framework for IDP management based on international standards and experience gained from the past.[57]

The report suggests that in addition to a national framework on internal displacement that is in line with international standards, drawing on the lessons learned from the 2004 tsunami can offer valuable insights and inform future protection and assistance programmes in the Maldives, where recurrent flooding and other natural disasters make displacement and relocation to safer islands a current reality.[58] Therefore, it is essential that climate change-induced displacement preparedness and measures must be in concurrence with a human rights-based approach and mechanisms for the welfare and well-being of the IDPs. Because, the coexistence of both IDPs and host communities, if it tended to prolong in temporary shelters, encouraged dependency, thus creating vulnerability, and always turns out to be a source of tension with host communities. Non-involvement of IDPs in the prioritization of needs and the planning stage was considered later to be the cause for the continued lack of engagement by IDP communities in managing their issues in the transition camps, the failure to form effective IDP committees and their lack of ownership in the reconstruction programmes.[59] Hence, the government must initiate measures to boost confidence – building among the IDPs to avoid the conflicting situation in Rehabilitation Camps.

Climate Change-Induced Migration: Voluntary or In-Voluntary?

After going through a lot of references and field-based study reports on climate change migration in the Maldives, one could surmise that despite being the high economic growth the all-inclusive developmental remained a challenge in the Maldives, there is no migration from the Maldives per se crossing the sovereign borders of the country or persecution as defined by the United Nations Convention of 1951. In 2015, authors Arnall and Kothari have also discussed inconsistencies among the Maldivian people's approach to having any relations or links between climate change and migration.[60] The authors showed that many Maldivians, those who are ordinary people, did not see sea level rise as being a sufficient reason to migrate. On the other hand, elites were more concerned about relocation or maybe fear being displaced due to climate change provided that the national government covered the costs of resettlement in full. At the same time, the younger generations foresee the migration induced by climate change as a potential opportunity to secure a better life elsewhere for economic prosperity.

It has been revealed that the pattern of migration in the Maldives is basically because of economic prosperities like secure jobs, quality life and education, and health facilities and avoiding the densely located colonies and locations which led to unemployment opportunities and poverty. Moreover, in recent years, the political instabilities of Maldives and the incremental increase in drug abuse and drug-related crimes also indirectly impact the pattern of migration. Whereas, many felt that climate change-induced migration is, for instance, environmental changes like sea-level rise and soil erosion, lack of space and population growth, dry weather and water shortage, climate variability and pollution of the environment.

In 2015, Arnall and Kothari provided a historical account of central government policies regarding internal migration in the Maldives. For decades, the government has been trying to consolidate the population from outer islands to a small number of islands on which larger communities would be built. Originally, the government's reason for population consolidation was given as economic sustainability and the provision of social services. Now, the government's reason for population consolidation is given as climate change.[61]

Even in the face of climate change discourse, people still do not wish to emigrate due to sea level rise and continue leaving in their houses because physical aspects of climate change have not impacted daily life. Even if the climate change impact becomes more pronounced, leaving the country permanently is not an acceptable option rather preference for moving within the Maldives along with family and community due to their commitment to land, family, and culture and creating and retaining their own, unique identity.[62] Maldivians, in general, are not known for migrating in search of livelihood and looking for opportunities in the western world in fear of losing their cultural and linguistic connections. Many times, it has been observed that they are apprehended for coping with the cultural and social assimilation in other societies and cultures. So whenever one could see or observe the migration by the Maldivians, it is not because of climate change but very much voluntarily.

Conclusion

In a nutshell, migration in the Maldives as mentioned before is not necessarily because of climate change but essentially it is voluntary, due the environment change. Very few consider sea level rise and soil erosion as a challenge. For Maldivians, environmental and climatic threats are not felt as acutely as other socioeconomic problems.[63] Moreover, the social history and empirical observations evidently illustrate the preference of Maldivians at present for internal migration. The general pathway followed is from Remote Islands to either capital or capital city Male, including Hulhumalé, a newly constructed island, for improved facilities in health, education, better employment opportunities and living standards. For the majority who wish to move internally, this is the final destination.

In the past two decades or more than that, many Maldivian economically affluent classes have started purchasing land in Lakshadweep, one of the Union Territories of the Indian Union and also in Kerala, one of the states of India. This migration is voluntary and a safe sanctuary for them as well as for the next generations. This kind of migration is taking place in Maldives as an alternative option available at their disposal at the moment for balancing their standard of life, especially, among the urban Maldivians who live in Male. This attitude suggests the proposition that 'migration as adaptation' is a viable option, despite having its advantages and disadvantages. Migration as adaptation does not mean forced or involuntary migration, so those who are migrating would not wish to be labelled as 'climate refugees' or 'climate change refugees'. In that case, it is not a migration which is taking place in the Maldives at least it doesn't fit into the international standard definition. But surely it is an internal displacement. Therefore, the Maldives has IDPs that are induced by climate change to some extent and also because of opportunities for economic prosperities.

Notes

1 The World Fact Book-2020, accessed from www.cia.gov/library/publications/resources/the-world-factbook/geos/print_mv.html on 22nd November 2020.
2 R. K. Pachauri and L. A. Meyer (eds.) (2014), *Climate change 2014: Synthesis report*. Geneva: IPCC, 151 pp, accessed from www.ipcc.ch/report/ar5/syr/#:~:text=This%20Synthesis%20Report%20is%20based,Fifth%20Assessment%20Report%20(AR5)on 22nd November 2020.
3 L. A. Nurse, R. F. McLean and A. G. Suarez (1998), "Small island states", in R. T. Watson, M. C. Zinyowera and R. H. Moss (eds.) *The regional impacts of climate change: An assessment of vulnerability. A special report of IPCC Working Group II*. Cambridge and New York: Cambridge University Press, 331–354.
4 Leonard A. Nurse and Graham Sem (2018), "IPCC report on small island states", accessed from www.ipcc.ch/site/assets/uploads/2018/03/wg2TARchap17.pdf website on 20th May 2021.

5 The World Population – 2021, accessed from www.worldometers.info/world-population/maldives-population/ on 4th June 2021.
6 Ibid.
7 Op. Cit. no. 1.
8 Bailey et al. (2015), "Estimating current and future groundwater resources of the Maldives", *Journal of the American Water Resources Association* (JAWRA), 51(1), 112–122 for details see website, https://onlinelibrary.wiley.com/doi/abs/10.1111/jawr.12236
9 J. Pernetta and G. Sestini (1989), *The Maldives and impacts of expected climate changes*. Nairobi: UNEP Regional Seas Reports and Studies 104, United Nations Environment Programme.
10 Former President of Maldives, Abdul. Gayoom, in the United Nations General Assembly 1976, p. 510, accessed from https://undocs.org/en/A/31/PV.26 on 10th October 2020.
11 Ibid.
12 John F. May (2014), *Maldives' population dynamics: Policy prospects for human growth and opportunity*. Washington: PRB, for details see, https://maldives.unfpa.org/sites/default/files/pub-pdf/Policy%20implications%20bookletWEB.pdf on June 2016.
13 Urmila Phadnis and Ela Dutt Luithui (1985), *Maldives: Winds of change in an Atoll State*. New Delhi: South Asian Publishers Pvt Ltd., 55–56.
14 Abdul Gayoom, in UNGA on 14 October 1985 for details see, A/40/PV.34 14 October 1985, p. 31.
15 For details see website, https://unctad.org/press-material/ldc-what-least-developed-country on 22nd November 2017, accessed on 14th November 2020.
16 Hans D. E. Kruijk and Martine Rutten (2007, August), "Vulnerability and poverty dynamics in the Maldives," Institute for International and Development Economics, IIDE Discussion Paper, p. 4 For details see, www.researchgate.net/publication/5164354_Vulnerability_And_Poverty_Dynamics_In_The_Maldives on 2nd October 2020.
17 Ibid.
18 In the early 1980s, the Maldives was one of the world's 20 poorest countries, with a population of 156,000. In 2012, with a population of more than 300,000, it is a middle-income country with a per capita income of over $6,300. The country has impressive improvements in health and education with a life expectancy of 74.8 and a literacy rate 98.4%. For details, see www.worldbank.org/en/results/2013/04/10/maldives-development-success-story on 13th November 2020.
19 The World Bank, Maldives: Overview, updated till 10 April 2020, for detail see, www.worldbank.org/en/country/maldives/overview on 18th September 2020.
20 Ibid.
21 Ibid.
22 Ibid, 54.
23 Ibid.
24 Nenad Jarić Dauenhauer (2017, 20 March), "On front line of climate change as Maldives fights rising seas," *NewScientist*, accessed from www.newscientist.com/article/2125198-on-front-line-ofclimate-change-as-Maldives-fights-rising-seas/ on 20th September 2020.
25 Ibid.
26 Ibid.

27 Maldives – Tidal Waves Apr 1987 UNDRO Situation Reports 1–3, for details, see https://reliefweb.int/report/maldives/maldives-tidal-waves-apr-1987-undro-situation-reports-1-3 on 10th September 2020.
28 Ibid.
29 Ibid.
30 Abdul Gayoom, 42 Session of UNGA A/42/PV.41 dated 20 October 1987, p. 27, https://research.un.org/en/docs/ga/quick/regular/42 on 10th September 2020.
31 Ibid, 29.
32 First National Communication of The Republic of Maldives to the United Nations Framework Convention on Climate Change, Published by Ministry of Home Affairs, Housing and Environment, (2001), p. 49. For details, see https://portals.iucn.org/library/node/26768 on 13th September 2020.
33 Maldives: Climate Change Policy framework, published by Ministry of Environment and Energy, August 2015, 8–9. For details, see www.environment.gov.mv/v2/en/download/4594 on 27th October 2020.
34 Ibid, 8–9.
35 'President presents Maldivian 'Climate Smart Resilient Islands Initiative' at UN Climate Action Summit as replicable and sustainable development model for SIDS' Press Release by Presidents office, Republic of Maldives, on 23 September 2019, Ref: 2019–743-UNGA. For details, see https://presidency.gov.mv/Press/Article/22213 on 26th September 2020.
36 Ibid.
37 Jack Board, Sustainability Fighting the tides: Maldives races to reclaim more land as sea levels rise appeared on 2 April 2022. For details, see www.channelnewsasia.com/sustainability/maldives-sea-level-rise-land-reclamation-2578871 on 22nd April 2022.
38 Op. cit., no. 35.
39 Ibid.
40 "Maldives: Rebirth of a community International Federation of Red Cross and Red Crescent Societies", accessed from http://w3.ifrc.org/what/disasters/response/tsunamis/dhuvaafaru.asp on 29th September 2020.
41 Ibid.
42 Ibid.
43 Ibid.
44 Ibid.
45 *Effects of the tsunami of 26 December 2004 on Rasdhoo and Northern Ari Atolls, Maldives*. accessed from www.researchgate.net/publication/285765939_Effects_of_the_tsunami_of_26_December_2004_on_Rasdhoo_and_Northern_Ari_Atolls_Maldives on 2nd October 2020.
46 Ibid.
47 Ibid.
48 Ibid.
49 Maldives News Bulletin, issue no 1181 Department of Tourism, Ministry of Tourism, Art and Culture Information 14–12–2008, For details, see www.maldives-info.gov.mv/home/files/bulletinx_det.php?id_news=1080 on 3rd October 2020.
50 Ibid.
51 Developing a Disaster Risk Profile for Maldives, United Nations Development Programme, (UNDP), May 2006, Volume; One, for details, see www.preventionweb.net/files/11145_MaldivesDisasterRiskProfileFinalRep.pdf on 3rd December 2020.
52 Ibid.

53 World Bank, Asian Development Bank, United Nations system, Republic of the Maldives: Tsunami impact and recovery, joint needs assessment (2005), para. 3.
54 Ibid.
55 Amit Ranjan, Rising Sea Levels: Threat for the Maldives, ISAS, NUS 8 December 2021 for details see, www.isas.nus.edu.sg/papers/rising-sea-levels-threat-for-the-maldives/ on 10th March 2022.
56 Chaloka Beyani (2012), *Report of the special rapporteur on the human rights of internally displaced persons*. Chaloka Beyani: Addendum. For details, see https://digitallibrary.un.org/record/720965?ln=en on 2nd December 2020.
57 Lessons learnt on IDP management in the Maldives, and the draft Framework on IDP Management in Maldives, for details, see www.ohchr.org/Documents/Issues/IDPersons/A.HRC.19.54.Add.1_en.pdf on 22nd September 2020.
58 Ibid.
59 Ibid.
60 A. Arnall and U. Kothari (2015), "Challenging climate change and migration discourse: Different understandings of timescale and temporality in the Maldives", *Global Environmental Change*, 31, 199–206, accessed from www.sciencedirect.com/science/article/abs/pii/S0959378015000138 on 23rd August 2020.
61 As Quoted in Robert Stojanov, Barbora Duží, Ilan Kelman, Daniel Němec and David Procházka (2017), "Local perceptions of climate change impacts and migration patterns in male, Maldives", *The Geographical Journal*, 183(4), 370–385, 377–378, https://doi.org/10.1111/geoj.12177 on 25th September 2020.
62 Ilan Kelman, Justyna Orlowska, and Himani Upadhyay, Robert Stojsnov, Christian Webersik, Andrea C Simonelli, David Prochazka, Daniel Nemec (2019), "Does climate change influence people's migration decisions in Maldives?" *Article in Climatic Change*, 153, 285–299, https://doi.org/10.1007/s10584–019–02376-y on 20th May 2020.
63 Robert Stojanov, Barbora Duží, Daniel Němec and David Procházka (2017, April), "Slow-onset climate change impacts in Maldives and population movement from islanders' perspective", Knomad Working Paper 20, p. 27. About 71 percent of respondents observed some shifts and changes in weather patterns within the most recent 10–15 years. Similarly, 37 percent of respondents worried about environmental challenges but out of it only (7.20%) consider sea level rise and soil erosion as challenge. Other remained lack of space for living and population overgrowth (17.87%), climate variability (5.48%) or dry weather and water shortages (3.75%) and pollution of environment (2.88%).

Chapter 8

Understanding Climate Change and Its Impact on Myanmar

Perspectives on Migration, Migrants and Legal Framework

Kaveri and Sumallya Mukhopadhyay

A survey conducted by the Union of Myanmar Ministry of Environmental Conservation and Forestry (MOECAF) delineates how various parts of the country have witnessed on an average 0.2 percent variation in weather in the past three decades.[1] In Myanmar, the future projections of further changes in weather pattern are quite uneven,[2] and intriguingly, this is the general trend worldwide.[3] Climate change has garnered critical attention, especially after UN Human Rights Committee ruled that governments must take into account cases of migration caused by climate crises.[4] In response to a lawsuit filed against the Government of New Zealand by Ioane Teitiota, an individual belonging to the Pacific nation of Kiribati, UN has stated that 'climate change represented a serious threat to the right to life'.[5] Interestingly, António Guterres, the UN secretary-general, in his recent report addressing the socio-economic impacts of COVID-19, urges governments to make policies keeping in mind air pollution, sea-level rise, deforestation and other climate emergency.[6] Understandably, climate change has acquired centrality in the discourses of international significance.

Climate change poses a unique threat in most developing countries, especially in the Asia-Pacific region. A recent report published by Intergovernmental Panel on Climate Change (IPCC) 2022 stated that Southeast Asia is one of the most affected regions by climate change, and if global warming continues, climate change would become more severe, with irreversible consequences to human life.[7] Processes such as loss of forest, soil degradation, sea-level rise, depletion of watersheds, floods, urban heat, wildfires, and droughts as well as biodiversity and habitat losses undermine the traditional livelihood pattern of individuals and their families;[8] resulting in displacement of masses of people. Thus, there is an urgent need to expand our ability to adapt, contingent on the threat we are facing. The climate crisis is already generating more frequent and severe disasters, accelerating food and water scarcity and global inequities, and wreaking havoc on people, ecosystems, economies and infrastructure.[9] It is believed that the growing demand for fresh water has the potential to be one of the primary sources of conflict in Asia-Pacific.[10] Lack of fresh water, in turn, can also have a detrimental

DOI:10.4324/9781003367802-9

effect on agricultural production, forcing individuals to migrate to find better means of livelihood. While many tend to migrate from rural to urban areas within a particular country, individuals also prefer to cross international borders to settle in different countries. For instance, the residents of Chapai Nawabganj, Satkhira, and Munshiganj districts in Bangladesh embrace migration as a livelihood strategy that involves a 'household-level decision to improve income [and] a quest for social mobility' in the face of regular riverbank erosion, unavailability of fresh water and salinity in soil.[11] Large swaths of Syrians from 2006 to 2011 experienced extreme drought, forcing many to leave their homes and migrate to Europe.[12] According to climatologists, the drought, to a large extent, engendered the conflict in Syria and contributed to the displacement of its citizens. U.S. secretary of state, John Kerry, substantiated this viewpoint when he said, 'You think migration is a challenge to Europe today because of extremism, wait until you see what happens when there's an absence of water, an absence of food, or one tribe fighting against another for mere survival'.[13]

The effects of climatic variance are felt over time, and it entails framing concerted policies to build community resiliency. Despite repeated warnings, often countries do not consider climate change as a severe problem. Even if there is a consensus among officials to actively pursue climate protection policies, effective implementation of such measures does not materialise in reality owing to the lack of infrastructural and institutional support. For example, there is a need to promote innovation in environmentally friendly technologies. Yet, there exists no structural incentive for individuals that will be conducive for them to invest in productive businesses.[14]

Against the backdrop of these observations, the chapter attempts to examine the causes and effects of climate change and migration in Myanmar. It begins by briefly outlining the fragile state of affairs in Myanmar due to the political and civil unrest brought by the coup in the country. It argues that state fragility and weak governance, sutured with recurring natural disasters and changes in weather patterns, contribute to the vulnerability of the civil society as well as the natural ecosystem in Myanmar. The chapter moves on to discuss the impact of various cyclones that made landfall in Myanmar and the ensuing framework of protection as adopted by the country. Irrespective of the policies, it appears that people resort to migration to find different methods to sustain themselves. The chapter attempts to see how people's lives are affected by climate change in Myanmar. It argues that while those who possess resources and social capital somehow manage to assimilate to the new surroundings, the vulnerability of those who are employed in the informal sector comes to the forefront. Migration also leads to rapid urbanisation, and it adversely affects the ecological balance of the society. In the following section, the chapter looks at the strategies taken by the government in Myanmar to harness community resilience against climate change, and the associative problems of having no international legal framework to address the issues of environmental and climate-related migrants. It highlights the various complications that migrants, as well as countries, come across due to the lack of any governing legal framework. By using Myanmar as a point of reference, it concludes by foregrounding that the introduction of an adequate legal framework will bring about innovative strategies to mitigate and adapt to climate change.

Climate Change and Myanmar: Understanding Its Impact

Myanmar is a Buddhist-majority country that, ever since its independence, has a history of conflicts with continuous civil unrest, state-sponsored ethnic cleansing, and genocide. More than five decades of military rule has resulted in a hostile ambience, disrupting the socio-political fabric of the civil society. The case of ethnic Rohingyas exemplifies this point. Since the late 1970s, Myanmar's discriminatory policies and targeted genocidal violence have forced hundreds of thousands of Rohingya Muslims to flee their homes in Myanmar. According to the United Nations High Commissioner for Refugees (UNHCR), in August 2017, more than 700,000 Rohingyas fled a severe military crackdown. Though there were no precise figures of Rohingyas fleeing to different countries, but so far Bangladesh is the largest recipient of these stateless refugees with approximately one million.[15] While, many have sought refuge in the ASEAN[16] and SAARC[17] countries and beyond as the 'new boat people'.[18] The Rohingya issue continues to be one of the major concerns in the country. However, what's an even bigger challenge for the country today is to deal with its domestic political tensions arising from the military overthrow of an elected civilian government to the arbitrary arrest of political activists and the use of violence to quell the protest, Myanmar is slipping into its dark past that portends a new cycle of political and humanitarian crisis.

Persistent socio-political conflict and violence, poverty and weak governance coupled with recurring natural disasters have contributed to the vulnerability of the human habitats as well as the natural ecosystem. According to the Regional Consultative Group (RCG) on Humanitarian Civil-Military Coordination for Asia and the Pacific, Myanmar is one of the five countries in Asia that is highly vulnerable to large-scale natural disasters (along with Bangladesh, Indonesia, Nepal and the Philippines).[19] In fact, in 2016, Myanmar was one of the countries that continued to perform poorly in the global Environmental Performance Index (EPI). Out of 180 countries, it was ranked 153. The rank highlights that it is among the worst in the Southeast and South Asian regions, marginally ahead of Bangladesh and Afghanistan.[20] And, in 2018, it ranted 138 on the EPI.[21] On the Human Development Index (HDI) (2019), Myanmar ranked 147 out of 189 countries.[22] According to the United Nations Office for the Coordination of

Humanitarian Affairs' (OCHA) Asia and the Pacific 2019 regional Focus Model, Myanmar ranks second only after Afghanistan among the most-hazard-prone countries that combine high vulnerability and low capacity to respond in the region.[23] And, on the Global Peace Index 2021 reported by the Institute for Economic and Peace, Myanmar ranks 131 out of 163 countries. Especially, after fall-out from a military coup in February 2021, Myanmar is now the least peaceful country in the region.[24]

It appears that Myanmar is particularly vulnerable to the effects of climate change that presents a palpable threat to its population.[25] As climate change dramatically alters landscapes that formerly sheltered the people and their economies, the availability of resources becomes a significant challenge. Irregularity in availability of resources can not only lead to power struggle and conflict, but it also results in forcible migration of individuals and their families. Demographically, Myanmar is the largest Southeast Asian country. It shares its border with India and Bangladesh in the northwest, China in the northeast, with Laos and Thailand in the east and southeast. The Andaman Sea and the Bay of Bengal are to its south and southwest. Its total size is 676,578 km^2, and the coastline of Myanmar is about 2,300 km long.[26] According to the mid-year UN data 2020, the overall population is approximately 54,409,800.[27] It is located in the tropical region, experiencing high temperatures, humidity and copious annual rainfall.[28] While the coastal regions are particularly exposed to tropical storms, cyclones, tsunamis and flooding are also a recurring phenomenon across different parts of the country. Myanmar is at risk from earthquakes, droughts and wildfires, and the mountainous regions experience landslides. Administratively, for decades, Myanmar has been politically and economically isolated from the rest of the world. As the country desires to develop its infrastructure and economy, it is putting its biodiversity and natural resources under substantial pressure.

Agriculture remains the country's largest economic sector, which employs approximately 61 percent of the country's workforce, thereby contributing to almost 36 percent of the country's total gross domestic product (GDP).[29] According to the World Bank report (2019), about 85 percent of the total population still resides in the rural areas and relies mostly on agriculture, fisheries and livestock as primary sources of income and subsistence.[30] The country's temperature is predicted to rise 1.3°C to 2.7°C by 2050,[31] affecting the yields of crops like rice, maize, wheat, groundnut and soybean. It can also lead to weed and pest proliferation.[32] In fact, occurrence of pests such as the golden apple snail (Pomacea canaliculate) which is linked to predicted increase in climatically suitable habitats in 2080, threatens the 28 top Asian rice-producing countries including Myanmar.[33] Additionally, it is important to note that the rising temperatures and expanding frequency and intensity of climatic conditions and events have affected and altered precipitation rates. These changes in precipitation patterns will result in short-term crop failures and long-term production can also decline.[34] The rise in sea levels has had an impact on agricultural production. It has given rise to a scarcity of food as well as loss of habitable land in the country. The agrarian losses have obvious negative consequences on the nation's economy, resulting in human suffering through increment in health problems, poverty, malnutrition and mortality rate. Additionally, rapid changes in temperature, precipitation, droughts, floods and erosion pose a significant threat to aquaculture.[35] While the extensive biodiversity is threatened by military actions, the abundant natural resources are hampered by large-scale resource extraction and infrastructure development such as dams, ports, roads and other connectivity projects. The Kaladan multi-modal transit project at its northwestern frontier, Sittwe port, Shwe Natural Gas Extraction Project besides other investments in Tamu-Kalea and Moreh-Kalewa-Yargi corridor and deep-sea port at Kyaukpyu and an industrial parks as well as the Belt and Road initiative (BRI) are some of the examples.[36] Speaking on Myanmar and its present problems, Sakia Sassen points out that the massive land acquisitions in the name of economic development have affected millions of people over the years. In 2016, the government usurped three million acres of Rakhine rural land in the national list of land allocations for economic development.[37] The situation is same in Thilawa[38] near Yangon and minority-dominated regions like the Shan, the Karen[39] and the Kachin.

The development-induced land acquisition not only adds to the existing conflict but also has a ripple effect in the displacement of the vast rural population, loss of habitat, and even alters the ecology. Lack of awareness and low adaptive capacity across the country has influenced a significant section of the population to migrate. It happens almost every year in Myanmar – within and across the borders – jeopardizing the future of those who tend to migrate.[40] Hence, one can attest that climate changes have a detrimental impact on developing countries like Myanmar, which, in turn, exacerbates the vulnerability of the population and triggers human movement.[41] In fact, the intersection between land grabs and climate change mitigation politics in Myanmar has also created new political opportunities for scaling up, expanding and deepening struggles towards 'agrarian climate justice'.[42]

The river system that originates in the Hindukush Himalayan region plays a crucial role in shaping the economy of the countries through which it transverses, right from Afghanistan to Myanmar.[43] These glaciers serve as the crucial water storage for the people living in the region. However, the effects of climate change are in itself visible with the glaciers melting in the Himalayas. These glaciers sustain Myanmar's main rivers like the Irrawaddy. Soon, with melting glaciers, there will be a sudden rise in water-level, triggering catastrophic flooding, soil-erosion and landslides. People may simultaneously suffer from loss of significant amounts of water. It would damage the biodiversity, natural habitat and local livelihoods.

Notably, the central dry zone is inhabited by one-third of the entire country's population. The region is particularly vulnerable to drought, straining the available water resources for domestic, agricultural and industrial usage. Water shortages are common in Magwe, Mandaly and Sagaing regions. Even the highland areas like Yangon, Shan, Chin, Rakhine, Kayan, Ayeyarwady and Bago are now facing similar predicaments due to climate change.[44] The chronic droughts have also affected the agro-diversity. Over the years, it has resulted in a significant aggravation in diseases and the spread of invasive species as well as wildfires induced by rising temperatures. As evident in Khindan, due to reduced agricultural productivity, people are forced to leave their villages. They tend to migrate from rural to urban areas such as to Yangon and Mandalay.[45] In fact, between 2009 and 2014, approximately 800,000 migrants arrived in Yangon. Most of them settled in the fast-growing peripheral industrial township – Hlaing Thar Yar, Dagon Seikkan and Mingalar Don.[46] Some of them have also left the country entirely[47] to seek better work opportunities elsewhere. IOM estimates about 70 percent of migrants living abroad are based in Thailand with Malaysia (15 percent), China (4.6 percent), Singapore (3.9 percent), and the USA (1.9 percent) accounting for rest of the numbers.[48]

Periodic flooding wreak havoc in Myanmar. From 1980 to 2011, about 50 percent of the total number of environmental disasters within the country was caused by floods followed by storms.[49] In 2015, Myanmar experienced massive floods and associated landslides that affected approximately nine million people.[50] And, direct damage to crops and indirectly reduced the yield by delaying the planting cost UD$13 million in the 2015 flood in Myanmar.[51] In fact, from 2016 to 2018, it is estimated that between 298,000 and 500,000 people have been forcibly displaced every year by natural disasters, mainly due to massive flooding and landslides.[52] Thus, for most living in Myanmar, natural disasters have become part of their everyday life.

Deforestation and land degradation are significant concerns that the country is confronted with due to ill-managed human activity and unsustainable development schemes. In recent years, the mangrove forest in Ayeyawady has severely suffered from uncontrolled deforestation and environmental degradation. And, the rates of loss in Myanmar were four times the global average from 2000 to 2012.[53] Felling of trees was done to expand agrarian projects, to get mangrove products, wood fuel and charcoal and to meet the over exploitative demand of the city of Yangon. In the past two decades, Myanmar has lost more than 3 percent of its forest ecosystems.[54] Additionally, the coastal landscape of Myanmar has strategic importance for trade, economy and security. The recent climatic disorders have intensified the frequency of natural disasters. As a result, the coastlines have become fragile in nature, and often the coastlines are affected by hydro-meteorological disasters like cyclones, storms and coastal flooding. The region is also exceptionally vulnerable to sea level rise. As IPCC has reported that the 'low lying coastal areas, small islands and deltas like those of the Irrawaddy, Salween,

Sittaung, and Kaladan rivers are at serious risk of sea level rise especially due to cyclones and floods'.[55] It has predicted that sea level rise will eventually displace millions of people from the densely populated fertile plains and coastal communities. It is expected that the sea levels will rise from 20 to 41 centimetres by 2050 and from 37 to 83 centimetres by the end of the century.[56] In turn, it will affect the entire Ayeyarwady delta and result in accelerated erosion of its seafront areas. It will not only lead to the loss of freshwater reserves but subsequently have an impact on the sociocultural and economic lives of the people living near the coastal regions, forcing millions from their homes to resettle in other areas. Cyclone Mala in 2006 affecting coastal and inland communities and townships is a case in point. The Ayeyarwady division and Rakhine state were the worst-hit regions. A total of 12,015 families were affected.[57] In 2007, Cyclone Akash, a tropical storm tide, caused coastal flooding. The Cyclone Nargis in May 2008, a destructive and category 4 cyclone, affected a total of 37 townships and displaced around 2.4 million people. It also destroyed Myanmar's coastline and Ayeyarwady Delta region,[58] making it among the ten most destructive cyclones in the history of human civilisation. Coastal lands were flooded and tidal surges inundated low lying areas, including the nation's most populous city, Yangon.[59] Myanmar's untimely intervention along with the uncooperative and apprehensive attitude towards international warnings, aid and assistance resulted in a humanitarian catastrophe that could have been averted.[60] The officials did not do an accurate counting of civilian deaths and prevented aid workers from entering the country, leaving people in a miserable state without food, water and medical supply. It is estimated that the country incurred approximately US$55 million damage and losses to the agricultural subsectors due to the cyclone.[61] After Nargis, in 2010, Cyclone Giri, led to the death of 45 people. The unrestrained effects of Giri resulted in 101,923 people being rendered homeless. At least 20,380 houses were destroyed, with a total of around 260,000 people getting affected and 7,081 hectares of agricultural land destroyed.[62] In 2015, Cyclone Komen, along with relentless rain, culminated in regions within the country getting inundated with floodwaters. It was estimated that more than 125 were killed by Komen and 1.5 million people displaced,[63] and approximately 687,000 acres of farmland had been damaged.[64] Again in 2017, severe Cyclonic Storm Mora made landfall in Myanmar. No official estimates were available on the total number of people affected. Mora primarily had affected regions where Rohingyas resided. Hence, humanitarian agencies were not able to visit the area to gather necessary information because of the ongoing military action against the Rohingyas. But it is believed that the cyclone destroyed 50,000 structures in the northern part of Rakhine State; more than 21,000 houses and shelters for internally displaced people were damaged, and a total of 21,504 homes were damaged in Maungdaw District.[65] Against the backdrop of countless natural disasters, evidently, the coastal communities continue to live under higher risk that affects their existence and livelihood. The informal sector was badly affected, especially the daily-wage labourers who depended on seasonal jobs in agriculture, rice mills, small-scale fishing, fish processing, salt production, woodcutting, community works and other resource-based economic activities.[66] Furthermore, communities had been experiencing severe effects of climate changes such as coral acidification, an upsurge in salinity in groundwater level, seawater intrusion that decrease the marine livelihood resources and increase frequency and occurrence of disasters. It forced coastal communities to migrate to look for better livelihoods in safer regions. As a consequence, the pattern of migration to other states, and even beyond the cartographic borders to foreign countries, had considerably swelled among the coastal communities. About 60 percent of the young population, mostly men, had migrated from the delta regions in search of better opportunities.[67] Interestingly, they preferred to move to Yangon rather than heading towards the local urban centres of Ayeryawaddy.[68]

In the wake of Cyclone Nargis, which devastated the country's infrastructure and economy, Myanmar adopted a national framework called the Myanmar Action Plan on Disaster Risk Reduction (MAPDRR). It aimed at making the country a 'safer and more resilient against natural hazards, thus protecting lives, livelihoods, and development gains'.[69] MAPDRR had identified 32 priority actions under four pillars: (1) risk information and awareness, (2) risk governance, (3) risk mitigation and preparedness and (4) response, rehabilitation and reconstruction. The priority actions wanted to strengthen the policy frameworks and systems for long-term risk reduction.[70] These four pillars of MAPDRR were aligned with four priority actions of the Sendai Framework for Disaster Risk Reduction.[71]

Later, in June 2013, the government adopted the Disaster Management Law, and its rules for implementation were promulgated in April 2015. Considering the significance of the coastal regions and the people who inhabit in those parts, the United Nations Organization had emphasized on Sustainable Development Goal 14. It aimed to 'conserve and sustainably use of oceans, seas and marine resources'[72] to protect the coastal ecosystems as well as the in habitants living nearby. However, Myanmar's languid effort on remedial and relief measures pointed out that the country was still not prepared to face the future challenges of climate change, especially about safeguarding the rights of the migrants. The disaster management law, reference handbook and other standing orders were not yet thoroughly tested or fully operational to plan and mitigate disaster risk. Also, it lacked inclusivity in terms of taking account of vulnerable groups – children, women, elderly and differently-able. Many national and international NGOs had highlighted that historically the country lacked the practice of recording data and maintaining information with regard to disasters and losses incurred,[73] affecting the long-term planning in disaster risk reduction and subsequent implementation. Myanmar's mistrust and suspicion towards international humanitarian agencies was another reason for its failure. Till date, no humanitarian agencies, media, global observers, independent researchers and other organizations like Médecins Sans Frontières except the United Nations (with executive limits) were allowed to travel and work without permission. Ineffective response to the disasters and post-disaster relief and recovery had resulted in forced displacement and migration, both internally and internationally.

Climate Change and Myanmar: Migration and Migrants

Other than negatively affecting biodiversity, the environmental and climatic changes also have significant repercussions in the lives of people. Climate changes can result in unemployment or a reduction in income. People also suffer due to the lack of access to food, water, healthcare and education. At times, they have to rebuild their lives from scratch. For those involved in agricultural production, the quantity and the quality of their harvests get severely compromised. The report by Reliefweb titled 'The Urgent Need to Prepare for Climate Displacement in Myanmar: Establishing a Myanmar National Climate Land Bank' discusses the difficulties faced by the people to restore and rebuild their lives due to inflation, especially in the post-disaster scenario.[74] As the costs are up, they are unable to access services like education, healthcare and housing. They are even unable to replace their lost livestock due to high costs. What complicates the matter is that the impacts of disasters vary from one nation to another and from one individual to another. The pre-existing hierarchy and stratification in societal milieu restrict access to resources, to better livelihood, and income opportunities, especially for those who occupy the lower strata of the society.[75] The stratifications exist on the basis of class, ethnicity, religion, caste, age, gender and differently-able.[76] One can argue that those discriminated against and marginalized are also unfavourably placed before natural disasters and their hazardous aftereffects. That they are forced to live under precarious conditions, make them more vulnerable to natural disasters as they are unable to cope with the crises. More often than not, they are forced to move and relocate far from their natural social habitat. In order to survive, they have to embrace various livelihood strategies, for they cannot return to their homes even if they want. However, individuals with wealth, education or otherwise privileged background are more likely to have the required resources to either adapt to the changing environment or migrate and re-establish their lives. As marginalized communities are most vulnerable, they are forced to bear the trauma of loss and relocation. Scott Leckie, in a report published in *The Guardian*, puts forth the concerns that 'in the developing world, climate migrants will end up being landless, migrating from rural areas and ending up in slums in the cities with severe increased poverty'.[77]

Significantly, their former livelihood strategies might not be feasible in the new surroundings as is case of many farmers and those working in fisheries, from rural areas like Ayeyarwady. Lack of alternative livelihood opportunities forces them to suddenly shift their occupation to non-agricultural casual labourers in urban centres of Yangon and Mandalay[78] and Pathein.[79] In fact, according to the World Bank report on *Myanmar Economic Transition amid Conflict: A Systematic Country Diagnostic*, even two years after Cyclone Nargis, indebtedness has doubled among labourers, small farmers and fishermen. It has aggravated the poverty, which, in turn, exacerbates impacts already experienced by climate change.[80]

Though migrants are not unaware of the conditions to which they can be subjected, more and more individuals migrate, employing it as an adaptation strategy to tackle the impacts of climate change. Migration forces them to rebuild their lives at an unknown location, which, in most cases, is a city. Some of them are left at the mercy of the state for their survival. Most of the time, they also face many legal complications; for instance, lack of documentation can result in employer refusing to employ migrants, leaving them unemployed or underemployed. Some get involved in criminal activities, and it can further make their lives miserable.[81] Thus, even after reaching the new locations, lives remain challenging for these migrants as most of them fail to access better livelihood opportunities. Often, they end up in industries or in informal sectors that do not ensure minimum wage, proper work timing and a safe work environment.

Alongside impediments in securing employment, migrants have limited access to housing for their families and education for their children. Health services prove equally degrading and inaccessible for these migrants in urban centres. Mostly, they live in overcrowded slums. These habitations are unscientifically built temporary shelters supported by bamboo, plywood and covered with tarp sheets with no proper sunlight. Overall, the ambience is quite unhealthy. The houses do not provide sufficient resistance against extreme weather conditions, and the settlements usually lack proper toilet, water, and electricity facilities. This segment of the population is not, however, a homogenous entity because within it are couched further layers. These layers consist of the women, children, elderly and differently-abled, whose mobility is either impeded by societal norms or they fail to contribute substantially owing to their physical condition. At times, desperation and ignorance also lead many to the nexus of forced labour, human trafficking[82] and sexual slavery.[83]

For the host communities that receive climate-induced migrants, the influx of people leads to overcrowding of cities and proliferation of slums and informal settlements. In 2017, according to the UN-Habitat, the population of the informal settlement or slums in Yangon reached around 350,000 people. The population too is constantly expanding.[84] At the same time, it also overburdens the use of local resources that triggers human prejudices against the migrants. The growing population has the potential to worsen health, educational and social indicators in the city. Since the communities in the city are themselves facing the harsh effects of climate change, the presence of the migrants is believed to threaten their existence. Hence, the migrant population is often targeted with vicious political campaigns, exacerbating the risk of physical attacks against them. They live under constant threat of forced eviction.[85] It leads to conflict and exclusion from the society. In fine, migration of people as a result of variability in climate changes the makeup of communities and cities resulting in political, economic and social problems. The changes disrupt the state's demography and bring about disequilibrium in resource management and security threat (both internal and external) to host states as well as the entire region (if migrants cross borders). While Sonia Shah argues that migration is actually an ancient and life-saving response to environmental changes and also not a source of fear but hope,[86] yet most countries, through anti-immigration policies, have begun to close their borders in the name of socioeconomic burden, further complicating the issue of forced displacement and migration.

Legality and Illegality of Environment and Climate Migrants

By using Myanmar as a point of reference, the chapter is trying to establish that climate change is one of the biggest challenges we are facing in the 21st century. Yet, climate-induced migration is a relatively recent issue of concern, emerging as part of the discussions on climate change as a global crisis. According to UNHCR, in mid-2021, the number of forcibly displaced people around the global is estimated to be 84 million. This number includes almost 26.6 million refugees, 4.4 million asylum seekers, and over 48.0 million internally displaced persons (IDPs).[87] The Internal Displacement Monitoring Centre in 2017 records that there are 18.8 million new disaster-related internal displacements. The Centre is a part of the Norwegian Refugee Council. Globally, approximately 33.4 million people were internal displacements because of conflicts and disasters in about 145 countries in 2019.[88] According to the Global Report on Internal Displacement 2020, total new displacement in Myanmar in 2019 is estimated around 270,000.[89] While the average expected number of future risk of displacement per year – for sudden-onset hazards is 569,140.[90] Mostly, displacements are caused by environmental hazards and the impacts of climate-induced disasters are internally felt and those affected remain within the national borders.[91] However, displacement beyond cartographically drawn borders is also a reality that occurs due to the country's inability to support and protect its people in times of conflict and violence.

The UN Guiding Principles on Internal Displacement does acknowledge natural or human-made disasters as a mechanism to force migration and displacement. It defines IDPs as

> persons or groups of persons who have been forced or obliged to flee or to leave their homes or places of habitual residence, in particular as a result of or in order to avoid the effects of armed conflict, situations of generalized violence, violations of human rights or natural or human-made disasters, and who have not crossed an internationally recognized State border.[92]

However, the Guiding Principles are not legally binding and the responsibility to protect IDPs falls upon the state; thus in practice, it cannot be held accountable for neglecting such requirements to protect IDPs. It further marginalizes a group that is already stigmatized.

The 2018 *Global Compact for Safe, Orderly, and Regular Migration* calls for humanitarian visas and temporary work permit for the climate migrants as well as planned relocation and prohibition on their forcible return.[93] The compact even proposes building a 'Platform on Disaster Displacement' and developing an 'Agenda for the Protection of Cross-Border Displaced Persons in the Context of Disasters and Climate Change' to address the issue. However, being a non-binding agreement, its credibility is often questioned. Despite the rising concern, there is no international legislation or legal framework to address environmental disasters. There is also no reliable data on the number of people on the move as a result of climate change. Climate change as a reason for migration is still considered debatable.[94] Hence, to offer protection to those who are exiled because of climate-induced migration appears quite problematic. These people are not legally recognized as climate or environmental refugees or migrants.[95] The everyday lives and concerns of the migrants are never brought into the picture of any policymakers. However, according to the UNHCR, by 2050, it is estimated that around 25 million to 1 billion people will be forced to leave their homes due to climate change and its resulting disasters.[96] But the questions remain: where will these people be rehabilitated? And how will their rights and dignity be ensured and respected? It is important to note that legally we have no consensus on what terminology can be used to describe individuals moving due to environmental and climatic factors. The 1951 Refugee Convention and its 1967 Refugee Protocol provide a definition for 'refugee', but its obligations of protection are not crafted by keeping climate change and natural disasters in mind. The current definition of refugee assures protection to individuals fleeing life-threatening situations based on the 'well-founded fear of being persecuted for reasons of race, religion, nationality, membership of a particular social group or political opinion'.[97] As is evident from the definition, the Convention does not consider environment or climate as a persecuting agent. Many scholars suggest that migration is always a result of multiple factors,[98] and it cannot be understood in isolation from other socio-economic and political factors. The need of the hour is to include environmental factors as well. It has been more than 50 years since the definition has had formally formulated. While the global circumstances have considerably changed, it is imperative to revise the definition to acknowledge the fact that climate change and environmental disasters are now a reality. It plays a deciding role in forcing people to migrate.

Even the International Organisation for Migration (IOM), along with the United Nations High Commissioner for Refugees (UNHCR) and the World Bank, now advocate for an explicit use of the term 'climate migrant' instead of 'climate or environmental refugee/ecological refugees'. For designating a person as a 'refugee' have legal ramifications as set out by the 1951 Convention and its 1967 protocol. Thus, the use of a specific term like 'migrant' will help in avoiding any legal complications, and it also provides a robust definition appropriate to the emerging global challenges. Often these terms are misused and are meant to identify the 'other' – the victim or the person who is not supposed to be at the new locations or at the host country; these terms, it seems, create barriers to economic stability, to social integration, and the necessary support needed to overcome the climate crises. Understandably, words and terminologies do matter. It justifies the way we treat people who are migrating to a new location in search of better livelihood and safer life.

Migration is often considered multi-causal, and, in all likelihood, the most vulnerable people do not possess any documentation that will prove non-political factors like climate and environmental factors as the sole reason for their migration. Documentation, after all, might be a necessary requirement if climate and environmental disasters are to be integrated into the existing refugee legislations. Thus, the issue has become quite problematic. The impacts of climate change are more abstract when compared, for example, homelessness, unemployment, poverty and malnutrition. Under the current legal framework, economic instability and food insecurity, owing to climate change, are not considered valid reasons to grant asylum and protection to someone. However, given the rising number of climate migrants around the world, it is urgent to protect these vulnerable individuals facing severe impacts of climate change and environmental disasters.

The case of Myanmar proves that there is a need to prepare a legal framework that studies climate-induced migration, granting it legitimacy at national and international forums. Myanmar is often disrupted by civil unrest, ethnic violence and ruthless army crackdown. The absence of legal framework simply aggravates the difficulties the migrants face. The army (Tatmadaw) enjoys special position as per the provisions of 2008 Constitution of Myanmar. The military holds 25 percent of the reserved legislative seats (both union and state) in the parliament. Hence, they have the power to legally block any constitutional amendments. Similarly, they hold key cabinet positions like interiors, defence and border security. With such important portfolios, the army always remains in a strong position in the country's governance and in the overall functioning of the administration.[99] Not to mention, the military coup, which sparked widespread protest and violence, has raised concerns about the country's prospects. As a corollary, the country's diplomatic relations with its neighbours and internationally have suffered. This included various sanctions and boycotts. Most recently the organizers of the COP26 (UN Climate Change Conference) turned away the five-member delegation, led by the junta's Ambassador Tun Aung Kyaw and Councillor Chit Win from Myanmar junta after it reached Glasgow to attend the ongoing conference.[100] This was the second time the junta was restricted at an international forum. ASEAN members had previously barred Myanmar's military chief, Min Aung Hlaing, from a summit in October 2021, citing the military's unwillingness to cooperate with the regional bloc to resolve the ongoing political and humanitarian crisis. The fragile state of affairs has not only disrupted socioeconomic development of the country but also resulted in discrimination and conflicts. It is believed that to shore up finances, the military may accelerate resource exploitation, putting one of the world's most climate-vulnerable countries at risk. Thus, the lack of democratic processes along antinomy and incongruity to corporate with regional and international agencies explain Myanmar's passivity towards the emerging humanitarian crisis.

Conclusion

Among the countries most vulnerable to the impacts of climate change, Myanmar's rich biodiversity and natural resources are coming under heightened pressure with unchecked and unsustainable development schemes. The variability in weather and alterations in climate have led to more intense and recurring cyclones, storm surges, floods, earthquakes, droughts and wildfires. These have caused enormous loss of life, damage to infrastructure and the economy. The phenomena of climate changes have led to rapid accretion of the movement of people, resulting in a drastic migrant crisis that can no longer be ignored. While the terms such as 'climate migrant' or 'environmental migrant' are still not accepted as legal categories, the underlying problem is that there is no international convention or framework that protects people displaced by climate change. Therefore, the vast scale of climate displacement, along with the lack of legal framework and adequate resources, demand formulation of innovative mechanisms to protect and mitigate the plight of climate migrants and help them to adapt and resettle with rights and dignity.

Moreover, lower-income countries like Myanmar often lack the financial, technological or institutional capacity and resources needed for adaptation planning.[101] Furthermore, the political instability and isolation brought by the military coup would exacerbate the situation in the country. Thus, if Myanmar wants to look forward to a new era of progress, it must ensure democratic progresses along both development and humanitarian plans keep in mind the vulnerable sections of its population. Reducing deforestation, redesigning agricultural practices, investments in renewable energy and environment-friendly development schemes along with reducing and preventing economic inequalities can be considered as critical solutions. Despite efforts to mitigate and build a climate-resilient society, the government's actions will be questioned as long as the problems of human rights abuses, ethnic cleansing and genocide remain unresolved.

The reality of climate change is such that it does not abide by the conceptualization of borders; rather, it has the potency to affect the entire world. The chapter argues that there is an urgent need to reframe our understanding of the crisis. Climate change is not a problem; instead, it is the most horrible symptom of an economic system that has been built to extract precious aspects of the planet and its people, starting from natural resources to human labour. We need to restructure our social and economic system as well as overcome our cultural and religious barriers. It will help us develop collective community resilience that can provide water, healthcare, food and housing facilities, and, most importantly, ensure equal rights and respect to all individuals.

Notes

1 Union of Myanmar Ministry of Environmental Conservation and Forestry. "Dry Zone Greening Department". 129, accessed from www.moecaf.gov.mm/user-page2.aspx?mid=26 on 26th July 2020
2 Ohn U. Win and P. Batchelor (2019, 20 September), "Climate change matters to Myanmar", *Myanmar Times*, accessed from www.mmtimes.com/news/climate-change-matters-myanmar.html on 24th July 2020.
3 LiveSciences, accessed from www.livescience.com/37057-global-warming-effects.html on 24th July 2020.
4 Amnesty International (2020), accessed from www.amnesty.org/en/latest/news/2020/01/un-landmark-case-for-people-displaced-by-climate-change/ on 24th July 2020.
5 Ibid.
6 UN Environment Programme News (2020), "Myanmar gear up for action on climate change", accessed from www.unenvironment.org/news-and-stories/story/myanmar-gears-action-climate-change on 22nd July 2020.
7 International Panel on Climate Change [IPCC] (2022), accessed from www.ipcc.ch/report/ar6/wg2/downloads/report/IPCC_AR6_WGII_FinalDraft_Chapter10.pdf [Draft Report] on 27th March 2022.
8 Richard E. Bilsborrow (2009), "Collecting data on the migration-environment nexus", in *Migration, environment and climate change: Assessing the evidence*. Geneva: International Organization for Migration, 121.

9 USAID (2022), Intergovernmental Panel on Climate Change (IPCC) 2022 [*Press Release*-February 28], accessed from www.usaid.gov/news-information/press-releases/feb-28-2022-intergovernmental-panel-climate-change-report
10 Peter Hefele and Vogel Johannes (2016), *At the limits of endurance climate change and resource conflicts as challenges to the Asia-Pacific region*. Germany: Konrad Adenauer Stiftung, p. 6.
11 Maxmillan Martin, Motasim Billah, Tasneem Siddiqui, Abrar Chowdhury, Richard Black and Dominic Kniveton (2014), "Climate-related migration in rural Bangladesh: A behavioural model", *Population and Environment*, 36(1), 90.
12 Colin P. Kelley, Shahrzad Mohtadi, Mark A. Cane and Richard Seager (2015, March), "Climate change in the fertile crescent and implications of the recent Syrian drought", *Proceedings of the National Academy of Sciences*, 112(11), 3241–3246, https://doi.org/10.1073/pnas.1421533112
13 "How climate change is behind the surge of migrants to Europe", accessed from http://time.com/4024210 on 29th June 2020.
14 Hefele and Vogel, *At the limits of endurance climate change and resource conflicts as challenges to the Asia-Pacific Region*.
15 UNHCR, India 2019, www.unhcr.org/rohingya-emergency.html
16 ASEAN stands for Association of Southeast Asian Nations.
17 SAARC stands for South Asian Association Regional Cooperation.
18 Chris Lewa (2008), "Asia's new boat people", *Forced Migration Review*, 30(1), 40–42, accessed from www.files.ethz.ch/isn/139358/FMR30full.pdf
19 Humanitarian Civil–Military coordination emergencies: Towards a Predictable Model. 2017. Regional Consultative Group (RCG) on Humanitarian Civil-Military Coordination for Asia and the Pacific, 6, accessed from www.acmc.gov.au/sites/default/files/201808/RCG_Humanitarian_Civil_Military_Coordination_in_Emergencies_Towards_a_Predictable_Model.pdf
20 Global Metric or the Environment (2016), "Environment performance index report 2016", accessed from https://wedocs.unep.org/bitstream/handle/20.500.11822/7501/Global_metrics_for_the_environment_The_Environmental_Performance_Index_ranks_countriespercentE2percent80percent98_performance_on_highpriority_environmental_issues-2016glob.pdf?sequence=3&isAllowed=y
21 Z. A. Wendling, J. W. Emerson, A. de Sherbinin, D. C. Esty, et al. (2020), *2020 environmental performance index*. New Haven, CT: Yale Center for Environmental Law & Policy, accessed from epi.yale.edu https://epi.yale.edu/epi-country-report/MMR
22 United Nations Development Programme, Human Development Reports, Myanmar 2020, accessed from https://hdr.undp.org/en/countries/profiles/MMR
23 Reliefweb (2019), "Asia and the Pacific: 2019 regional focus model report-May 2019", accessed from https://reliefweb.int/report/world/asia-and-pacific-2019-regional-focus-model-may-2019
24 Institute for Economics & Peace. Global Peace Index 2021 (2021, June), "Measuring peace in a complex world", Sydney, accessed from www.visionofhumanity.org/wp-content/uploads/2021/06/GPI-2021-web-1.pdf
25 MyanmarCcAlliance, accessed from http://myanmarccalliance.org/en/climate-change-basics/impact-percent20of-climate-change-and-the-case-of-myanmar/
26 accessed from https://link.springer.com/referenceworkentry/10.1007percent2F978-1-4020-8639-7202
27 World Meter, accessed from www.worldometers.info/world-population/myanmar-population/

28 United Nations Office for Disaster Risk Reduction (2020), "Disaster risk reduction in Myanmar status report 2020", accessed from www.undrr.org/publication/disaster-risk-reduction-myanmar-status-report-2020
29 Asian Development Bank (2012), *Greater Mekong subregion atlas of the environment*, 2nd ed., accessed from www.adb.org/sites/default/files/pub/2012/gms-atlas-environment-2nd-edition.pdf
30 World Bank (2019), "Myanmar economic transition amid conflict: A systematic country diagnostic report", accessed from https://documents1.worldbank.org/curated/en/507421574785059413/pdf/Myanmar-Economic-Transition-amid-Conflict.pdf
31 Khin Khin Ei (2020, 11 January), "Climate migration in Myanmar", *Mizzima News*, accessed from www.mizzima.com/article/climate-migrations-myanmar
32 World Bank, accessed from https://climateknowledgeportal.worldbank.org/country/myanmar-burma/impacts-agriculture
33 International Panel on Climate Change [IPCC] (2022), accessed from www.ipcc.ch/report/ar6/wg2/downloads/report/IPCC_AR6_WGII_FinalDraft_Chapter10.pdf [Draft Report] on 27th March 2022.
34 World Bank, accessed from https://climateknowledgeportal.worldbank.org/country/myanmar-burma/impacts-agriculture
35 International Panel on Climate Change (2022), "Climate change 2022 impact, adaptation and vulnerability: Summary for policymakers", accessed from www.ipcc.ch/report/ar6/wg2/downloads/report/IPCC_AR6_WGII_FinalDraft_FullReport.pdf on 27th March 2022.
36 Kaveri (2020), "The politics of marginalization and statelessness of the Rohingyas in India", in Nasreen Chowdhory and Biswajit Mohanty (eds.) *Citizenship, nationalism and refugeehood of Rohingyas in Southern Asia*. Singapore: Springer, 80.
37 S. Sassen (2017, 15 September), "The assault on the Rohingya is not only about religion – it's also about land", *Huffington Post*, accessed from www.huffpost.com/entry/rohingya-land-grabmilitary_b_59b96400e4b02da0e13e79f4?section=us_theworldpost
38 Land lost, families uprooted as Myanmar pushes industrial zones. Thomson Reuters Foundation, accessed from https://news.trust.org/item/20190320004828-dp6po/
39 Human Right Watch, The Farmer Becomes the Criminal Human Rights and Land Confiscation in Karen State Report, 2016 at www.hrw.org/report/2016/11/03/farmer-becomes-criminal/human-rights-and-land-confiscation-karen-state on 16th February 2021.
40 Refugee International Report (2016), "Accelerating threats from climate change disasters and displacement in Myanmar: A field report", accessed from www.refugeesinternational.org/reports/2016/myanmar
41 Vikram Odedra Kolmannskog (2008), *Future floods of refugees: A comment on climate change, conflict and forced migration report*. Oslo: Norwegian Refugee Council, accessed from www.nrc.no/globalassets/pdf/reports/future-floods-of-refugees.pdf
42 Y. Sekine (2021), "Emerging 'agrarian climate justice' struggles in Myanmar", *The Journal of Peasant Studies*, 48(3), 517–540, https://doi.org/10.1080/03066150.2020.1839054
43 D. Carrington (2019, 4 February), "Third of the Himalayan ice cap doomed, finds report", *The Guardian*, accessed from www.theguardian.com/environment/2019/feb/04/a-third-of-himalayan-ice-cap-doomed-finds-shocking-report

44 Moe Myat Aung (2018, 8 March), "Villages brace for water shortage this summer", *Myanmar Times*, accessed from www.mmtimes.com/news/villages-brace-water-shortages-summer.html
45 Ki, "Climate migration in Myanmar".
46 Ibid.
47 L. Hogan (2018, 1 November), "We feel like hermit crabs': Myanmar's climate dispossessed", *The Guardian*, accessed from www.theguardian.com/global-development/2018/nov/01/we-feel-like-hermit-crabs-myanmar-climate-dispossessed
48 International Organisation of Migration, accessed from www.iom.int/countries/myanmar
49 AHA Centre Report. 2015. Country Report Myanmar: Natural Disaster Risk Assessment and Area Business and Continuity Plan Formulation for Industrial agglomerated Areas in the ASEAN Region, accessed from https://openjicareport.jica.go.jp/pdf/1000023395.pdf
50 Refugee International Report, "Accelerating threats from climate change disasters and displacement in Myanmar".
51 International Panel on Climate Change, "Climate change 2022 impact, adaptation and vulnerability".
52 Myanmar Internal Displacement Monitoring Centre (2018), accessed from www.internal-displacement.org/countries/myanmar
53 International Panel on Climate Change [IPCC] (2022), accessed from www.ipcc.ch/report/ar6/wg2/downloads/report/IPCC_AR6_WGII_FinalDraft_Chapter10.pdf [Draft Report] on 27th March 2022.
54 Myanmar Climate Change Alliance (2016), accessed from http://myanmarccalliance.org/en/climate-change-basics/impact-of-climate-change-and-the-case-of-myanmar/
55 The Burma Environment Working Group Report (2011), "Burma's environment: People, problem, policies", accessed from https://earthrights.org/wp-content/uploads/Burmas-Environment-People-Problems-Policies.pdf
56 Reliefweb (2018), "The urgent need to prepare for climate displacement in Myanmar: Establishing a Myanmar national climate land bank", accessed from https://reliefweb.int/sites/reliefweb.int/files/resources/DIS5757%20Myanmar%20National%20Climate%20Land%20Bank%20report%20v3_1%20ISSUU.pdf
57 International Federation of Red cross and Red Crescent Societies brief, accessed from www.ifrc.org/docs/appeals/06/MDRMM00101.pdf
58 International Federation of Red cross and Red Crescent Societies (2011), "Myanmar: Cyclone Nargis 2008 facts and figures", accessed from www.ifrc.org/en/news-and-media/news-stories/asia-pacific/myanmar/myanmar-cyclone-nargis-2008-facts-and-figures/
59 International Panel on Climate Change [IPCC], Climate Change (2013), *The physical science basis: Working Group I contribution to the fifth assessment report of the Intergovernmental Panel on Climate Change*, ed. Thomas F. Stocker, Dahe Qin, Gian-Kasper Plattner, Melinda M. B. Tignor, Simon K. Allen, Judith Boschung, Alesxander Nauels, Yu Xia, Vincent Bex and Pauline M. Midgley. Cambridge and New York: Cambridge University Press, 1273, accessed from www.ipcc.ch/site/assets/uploads/2018/02/WG1AR5_all_final.pdf
60 Burma Centre Prague (2015), "Cyclone Nargis", accessed from www.burma-center.org/en/burma/history/cyclone-nargis/
61 Food and Agriculture Organisation of United Nations (2015), "The impact of natural hazards and disasters agriculture, food security and nutrition", accessed from www.fao.org/3/a-i5128e.pdf

62 Accessed from https://reliefweb.int/disaster/tc-2010-000211-mmr
63 United Nations Office for the Coordination of Humanitarian Affairs, Myanmar Floods and Landslides 2015, 2015.
64 Episcopal Relief and Development (2015), accessed from www.episcopalrelief.org/press-resources/responding-to-cyclone-komen-in-burma-myanmar/
65 Relief Web (2017), "Tropical cyclone Mora – May 2017", accessed from https://reliefweb.int/disaster/tc-2017-000058-bgd
66 Food and Agriculture Organisation of United Nations, "The impact of natural hazards and disasters agriculture, food security and nutrition".
67 Livelihoods and food security Funds Report (2016), accessed from www.lift-fund.org/sites/lift-fund.org/files/publication/Internalpercent20Migrationpercent-20FINALpercent20ENG.pdf
68 Accessed from www.mmtimes.com/business/24067-as-labourers-leave-myan-mar-delta-farmers-struggle-to-mechanise.html
69 Refugee International Report, "Accelerating threats from climate change disasters and displacement in Myanmar".
70 Accessed from www.mm.undp.org/content/dam/myanmar/docs/Publications/EnvEngy/UNDP_MM_MAPDDR_2017_ENG_web.pdf
71 Sendai Framework for Disaster Risk Reduction 2015–2030, also known as the Sendai Framework, is an agreement which is adopted by UN member states at the World Conference on Disaster Risk Reduction held in Sendai, Japan, in March 2015. It is a roadmap with concrete actions to protect development gains along with making communities safer and more resilient to disasters. It recognizes that the nation's primary role is to reduce disaster risk, but that responsibility has be shared with other stakeholders including local government, the private sector and other stakeholders. It is the UNDRR that has the task to support the implementation, follow-up and review the Sendai Framework, accessed from www.undrr.org/implementing-sendai-framework/what-sf
72 United Nation, accessed from https://sdgs.un.org/goals/goal14
73 Oxfam (2013), "Review of Myanmar's Disaster Management Law from the angle of inclusivity", accessed from https://oxfamilibrary.openrepository.com/bitstream/handle/10546/312201/rr-myanmar-disaster-management-law-050214-en.pdf;jsessionid=EBF0ECA230AF17F4C7A5E2F693E83923?sequence=1
74 Reliefweb, "The urgent need to prepare for climate displacement in Myanmar".
75 Sumallya Mukhopadhyay (2019), "Thinking of migration through caste", *Journal of Migration Affairs*, 2(1), 127, https://doi.org/10.36931/jma.2019.2.1.113-131
76 Oxfam, "Review of Myanmar's Disaster Management Law from the angle of inclusivity".
77 Hogan, "We feel like hermit crabs".
78 Livelihoods and Food Security Funds Report (2016), accessed from www.lift-fund.org/sites/lift-fund.org/files/publication/QSEM%205%20%28English%29%20LOW%20RES%20FINAL.pdf
79 World Bank (2014), "Another Nargis strikes everyday: Past Nargis social impact monitoring five years on", accessed from www.gfdrr.org/sites/default/files/publication/Another-Nargis-Strikes-Every-Day.pdf
80 World Bank Report (2019), "Myanmar economic transition amid conflict: A systematic country diagnostic", 14, accessed from http://documents1.worldbank.org/curated/en/507421574785059413/pdf/Myanmar-Economic-Transition-amid-Conflict.pdf
81 Eben Forbes (2019), "Migration, informal settlement, and government response: The cases of four township in Yangon, Myanmar", *Moussons*, 33(1), 98.

82 International Organisation of Migration, accessed from www.iom.int/countries/myanmar
83 Refugee International Report, "Accelerating threats from climate change disasters and displacement in Myanmar".
84 Forbes, "Migration, informal settlement, and government response", 113.
85 Ibid.
86 Sonia Shah (2020), *The next great migration: The beauty and terror of life on the move*. New York: Bloomsbury Publishing.
87 UNHCR fact sheet 2021, accessed from www.unhcr.org/refugee-statistics/
88 The Internal Displacement Monitoring Centre (2020), "Global report on internal displacement 2020", accessed from www.internal-displacement.org/global-report/grid2020/
89 Ibid.
90 Ibid.
91 UNHCR, India, accessed from www.unhcr.org/climate-change-and-disasters.html
92 United Nations Guiding Principles on Internal Displacement, accessed from www.unhcr.org/43ce1cff2
93 Global Compact for Migration (2018), accessed from https://refugeesmigrants.un.org/migration-compact
94 Thea Philip (2018), "Climate change displacement and migration: An analysis of the current international legal regimes deficiency, proposed solutions and a way forward for Australia", *Melbourne Journal of International Law*, 19(2), accessed from http://classic.austlii.edu.au/au/journals/MelbJIL/2018/22.html
95 Ibid.
96 Baher Kamal (2017), "Climate migrants might reach one billion by 2050", *ReliefWeb*, accessed from https://reliefweb.int/report/world/climate-migrants-might-reach-one-billion-2050
97 1951 Refugee Convention, Article 1, accessed from www.unhcr.org/3b66c2aa10
98 Philip, "Climate change displacement and migration".
99 Kaveri, "The politics of marginalization and statelessness of the Rohingyas in India", 78.
100 J. Liu and R. Wallace (2021, 1 December), "Climate danger grows in vulnerable Myanmar after military coup", *Aljazeera*, accessed from www.aljazeera.com/news/2021/12/1/myanmar-climate
101 Eranga K. Galappaththi, Vasantha B. Susarla, Samantha J. T. Loutet, Stephanie T. Ichien, Amanda A. Hyman and James D. Ford (2020), "Climate change adaptation in aquaculture", *Reviews in Aquaculture*, 12(4), 2160–2176, https://doi.org/10.1111/raq.12427

Chapter 9

Climate Change and Human Mobility in Nepal

Rajesh Kharat and Rishi Gupta

Backdrop

The history of human mobility is as old as the history of humanity.[1] However, in the past century, human mobility has seen different causes and concerns, including political instability, conflicts and climate change among others. Since human mobility is induced by several factors, mobility has also been categorized into different forms such as refugees, migration, statelessness and displacement. Among many reasons for human mobility, livelihood and conflicts continue to be the cardinal reasons with different proximities and impacts. In South Asia, the problems of refugees, migrants, stateless and displaced persons have become severe. It has witnessed the most significant movement of people in recorded history, both within the national boundaries and across them.[2] While discussing human mobility in the context of Nepal in South Asia, it is no exception. Today, Nepal is witnessing high-level human mobility within and outside Nepal where displacement is seen as an extreme manifestation of disaster risks resulting in a high-level vulnerability. Lack of resilience is incredibly high, resulting in natural disasters of all levels. These disasters compel people to leave their homes and livelihoods to survive. The magnitude of displacement is undoubtedly related to extreme natural events.[3] For instance, Nepal has been affected by two major earthquakes in 1934 and 2015, resulting in major human mobility in search for safety and survival.

Compared to countries like Chile, which have used natural disasters as a lesson to improve building codes and land-use plans, Nepal has struggled to improve its housing and infrastructure stock quality.[4] The last two significant earthquakes in the 1980s affected over 200,000 people.[5] On 18 August 2008, a breach of the Kosi River embankment caused flash flooding that displaced around 45,000 people from the Sunsari District in Nepal and affected about three million people from 1,704 villages in the neighbouring North Bihar in India. In the flood's aftermath, some displaced persons from Nepal travelled to India to flee from the deluge.[6] In April 2015, an earthquake of 7.8 magnitudes struck Nepal. With its epicentre in the Gorkha

DOI:10.4324/9781003367802-10

district of Nepal, the earthquake and its aftershocks claimed nearly 9,000 lives, injured more than 16,000 and destroyed hundreds of thousands of homes across the country.[7] In addition to the human suffering it caused, the earthquake had an immediate economic impact of "as much as half of Nepal's USD 20 billion GDP".[8] "The ensuing internal displacement had further consequences for the economy that until now has not been quantified".[9]

While human mobility has become a common phenomenon around the world, establishing a direct correlation between climate and human mobility is often done through the analysis of the impact of natural disasters or a long-standing conflict. However, the 2022 Intergovernmental Panel on Climate Change (IPCC) report categorically stated that "climate-induced hydrological changes can, through slow-onset (e.g., drought) or rapid onset (e.g., flood) events, influence human mobility and migration through effects on the economy and livelihoods".[10] By putting these observations in the context of Nepal, the related impacts of regular floods in Southern Nepal can be observed in the patterns of human mobility in Nepal. In this context, it is essential to study topography and Nepal's geographic location to understand climate-induced human mobility in Nepal.

Topography of Nepal

Nepal lies between the Tibet autonomous region of China and the federal states of India – Uttarakhand, Uttar Pradesh, Bihar, West Bengal and Sikkim. Nepal's geographical location establishes its geo-strategic forms connected with the Gangetic belt, a very fertile and abundant natural resource. Rivers, lakes, mountains, minerals and forests are the natural resources of Nepal. These resources are extremely important for industrialisation and economic development, which shows the strength and assets of the nation. Nepal has 83,000 MW[11] hydro potential, the second-largest country after Brazil. At a time, scarcity of water and energy is high at the global level, such potentiality of Nepal draws the attention of economically powerful countries. Most of the rivers in Nepal flow from North to South. There are more possibilities for developing multipurpose projects in irrigation, river transport, hydropower production, flood control and ecosystem preservation. With two mighty economies – India and China – their energy demand is higher than ever in the neighbourhood. They need colossal energy to pursue their industrialisation process, economic growth and produce surplus powers.[12] However, the hydro-energy potential of Nepal remains underused due to its no long-term utility policies, plans, unstable government and corruption.[13]

In terms of topography, the mighty Himalayan ranges and their bases make up more than 15 per cent of the total area of Nepal. These ranges are home to some of the unique topographical conditions found across the world. These Himalayan ranges host the most significant peak in the world – Mount Everest. As home to rare wild medicines and herbs, the hill region is inhabited by less than 10 per cent of the total population considering the difficult habitation and land routes.[14] The hill region covers approximately 65 per cent of Nepal's entire land and is inhabited by 45 per cent of the population.[15] Terai (lowland) is the third topographical category that works as the country's food and grain lifeline. Located in the Southern plains of Nepal, the region is very fertile and home to several important rivers like Kosi, Gandaki and Karnali, which finally join the Ganges in India and fall into the Bay of Bengal. The region is providing suitable weather conditions for the crops. It occupies 21 percent of the total land of Nepal with 50 percent population. It is the backbone of Nepal in the context of the economy.[16]

Climate Change Vulnerabilities and Human Mobility

It has been observed globally that climatic changes have contributed to physical and biological systems in many parts of the world. For instance, the shrinkage of glaciers, changes in rainfall frequency and intensity, shifts in the growing season, early flowering of trees and emergence of insects and shifts in the distribution range of plants and animals in response to changes in climatic conditions.[17] In the context of Nepal,

> the climate varies from the tropical to the arctic within the 200 km span from south to north. Much of Nepal falls within the monsoon region, with regional climate variations largely being a function of elevation. National mean temperatures hover around 15°C.[18]

It is increasing from north to south except for mountain valleys. The average rainfall is 1,500 mm, with rainfall increasing from west to east. The northwest corner has the least rainfall, situated as it is in the rain shadow of the Himalayas.[19] Despite abundant rainfall, its distribution is uneven and a matter of grave concern; for example, there is constant flooding during Monsoons, whereas during the summer, droughts are not uncommon in certain regions in other parts of the year.

In terms of Global Warming concerning Nepal,

> The global emission of greenhouse gases is negligible at per-capita CO_2 emission of 0.13 tons, but Nepal still faces the consequences of global warming because of the geographical and climatic conditions, high dependence on natural resources and lack of resources to cope with the changing climate.[20]

The average temperature in Nepal is rising by 0.5 degrees Celsius per decade.[21] However, such a minimal change in air temperature can also lead to the rapid melting of glaciers and Glacier Lakes.[22] For instance, a World

Wildlife Fund (WWF) Nepal Program study in 2005 indicated that "the Khumbu Glacier, a popular climbing route to the summit of Mt Everest, has retreated over 5 km".[23]

Agriculture and Floods

Agriculture is one of the significant sources of Nepal's gross domestic product (GDP). It accounts for 24.256 per cent of the GDP after the service sector.[24] It is estimated that two-thirds of the Nepalese people are engaged in agricultural activities.[25] In the past five decades, the agricultural productivity in Nepal has come down to an extreme level. For instance, in 1975, agriculture was the most significant contributor to the national economy. However, in low riparian areas (southern belts), annual floods have primarily contributed to human agony.

Along with natural monsoon season rains, Nepal has two glacial lake outbursts – flood and the Bisyari (breaking of dams caused by landslides falling directly into rivers).[26] With Nepal located on the foothills of the Himalayas, it is home to "2,323 glacial lakes covering 75 sq. km".[27] As reported, globally, "glaciers have retreated rapidly in the second half of the 20th century, forming, in many cases, ice-core moraine-flanked lakes of melted water".[28] As a result, rubble dams are broken, leading to draining rivers and naturally created reservoirs. Therefore, the glacial lake outburst floods have caused massive damage to properties, and local infrastructure, loss of lives and displacement. It has forced the poor to opt for other professions, such as moving to other countries and searching for employment. Nepal witnessed a sharp rise in demand for foreign employment with the advent of globalization in the 1990s. A recent report by the Central Department of Environmental Science at Tribhuvan University in Nepal points to some alarming indicators. The report adds:

> The climate risks are high in Nepalese agriculture as the farming faces several hazards, exposure to extreme weathers and farmers are vulnerable. Nepalese agriculture and nutrition face many climate-induced hazards and extreme trends, particularly drought, crop diseases, livestock diseases, cold waves, inundation, riverbank cutting, and flood. Most of the farms are exposed to one or the other hazards. The exposure of the agriculture system to climate change is very high due to farmlands under challenging terrains, limited irrigation schemes, poor road accessibility, large but low productive rangeland-based livestock population, poor market network, traditional livestock sheds and heavy dependency on conventional agriculture for livelihood. Impacts of climate change are visible in crop and livestock production, fisheries and malnutrition. Land and labour productivity and competitiveness are low; adoption of improved technology is slow. Increasing temperature and extreme variability in rainfall have significant implications for the agriculture sector.[29]

The adaptation to climate change vulnerabilities is considerably a new phenomenon in Nepal. The Government of Nepal has assigned the National Adaptation Programme of Action (NAPA) to better the agriculture-related requirements affected by climate change in terms of finding suitable technology, equipment and weather forecasts with a fund of USD 95 million. As the technology is imported from other countries, management of regular drought requires continuous engagement between farmers, government and technology.[30] However, the "Nepal Tarai and the Gangetic plain are somewhat isolated from technological and economic globalisation but nonetheless are affected indirectly".[31]

Nepal is a water-rich country which has been divided into various river basins.[32] Among these basins, six basins are most affected by floods, which has/had induced human mobility. In this context, the Asian Development Bank, in its study on floods in Nepal, states:

> Flooding has concentrated mainly in six river basins – West Rapti, Mawa-Ratuwa, Lakhandehi, Mohana-Khuriya, East Rapti, and Bakraha. In the more than two decades that have passed, these river basin areas have suffered through more than 200 floods. Over 143,000 people were affected, with 273 reported deaths, and just under 4,300 households were ruined. The flood risk is expected to increase as more people migrate to the Terai region in search of farming livelihoods.[33]

Historically, Nepal has witnessed inward migration from the downhills. The basins mentioned earlier affected by the floods have also been the centre of human mobility. In the 1950s, floods caused the outbreak of Malaria, which saw major human mobility from lower hills to the Terai (lower) region. For instance, "The floods of July 21 and 25, 1998 displaced 25 households of Pokhara tole. After the flood, more than 150 households migrated, and the trend continued until 2003. Everyone living in the *Purano Basti* (old colony) of Bhasedwa migrated elsewhere".[34] A major post-flood assessment by the Planning Commission of Nepal observes that "with the increasing impact of climate change, floods are likely to occur frequently in Nepal".[35]

Water Resources and Energy

Nepal has a bright future when it comes to water resource development. Yet only around 7 per cent of the overall accessible water has been used thus far. Farming is the most water-intensive industry, making over 96 per cent of total flows, compared to 3.8 per cent for the household sector and relatively little for the manufacturing industry.[36] Wood is a crucial energy source in the power sector, accounting for 80 per cent. Hydropower, on the other hand, has a 63 per cent share of overall electricity consumption. Climate change and unpredictability influence natural resources, energy production, electricity consumption and the design of hydro energy infrastructure. In terms of resource wealth, climate change/variability affects the spatial-temporal availability of water availability in various ways, including accelerating evapotranspiration and measuring evapotranspiration. However, the expected future of hydropower plants has negative impacts as well.

Meanwhile, the energy output is dependent on a variety of factors, including the rate of the warming trend and plant location, among others. The water inflow to the dam is also affected by rainfall fluctuation, a common phenomenon in Nepal. The hydro-energy industry is being impacted not just by changes in hydrology but also by increased water-led disasters such as silt deposition, geo-hazards and floods – any significant shift within the occurrence of droughts and floods in the water supply and water availability. The seasonal timing of the water supply would necessitate adaptations that can be expensive, not just financially but also throughout social lives. Also, uncertainty over the availability of energy in Nepal had led to the non-establishment of industries in Nepal. On the technological front, Nepal imports technology and machinery from their countries. However, sustained energy production of its own will positively impact the industrialisation of Nepal. While industrialisation in the lower hills and upper hilly regions is a challenge, it will help employment-induced mobility within Nepal.

Earthquake

In April 2015, Nepal witnessed a major earthquake of 7.8 magnitudes. The last earthquake of such velocity took place in 1934. The earthquake claimed more than 9,000 lives and 22,000 injured, and to date, there are thousands of families who have felt the pain of losing their loved ones to the earthquake. While the state could have learnt lessons from the 1934 earthquake and prepared for the earthquake by coordinating with the global seismologic agencies as it is located in the Himalayan region, the lack of emergency response doubled the loss of lives. Till 2015, Nepal did not have a well-equipped natural disaster response team. The proximity of damage in the Gorkha district was higher than in any other region as it was the earthquake's epicentre. With early preparation in place for better emergency health facilities, infrastructure and trained human resources. Instead, Nepal lost several precious hours waiting for global humanitarian help to reach. The earthquake damaged health, food and freshwater facilities. The women and girls were the most affected as they had no financial independence to immediately fill the house's loss. Therefore, they lived in deplorable unhygienic tents for months. In 2017, the Planning Commission of Nepal estimated that 72,784 pregnant and 61,715 lactating women were in dire need of immediate health services.[37]

On the other hand, the post-disaster recovery saw another looming challenge of missing human resources, especially in the Gorkha district, which was the earthquake's epicentre. Soon after the earthquake, the Government of Nepal requested almost all the Gulf countries to allow Nepalese migrant workers to return home. Meanwhile, several workers stayed back in the host countries as they could not afford to come back after visiting their homes. The absence of human resources was an outcome of the tradition of migration in Nepal to third countries. Also, the internal displacement caused by the earthquake doubled the challenges in terms of loss of property, business/employment, schools, health and food.

Biodiversity and Ecosystem

Deforestation, changes in the gaging habitat for animals, the absence of gaging lands, deforestation, pollution, wildfire and fragile ecosystem eventually impact the monsoon cycle. Floods have become a common phenomenon in the Terai region of Nepal, where droughts, non-monsoon rains and earthquakes shatter the lives in the hills. Many studies have highlighted the impact that the "topography of the Terai makes the entire region more vulnerable to flooding and inundation".[38] These flash add (it adds) floods and droughts have severely affected Nepal's biodiversity. The country is marked as one of the world's top biodiversity hotspots, including rich climatic zones, glaciers, and home to rare species and medicinal plants. With the biodiversity changes, the permanent habitat of birds, animals and humans has turned into mobility-oriented. Deforestation has led to endangering of rare species which can only survive in the Himalayan biodiversity. In 2017, a study titled, *The Impact of Climate Change on Biodiversity in Nepal* highlights the impact of climate change and deforestation, add:

> In the Chitwan-Annapurna Landscape (CHAL) of central Nepal, the forest area remained unchanged (35.5%) between 1990 and 2010, whereas forest area in Nepal's Kailash Sacred Landscape (KSL) declined 9% from 1990 to 2009. Deforestation is still a significant problem in the Siwalik and Terai region. In KoshiTappu Wildlife Reserve, a Ramsar site in eastern Terai, the forest area declined 94% from 1976 to 2010.[39]

During the decade-long Maoist insurgency in Nepal, forests had become home to illegal poaching and unwanted exploitations. Since the Maoist guerilla fighters used forests as their hideouts to sustain their financial needs, poaching and illicit animal trading emerged as a dire challenge to wildlife in Nepal. The National Parks and Wildlife Conservation (NPWC), responsible for the protected areas in Nepal, had reported that by 2004, forty-seven physical structures of the NPWC had been destroyed by the Maoists to continue their illegal practices.[40] Therefore, protecting biodiversity through different departments, including forest, water, and climate, is the highest necessity for climate protection.

On the ecosystem front, large-scale climate prediction systems are based on the changes in the Himalayas. While the global community is looking at the melting of the Himalayan glaciers to verify global warming, Nepal faces immediate challenges like flash floods and falling agricultural productivity. In 2009, the Government of Nepal attracted the world's attention by holding its cabinet meeting on climate at the base camp of Mount Everest.[41] Even though the government sent a symbolic message to the global community regarding a changing ecosystem in the Himalayan region, Nepal's political instability has kept the climate in the back seat for the past 30 years. The Stockholm Environment Institute, in its 2011 report on Nepal, cited three consequences of climate change in Nepal:

1) Impacts on people's livelihoods and economy from erratic and uncertain weather conditions;
2) Increased natural hazards, including landslides, floods and Glacial Lake Outburst Floods (GLOFs);
3) Negative consequences for key economic sectors like agriculture and hydropower. All of these impacts are likely to have long-term consequences for the country's economy, food security and biodiversity, and irreversible damage to ecosystem services and environmental flows.[42]

Agriculture is one such area that has direct consequences on human mobility in Nepal. For instance, in the past century, agriculture was the central pillar of the Nepalese economy till the 20th century. With the rise of the Maoist insurgency in Nepal in 2001, Nepal witnessed internal mass displacement. As a result, farmers in the hills and Terai moved to urban areas to seek safety and livelihood. While the country could accommodate a new workforce to a limit, people began to migrate overseas, especially to the Gulf and Nordic countries, South-East Asia and Australia. As a result, remittances have surpassed agricultural contributions to GDP. In 2018, remittances accounted for 28 per cent of the Nepalese GDP.[43] In recent years, outward migration has become the most sought-after means of employment. The service sector has also become a rising industry in Nepal. Therefore, agriculture is being replaced by other economic drivers where climate continues to play a cardinal role.

The global phenomena of internal displacement are not new to Nepal. Nepal already witnessed the widespread displacement of people with the incremental increase in armed conflict between the Maoists and government armed forces.[44] But the recent earthquake in April 2015 has taught a lesson not only to the state actors but also to the international actors like UNDP. To cite one of the rescue operators, who were on the Mission, Daniel

Buckley, Climate Change Policy and Finance analyst, UNDP Sustainable Development Group, said:

> As a UNDP climate change policy specialist based in New York, I was on a mission to Kathmandu when the earthquake struck. My mission was to design a project to enable Nepal to access increased climate finance. With such funding, Nepal could better adapt to climate impacts in vulnerable sectors of the economy while putting the country on a low-carbon development path that encourages sustainable livelihoods.[45]

He further adds:

> When I first arrived in Nepal, many remarked on the unusually early rains. A growing body of evidence suggests climate change affects the monsoon's arrival and intensity. Nepal must now prepare for monsoons that may come too early or too late. Erratic rainfall patterns and amounts may bring above-normal quantities of precipitation that cause deadly floods, endangering lives and crops. Decreased rains in water-stressed regions may force migration to already crowded cities and increase food insecurity.[46]

The aforementioned statements explain Nepal's vulnerability to climate change, especially in the mountain areas, leading to more and more displacement in search of livelihood, food and shelter. Nepal, being one of the LDCs, could face more challenges to its socio-economic setup. There are many incidents, particularly in the Nepal-Tibet borders where the borderland communities have lost their lives, sources of livelihood like the agriculture sector, animal husbandry, small business-like trade and transport and other minuscule opportunities to survive.

Climate Policies

Nepal is under immediate threat of climate change as rising temperature melts the snow at an alarming rate that can bring disastrous consequences by the end of this century.[47] Considering the danger that climate change poses, timely solutions must meet the challenge. To do so, countries across the world facing climate crisis have come up with convenient policy frameworks seeking global/local attention, cooperation, action and response. However, Nepal has fallen short in this regard despite witnessing climate-induced challenges such as floods and earthquakes. The weak design of climate policy is a result of unstable governments. However, for the first time in the history of Nepal's efforts in reducing the impact of climate change, the Government of Nepal established a Climate Change Council under the chairmanship of the prime minister. The council included experts, scientists, researchers and policy planners. A Climate Change Management Division was also established in the Ministry of Forest and Environment. The division has been made responsible for addressing all levels of climate-change issues and coordinating public, private and international agencies, groups and individuals. The National Planning Commission of Nepal has also brought a Climate Change Budget Code to allocate annual funding for the cause of climate change.

Between 2008 and 2021, more than eight different governments have come into power. No government has been able to further or implement the policies. Political instability had almost jeopardised the country's policy planning. For instance, the UN Green Climate Fund was formed in 2010, but Nepal could attain its first share in grants only in 2019.[48] The mismatch between availability and availing funds is a gap widened due to many factors, among which unstable governments is also an important reason. The policy visualisation of climate change through the lens of scientific research, climate justice, development, hunger, poverty and proposed options for a prosperous Nepal is of utmost need. In 2011, the Government of Nepal came up with a climate change policy to address the adverse impact of climate change in the country. It was one of the rare occasions when Nepal released an essential document on climate. The policy's cardinal features were the objectives of the policy aiming to reduce greenhouse gas emissions by providing alternate energy sources, including its abundant hydro energy, building programmes for public awareness regarding the uses of clean energy and better management of the natural resources and low-carbon emissions. To execute these, the government has also established an Alternative Energy Promotion Center to facilitate the country's Clean Development Mechanism. The policy had further been revised in 2019. The new policy has been brought in line with the country's 2015 constitution, which guarantees fundamental rights to its people to live in a clean and healthy environment.

The creation of domestic policy based on international compulsions is to achieve the desired funding under international mechanisms. Drawing attention to the severity of climate change issues in a small state like Nepal requires immense work from the government of small states. Nepal has been taking active steps in displaying its climate-conscious image; the Government of Nepal under Madhav Kumar held a cabinet meeting at Everest Base Camp, whose slogan was "Save the Himalayas" with a 10-point Everest Declaration.[49] In April 2020, the Government of Nepal organized *Sagarmatha Sambad* (Everest Dialogue) to bring global attention to the climate vulnerability of Nepal. However, it was cancelled due to the COVID-19 pandemic:

> The first *Sambad* was to be convened on April 2–4, but it has been postponed due to the pandemic. Although Nepal has invited the US, India and China to participate in the deliberations, a no-show for Nepal at the Climate Summit says a thousand words of an increasing unease in Washington DC towards Nepal. For the record, Nepal has prioritised

climate change as a "national security threat" in its first-ever National Security Policy 2016; it stands as a political manifestation to seek international funds for the cause.[50]

The climate policies in Nepal have never been determined entirely from within the country and were influenced by international actors.[51] In developing countries, including Nepal, donors shape spaces for participation and negotiation around climate policy. In 2014, Nepal made a joint statement on SAARC's behalf for equity and CBDR-RC, asking rich nations to reduce their emissions. At the local level, the climate change policy in 2011 defended community rights in adaptation techniques by entitling local communities to up to 80 per cent of the total climate change funds and initiating community-based adaptation actions.[52] It also promoted climate adaptation through technology development, capacity building and access to financial resources. However, the policy doesn't identify a clear implementation path and make local communities only passive partner.

Climate Change Adaptation and Disaster Risk Management in Agriculture is another policy brought in by the Government of Nepal. Priority Framework for Action 2011–2020 provides a road map for the MOAC towards proactive climate adaptation and climate risk management in the agriculture sector.[53] Also, of the eight strategic pillars of the Forestry Sector Strategy, 2016–2025, climate change mitigation and resilience are essential aspects.[54] The National REDD+ Strategy, 2018 also aims to reduce carbon emissions and achieve ecosystem resilience through mitigation and adaptation.[55] The National Adaptation Plans (NAPs) 2015 focuses on building adaptive capacity and integrating climate change adaptation at different levels in existing policies/plans.[56] The 2015 Nepalese constitution and Local Government Operation Act, 2017, have given the local bodies (Gaunpalika/Nagarpalika) responsibility to undertake climate change adaptation activities.[57] Nepal's major climate policies and frameworks emerged during 2008–12, along with its first Constituent Assembly election in 2013. The major policies, the National Adaptation Programme of Action (NAPA), "came with the support of United Nations Development Programme (UNDP) and the Climate Policy, the WWF rather than national and local deliberations with affected people and political representatives".[58]

Additionally, the two major institutional structures involved in climate policy-making in Nepal are the Climate Change Council (CCC), formed in 2009 and the Multi-stakeholder Climate Change Initiatives Coordination Committee (MCCICC) during the NAPA process in 2010.[59] The MCCICC has no community representation provision.[60] The committees involve members of the government, experts and civil society.

> The CCC is the highest-level body, chaired by the Prime Minister and provides long term policy and strategic guidelines for climatic change

activities in the country, while the MCCICC formed under the Ministry of Environment aims at contributing to the climate change-related programmes in Nepal.[61]

The NAPA 2010 identified climate change adaptation as an urgent priority programme for different sectors. However, there are some drawbacks to the plan, such as limited importance to institutional reforms and the capacity building of the local bodies for implementation. The NAPA 2010 is critiqued as "an incomplete and toothless" document biased in favour of central-level prejudices, as out of the nine prioritised activities envisaged, only four are community-centric.[62] The delay in the creation of NAPA occurred due to poor understanding among donors (Global Environment Facility), facilitator (UNDP) and the implementor (Nepal's Ministry of Environment) of the plan.[63]

With government procedures for adaptation in place, the local population has also adapted to the climate stresses. Autonomous adaptation includes individual or collective responses that people, communities, businesses and other agencies undertake on their own in response to the opportunities and constraints they face as the climate changes. In Nepal, autonomous adaptation occurs mainly in the poor-documented informal sector.[64]

Working Policies on Climate Change

Under a unified policy on climate change, the Government of Nepal has introduced specific sectoral policies, strategies and working policies. These particular departments prepare these policies and strategies under the Ministries of Agriculture, Environment, Tourism, Food and Health.

Forest, Biodiversity and Watershed Conservation

The policy aims to minimise the carbon footprint and increase sustainable forest management. Also, it seeks to protect biodiversity through the means of green practices. Although the policy exists, it is still lagging on the action plan, which is affected mainly by the coordination between the government's different agencies.

Agriculture and Food Security Policy

The agriculture and food security policy covers a large spectrum of issues from food security to livelihood, nutrition and sustainable and green agricultural practices. It aims to adopt welfare programmes for the poor and marginalised communities, the rights of the ethnic groups and protect the traditional modes of clean and sustainable ways of farming.

Water Resources and Energy Policy

Nepal has an abundance of the wealth of water. It has an estimated 42,000 MW hydropower potential which has hardly been exploited.[65] It is partly due to the absence of a stable political environment that can successfully implement the policies and join third-world countries to exploit the potential. Since Nepal lacks on the technological front, it has neighbours like India interested in exploiting hydro energy to be used by both countries. However, amidst the rising political tensions with India, projects like Mahakali have not moved any further in last two decades.

Additionally, Nepal has further brought in a Rural and Urban Habitat Policy; Industry, Transport and Physical Infrastructure Policy; Tourism and Natural and Cultural Heritage Policy; Health, Drinking Water and Sanitation Policy; Disaster Risk Reduction and Management Policy; Gender Equality and Social Inclusion; Livelihoods and Good Governance Policy; Awareness Raising and Capacity Building Policy; Research, Technology Development and Expansion Policy; and Climate Finance Management Policy. Other than the policy framework, the institutional framework on climate change is responsible for closely examining the federation's role, Province a Local Level, in implementing the National Climate Policy.[66]

Challenges to Implementation of Policies

In 2016, climate change was added as the national security threat in its first-ever National Security Policy. The policy is a comprehensive document that analyses Nepal's national security challenges and places climate change among the traditional security understanding as a milestone achievement. While the national security apparatus of Nepal has mostly been based on the conventional understanding of national security and considered the dedicated domain of the security forces, the inclusion of non-traditional security threats such as climate change, natural disasters, floods and droughts was introduced as part of the 1994 United Nations Human Development Report which had for the first time emphasised on the non-traditional security threats. While Nepal's government has introduced the 2016 National Security Policy and other policies on climate change, they lack a plan of action. For instance, despite being revised in 2018, the National Security Policy is projected as a political tool for seeking funds from international agencies. During an interview, a high-level officer in the Nepal Army revealed that by bringing climate change into the national security policy, the government had projected climate change as a tool to get humanitarian findings. In reality, these funds are not used correctly, and poor policy planning, political instability, corruption, lack of action plan, mismanagement of resources and coordination between different departments.

Climate Change, Human Mobility and Human Rights

Human mobility is often induced by climate change, which results in the direct denial of people's fundamental rights.[67] Natural disasters cover an entire episode of human lives where fundamental rights are violated or withheld by the state. Denial of basic services such as medical, freshwater, mental health, menstrual hygiene, education or food makes a dent in the right to life with dignity. The absence of a proper mechanism to address natural disasters in light of the country's critical seismological and meteorological location troubles the vulnerable population to meet the emergency response. In this light, this section discusses the Nepal earthquake as a product of climate change and its eventual impact on the life of the public. It also establishes the relationship between natural disasters and the citizens' fundamental rights that stand pale or denied in the wake of an earthquake, tsunami or flood.[68]

Right to Life with Dignity

The right to life with dignity was added to the Universal Declaration of Human Rights in 1950.[69] It was laid in access to health, food, water, work and education. While such declarations have made it easier for international agencies to set universal parameters to protect an individual's rights, the state's failure to provide basic services leads to violations. For instance, during the 2015 earthquake, Nepal fell short of managing the emergency crisis initially; it also failed to provide help to the affected and vulnerable. In the aftermath of the 2015 earthquake, human mobility was on the rise as no primary sources of income generation were available locally.[70] At the same time, the state should have made prior policy planning to provide immediate relief to the affected population. However, an outward migration was.[71]

Health

Since disasters are considered the windows that bring vulnerability to the front, Nepal's 2015 earthquake was an eye-opener to the existing inequalities in Nepalese society. The United Nations Human Development Report of 2015 ranked the country at 145. It was 108 in the Global Innovation Index and ranked second-lowest in human development.[72] The maternal mortality rate stood at 190 deaths per 1 lakh births.[73] Amidst such low health indicators, an earthquake of high magnitude was life-threatening and challenging. As per the 2011 census, Nepal had 102 total health facilities across the country.[74] However, the state-run hospitals and local healthcare units lacked the fundamental infrastructure to provide emergency services to the earthquake's affected people. The UN estimated that "662 (83.5 per cent) of the 793 public health facilities in the 14 most-affected districts were destroyed or partially damaged".[75] After major health facilities were destroyed by the earthquake in the 14 most-affected districts of Nepal, emergency services were provided by third countries, including India, China, Japan and other international agencies, including the United Nations, Doctors Beyond Borders and Red Cross. Women's health was a critical challenge for all as pregnant and lactating women had to be provided with immediate help. Other than the climate-induced human displacement due to earthquakes, mental health was also a challenge to Nepal.[76] The earthquake also left a long-term impact on the mental health of the population. Several studies on natural disasters have reported that mental health is on the least priority list for several countries in South Asia. In Nepal, the World Health Organization and the International Organization for Migration reported that Nepal's capacity to address mental health care in the post-earthquake was dire.[77] Therefore, in the cycle of climate change, health needs to be seen as a fundamental need. It is understood that a natural disaster may destroy health infrastructure, but the country has to be prepared for emergency health response in ratio to the population.[78]

Education

The Gorkha earthquake destroyed the educational infrastructure of the country. In its preliminary report on the impact of the earthquake on education, the United Nations Children's Fund reported that at least "950,000 children will not be able to return to school unless urgent action is to provide temporary learning spaced and repair the school buildings".[79] It also added that at least 24,000 classrooms were damaged. While the large-scale displacement due to the earthquake had brought life to a standstill, issues like education were minute but remained challenging.

Housing and Livelihood

Affected and damaged by the earthquake, an estimated 750,000 houses were the affected population's immediate requirements. Housing was the most significant physical loss for the country. To reconstruct these houses, Nepal organised an International Conference to bring international donors to contribute. Other than India, China, the United States, and Canada, the international Agencies pledged US$4.1 billion for reconstruction purposes. Meanwhile, the internal displacement further increased the requirement for housing facilities. An estimated number of IDPs living in 409 camps grew to 117,000 by the beginning of June 2015.[80] While the process to provide homes back to the affected population continues to date, it has/had a long-lasting impact on the population's livelihood. As Nepal is a non-industrial economy and today, remittances, agriculture and service sectors stand as the

Nepalese GDP's three main pillars. Since migration studies have found labour migration a preferred occupational option to seek employment in post-disaster situations, Nepal experienced a similar pattern of labour migration. Among the 14 most affected districts of Nepal, an average of 5 per cent was already working abroad, and remittances were the primary source of income. The Central Department of Population Studies at the Tribhuvan University in Nepal estimated that at least 3.4 per cent of people in the rural and 1.6 per cent of people in the urban areas chose to migrate for work.[81] The quest to migrate was majorly driven by the lack of opportunities within the country in the post-earthquake phase. To build a house and achieve these, migration became one of the choices for internally displaced people.

Conclusion

The plight of Nepali citizens as internally displaced persons is not a new phenomenon. Climate-induced natural disasters like floods, landslides, hostile living conditions, scarcity of sources of livelihood and the spread of epidemics like Malaria in the hills and mountainous region have compelled Nepalese to migrate and displace from one region to another. While people in the upper-lower and lower belts of Nepal are used to adjusting themselves to the conditions wherever such calamities occur, it affects livelihood and employment. Climate change-induced human mobility is not by choice but by circumstances, and it has a lasting impact on the future of lives. Human mobility results in *ad hoc* displacement, emergency evacuation, and migration to neighbouring countries, and sometimes planned evacuations are re-settlements are made. However, in the absence of long-term impact plans, strategies, proper technology regarding infrastructure development, and a stable government, climate change will continue to remain unprioritised. Nepal has been facing floods and earthquakes as the two critical vulnerabilities, yet no mechanism has been deployed so far. For instance, Nepal is still facing post-earthquake recoveries and faces the challenge of a lack of funds. The non-existence of disaster management planning has increased the impact of disasters like an earthquake on people and infrastructure. Nepal has brought in a few policies to chalk out climate concerns, but they require proper attention and actionable planning.

Meanwhile, it needs to be noted that despite a correlation established by some of the studies between climate change and human mobility in Nepal, the lack of substantial work from the Government of Nepal makes the issue less attentive. Nepal's Department of Meteorology and Hydrology observed Nepal's average "maximum temperature has risen by 0.056 degree Celsius. Also . . . the average maximum temperatures in all seasons in Nepal have increased for the period 1971–2014".[82] In this context, a correlation can be established between migration from hills and Terai within Nepal and outside. Yet, it will need substantial attention from the Government of Nepal considering the proximity and coverage of the aimed studies. The 2015 earthquake and annual floods are a common phenomenon, witnessing large-scale human mobility in Nepal, and they demand close consideration at the policy and execution level.

Notes

1 Partha Ghosh (2003), *Migrants, refugees and the stateless in South Asia*. New Delhi: SAGE.
2 Ibid.
3 Justin Ginnetti and Chris Lavell (2015), "The risk of disaster-induced displacement in South Asia: Disasters, climate change and displacement", *Internal Displacement Monitoring Centre*, 8, accessed from www.internal-displacement.org/sites/default/files/publications/documents/201504-ap-south-asia-disaster-induced-displacement-risk-en.pdf on 9th November 2020.
4 Ibid, 40–41.
5 Hemchandra Chaulagain, Dipendra Gautam and Hugo Rodrigues (2018), "Revisiting major historical earthquakes in Nepal: Overview of 1833, 1934, 1980, 1988, 2011, and 2015 seismic events", in Dipendra Gautam and Hugo Rodrigues (eds.) *Impacts and insights of the Gorkha earthquake*. New Delhi: Elsevier, 1–2.
6 R. K. Shrestha, R. Ahlers, M. Bakker and J. Gupta (2010), "Institutional dysfunction and challenges in flood control: A case study of the Kosi flood 2008", *Economic and Political Weekly*, 45(2), 45–53.
7 IDMC (2018a), "Lost production due to internal displacement: The 2015 earthquake in Nepal", *Internal-Displacement*, accessed from www.internal-displacement.org/sites/default/files/publications/documents/20180625-economic-impacts-nepal.pdf on 7th April 2021.
8 UNISDR (2015, 25 April), "Gorkha earthquake disaster risk reduction situation report", *United Nations Office for Disaster Risk Reduction*, accessed from www.preventionweb.net/files/44592_gorkhaearthquakedisasterriskreducti.pdf on 3rd April 2021; Also see IDMC (2018b), "The ripple effect: Economic impacts", *Internal Displacement Monitoring Center*, accessed on https://reliefweb.int/sites/reliefweb.int/files/resources/63238_20180625economicimpactsnepal.pdf on 16th May 2021.
9 IDMC, 2018b, Ibid.
10 IPCC Report 2022, 4, accessed from www.ipcc.ch/report/ar6/wg2/downloads/report/IPCC_AR6_WGII_FinalDraft_FullReport.pdf on 9 April 2022.
11 R. Jha (2010), "Total run-of-river type hydropower potential of Nepal", *Journal of Water, Energy and Environment*, 7(7), 8–13, accessed from https://doi.org/10.3126/hn.v7i0.4226 on 29th December 2020; Note: "The total hydropower potential of Nepal was assessed as 83,500 MW in 1966 by Dr Hari Man Shrestha during his PhD research work in former USSR". As cited in "Raghunath Jha, (January 2011) Total Run-of-River type Hydropower Potential of Nepal Hydro Nepal Journal of Water Energy and Environment".
12 Rajan Bhattarai (2003), *Geopolitics of Nepal and international responses to conflict transformation*. Kathmandu: Friends for Peace.
13 Ivar Kolstad and Tina Søreide (2008), "Corruption in natural resource management: Implications for policy makers", *Resources Policy*, 34, 14–26, https://doi.org/10.1016/j.resourpol.2009.05.001

14 CIT (2020), Geography of Nepal, accessed from http://web.gps.caltech.edu/~avouac/nepal_trip/geography.htm#:~:text=Nepal%20is%20topographically%20divided%20into,of%20the%20total%20land%20area on 9th November 2020.
15 Ibid.
16 R. Shrestha, Nanda (1997), *In the name of development: A reflection on Nepal.* New York: University Press of America.
17 Sarita Lama and Bhupendra Devkota (2009), "Vulnerability of mountain communities to climate change and adaptation strategies", *Journal of Food Agriculture and Environment*, 10, 65.
18 Shardul Agrawala, et al. (2003), "Development and climate change in Nepal: Focus on water resources and hydropower", *OCDE. Organisation for Economic Co-operation and Development and Organisation de Coopération et de DéveloppementEconomiques*, accessed from www.oecd.org/countries/nepal/19742202.pdf on 7th December 2020.
19 Ibid, 12.
20 Lama and Bhupendra, op. cit., 65.
21 Sunil N. Lohani (2007, 26 December), "Climate change in Nepal: Shall we wait until bitter consequences?", *Journal of Agriculture and Environment*, 8, 38–45, https://doi.org/10.3126/aej.v8i0.725
22 A. B. Shrestha and R. Aryal (2011, 17 November), "Climate change in Nepal and its impact on Himalayan Glaciers", *Regional Environmental Change*, 65–77, https://doi.org/10.1007/s10113-010-0174-9.
23 Lama and Devkota, op. cit.
24 World Bank (2021), *Agriculture, forestry, and fishing, value Added (% of GDP) – Nepal.* World Bank, accessed from https://data.worldbank.org/indicator/NV.AGR.TOTL.ZS?locations=NP on 7th May 2021.
25 GoN (2021), *Agriculture sector profile.* Kathmandu: Office of the Investment Board, Government of Nepal, 5, accessed from https://ibn.gov.np/wp-content/uploads/2020/04/Agriculture-Sector-Profile.pdf on 7th May 2021.
26 GoN (2017), *Post flood recovery assessment report. Flood assessment, national planning commission.* Kathmandu: National Planning Commission, Government of Nepal, accessed from https://reliefweb.int/sites/reliefweb.int/files/resources/PFRNA%20Report.pdf on 9th November 2020.
27 P. Mool, S. K. Bajracharya and S. R. Joshi (2001), *Inventory of glaciers, glacial lakes and glacial lake outburst floods: Monitoring and early warning systems in the Hindu Kush-Himalayan Region Nepal.* Kathmandu: International Center for Integrated Mountain Development ICIMOD; Ajaya Dixit (2020), *Climate change in Nepal: Impacts and adaptive strategies*, accessed from www.wri.org/our-work/project/world-resources-report/climate-change-nepal-impacts-and-adaptive-strategies on 9th April 2021.
28 Ibid.
29 CDES-TU (2018), *Climate change vulnerability, impact, and adaptation assessment.* Kathmandu: Central Department of Environmental Science, Tribhuvan University, accessed from www.mofe.gov.np/search/#notice184 on 30th March 2021.
30 Ibid.
31 Ajaya Dixit, Madhukar Upadhya, Anil Pokhrel, Kanchan Mani Dixit, Deeb Raj Rai and Madhav Devkota (2007), *Flood disaster impact and responses in Nepal Tarai's marginalised basins in working with the winds of change: Towards strategies for responding to the risks associated with climate change and other hazards* (2nd ed.). Kathmandu: Institute for Social and

Environmental Transition-International and Institute for Social and Environmental Transition-Nepal.

32 WEPA (2020), "Water environment partnership in Asia", accessed from www.wepa-db.net/policies/state/nepal/state.htm on 9th December 2020.

33 Asian Development Bank (2020), *Protecting valuable agricultural lands from destructive floods in Nepal*. Asian Development Bank, accessed from www.adb.org/news/features/protecting-valuable-agricultural-lands-destructive-floods-nepal on 6 May 2021.

34 Ajaya Dixit, Madhukar Upadhya, et al., op. cit.

35 GoN, 2017, op. cit.

36 CDES-TU, 2018, op. cit.

37 GoN, 2017, op. cit.

38 Basistha Raj Adhikari (2013), "Flooding and inundation in Nepal Terai: Issues and concerns", *Hydro Nepal*, 13, 59–69; M. J. Creed, H. D. Sinclair, D. Gautam, N. Gourmelen, A. G. L. Borthwick and M. Attal (2020), "Dynamic flood topographies in the Terai region of Nepal", *Earth Surface Processes and Landforms* (John Wiley & Sons Ltd.), 45, 3092; Santosh Pathak, Hari Krishna Panta, Thaneshwar Bhandari and Krishna P. Paudel (2020), "Flood vulnerability and its influencing factors in Nepal", *Natural Hazards*, 104, 2178.

39 Aishwarya Bhattacharjee, José D. Anadón, David J. Lohman, Tenzing Doleck, Tarendra Lakhankar, Bharat Babu Shrestha, Praseed Thapa, Durga Devkota, Sundar Tiwari, Ajay Jha, Mohan Siwakoti, Naba R. Devkota, Pramod K. Jha and Nir Y. Krakauer (2017), "The impact of climate change on biodiversity in Nepal: Current knowledge, lacunae, and opportunities", *Climate*, 5(4), 80, https://doi.org/10.3390/cli5040080.

40 Nabin Baral, M. S. Heinen and T. Joel (2005), "The Maoist people's war and conservation in Nepal", *Politics and the Life Sciences*, 24(1), 2–11.

41 Sabita Thapa, Lisa Schipper, Moon Shrestha, Santosh Nepal, Anna Taylor and Tahia Devisscher (2011), *Nepal ecosystems, development, and climate adaptation improving the knowledge base for planning, policy and management*. Stockholm: Stockholm Environment Institute, 1–26, accessed from www.weadapt.org/sites/weadapt.org/files/legacy-new/placemarks/files/5028cb4cb0926final-nepal-report-sei-asia-march-2011.pdf on 9th November 2020.

42 Ibid.

43 World Bank, 2021, op. cit.; Rishi Gupta (2020, 9 April), "Covid-19 in Nepal: Low numbers don't tell the whole story", accessed from https://southasianvoices.org/covid-19-in-nepal-low-numbers-dont-tell-the-whole-story/ on 9th April 2020.

44 Bandana Shrestha and Som Niroula (2005), "Internally displaced persons in Nepal", *Peace and Democracy in South Asia*, 1(2), 44–55; Ritendra Tamang (2009), "Internally displaced persons in Nepal: Neglected and vulnerable", *Asian Social Science*, 5(6), https://doi.org/10.5539/ass.v5n6p3

45 Daniel Buckley (2015, 29 April), "Nepal: A lesson in the risks climate change poses to disaster-prone countries", *United Nations Development Programme*, accessed from www.asia-pacific.undp.org/content/rbap/en/home/blog/2015/4/29/-Nepal-A-lesson-in-the-risks-climate-change-poses-to-disaster-prone-countries.html on 30th March 2021.

46 Ibid.

47 World Wide Fund for Nature (2020), "Climate change and global glacier decline", *World Wide Fund for Nature*, accessed from https://wwfeu.awsassets.panda.org/downloads/glacierspaper.pdf on 9th May 2021; A. J. McMichael, et al. (2003), "Climate change and human health: Risks and responses", *World*

Health Organization, accessed from www.who.int/globalchange/publications/climchange.pdf on 22nd April 2021.

48 Sumit Vija, Robbert Biesbroeka, Annemarie Grootb and Katrien Termeera (2018), "Changing climate policy paradigms in Bangladesh and Nepal", *Environmental Science & Policy*, 81, 77–85.

49 Kamal Dev Bhattarai and Sujata Karki (2020, 27 January), *Nepal gets serious about climate change*. accessed from https://thediplomat.com/2020/01/nepal-gets-serious-about-climate-change/ on 14th December 2020.

50 Rishi Gupta (2021, 3 May), "Nepal gets the cold shoulder", *The Pioneer*, accessed from www.dailypioneer.com/2021/columnists/nepal-gets-the-cold-shoulder.html on 5th May 2021.

51 Hemant R. Ojha, Sharad Ghimire, Adam Pain, Andrea Nightingale, Dil B. Khatri and Hari Dhungana (2015), "Policy without politics: Technocratic control of climate change adaptation policy making in Nepal", *Climate Policy*, 16(4), 415–433.

52 UNDP (2011), *Nepal's climate change policies and plans: Local communities' perspective – January 2011*. HELVETAS Swiss Interco-operation Nepal, accessed from www.adaptation-undp.org/sites/default/files/downloads/nepals_climate_change_policies_and_plans_2011.pdf on 21st December 2020.

53 GoN (2012), *Climate change adaptation and disaster risk management in agriculture – priority framework for action 2011–2020*. Kathmandu: Climate, Energy and Tenure Division, accessed from www.dpnet.org.np/public/uploads/files/CCA%20and%20DRM%20in%20agriculture%202019-07-25%20 11-00-31.pdf; Sundar Kumar Sharma (2011), "The political economy of climate change governance in the Himalayan Region of Asia: A case study of Nepal", *Procedia-Social and Behavioral Sciences*, 14, 129–140.

54 MoFSC (2016), *Forestry sector strategy 2016–25*. Kathmandu: Ministry of Forestry, Soil and Climate, accessed from http://mofe.gov.np/downloadfile/Forestry%20Sector%20Strategy%20%20(2016–2025)_1526466721.pdf on 9th December 2020.

55 MoFE (2018), *Nepal national REDD+ strategy (2018–2022)*. Kathmandu: Ministry of Forests and Environment.

56 UN (2012), *National adaptation plan: Technical guidelines for the national adaptation plan process*. United Nations Framework Convention on Climate Change, accessed from https://unfccc.int/files/adaptation/cancun_adaptation_framework/application/pdf/naptechguidelines_eng_high__res.pdf on 8th December 2020.

57 Sundar Kumar Sharma (2011), "The political economy of climate change governance in the Himalayan Region of Asia: A case study of Nepal", *Procedia-Social and Behavioral Sciences*, 14, 129–140.

58 Ojha et al., 2015, op. cit.

59 Nanki Kaur (2015), *Climate change planning in Nepal*. The Green Growth Best Practices, accessed from www.greengrowthknowledge.org/sites/default/files/downloads/best-practices/GGBP%20Case%20Study%20Series_Nepal_Climate%20Change%20Planning.pdf on 30th November 2020; Pashupati Nepal (2019), "Mainstreaming climate change adaptation into sectoral", *The Geographical Journal of Nepal*, 12(1).

60 Asian Development Bank (2021), *Linked document 4C: ADB support for climate change adaptation and mitigation in Nepal*. Asian Development Bank, accessed from www.adb.org/sites/default/files/linked-documents/Linked-Document-4c-ADB-Support-for-Climate-Change-Adaptation-and-Mitigation-in-NEP.pdf on 30th March 2021.

61 Dil Khatri, et al. (2015), *Climate change, local politics and institutional responses in Nepal: A synthesis of research findings*. Kathmandu: Forest Action Nepal.

62 UNDP, 2011, op. cit.
63 Ibid.
64 Dixit, *Climate Change in Nepal.*
65 Ramesh Prasad Bhatt (2017), "Hydropower development in Nepal – climate change, impacts and implications", in Basel I. Ismail (ed.) *Renewable hydropower technologies*, Intech Open, accessed from www.intechopen.com/books/renewable-hydropower-technologies/hydropower-development-in-nepal-climate-change-impacts-and-implications.
66 MoFE, 2018, op. cit.
67 OHCHR (2018, 22 March), "The slow onset effects of climate change and human rights protection for cross-border migrants", accessed from www.ohchr.org/Documents/Issues/ClimateChange/SlowOnset/A_HRC_37_CRP_4.pdf on 24th November 2020.
68 Elizabeth Ferris (2010, 3 March), "Natural disasters, conflict, and human rights: Tracing the connections", accessed from www.brookings.edu/wp-content/uploads/2016/06/0303_natural_disasters_ferris.pdf on 8th November 2020.
69 UN (1948), *Universal declaration of human rights*. United Nations, accessed from www.un.org/en/about-us/universal-declaration-of-human-rights on 7th April 2021.
70 Nansen Initiative (2015, February), "Climate change, disasters, and human mobility in South Asia", accessed from www.unisdr.org/preventionweb/files/61746_climatechangedisastersandhumanmobil.pdf on 4th May 2021.
71 Sonja Ayeb-Karlsson (2015, 6 July), "Nepal earthquake: Preparing and planning for the next disaster", accessed from https://ehs.unu.edu/blog/articles/nepal-earthquake-preparing-and-planning-for-the-next-disaster.html on 14th October 2020.
72 UNDP (1994), *Human development report 1994*. New York: Oxford University Press, 1–226.
73 Ibid.
74 CBS (2014), *Population monograph of Nepal*. Central Bureau of Statistics (CBS), accessed from http://cbs.gov.np/image/data/Population/Population%20Monograph%20of%20Nepal%202014/Population%20Monograph%20of%20Nepal%202014%20Volume%20I%20FinalPrintReady1.pdf on 8th January 2021.
75 Sophie Goyet and Rajan Rayamajhi (2017), "Post-earthquake health-service support, Nepal", accessed from www.who.int/bulletin/volumes/96/4/17-205666/en/ on 7th November 2020.
76 IDMC, 2018b, op. cit.
77 IOM (2016, 26 June), "Nepal: Thousands remain displaced from earthquake, exposed to impact of coming monsoon season", *International Organization for Migration*, accessed from www.iom.int/news/nepal-thousands-remain-displaced-earthquake-exposed-impact-coming-monsoon-season on 1st June 2021.
78 Elisa Lai (2017, 7 August), "Displacement and migration induced by 2015 Nepal earthquake", accessed from https://medium.com/@elailai94/displacement-and-migration-induced-by-2015-nepal-earthquake-33deebf8ba48 on 1st June 2021.
79 UNICEF (2015, 7 May), "Nepal Earthquake: Education for nearly 1 million children in jeopardy – UNICEF", accessed from www.unicef.org/rosa/press-releases/nepal-earthquake-education-nearly-1-million-children-jeopardy-unicef on 1st June 2021.
80 Lai, 2017, op. cit.

81 Ganesh Gurung (2018), *2015 earthquake as a driver of labour migration*. Kathmandu: South Asia Watch on Trade, Economics and Environment (SAWTEE).
82 Chandan Kumar Mandal (2017, 27 August), "Average annual temp rose by 0.056-degree Celsius in the past 4 decades", *Kathmandu Post*, accessed from https://bit.ly/3ugFPTd on 1st June 2021.

Chapter 10

Pakistan's Climate Migrants Beyond Mediatized Fictions

Farooq Sulehria

Introduction

Though the exiting discourses on global migration do not count fast-changing environmental patterns as the sole or primary cause behind the human displacements, yet climate change is increasingly and justifiably factoring in emerging migration-related discourses, as well as media narratives, as an exacerbating component. That climate is a threat multiplier is largely accepted.[1]

Aforementioned statement *in toto* applies to the case of Pakistan, a country categorized by the 2018 Long Term Climate Risk Index as the 7th most affected land. Likewise, United Nation's Intergovernmental Panel on Climate Change (IPCC) in its 2022 report placed Pakistan in highly vulnerable countries. Earthquakes, flash floods, droughts and landslides not merely take a tragic toll on human life but also inflict huge financial costs on Pakistan's fledging and struggling economy: $2 billion annually.[2] Table 10.1 demonstrates the enormity of Pakistan's climatic apocalypse on a global scale: of the five biggest natural catastrophe, globally, during 2000–2010, two afflicted Pakistan. In 2022, Pakistan was yet again making global headlines owing to devastating flood in summer 2022. While one-third Pakistan was submerged, flash floods strafed 33 million people and displaced another 8 million. Besides 1739 deaths, these floods damaged infrastructure and livelihoods worth $16 billion.[3] A glimpse into infrastructural and economic damage: 13,115 kilometre-long stretch of roads, 439 bridges and 2.2 million houses were washed away besides 1,164,270 livestock.[4] Crops over 4 million acres were wrecked invoking fears of mass hunger.[5]

As regards the migration induced by climatic calamities, two major events symbolize the scale of the problem under consideration. In 2005, a catastrophic earthquake that jolted North Pakistan and adjacent districts in Pakistan-administered Jammu and Kashmir, left over 80,000 dead besides displacing four million people.

Likewise, in 2010, one-fourth of Pakistan's landmass was submerged when the routine monsoon downpour kept showering down for weeks. Only in

DOI:10.4324/9781003367802-11

Swat valley, perched in the Hindukush foothills, over a million people were rendered homeless (in total, 14 million were re-located on temporary basis). In either case, a sizeable number of displaced people did not return to their lost homes. Reasons abound and will be highlighted in a while.

Meantime, the state in Pakistan is ill prepared to deal with the climate-induced migration which needless to say is an unfolding catastrophe with huge social, political and economic consequences. And this is exactly what this chapter argues on two counts.

For the first, Pakistan is not investing required financial resources to deal with climatic changes and related human migrations. Largely, Pakistan counts on international community. The international gaze, in turn, is often drawn to mediatized human catastrophes of immediate nature.

Secondly, instead of introducing strategies and preparing the citizens to cope with climate challenges, worsening environmental crises are blamed on 'arch enemy' India: while floods during monsoon are described as 'water terrorism' by India which happens to be the upper riparian, smog in the winter season is attributed to burning of stubble in the adjacent Indian state of the Punjab.

This chapter is also aimed at flagging up socio-political consequences of hosting refugees and migrants. Pakistan is a country where human migrations, since its inception in 1947, has generated bloody ethnic conflicts. Hence, it is imperative to learn some lessons and draw conclusions to avoid future tragedies.

However, to demonstrate the aforementioned thesis, this chapter also maps the sheer scale of Pakistan's environmental challenges and documents inadequate institutional arrangements to deal with climate-related calamities and displacements.

Accordingly, this chapter is organized in the following manner. Section 1 maps Pakistan's burgeoning climate challenge and the migratory waves it entails. Section 2 deals with inadequate preparation to deal with climate-induced challenges including migration. Before Conclusion, the socio-political consequences of climate-migrations are explored in Section 3. Section 3 also draws on Thomas Homer-Dixon's[6] conceptualization of 'environmental scarcity' to establish a link between climate change, migration and conflict.

Section 1: Pakistan's Climate Challenge and Future Migrations

Pakistan's history is marked by multi-dimensional crises: political instability, corruption, terrorism, unaccountable power elite, ethnic conflicts, sectarian strife, population explosion, external debt and separatism.

Not merely these problems have been lingering on, a drastic in-the-face climate change 1980s onwards has aggravated all the crises mentioned earlier. "Pakistan's biggest threat isn't terrorism – it's climate change," reads a

Foreign Policy headline.[7] Though the *Foreign Policy* headline sounds cruel (calamities and tragedies should not be hierarchized) yet the message cannot be ignored. Only in the past two decades, natural calamities have twice paralyzed Pakistan – as mentioned earlier, October 2005 earthquake and July 2010 flash floods. Worst in 80 years, July 2010 floods claimed 1,800 lives and the country suffered an economic loss worth US$10 billion.[8]

However, floods almost an annual phenomenon in Pakistan like the rest of South Asia and earthquake are not the only challenges. The United Nations International Strategy for Disaster Reduction (UNISDR) identifies the following five categories of natural disasters threatening Pakistan:

> Geophysical (earthquake, tsunami), hydrological (floods, landslides, avalanches), metrological (storms, cyclones, extreme temperature, dust storms), climatological (drought, glacial lake outburst flood [glof]), biological (epidemics and pandemics).[9]

One region or the other is routinely hit by one of the five calamities during every season of the year. While the annual monsoon seasons synonymize floods, glofs and landslides make headlines during the autumn. Heatwaves during the summer is yet another established fact. For instance, the heatwave in Karachi, country's largest metropolitan with roughly 20 million residents, left 1200 dead in 2015.[10] Another 65,000 were hospitalised.[11] The country has weathered 15 cyclones between 1971 and 2010.[12] The cyclone that hit, in 2010, Thatta and Badin districts on the coast of Arabian sea claimed 168 lives, wiped out 73 settlements and destroyed 11000 cattleheads besides destroying 1800 fishing boats. In total, 0.6 million people were affected.[13]

Table 10.1 A comparison of Pakistan's major disasters 2000–2010 with global international calamities

	Pakistan floods 2010	*Pakistan earthquake 2005*	*Katrina cyclone USA 2005*	*Nargis cyclone Myanmar 2008*	*Indian Ocean tsunami 2004*	*Haiti earthquake 2010*
Deaths	1,985	73,338	1,836	84,537	238,000	230,000
Population affected (in million)	20.2	3.5	0.5	2.4	2.2	3.2
Area affected (square km)	132, 000	30,000	NA	23,500	NA	13,226

Source: NDMA Annual Reports 2010–2018. Available at http://web.ndma.gov.pk/publications.php

Drought, according to the National Disaster Management Authority (NDMA), prevails for two to three years in southern parts of the country, affecting three of the four provinces. NDMA's annual report for 2011 notes, "Serious drought periods in 1998–2002 affected livelihoods, resulted in human deaths, forced tens of thousands people to migrate and also destroyed a large number of cattleheads. The drought led to 120 casualties".[14]

If we only take extreme weather conditions into account, Pakistan suffered 152 such events during 1999–2018. These extreme weather incidents claimed 9,989 lives besides inflicting an economic damage worth US$3.8 billion.[15] During the first decade of present century, two of the six most devastating natural catastrophes, globally, hit Pakistan.

While earthquake in 2005 proved most fatal in terms of causalities and destruction, yet it is the phenomenon of floods that pose actual climatic challenge in terms of economic damages, development and climate-induced migration. Table 10.2 demonstrates that floods rank as the number one natural disaster, while Table 10.3 demonstrates not merely the frequency

Table 10.2 Natural disasters 1987–2011

Disaster	*Ranking*	*Deaths*	*People affected (in millions)*	*Economic damages ($000)*
Floods	1	14,206	68	12, 746,030 (excluding 2011 floods)
Earthquake	2	142,812	1.2	5,019,255
Drought	3	223	2.2	247,000

Source: NDMA Annual Reports 2010–2018. Available at http://web.ndma.gov.pk/publications.php.

Table 10.3 Floods 2010–2018

Year	*Deaths*	*Affected people (in millions)*
2010	1,984	20
2011	520	9.2
2012	571	4.8
2013	333	1.4
2014	367	2.5
2015	238	1.5
2016	484	N.A.
2017	271	N.A.
2018	137	N.A.

Source: NDMA Annual Reports 2010–2018. Available at http://web.ndma.gov.pk/publications.php.

of their occurrence but also the human displacement they cause. This displacement contributes to migration, in turn. The case of July 2010 floods, explored in the next sub-section, will further demonstrate the danger posed by recurring deluge in the wake of monsoon seasons.

The case of 2010 Floods: "Pakistan's flood crisis as bad as African famines, UN says," British *Guardian* reported.[16] The orientalist tone of the *Guardian* headline notwithstanding, the July 2010 floods were devastating. The NDMA declared the deluge "worst ever disaster in the history of Pakistan".[17] The then UN general secretary Ban Ki-moon visited Pakistan and declared the crisis a "slow motion tsunami" and a "global disaster".[18] As Table 10.1 demonstrates: the number of people affected (20 million) outnumbered the other five global disasters during the first decade of the present century. Out of country's 141 districts, 78 were submerged: 29 of them severely and 49 moderately.[19] In other words, 132,000 square kilometres of country's landmass had been flooded. Notably, 2.1 million hectares of cultivated land was destroyed.[20] Crop worth one billion dollars was destroyed.[21]

A cursory look at the damage to infrastructure and economy will demonstrate more concretely the devastation floods wrought. The NDMA estimated: 10,436 educational institutions were destroyed; 515 health facilities were lost; 1.6 million houses were damaged; and 6,841 water and sanitation schemes were inundated. Energy sector was badly mauled: 92 power plants, 32 grids besides 3000 kilometre supply lines were damaged. Moreover, 1.5 million livestocks and 90 banks (10 ATM) were also destroyed.[22]

Roads, bridges, flood protection embankments, warehouses, businesses, factories, in short an entire society was liquidated. While the immediate affectees are the real victims, the entire country pays the price. According to NDMA estimates, the damages were to the tune of Rs 855 billion. In other words, 5.8% of the country's GDP (in 2009–10) had been swept by the overflowing rivers into the Arabian Sea.[23] Therefore, *Foreign Policy* justifiably notes, "During 2011–15, economy grew at 2.9%, it could be 6.5% if flooding had not caused economic and human loss".[24]

Paradoxically, a country regularly hit by floods is simultaneously running dry. Water stressed since 1990, Pakistan will be facing water scarcity by 2025.[25] Country's first "National Water Policy" introduced in 2018, notes: "Per capita surface water availability has declined from 5,259 cubic meters per year in 1951 to around 1,000 cubic meters in 2016". By 2025, the aforementioned equation will drop to 860 cubic metres per capita. When the availability is below 1,000 cubic metres per capita, a country is considered water scarce.[26] "Pakistan is not water secure," screams a World Bank report.[27] Likewise, the International Monetary Fund (IMF), in 2018, ranked Pakistan third among the countries facing water shortage.[28] By 2047, when Pakistan turns hundred, the situation will be even grave because the climate warming will drive up the water demand by 5% to 15%.[29] While one lacks a concrete definition of climate refugees and lack of data is a global problem when it comes to climate refugees,[30] one cannot authentically present actual figures especially in the case of Pakistan where scholarly studies on climate migration (to be cited in a while) are rare. The NDMA annual reports, otherwise useful in mining data regarding the climate disasters, do not cite any data either. Likewise, the Ministry of Climate Change has not conducted any such research. Saeed et al.[31] observe,

> In the case of Pakistan, which is the fastest urbanizing country in South Asia, the phenomenon of rural-to-urban migration is emerging as a major challenge. However, lack of research in the area leaves a knowledge void that hinders meaningful policy making and its implementation.

"Climate change triggers widespread migration in Pakistan", reports *The Express Tribune*, a leading English daily.[32] The report quotes Muhammad Saleem, a spokesperson for the Ministry of Climate Change, to claim that 70% of the July 2010 internally displaced persons (IDPs) did not return to their original homes.[33] Citing international surveys, Saleem claimed that 700,000 migrate from the countryside to urban centres annually. One contributing factor, he claims, is climate change. After all, according to Saleem, "Almost 50% of Pakistan's population is increasingly becoming vulnerable to climate change". Pakistan's population is 220 million presently. *The Express Tribune* also quotes Amar Guriro, an expert on climate-induced migration. Guriro estimates that climate change has forced 30 million people to migrate during 2009–19.[34] "Climate-induced migration has spread across much of Pakistan, as droughts, floods, and sea intrusion disrupt local communities," claims Suliha Nazar in a report for *Foreign Policy*. According to Nazar, 80% of the five million once living along the banks of the Delta have migrated while "sea-level rise is expected to produce 35–40 million climate refugees".[35]

Aforementioned journalistic discourses have also been substantiated by academic and scholarly studies. Moreover, scholarly research has also established a link between the climate change and migration. Mueller et al.,[36] for instance, in their much-cited and rigorous study on the Pakistani case of climate migration claim that floods and heat stress are contributing to long-term human migration in Pakistan. Muller et al.'s findings were also substantiated by micro-level studies by the Environment and Climate Change Unit (ECCU) of the Sustainable Development Policy Institute (SDPA), Pakistan's leading Islamabad-based think tank. Under a project titled, PRISE, field surveys were conducted in Dera Ghazi Khan (a district in the Punjab province but bordering Balochistan province), Faisalabad (Punjab province) and Mardan (Khyber Paktunkhwa province).[37] While evidence of climate-related migration was found in all three cases, the strongest evidence emerged, understandably, from Dera Ghazi Khan district since this district has been hard hit by floods as well as droughts.[38]

"The impact of climate change was found to be indirect in its nature," asserts Siyal, one of the researchers involved in the field surveys. Three factors contributed to migration, according to this study. One, the impact of climate change on health (epidemics, destruction of hospitals). Secondly, destruction of agriculture owing to floods and droughts. Finally, damage to livelihoods, private property and infrastructure.[39] Likewise, Majid and Zahir have also demonstrated not only a depressing effect on the farm productivity in the provinces of Punjab and Sindh as a result of climatic stress, but they have also established a link between climate change and migration.[40] Is Pakistan even half-ready to deal with the gathering storm? The next section is an attempt to answer this question.

Section 2: State Inadequately Prepared to Deal With Migration

Pakistan is signatory to 14 conventions and agreements on environment and climate change. In 2015, it also established a Ministry of Climate Change. Is Pakistan, as a state and society, ready to brace the gigantic challenge posed by the climatic change? In trying to answer this question, this section begins by looking at official policy making in relation to both climate change and climate-induced migration. Next, it will explore the question of climate change in relation to state and society dynamics and will briefly flag the highly problematic role of media. Pakistani media, censored-and-manipulated by the state,[41] is important to mention because media discourses on climate-related problems will help indicate Pakistan's preparedness to changing realities.

In recent years, certain climate-friendly measure has generated a goodwill for Pakistan's international image. Such measures have also, on the domestic front, centre-staged the climate question. For instance, a ban was imposed on single-use plastic in the federal capital, Islamabad, in August 2019. The ban was further extended to the largest province, the Punjab. Sindh, the second largest province, also announced to implement a similar ban.[42] Such a ban has been announced previously but was hardly implemented. However, this time, at least in the federal capital a compliance has been largely successful. Likewise, a billion-tree project to reverse deforestation in Khyber Pakhtunkhwa province had been flaunted by the present government, led by the then Prime Minister Imran Khan, as its commitment to green politics. In his statements and media talks, Khan while in opposition would point out deforestation in Pakistan and climate disaster. This billion-tree project was launched in 2014 by the Khyber Pakhtunkhwa provincial government, led by Imran Khan's party, Pakistan Justice Party (PTI). Since at least 2008, the two other mainstream parties the Pakistan People's Party (PPP) and the Pakistan Muslim League-Nawaz (PML-N) have also been promising in their election manifestos a commitment to fight back the climate change.

Only a separate research can establish whether certain climate-friendly policies introduced by various governments in the last decade have been a response to global commitments, with an eye on donor-money, or a genuine fulfilment of election promises and response to public pressure. The silver lining, however, is the fact that there have been state-level initiatives to combat the climate change. As far as policy making is concerned, there is a ground for optimism as well as pessimism. An optimistic development is the acknowledgement of climate emergency at the official level. In this regard, according to Siyal,

> The acceptance of the Climate Change Bill by the National Assembly [the lower house of federal parliament] in 2016 and the Senate [the upper house] in 2017 gives a clear signal that steps supported by an allocation of funds are being taken to address it.[43]

While the Pakistan Climate Change Act 2017 covers a lot of climate-related aspects, from mitigation to gender, it simply avoids the problem of climate migration. Likewise, a 'National Climate Change Policy' was presented by the Ministry of Climate Change in 2012 but it was also silent on the question of climate-induced migration.[44]

In their working paper on climate-induced rural-to-urban migration, Saeed et al. also note:

> The issue of migration receives little attention in Pakistan's rural-urban development planning. For example, while the prevalence of poverty in rural and urban areas largely influences migration and urbanization patterns, the Government's Poverty Reduction Strategy Paper (PRSP) and recently approved Vision 2015 fail to provide any strategy relevant to current and future migration.[45]

They also mention the draft National Emigration Policy that exists which only discusses international migration and does not take into account the question of migratory patterns in relation to internal migration, let alone climate-related displacement.[46] It is worth pointing out that Pakistan's agricultural sector is country's largest employer: 44% of the total workforce while 68% of the rural workforce is absorbed by the agricultural sector. A large section in the agriculture sector is engaged in subsistence farming. Likewise, pastoralism is commonplace.[47]

Research shows a link between heat stress and declining farm productivity.[48] It is evident as Section 1 also demonstrates, climate change with adverse effects on agriculture sector is inevitably triggering waves of migration. That Pakistan is already world's sixth-largest populated country with a history of bitter ethnic conflicts and ongoing ethnic tensions (to be explored in Section 3), the mere number of people involved in any displacement will be huge. A case in point is July 2010 flooding whereby 20 million people were hit. Fourteen million people were re-located temporarily,[49] 200,000 of them in IDP camps funded by the international donors.[50] According to UNDP,[51] the average costs for annual adaptation to climate change range between $6 billion and $14 billion upto 2050. Before the UNDP estimates, the National Sustainable Development Strategy also estimated US$6 billion to US$14 billion annual spending in order to adapt to climate change.[52] In other words, at average, Pakistan needs to spend US$10 billion annually. Pakistan's spending on combating climate change is increasing as is evident by UNDP-conducted audit of Pakistan's climate public expenditure for 2010–14. During this period, total federal climate-related expenditure was 5.8% to 7.6% of the total expenditures.[53] However, it is far from adequate. International aid can rescue Pakistan by bridging the gap between required finances and needs. However, such global funding is not forthcoming adequately. At 26th Conference of Parties (COP-26), held in Glasgow in 2021, for instance, the UK, the USA, France and Germany jointly pledged US$8.5 billion for South Africa to move away from coal while Pakistan received nothing to shelve two coal plants. This despite the fact that Pakistan submitted an ambitious plan to cut carbon emissions by signing Global Methane Pledge even if Pakistan contributes only 1% of global greenhouse emissions.[54]

Understandably, Bhatti et al.[55] and Malik et al.[56] consider Pakistan ill-prepared to cope with climate change. Likewise, *Foreign Policy* observes: "Since Pakistan is not financially secure enough to afford climate change implementation programs on its own, it needs assistance from foreign entities as well as climate change experts who can design comprehensive programs, bearing in mind the government's limitations".[57] However, such externalization of climate change policy will only aggravate a periphery country's dependence on the metropolitan. Yet another problem with climate change policy in Pakistan's case is state's refusal to play its pedagogic role. On the one hand, only 2% of the federal climate change budget is spent on awareness, on the other, state manipulated media have found in annual flooding a new tool to otherify India. "Self" is, at least in part, constructed in relation to the "other". By externalizing and ascribing floods, country's biggest climate challenge in the context of this chapter, to India (the "other"), a self-image is built whereby Pakistan is delineated as climate-innocent if not climate-friendly. The way Pakistani media explain Pakistan's annual problem of floods is indicative of state's lack of seriousness to play its pedagogic role.

A new term, "water terrorism", has been popularized by the print media as well as screaming news channels with near-universal audience-outreach in Pakistan. A personal anecdote will demonstrate the hollowness of deploying the water-terrorism discourse and lack of its credibility. A personal friend working for ARY news channel was reporting live on India's sudden release of river waters causing floods in the river Ravi. Incidentally, while listening him, I was driving over the Ravi bridge and the muddy-as-usual Ravi bank was visible. There were no signs of floods even 150 kilometres north of Lahore because I immediately spoke to my brother in district Sialkot which, being on the Jammu border, is usually the first district to suffer. My village, often inundated during monsoon, is located 50 kilometres east of Sialkot. Hence, my worry was natural. The Ravi was empty even next to Sialkot. In short, the news was simply fake. Even July 2010 floods were blamed on India by rabidly rightwing TV commentators. True jingoistic sections of Indian media and the present Indian government, headed by Narendra Modi, has often passed the threat to use river waters as a bargaining tool.[58] Also, one cannot rule out that India never engages in subversive water wars. Yet blaming India for Pakistan's climate change is a self-destructive exercise. Fortunately, consciousness in Pakistan regarding climate change has improved. In 2007–08, only 34% Pakistanis were aware of climate change and 24% considered it a threat. By 2015, Pakistan was one of the 19 countries where a majority considers climate change a top global threat.[59] The youth in particular is expressing concern, like rest of the world. Pakistan, in fact, surprised itself when in 2019, responding to the call of global teen activist from Sweden, Greta Thunberg, more than 27 cities and towns took part in the protest all over the country, including Mardan, Jhang, Turbat, Kotli, Bagh, Killa Abdullah, Chitral and Ghotki.[60] In Lahore, Pakistan's second-largest city, over 5,000, mostly school students, took to the streets.

Section 3: Socio-political Consequences

As argued earlier, the link between climate change and migration is evident and understandable. In the context of Pakistan, where climate change is assuming apocalyptic proportions, migration entails bitter ethnic conflicts.

The case of Pakistan, in fact, testifies to the theoretical framework Homer-Dixon offers to conceptualise the role climate change plays in tickling waves of migration and triggering ethnic conflicts. The key concept here is environmental scarcity. Defined as "scarcity of renewable resources, such as cropland, rived water, and fish stocks,"[61] environmental scarcity, according to Homer-Dixon, is caused by the degradation of renewable resources (supply-induced). The increased demand for these resources (supply-induced) or their unequal distribution (structural) triggers conflict. While the three sources of environmental scarcity often interact as well as reinforce each other, Homer-Dixon flags two particular interaction: (a) resource capture and (b) ecological marginalisation.

Resource capture occurs when growing population places stress on renewable resources in the form of their depletion. Hence, this tension between supply and demand triggers the structural forces (power-wielding groups) to shift the distribution of resources in their favour. Not merely these clusters of powerful people capture the resource, they also exploit the control of these resources to accumulate wealth and further consolidate their power. Hence, resource capture intensifies environmental scarcity. Likewise, ecological marginality occurs when an unequal access to renewable resources, combined with an increase in population, forces people to migrate. The depletion of renewable resources drives people to move to such ecologically fragile regions as steep upland slopes, areas risking desertification, tropical rainforests or sometimes to low-quality urban territories.

While ecological marginality is one source of climate migrations, environmental scarcity (reinforced by resource capture and ecological marginality) generates migratory trends also because local agriculture and economic production is bearish. Understandably, climate victims move on to greener pastures. Meantime, environmental scarcity strengthens group identities based on such affiliations as ethnicity, religion, class and so on: a process defined by Homer-Dixon as social segmentation. Social segmentation, in turn, intensifies competition and undermines social harmony. Above processes also increase demand on the state, stimulate predatory behaviours and depress tax collection. Hence, the state's administrative capacity erodes while its legitimacy is challenged. Consequently, insurgencies, ethnic conflicts and possibilities of coups d'etat emerge.

Anchored in Homer-Dixon's analysis, this section demonstrates the link between environmental scarcity, climate migration and ethnic conflict. Homer-Dixon, himself, notes:

> In Pakistan, shortages and maldistribution of good land, water, and forest in the countryside have encouraged millions of poor to migrate into major cities, such as Karachi and Hyderabad. The conjunction of this in-migration with high fertility rates is causing city populations to grow at an astonishing 4% to 5% a year, producing fierce competition – and often violence – among ethnic groups over land, basic services, and political and economic power.[62]

Long before climate migrations, the country had witnessed huge migrations owing to geo-political history of the region. Carved out of India in 1947 as East Pakistan (now Bangladesh) and West Pakistan (present Pakistan), the country was at war with itself from the day one, literally and figuratively, on ethnic basis. While the East Pakistan was agitating against the Western wing on imposition of Urdu as the national language or establishing Karachi as the capital, the ethnic tension in West Pakistan was even acute.

Urdu-speaking migrants from Delhi, Uttar Pradesh and Bihar largely settled in Karachi, Hyderabad and Sukkur, the three largest towns in the Sindh province. Owing to complicated historical twists, Urdu-speaking migrants, called Mohajirs in vernacular, along with the Punjabi elite, emerged as the ruling clique also because Punjabis and Mohajirs dominated the military and bureaucratic apparatuses. Besides East Pakistan, the people of Sindh also resented repatriation of Mohajirs because the evacuee land and property left behind by Hindus who migrated to India, was allotted to newly arrived Mohajirs instead of the Sindhis. Between 1947 and 1951, eight million moved from India to Pakistan: 20% of them into Sindh. A large majority settled in Karachi. According to 1951 census, 55% of the Karachi population was Mohajir.[63] The then chief minister of Sindh, in protest, resigned.

The conflict later turned into bloody riots. First serious ethnic-based unrest that engulfed was witnessed in the 1970s, when the government of Zulfiqar Ali Bhutto – Bhuttos are native Sindhis – introduced a language bill whereby Sindhi language was also granted an official status as the language of Sindh. Mohajirs agitated and ensuing riots claimed over a dozen lives.[64],[65] That Karachi was initially country's capital (federal capital was later moved to purposely built town of Islamabad in 1964), port city and the industrial power-house of the country, youth from the Punjab and Khyber Pakhtunkhwa provinces, in their millions, migrated to Karachi in search of greener pastures. Ironically, Sindhis and Baluch constituting a majority in Karachi in 1947 had been reduced to 7% and 4%, respectively, by the 1990s.[66] Mohajirs who dominated, demographically, already felt besieged by the Bhutto era language bill and quota system, were now finding Punjabis and Pakhtuns (or Pukhtoons), as the new challenges. The Mohajirs launched Mohajir National Movement (MQM), with an armed wing. From the mid-1980s onwards, Karachi was a battleground for ethnic strife. In 1995, total 1,742 Karachites were killed,[67] while 2,300 lives were claimed by ethnic violence in 2011.[68]

Rioting had an economic cost too. A working day lost by strike would cost 1.3 billion rupees ($38 million). In 1995, thirty-four days were lost owing to strikes imposed by ethnic-conflict.[69]

Almost four decades down the line, Karachi remains restive on ethnic grounds. Climate-induced migration from rural Sindh to Karachi is further complicating the situation. According to Bloomberg, Karachi as an example of climate change and conflict.[70] Meantime, in 1971, East Pakistan went independent, after a bloody war of liberation. The ethnic tensions had exacerbated to an extent that the two wings could not co-exist together anymore. In the 1970s, a second wave of migration ignited new tensions. This time, Afghanistan was the source of refugees arriving Pakistan in their millions. That most of the Afghan refugees were settling in Khyber Pakhtunkhwa and Balochistan provinces, it was Baloch who resented.

Balochistan, geographically the largest of four provinces, has a miniscule population share in Pakistan. With over seven million residents, Balochistan is not even the size of Karachi or Lahore. On top of that, Balochistan province is ethnically divided. The districts bordering Afghanistan are inhibited by Pakhtun tribes. Afghan refugees arriving Balochistan were, as is well known, also ethnically Pakhtuns. The Baloch viewed it as a design by the Punjabi elite to turn Baloch into a minority in their own province. Balochistan has seen four waves of militant separatism, fourth phase is still going on. Baloch resent that the Punjab exploits the Balochistan resources. No doubt, Balochistan is resource rich but indeed under-developed. That Afghan conflict has not come to an end, the question of Afghan refugees has assumed new dimensions. "The presence of large number of Afghan refugees in Pakistan's Khyber Pakhtunkhwa is seen by the Pakistani military as a security risk that aggravates drug trafficking, smuggling and terrorist activities," observe Kaur and Kaur.[71] This outsider view of this problem is not indeed misplaced. The situation is actually much more complex and space will not allow to explore it all. In short, the question of Afghan refugees has become a source of tension in Balochistan as well as Khyber Pakhtunkhwa where in general every crime, petty or otherwise, is blamed on Afghan refugees.[72]

Yet another case of migration-and-ethnic tensions was on display in the wake of 'war-on-terror' scenario. The region formerly called Federally Administered Tribal Areas (FATA), consisting of six districts, became theatre of a multi-pronged violent conflict between the Taliban factions, Pakistan military and local tribes. In the post-9/11 period, over three million people became IDPs. FATA, bordering Afghanistan, is inhabited by ethnically Pashtun tribes. Owing to tribal ties, one natural destination for the IDPs was Karachi. However, not merely Mohajirs in Karachi were suspicious of newly arriving Pashtun IDPs, the Sindh government also protested. In fact, Sindhi nationalist outfits staged public demonstrations and initiated an agitation against hosting Pashtun IDPs. The Punjab province was also reluctant. Pashtun profiling in Lahore, the capital of Punjab province, has become a new phenomenon. Finally, IDP camps were established in Khyber Pakhtunkhwa districts owing to ethnic affinity between FATA and the province. Imagine couple of more deluge on the scale of July 2010 flood. If one takes into economic losses suffered by the four provinces, the breakdown will be as follows: Sindh: 43%, Punjab: 26%, Khyber Pakhtunkhwa: 12%, Balochistan: 6% (rest: federally administered areas including Pakistani administered Kashmir).[73]

As mentioned earlier, July 2010 floods displaced 14 million people. This is more than what Afghan war and 'war-on-terror' combined contributed in terms of refugees. In short, migrations to be triggered by climatic change in Pakistan need serious attention not merely for humanitarian and economic reasons. In the context of Pakistan, human migration has very serious consequences for country's political stability. The case of Attabad lake, in Gilgit-Baltistan region, highlights that climatic changes and human displacement may imply increased state repression. Attabad is a village in Hunza Nagar district. In 2009, the village was declared hazardous in the light of reports filed by Geological Survey of Pakistan. Consequently, 103 families were rescued by the NDMA. On January 2, 2010, a massive landslide wiped neigbouring village Sarat, leaving 20 dead while blockage of Hunza river turned Attabad to a lake. The victims of Attabad incident, in due course, started agitating for their rehabilitation and other rights. One such demonstration was fired upon by the police. A youth and his father were shot dead. This triggered further protest. Baba Jan, a youth activist, became symbol of the movement. Consequently, Baba Jan and four of his fellows were implicated in terrorism cases. While two were later set free but Baba Jan and the other two were sentenced to jail terms of upto 90 years (they were released in 2021 after a mass agitation). For ten years, these climate activists were behind the bar while initially they were subjected to horrible physical and mental torture too.[74] Criminalisation and militarization of social movements in the post-colonial states, particularly in South Asia, is not unique. However, climate migration is adding yet another dimension to this dynamic. While Attabad is merely one case, similar cases can be cited from other regions and provinces.

There is a gender aspect to migration as well.[75] Saeed et al.[76] note that rural to urban migration implies that women on the countryside have to take up new roles that previously were assigned to the men. Since men are moving to towns, women share in village labour has further increased. In the context of Pakistan, climate-related politics has huge consequences for the civil-military relations. The Pakistan military is often viewed and portrayed as a state within the state with phenomenal political, corporate and business stakes. Besides having ruled the country directly for over 30 years, military continues to assert itself in politics, foreign policy and economy. Understandably, rescue operations in the case of natural catastrophes – almost an annual ritual in Pakistan – become an event for the military to present itself as the force that rescues people during the times of calamities. Its saviour image is reinforced through structural means too. For instance, 40 percent of the NDMA employees are military personnel.[77] Of the seven chairperson, NDMA has seen hitherto, six were military generals. That media are effectively controlled and manipulated by the military further helps to glorify military's image as the saviour every time military is engaged in any rescue effort. Rescue efforts, centre-staging military, are reported ad nauseam on news channels as well as flashed on front pages of the mainstream broadsheets. Meantime, media keep portraying the civil leadership as corrupt, inefficient and incapable of delivering anything tangible.

A corollary to this equation is the role of Jihadi outfits such as Lashkar-e-Tayyaba (LeT). During, for instance, the earthquake in 2005 or July 2010 floods, not merely the Let and its jihadi cousins were actively engaged in rescue operations, their role was glorified in the media. Ironically, these outfits were officially proscribed and had ceased to exist. These outfits are viewed as proxies of the military and democratic forces in the country view these outfits as subversive elements patronized to undermine democracy in Pakistan. To sum up: climate disasters, climate-induced migration, and associated structures or their political economy in Pakistan is an explosive and loaded topic.

Conclusion

Phenomenal climatic changes are throwing up multiple challenges, including human migration. For a periphery economy like Pakistan, the climate question assumes an urgency and enormity of highest proportion. It is one of the global hotspots. That two of the six global climatic catastrophes inflicted Pakistan during the first decade of this century, is indeed suggestive.

The evidence documented earlier further demonstrates that the key threat in the context of climate-induced migration is the annual flooding. Between 1987 and 2011, sixty-eight million people were affected by the floods while the water gone wild inflicted an economic penalty of US$12,746,030,000 (excluding 2010 floods which inflicted an economic damage to the tune of US$10 billion). Hence, a very important finding is: floods constitute Pakistan's biggest challenge in terms of economic damage, development and climate-induced migration.

To stem the tide of climate-induced migration and address the question of climate-related changes, Pakistan lacks the financial resources. For the next three decades, that is, till 2050, the country is required to spend US$10 billion on annual basis, according to the United Nations Organization (UNO). Though Pakistan is tendentially increasing its spending to address the challenges posed by climate change yet the shortfall is spending is markedly enormous. Hence, the international community has to chip in generously.

Likewise, the state in Pakistan has not played the pedagogic role adequately. On the one hand, the emphasis remains on building an infrastructure to deal with climate change and climate-induced migration, on the other, country's biggest climate challenge, that is, flooding has been exploited to otherify India for the sake of politics. The role of mainstream media, in otherfying India instead of enlightening the citizenry as to the actual threat of climate change, deserves a separate full-length study. However, indicative of Pakistan's inadequate response to emerging climate challenges, media have played a subversive role. This also mirrors the lack of stress on state's pedagogic role in relation to climate change.

Finally, in view of the ethnic tensions that mark the polity in Pakistan a democratically developed strategy should be in place on emergency basis to accommodate internal migrations to be caused by climate change. Else, the climate change will add fuel to ethnic conflict that has stymied development in the Sindh province and keeps Karachi, country's industrial and financial power house, on the edge.

In the light of aforementioned findings, a few recommendations are in place here.

1 The state in collaboration with the international community take emergency measures to prepare short-term as well as long-term plans to cope with climate-related migration. In the immediate future, contingency plans should be in place so that the towns can embrace migrating population without violently disconfiguring country's ethnic make-up in any province. In the long run, institutional mechanisms should be built anew. An integral approach to climate change and climate-induced migration is a forgone conclusion. In the long run, empowering of local communities in order to build their resilience in the face of climate change is pivotal. This involves material infrastructure as well as educational projects to equip the communities to deal with floods, droughts, cyclones, landslides and earthquakes.
2 There is a huge lack of research on the topic. The dire need to improve the empirical basis for meaningful policy-making hardly needs to be stressed anymore. Planning is impossible without adequate and reliable data. Likewise, robust modelling and case studies should be explored in the context of Pakistan. This process should involve development and climate experts as well as local communicates.
3 Enhanced resource allocation is yet another forgone conclusion. However, in view of Pakistan's economic status and myriad economic woes, the state in Pakistan is not likely to do much. Therefore, harnessing global support to build institutional and infrastructural mechanisms to deal with future climate challenges, including migration, is key to any future planning.
4 The state in Pakistan should take its pedagogic role more earnestly. Not merely media, the state needs to deploy all the means on its disposal to educate the citizenry in order to deal with climate change. Besides media campaigns, climate should be included in the school curriculum. On war-footings, there should be mass rehearsals to deal with floods, earthquake and so on so that the communities are prepared to deal with any eventuality.
5 Environmental scarcity is closely linked with population growth. The population growth rate in Pakistan remains highest in South Asia (2.4%). Climate, development policies and preservation of renewable resources are all undermined by a fast multiplying citizenry in Pakistan. Hence, like many other areas, population control is also an urgent imperative.

Notes

1 V. Mueller, C. Gray and K. Kosec (2014), "Heat stress increases long-term human migration in rural Pakistan", *Nature Climate Change*, 4(3), 182–185, https://doi.org/10.1038/nclimate2103.

2 Basharat Saeed and Harmain Rukh (2017), *Loss & damage from drought in Pakistan: Notes from Tharparkar*. Islamabad: LEAD Pakistan, accessed from www.lead.org.pk/lead/Publications/Loss%20&%20Damage%20from%20Drought%20in%20Pakistan%20-%20Notes%20from%20Tharparkar.pdf on 8th July 2020.
3 NDMA (National Disaster Management Authority) (2022, 18 November), *Monsoon SITREP#158*. Islamabad: National Disaster Management Authority, Government of Pakistan, accessed from https://cms.ndma.gov.pk/storage/app/public/situation-reports/November2022/N2n1eEarMt6q6Rb8ZYwn.pdf on 9th December 2022; Ministry of Planning Development & Special Initiative (2022), *Pakistan floods 2022. Post-disaster needs assessment*. Islamabad: Ministry of Planning Development & Special Initiative, Government of Pakistan, accessed from https://thedocs.worldbank.org/en/doc/4a0114eb7d1cecbbbf2f65c5ce0789db-0310012022/original/Pakistan-Floods-2022-PDNA-Main-Report.pdf on 9th December 2022.
4 Ibid.
5 M. Ahmed and M. Farooq (2022, 26 September), "Pakistan floods raise fears of hunger after crops wrecked", *The Diplomat*, accessed from https://thediplomat.com/2022/09/pakistan-floods-raise-fears-of-hunger-after-crops-wrecked/ on 9th December 2022.
6 Thomas F. Homer-Dixon (1999), *Environment, society, and violence*. Princeton: Princeton University Press.
7 Suliha Nazar (2016), "Pakistan's biggest threat isn't terrorism – its climate change", *Foreign Policy*, accessed from https://foreignpolicy.com/2016/03/04/pakistans-big-threat-isnt-terrorism-its-climate-change/ on 23rd June 2020.
8 NDMA (National Disaster Management Authority) (2011), *Annual report 2011*. Islamabad: National Disaster Management Authority, Government of Pakistan.
9 UNISDR (United Nations International Strategy for Disaster Reduction) and (Centre for Research on the Epidemiology of Disasters) CERD (n.d.), *The human cost of weather related disasters*, accessed from http://web.ndma.gov.pk/publications/S1995-2015.pdf on 29th October 2020.
10 Nazar, op. cit.
11 M. Hussain, A. R. But, F. Uzma, R. Ahmed, S. Irshad, A. Rehman and B. Yousaf (2019), "A comprehensive climate change impacts, adaptation, and natural calamities in Pakistan", *Environmental Monitoring and Assessment*, 192(48), https://doi.org/10.1007/s10661-019-7956-4.
12 NDMA, 2011, op. cit., 2.
13 Ibid., 2.
14 NDMA, 2011, op. cit.
15 Anadolu Agency (2019, 8 December), "Climate change triggers widespread migration", *The Express Tribune*, accessed from https://tribune.com.pk/story/2113842/1-climate-change-triggers-widespread-migration-pakistan/ on 24th June 2020.
16 Declan Walsh (2011, 27 January), "Pakistan's flood crisis as bad as African famines, UN says", *The Guardian*, accessed from www.theguardian.com/world/2011/jan/27/pakistan-flood-crisis-african-famines on 4th July 2020.
17 NDMA (National Disaster Management Authority) (2010), *Annual report 2011*. Islamabad: National Disaster Management Authority, Government of Pakistan, 13.
18 Mila Sanina (2010, 20 August), "Pakistan crisis a 'slow-motion tsunami', UN chief says", *CNN*, accessed from https://edition.cnn.com/2010/WORLD/asiapcf/08/20/pakistan.floods/index.html on 4th July 2020.

19 NDMA, 2010, op. cit.
20 Ibid., 14.
21 Muller et al., 2014, op. cit.
22 NDMA, 2010, op. cit., 14.
23 Ibid., 14–15.
24 Nazar, 2016, op. cit.
25 Shah Meer Baloch (2018), "Water crisis: Why is Pakistan running dry?", *DW*, accessed from www.dw.com/en/water-crisis-why-is-pakistan-running-dry/a-44110280 on 8th September 2020.
26 Ministry of Water Resources (2018), *National water report*. Islamabad: Government of Pakistan, p. 1, accessed from http://waterbeyondborders.net/wp-content/uploads/2018/07/Pakistan-National-Water-Policy-2018.pdf on 8th July 2020.
27 Young William, Anwar Arif, Bhatti Tousif, Borgomeo Edoardo, Davies Stephen, William Garthwaite III, William Raymond, Gilmont Efrem Michael, Leb Christina, Lytton Lucy, Makin Ian and Saeed Basharat Ahmed (2019), *Pakistan: Getting more from water (English)*. Water security diagnostics. Washington, D.C.: World Bank Group, p. xv, accessed from http://documents.worldbank.org/curated/en/251191548275645649/Pakistan-Getting-More-from-Water
28 Baloch, 2018, op. cit.
29 World Bank (2019), *Pakistan: Getting more from water*, accessed from http://documents1.worldbank.org/curated/en/251191548275645649/pdf/133964-WP-PUBLIC-ADD-SERIES-22-1-2019-18-56-25-W.pdf on 8th July 2020.
30 Simrit Kaur and Harpreet Kaur (2018), "A storm of climate change is brewing in South Asia", *Lethal Heating*, accessed from http://lethalheating.blogspot.com/2018/06/a-storm-of-climate-change-migration-is.html?m=1 on 23rd June 2020.
31 F. Saeed, K. M. Salik and S. Ishfaq (2016), *Climate induced rural-to-urban migration in Pakistan: Working paper*. Islamabad: SDPI, p. 14, accessed from https://sdpi.org/sdpiweb/publications/files/Climate-induced-rural-to-urban-migration-in-Pakistan.pdf on 4th July 2020.
32 Anadolu Agency, 2019, op. cit.
33 The NDMA claimed that 97 percent of the population displaced by July 2010 flood had returned to their homes (NDMA, 2010, op. cit.). The huge discrepancy between the claims made by the NDMA report and the statement by the Ministry of Climate Change's spokesperson can be understood if we take the following into account: NDMA being a government department focuses on showing efficiency instead of engaging in any long-term scholarly ambitions. On the other hand, the Spokesperson has also uttered a statement to the press without much nuance involved.
34 Anadolu Agency, 2019, op. cit.
35 Nazar, 2016, op. cit.
36 Mueller et al., 2014, op. cit.
37 Ghamz e Ali Siyal (2017), "Analysing the reality of climate-induced migration in Pakistan's semi-arid regions", *LSE Website*, accessed from https://blogs.lse.ac.uk/southasia/2017/07/06/analysing-the-reality-of-climate-induced-migration-in-semi-arid-regions-of-pakistan/ on 28th April 2021.
38 Ibid.
39 Ibid.
40 H. Majid and H. Zahir (2013), "Farmer adaptability to climate change: The role of socioeconomic factors in agricultural productivity". IDRC-CRDI climate change in Pakistan: Working paper series no. 1, IDRC, Ottawa.
41 Farooq Sulehria (2019), "From overdeveloped state to praetorian Pakistan: Tracing the media's transformations", in McCartney and S. A. Zaidi (eds.) *New*

perspectives on Pakistan's political economy. New Delhi: Cambridge University Press, 241–255.

42 Baloch, 2018, op. cit.

43 Siyal, 2017, op. cit.

44 Ministry of Climate Change (2012), *National climate change policy*, accessed from www.mocc.gov.pk/moclc/userfiles1/file/Moclc/Policy/National%20Climate%20Change%20Policy%20of%20Pakistan%20(2).pdf on 5th July 2020.

45 Saeed et al., 2016, op. cit., 14.

46 Ibid.

47 Ibid., 15.

48 D. Qin, G. K. Plattner, J. Boscchuung, A. Nauels and P. M. Midgley (2014), "Climate change 2013: The physical science basis", in T. Stocker (ed.) *Contribution to the fifth assignment report of the intergovernmental panel on climate change*. Cambridge: Cambridge University Press, 15–35.

49 Mueller et al., 2014, op. cit.

50 Walsh, 2011, op. cit.

51 UNDP (United Nations Development Programme) (2015), *Pakistan: Climate public expenditure and industrial review (CPEIR)*. Islamabad: UNDP Pakistan, p. 12, accessed from file:///C:/Users/Farooq/AppData/Local/Temp/UNDP%20 Climate%20Report%20V9.pdf on 5th July 2020.

52 Saeed and Rukh, 2017, op. cit.

53 UNDP, 2015, op. cit., 25.

54 S. A. Ramay (2021, 6 December), "COP-26 lessons for Pakistan", *The News*, accessed from www.thenews.com.pk/print/914463-cop-26-lessons-for-pakistan on 16th April 2022. Also, see: M. Qasim (2021, 24 November), "Cop 26 & Pakistan", *Daily Dawn*, accessed from www.dawn.com/news/1659941 on 16th April 2016.

55 M. Bhatti, K. Balkhair, A. Masood and S. Sarwar (2018), "Optimized shifts in sowing times of field crops to the projected climate changes in an agro-climate zone of Pakistan", *Experimental Agriculture*, 54(2), 201–213.

56 S. M. Malik, H. Awan and N. Khan (2012), "Mapping vulnerability to climate change and its repercussions on human health in Pakistan", *Global Health*, 8(31), https://doi.org/10.1186/1744-8603-8-31.

57 Nazar, 2016, op. cit.

58 After the "Uri attack" on Indian troops in 2016 in Kashmir, New Delhi blamed Pakistan-based militant outfit Jaish-e-Muhammad (JeM) for the attack. The Uri attack led escalation on the Line of Control (LoC), and tension between India and Pakistan. At the time, Indian prime minister, Narendra Moodi stated: "Blood and water cannot flow together". To quote Indian columnist Mohan Guruswamy. "By implication he was suggesting that India could retaliate by turning off the spigot of the three western rivers of the Indus basin that flow unhindered into Pakistan and sustain most of its agriculture". See: Mohan Guruswamy (2019), "PM Modi's empty and ill-informed threat to stop flow of water to Pakistan", *National Herald*, accessed from www.nationalheraldindia.com/opinion/pm-modis-empty-and-ill-informed-threat-to-stop-flow-of-water-to-pakistan on 25th October 2020. One may quote may such examples.

59 Nazar, 2016, op. cit.

60 Abdus Samad Khan (2019, 21 September), "Climate strike: Thousands march across Pakistan to protest against climate change", *The Nation*, accessed from https://nation.com.pk/21-Sep-2019/climate-march-thousands-march-across-pakistan-to-protest-against-climate-change on 4th July 2020.

61 Homer-Dixon, 1999, op. cit., 8.

62 Ibid, 12.

63 Farhat Haq (1995), "Rise of the MQM politics in Pakistan: Politics of ethnic mobilization", *Asian Survey*, 35(11), 990–1004.
64 Ibid, 992–993.
65 First ethnic riots in Karachi were witnessed in 1964–65 when Mohajirs and Pashtuns clashed. See Moonis Ahmer (1996), 'Ethnicity and state power in Pakistan: The Karachi crisis", *Asian Survey*, 36(10), 1031–1048, p. 1032.
66 Haris Gazdar (2011), "Karachi battles", *Economic and Political Weekly*, 14(38), 19–21, p. 20.
67 Laurent Gayer (2012), "Political turmoil in Karachi: Production and reproduction of ordered disorder", *Economic and Political Weekly*, 47(31), 76–84, p. 76.
68 Mashail Malik and Niloufer Siddiqui (2019, June), "Exposure to violence and voting in Karachi, Pakistan", US Institute of Peace. Special Report no. 450, p. 4, accessed from www.usip.org/publications/2019/06/exposure-violence-and-voting-karachi-pakistan on 28th April 2021.
69 Ahmer, 1996, op. cit., 1035.
70 Thor Benson (2018, 21 March), "The cities at risk of climate-driven conflict", *Bloomberg*, accessed from www.bloomberg.com/news/articles/2018-03-21/the-worrying-link-between-climate-change-and-conflict on 23rd June 2020.
71 Kaur and Kaur, 2018, op. cit.
72 The Afghan refugees face xenophobia, harassment, police blackmail. Devoid of rights and economic possibilities, their plight in Pakistan as well as Iran (where they are in an even more precarious situation) deserve a separate study.
73 NDMA, 2010, op. cit., 15.
74 Ibid, 28–30; Kiran Nazish (2012), "Baba Jan: One year in jail (an interview)", *Naked Punch*, accessed from www.nakedpunch.com/articles/150 on 7th July 2020.
75 For details, A. Qaisrani and S. Batool (2021), "Vulnerabilities of rural women to climate extremes: A case of semi-arid districts in Pakistan", in A. Hans, N. Rao, A. Prakash and A. Patel (eds.) *Engendering climate change: Learnings from South Asia*. Islamabad: Routledge, 19–37.
76 Saeed et al., 2016, op. cit.
77 Muhammad Saqib Tanvir (2020), "Ground per kam karnay walay ahlkar fauj kay hain", *Daily Independent Urdu*, accessed from www.independenturdu.com/node/40686

Chapter 11

Climate-Induced Migration in Sri Lanka

Vulnerability, Mobility, and Resilience

Dennis Mombauer and Vositha Wijenayake

Introduction

The South Asian region has seen human mobilities throughout history,[1] with people migrating within or across borders due to a variety of demographic, socio-economic, and political factors,[2] including damaged infrastructure, land degradation, eroding income opportunities, lack of alternative coping mechanisms, conflict, land access issues, development, employment, kinship, and access to health and education services.[3]

In Sri Lanka, migration streams have flowed towards urban centres, export processing zones, and countries in the Middle East and East Asia since at least the 1970s, when less restrictive economic policies allowed young people to migrate out of rural areas.[4] In addition to socio-economic and demographic factors, recent decades have seen climate change emerging as a major underlying driver that influences migration patterns in Sri Lanka and exacerbates existing economic, demographic, social, and environmental migration drivers.[5]

This new nexus between climate change and migration is complex and so far lacks a solid body of research and data.[6] Human mobilities in Sri Lanka are determined by a multidimensional field of tension in which climate change can act either as a direct driver or as an additional stressor and compounding factor that forces vulnerable populations to move.[7]

Climate-induced migration occurs as a result of constraints to livelihoods and creates a need for financial assistance and resource management to ensure that depletion or over-exploitation of resources does not cause additional conflicts and crisis.[8] Most notably, poor and rural communities in Sri Lanka lack resilience and are drained by a complex interplay of push and pull factors. This creates challenges and opportunities for areas with high in- and out-migration and for different populations: migrants, their family members, communities staying behind, and host populations.[9]

DOI:10.4324/9781003367802-12

Country Context

Sri Lanka is a tropical island nation with a land area of 62,705 square kilometres, a population of 21.67 million, and a gross domestic product (GDP) of approximately US$88.9 billion in 2018.[10] Almost 58% of the GDP is provided by the services sector, while other important economic sectors include agriculture, manufacturing, the plantation industry, and tourism.[11]

Sri Lanka enjoys a high standard of living as measured by key development indicators. Sri Lanka is one of only two upper-middle-income countries in South Asia[12] and ranks comparatively high on the Human Development Index, the Gender Development Index, for life expectancy, estimated gross national income per capita, expected and mean years of schooling, and adult literacy rate (91.71%).[13]

Furthermore, Sri Lanka has achieved near-total rural electrification (97%) as well as widespread access to drinking water and basic sanitation facilities.[14] Disregarding the Maldives, Sri Lanka's coefficient of human inequality, its gender inequality index, multidimensional poverty index, and maternal mortality ratio are the lowest in the region. It has also been certified as malaria-free by the World Health Organization in 2016.[15]

Despite these advances, Sri Lanka remains a developing country with 4.1% of the population living below the national income poverty line and 14.3% vulnerable to multidimensional poverty.[16] Total 38.9% of the country's employed population is engaged as vulnerable unpaid family workers and own account workers,[17] and 11.9% of households nationwide are vulnerable to multidimensional poverty and could be pushed below the poverty line by economic shocks such as job loss, severe illness, injuries, and loss of livelihood.[18] Vulnerability to multidimensional poverty varies significantly between districts (going up to almost 20% in Polonnaruwa

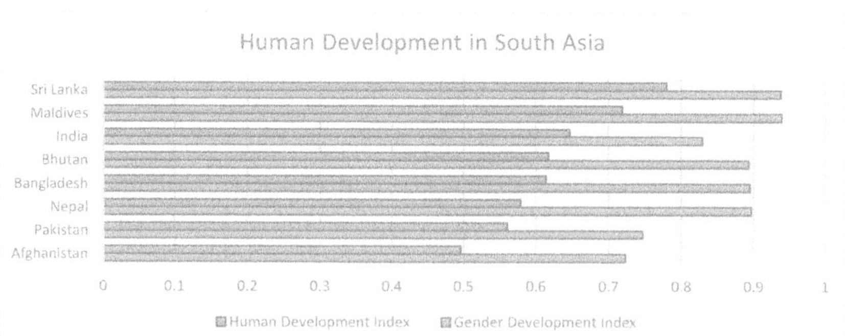

Figure 11.1 Human development in South Asia

Sources: United Nations Development Programme. (2019). Human Development Report 2019. New York, USA: United Nations Development Programme.

Table 11.1 Monsoon seasons and rainfall distribution

Months	*Season*	*Rainfall (mm)*	*Rainfall (%)*
March–April	First inter-monsoon season (FIM)	268 mm	14%
May–September	Southwest monsoon season (SWM)	556 mm	30%
October–November	Second inter-monsoon season (SIM)	558 mm	30%
December–February	Northeast monsoon season (NEM)	479 mm	26%
Overall mean annual rainfall:		1,861 mm	100%

Source: Ministry of Mahaweli Development and Environment. (2015). National Adaptation Plan for Climate Change Impacts in Sri Lanka: 2016–2025.

and Moneragala) and sectors, with the estate sector being more than four times as vulnerable as the urban sector and 1.76 times as vulnerable as the rural sector.[19]

Sri Lanka has a significant regional variation in temperature, and the country can be divided into three distinct climatic zones: the wet zone in the South-eastern part and the central hill country, the dry zone centred around the Northern and Eastern regions, and the intermediate zone. As temperatures across all of these zones are relatively constant throughout the year, climate patterns are determined by variations in precipitation caused by two distinct monsoon seasons.[20]

Climate Risks and Vulnerabilities

Climate data and projections show a clear trend of overall warming temperatures, less predictable precipitation patterns, sea level rise, and increasing weather extremes throughout South Asia.[21] In Sri Lanka, around nineteen million people – 90% of the entire population – live in areas that are poised to become moderate to severe hotspots as early as 2050 under an RCP 8.5 carbon-intensive scenario. In these areas, changes in average temperature and precipitation are set to negatively impact living standards by 7.1% in moderate and 10.5% in severe hotspots.[22]

Sri Lanka already suffers various impacts of climate change, including flash floods and flood surges, droughts and prolonged dry spells, landslides, erratic precipitation patterns, heatwaves, high winds, storms and cyclones, sea level rise, ocean acidification, saline intrusion, soil degradation, and hotter night temperatures.[23] In the past decade alone, Sri Lanka has experienced Cyclone Roanu in 2016; historic droughts in 2015–16 and 2016–17; and major floods in 2010, 2011, 2014, 2016, and 2018 which affected hundreds of thousands of people.

These climate impacts severely threaten communities especially in the dry zone and the densely populated coastal belt, compromising livelihoods related to fisheries, agriculture, livestock, forestry, and tourism, as well as posing increasing dangers from extreme weather events and disasters such as floods, storm surges, and tropical cyclones.[24] Between 1990 and 2018, recurring disasters have caused recorded damages of nearly US$7 billion and additional costs arising from unrecorded local events, smaller scale events, and long-term impacts such as monsoon collapse and soil degradation.[25]

Floods and storms cause the highest direct damages to property and assets (US$2.5 billion and US$400 million between 1990 and 2018, respectively) and are together responsible for 99% of such damages caused by disasters. Slow-onset disasters such as droughts, however, affect larger numbers of households and have severe socio-economic ripple effects. In addition, there are also indirect costs, such as an additional strain on the national healthcare system of an estimated US$52.8 million annually due to floods and droughts, as well as non-economic losses and damages.[26]

A Rural Economy

Despite the decline of its GDP contribution to 7.4% in 2019,[27] the agriculture sector still provides employment for more than two million people, a quarter of Sri Lanka's total employed population.[28] The dominant crop is paddy which was cultivated on over one million hectares and produced almost four million metric tonnes in 2018.[29] The majority of agricultural operators, approximately 1.65 million people, are smallholders farmers who cultivate less than two hectares on average but provide 80% of the country's total annual food production.[30]

According to the 2012 census, Sri Lanka's urbanization rate is 18.2%,[31] ranking it near the bottom in global comparison, although other estimates suggest that urbanization might in fact be as high as 35%, 45%, or even 50%.[32] In any case, a vast proportion of Sri Lanka's population remains rural and relies on agriculture for their main or only source of livelihood, income, and food security, making them particularly vulnerable to the adverse impacts of climate change.[33]

Floods, droughts, storms, and landslides are exacerbated by climate change and are projected to further increase in frequency and severity over the coming decades.[34] Sri Lanka's farmers struggle with droughts, floods, and alternating floods and droughts that lead to progressive soil depletion, water scarcity, and erosion of ecosystem services. Reduced crop yields, failing harvests, health impacts such as kidney disease, loss of income, and lack of alternative livelihoods in rural areas present strong push factors and drive out-migration either on a seasonal or long-term basis.[35]

In particular, drought has become a determining factor for rural-urban migration in Sri Lanka and is among the most pressing issues identified by the agricultural community. In 2016 and 2017, the country went through the worst drought in forty years which affected twenty districts and approximately 1.8 million people.[36] It is important to note that drought has multiple overlapping dimensions – meteorological, hydrological, agricultural, socio-economic – which are relevant for Sri Lanka and especially the country's dry zone.[37]

Changing weather patterns trigger prolonged dry spells and render precipitation patterns more erratic and less reliable, but it is the rural population's poverty and vulnerability to poverty, its lack of access to technology, gaps in knowledge and awareness, and the need for better land and water management that make droughts so devastating and dangerous.[38] Much of the country's ancient irrigation infrastructure[39] has fallen into varying states of disrepair, and the system of major and minor cascading tanks no longer work effectively in many areas.[40]

Out of twenty livelihood zones identified in a consolidated livelihood mapping exercise conducted by the Government of Sri Lanka and the World Food Programme in 2014, only five livelihood zones were classified as food secure. The remaining livelihood zones were classified as either food insecure in a bad year (30%), seasonally food insecure (30%), or chronically food insecure (15%). Similarly, only two zones were classified as having a very low sensitivity to changes in climatic patterns, with another 40% having low sensitivity and the remaining 50% either moderately or highly sensitive to climatic changes.[41]

If climate change impacts continue to increase in frequency and severity, the resulting monsoon collapse, sea level rise, and climatic shift are projected to further compromise food security and income across Sri Lanka.[42]

Migration Dynamics in Sri Lanka

Migration is defined as the process of moving within or across borders, either temporarily, seasonally, or permanently. It is commonly associated with an element of choice and is considered to be voluntary in nature as opposed to displacement, which refers to instances where people are forced to move within or across borders.[43]

> Environmental migrants are persons or groups of persons who, predominantly for reasons of sudden or progressive change in the environment that adversely affects their lives or living conditions, are obliged to leave their habitual homes, or choose to do so, either temporarily or permanently, and who move either within their country or abroad.[44]

The Constitution of the Democratic Socialist Republic of Sri Lanka guarantees every citizen the "freedom of movement and of choosing his residence within Sri Lanka" under the Fundamental Rights listed in chapter III, paragraph 14.[45] There has always been human mobility around the island, and around one-fifth of the population consists of internal migrants. According to 2016 government statistics, one out of every eight households has at least one internal migrant residing elsewhere in the country, and one out of every fourteen households has an international migrant, with remittances being sent back by both kinds of migrants.[46]

Besides marriage and reuniting with family members, economic reasons are the major drivers of internal and international migration in Sri Lanka. There are four main types of migration dynamics in Sri Lanka: permanent internal migration, temporary disaster displacement, departures for foreign employment, and cyclical economic migration. Except for departures for foreign employment, all of these movements take place within Sri Lanka's borders and across districts and provinces, with the direction predominantly from rural to urban areas, although rural-rural and urban-urban migration take place as well (SLYCAN Trust, 2019b).

In addition, there are additional international migration streams, such as student migration, refugees, and inbound migration of foreign citizens, but there is not sufficient proof to establish a close link to climate change impacts within Sri Lanka.[47]

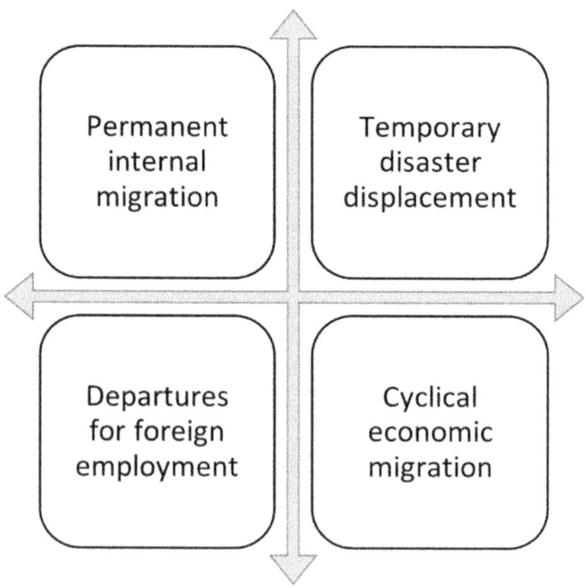

Figure 11.2 Major migration streams in Sri Lanka

Source: Prepared by the authors.

Permanent Internal Migration

As recorded in Sri Lanka's 2012 census of population and housing, the total number of internal migrants in Sri Lanka came to 4,115,363. One in seven Sri Lankans is an inter-provincial migrant, one in five an inter-district migrant.[48] Besides marriage (30.89%) and accompanying a family member (18.82%), employment (20%) is the main reason given for migration. In many cases, this move is permanent, and around 65% of migrants remain in their new districts for at least five years.[49]

Sri Lanka's internal migrants mainly come from the agricultural provinces, including the Central Province, Southern Province, North Western Province, and North Central Province.[50] Inadequate arable land, economic constraints, low productivity, personal attitudes, and climate change impacts[51] funnel many people in these areas into a "poverty trap," where low resource endowment leads to low productivity which in turn leads to low income and further erosion of resources.[52]

In Colombo district, 42% of migrants, approximately 280,000 people (almost 7% of all migrants in Sri Lanka) have come for employment. Almost one-third (31.32%) of all internal migrants in Sri Lanka live in Colombo district and Gampaha district, with other large migrant populations in Kalutara (234,102 people), Kurunegala (241,058 people), and Kandy (235,206 people).[53]

With the exception of Kurunegala, these are the most urban districts in Sri Lanka, with urbanization rates of 90.51% in Colombo, 67.32% in Gampaha, 62.09% in Kalutara, and 56.98% in Kandy districts.[54] Cities are the economic centres of Sri Lanka, and the Western Region Megapolis and the eight other provincial capitals together account for 71% of Sri Lanka's GDP. These cities offer employment and other economic opportunities, for example, in construction or the textile industry, which serve as powerful pull factors.[55]

Temporary Disaster Displacement

Within South Asia, Sri Lanka has been identified by the Internal Displacement Monitoring Centre as the country with the highest relative risk of being displaced by disasters in 2015. On an annual basis, 15,000 out of every million inhabitants are at risk of being displaced by disasters. In 2018 alone, almost two million people were affected by droughts, 190,000 people were affected by floods, and 18,000 people were affected by strong winds.[56]

Between 1980 and 1990, climate-related disasters impacted an average of 400,000 people per year in Sri Lanka, a number that has risen to 750,000 per year between 2000 and 2013.[57] In 2016, one in every eleven households was affected by natural disasters,[58] and in 2019, the Internal Displacement

Monitoring Centre counted 87,000 new disaster displacements in Sri Lanka.[59]

Sudden-onset events such as cyclones, flooding, or landslides cause people to lose their land, home, and possessions, and force them to move out of the affected area into temporary shelters and relief sites. While many will eventually move back to rebuild their destroyed assets and livelihoods, those whose homes and livelihoods (particularly agriculture) have been permanently lost or damaged can find themselves forced to move permanently in search of work in order to survive.[60]

As the movement in these cases is unplanned, not out of choice, and disproportionately affects poor rural populations, people end up in informal settlements in the outskirts of urban areas. Forty percent of Sri Lanka's poor inhabit such informal settlements around the urban areas of the capital region, rendering them highly vulnerable to infectious diseases,[61] further flooding events, and displacement as these settlements tend to lack resilient infrastructure and basic sanitation.[62]

Departures for Foreign Employment

International labour migration is one of the major migration streams for Sri Lanka and has been an important contributor to the national economy for decades. 2018 saw approximately 211,000 departures for foreign employment divided into 61% men and 39% women, the majority of which went as skilled labourers (32%), housemaids (31%), or unskilled labourers (24%).[63] The main countries of destination are situated in the Middle East,

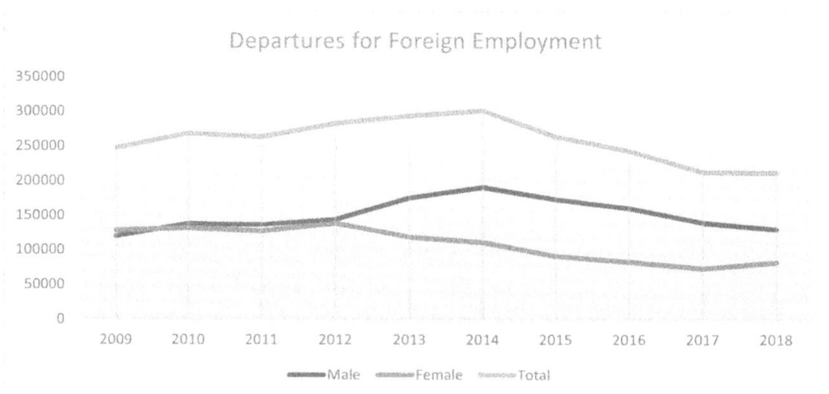

Figure 11.3 Departures for foreign employment

Sources: Department of Census and Statistics. (2020). Statistical Data Sheet 2019. Battaramulla, Sri Lanka: Ministry of Finance, Economy and Policy Development; Sri Lanka Bureau of Foreign Employment. (2018). Different Perspectives of Departure Details. Colombo, Sri Lanka: Sri Lanka Bureau of Foreign Employment.

with Saudi Arabia, Qatar, the United Arab Emirates, and Kuwait being the most common.[64]

Overall departures for foreign employment have stayed between 210,000 and 300,000 since the end of the Civil War in 2009, with a slight downward trend over the entire ten-year period. At its peak, the proportion of women among Sri Lanka's migrant workers stood at over 75%.[65] However, while more women than men departed in 2009, the proportions reversed to 61%–68% men and 34–39% women in recent years.[66]

This change can be partially attributed to policy changes instituted with the family background report circulars 2013 which mandated compulsory family background checks and made it harder for women to migrate abroad, especially if they have children.[67]

Migrant worker remittances are a key source of income for Sri Lanka, and the country receives the fourth highest amount of remittances in South Asia, accounting for 10% of the total GDP, over half of which stems from the countries of the Gulf Cooperation Council.[68] In 2016, one in every eight Sri Lankan households received internal remittances, and one in every eleven households received foreign remittances.[69]

The rapid growth and high absolute value of remittances indicate the reliance of Sri Lanka's national economy on foreign employment.[70] Most labour migrants are from districts that simultaneously serve as destinations for internal migration: Colombo (13.1%), Gampaha (10.3%), Kandy (9.7%), Kalutara (5.4%), or Kurunegala (8%).[71] Despite their attractiveness as sources of employment opportunities, districts such as Kalutara, Kurunegala, and even Gampaha are also highly affected by climate impacts including floods and droughts. However, due to the much higher economic diversification and better infrastructure in these urban areas, migrants remain motivated to move toward them.[72]

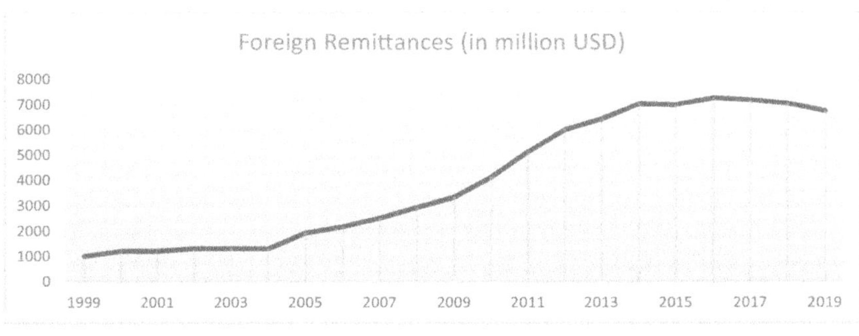

Figure 11.4 Foreign remittances to Sri Lanka

Source: International Labour Organization, Labour Migration Branch. (2019). Review of law, policy and practice of recruitment of migrant workers in Sri Lanka. Geneva, Switzerland: International Labour Organization.

Currently, the extent to which climate change influences these labour migration movements is not well-documented. An ongoing research surveyed a number of female migrant workers in Kuwait and found that 60% of them – with an average monthly pre-departure household income of LKR 12,300 (approximately USD 66) – had experienced weather impacts on their livelihoods in the form of heavy or prolonged rains. It is probable that this is widespread and affects especially the poorest and most vulnerable households.[73]

Cyclical Economic Migration

The fourth and last main type of migration dynamic in Sri Lanka is routine internal economic migration that takes place in cyclical or seasonal patterns aligned to the agricultural calendar and is caused by climate impacts on agricultural livelihoods.[74]

Rising temperatures, prolonged dry spells, droughts, land degradation, and increasingly erratic rainfall patterns place immense pressure on the rural economy and the patterns of village life. The rural economy depends on agriculture and sufficient irrigation, as people are engaged in tank-irrigated lowland paddy cultivation (supplemented by onion, chilli, corn, and pulses during the minor Yala season) or grow vegetables and other crops, such as legumes, coarse grains, vegetables, and fruit, in rainfed upland and home garden cultivation, often integrated with additional small-scale livestock farming. Only a small percentage of the rural population works in public institutions or private organizations, and a decline in agriculture leaves the vast majority without livelihood options.[75]

In most areas of Sri Lanka, smallholder farmers require two successful harvests per year to generate enough income to keep themselves and their family above the poverty line.[76] Protracted climate impacts and recurring disasters drain assets such as savings, land, cattle, or tools, and once other coping strategies – sale and pawning of household assets, borrowing money, taking loans, or using government relief funding – are exhausted, migration to find alternative work is left as the only option.[77]

In a 2018–19 survey across farming communities in Trincomalee district conducted by SLYCAN Trust, a near-total majority (97%) was engaged in predominantly rainfed (55%; other farmers rely on river-based irrigation, wells, or small tanks), small-scale (average of 2.7 acres of paddy), low-income agriculture. Virtually all farmers (97%) reported impacts from droughts and heat while 89% had additionally experienced changes in rainfall patterns, leading to the migration of household members in 80% of surveyed households.[78] Another survey in Rathnapura district found that more than 11% of the total population had migrated out of the district due to declining livelihoods, with a five to one ratio of male to female migrants.[79]

These findings are mirrored in other districts across Sri Lanka's dry zone, where climate-sensitive agriculture is the only major source of employment. The main characteristic of this rural-urban migration is its circular nature, where migrants leave their place of permanent residence with the intention of returning in regular intervals or after a certain amount of time. They move to urban centres for employment opportunities and to earn additional income, but there is no permanent settlement and no planned family reunification. In the Trincomalee survey, 62.5% of households with a migrating family member reported that this person would come back once per month or once every couple of months to stay for several days or a week in their home community while supporting it with remittances for the rest of the year.[80]

As these migrants predominantly stem from farming communities and have not undertaken alternative vocational training, they are forced to engage in unskilled labour in low-paying and often dangerous fields such as construction.[81] Due to the rise in internal migration numbers, there is now also a surge in demand for employment that makes it increasingly difficult for new migrants to find work. In Colombo, approximately 45% of income-earning household members are engaged in unskilled employment, and about 9% of households have no source of regular income at all.[82]

Due to the significant barriers for women attempting to access the urban labour market and socio-cultural preconceptions and traditions,[83] there is a strong gender component connected to this type of migration. The overwhelming majority of cyclical economic migrants in Sri Lanka are adult males while women, children, the disabled, and the elderly stay behind in rural areas.[84]

The Nexus of Climate Change and Migration

The linkages between climate change and migration in Sri Lanka are complex and present significant gaps in data and research. However, the impacts of climate change in Sri Lanka are significant, and there is a clear causal relationship between them and the reduction of agricultural yields, incomes, and livelihoods.[85]

It is assumed that the severe and wide-ranging impacts of climate change on Sri Lanka and especially the rural sector affect all four types of migration dynamics.[86] However, this is well-documented only for temporary disaster displacement, where the increasing occurrence and intensity of disasters such as floods and storms can be directly linked to climate change. For the remaining three types, climate change is not causing migration on its own but instead functions as an underlying driver of "climate mobilities"[87] in Sri Lanka.

While sudden onset disasters like floods and landslides, which are increasing in frequency and intensity, lead to forced displacement, slow-onset impacts affect entire areas over larger timescales and amplify existing push and pull factors.[88] The rise in temperatures, saline intrusion, unreliable rainfall patterns, dry spells, and droughts lead to land degradation and reduced yields from agricultural crops, livestock, fisheries, and forestry. This reduction in agricultural potential and ecosystem services, in conjunction with health impacts and water scarcity, impacts livelihoods and creates a strong incentive for labour migration.[89]

The rural economy in Sri Lanka's dry zone revolves around agriculture, and many families already live on the verge of multidimensional poverty or have to pay off loans for seeds and equipment. Climate change can tip the scales and render small-scale agriculture, home gardening, tank fisheries, and other rural income sources unviable, forcing families to either find other employment, fall into poverty, or move away.[90]

Sri Lanka's migration streams, both short- and long-term, lead from rural areas to urban areas or abroad. While people have strong cultural and familial ties to their home regions and a basic support system, the loss of their livelihoods forces them to seek alternative income opportunities. In many rural areas, the economy has a very low degree of diversification and no secondary employment options.

A lack of awareness about climate change impacts among farmers, agricultural extension officers, and local government officials presents an obstacle to both data collection and the implementation of adaptation measures.[91]

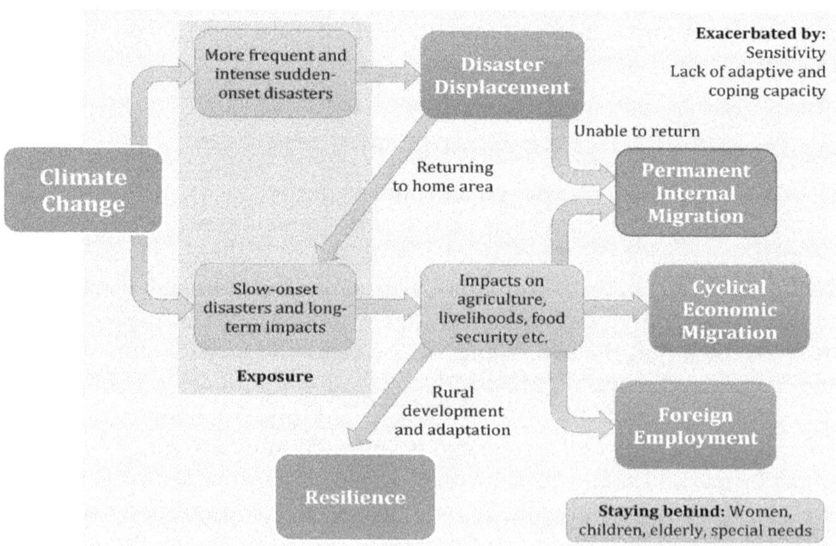

Figure 11.5 Human mobility dynamics and climate change in Sri Lanka

Sources: Prepared by the authors.

Farmers cultivate the same crop combinations and take up loans to support their livelihoods even in the face of recurring droughts and dry spells.[92] While they experience the impacts of climate change, many farmers are not aware of climate change as a technical term. However, a strong majority reported incidences of droughts and shifts in rainfall patterns, changes in the annual amount of rain, temperature increase and reduction of water retention in cultivation soil, salinity, and increases in underground water scarcity, as well as pests and diseases in cultivation.[93]

To date, there is a lack of data on temporary internal labour migration, and it is hard to establish its exact relationship to climate change. Sri Lankan government authorities such as the Disaster Management Centre currently collect data on temporary disaster displacement, but not on temporary and permanent migration related to climate change, on the relationship between household characteristics (such as income availability, livelihoods, and access to food and water) and climate-induced migration, or on the impact of slow-onset events on migration dynamics.[94]

Therefore, it is not empirically possible to distinguish between climate migrants and non-climate migrants in Sri Lanka. However, this does not discard the potential for climate change to disrupt lives and livelihoods,[95] or the existence of climate change as one of the underlying drivers of migration in Sri Lanka.[96]

As a result, the solution to climate-induced migration will revolve around identifying risks and vulnerabilities, reducing exposure, and strengthening adaptive and coping capacities especially of the millions of Sri Lankans who live in rural areas and are dependent on climate-sensitive agriculture. Resilient and diversified livelihoods, reliable access to food and water, effective health services and infrastructure, and a social safety net can alleviate both push and pull factors.[97]

Existing Legal and Policy Frameworks

A need for effective laws, policies, and institutions as well as policy coherence has been pointed out as priorities to address "climate fragilities" and the impacts of climate change.[98] Sri Lanka has a number of domestic and international laws, policies, plans, and strategies that are relevant to climate change, rural development, disaster risk reduction, disaster management, environmental degradation, displacement, and migration.

While the government and non-government actors such as civil society organizations and other stakeholders are providing support and relief to vulnerable parts of the population, there are existing gaps and needs as well as opportunities to strengthen the existing legal and policy framework to better integrate climate migration into national and international processes on climate change, sustainable development, and disaster risk reduction and management.[99]

Labour and Migration Policies

Sri Lanka has a robust framework for labour migration that was solidified with the Colombo Process in 2003, the National Labour Migration Policy in 2008, and the National Migration Health Policy and Action Plan in 2013.[100] An over-arching Safe Labour Migration Programme was established by the government in 2016, and a minimum wage of US$00 for migrant workers was instituted in 2017.[101] In its "Vision 2025," Sri Lanka aims to "balance policies to promote out-migration with domestic labour market needs."[102]

The Sri Lanka National Migration Health Policy covers outbound, inbound, and internal migrants and makes reference to "diverse reasons" that drive these migration dynamics. In addition to the health risks and impacts to outbound migrants, the policy identifies significant negative impacts on the health status of family members left behind (mainly women, children, and the elderly) and recognizes an urgent need to examine and respond to their mental and physical health needs, including the prevalence of common mental disorders such as depression, sleeping disorders, and anxiety along with child psychopathology such as behavioural, conduct, and emotional disorders.[103]

Furthermore, the policy also addresses the need to care for the vulnerable children of migrant workers on a regular basis and to establish a coordination mechanism between education authorities and the authorities responsible for migrant care. The health of internal migrants is an inadequately addressed area of migration and has been identified as a significant public health challenge.[104] Despite the existence of the frameworks mentioned

Table 11.2 Labour migration governance in Sri Lanka

Relevant government entities	Ministry of Foreign Employment Sri Lanka Bureau of Foreign Employment Sri Lanka Foreign Employment Agency National Steering Committee on Migration Health Association of Licensed Foreign Employment Agencies
Key domestic policies and laws	Immigrants and Emigrants Act No. 20 of 1948 Sri Lanka Bureau of Foreign Employment Act No. 21 of 1985 National Labour Migration Policy for Sri Lanka (2008) Sri Lanka National Migration Health Policy (2013) Family Background Report Circulars (2013)
International processes	Convention on the Rights of the Child (ratified 1991) UN Migrant Workers Convention (ratified 1996) ILO Multilateral Framework on Labour Migration (2006) UN Trafficking Protocol (ratified 2015) ILO General Principles and Operational Guidelines for Fair Recruitment (2016) Sustainable Development Goals (especially indicators 10.7.1, 10.7.2, 10.C.1, 16.2.2, 17.3.2, and 17.18.1)

Sources: Prepared by the authors.

earlier, there are also migrants who attempt to find new livelihoods and escape poverty through different means and without acquiring work and travel documentation, which results in difficulties abroad and puts them at risk of exploitation and abuse.

Sri Lanka is involved in a number of international processes regarding migration, including as founding member of the Colombo Process and as chair of the Abu Dhabi Dialogue. The country has ratified the Convention on the Rights of the Child in 1993 and the International Convention on the Protection of the Rights of All Migrant Workers and Members of Their Families in 1996. However, as of 2020, the 1949 ILO Migration for Employment Convention, the 1951 Convention relating to the Status of Refugees, the 1954 Convention relating to the Status of Stateless Persons, the 1961 Convention on the Reduction of Statelessness, 1961, and the 1975 ILO Migrant Workers (Supplementary Provisions) Convention have not been ratified by Sri Lanka.[105]

Safe migration is not integrated with climate change adaptation, loss and damage, sustainable development, and disaster risk reduction in Sri Lanka. The National Labour Migration Policy for Sri Lanka does not address climate change or disaster displacement,[106] while the National Migration Health Policy acknowledges that "outbound migrants comprise the flow of population moving out of Sri Lanka for diverse reasons," but does not specifically refer to climate change.[107]

Disaster Risk Reduction and Disaster Management

Similar to labour migration, Sri Lanka has a solid framework to handle climate-induced disasters, provide early warning, distribute relief, and evacuate people.[108] The Disaster Management Centre publishes daily weather reports and updates on disaster losses, including figures on displacement and property losses and damages,[109] and a number of online portals (DesInventar, Sri Lanka Disaster Resource Network, RiskInfo) have been developed to collate geospatial data, hazard maps, risk assessments, impact analyses, and other relevant data.[110]

On the policy level, the Government of Sri Lanka has committed to integrate disaster risk reduction across sectors, and "[investment] in flood and drought mitigation has become a crucial element in spatial planning and area development plans."[111]

Sri Lanka has also been operating risk transfer instruments for the agricultural sector since 1958, with national-level public crop insurance schemes that protect farmers from a number of climate- and non-climate-related hazards (including wild elephants). In addition, a national disaster insurance scheme operated by the National Insurance Trust Fund insures every house in Sri Lanka against natural disasters and triggers compensation payouts in case of destruction.[112] While there are gaps in awareness

Table 11.3 Disaster management in Sri Lanka

Relevant government entities	Ministry of Defence National Council for Disaster Management Disaster Management Centre National Disaster Relief Services Centre Department of Meteorology National Building Research Organization National Insurance Trust Fund
Key domestic policies and laws	Sri Lanka Disaster Management Act No. 13 of 2005 National Policy on Disaster Management (2013) National Emergency Operations Plan (2013) National Disaster Risk Management Plan 2013–2017 Comprehensive Disaster Management Programme 2014–2018 Nationally Determined Contributions (2016) National Adaptation Plan for Climate Change in Sri Lanka (2016) National Disaster Risk Management Plan 2018–2030
International processes	Warsaw International Mechanism for Loss and Damage associated with Climate Change Impacts (especially the Task Force on Displacement) Sendai Framework for Disaster Risk Reduction

Sources: Prepared by the authors.

and acceptance of these insurance schemes, Sri Lanka is demonstrating a commitment to diverse risk reduction and risk management strategies that can shield its vulnerable population from livelihood loss and the impacts of climate change.[113]

Climate Change and Migration

Sri Lanka has two main documents outlining its commitments for climate change mitigation and adaptation under the United Nations Framework Convention on Climate Change (UNFCCC) and the Paris Agreement, namely its Nationally Determined Contributions (NDCs) and its National Adaptation Plan for Climate Change in Sri Lanka 2016–2025 (NAP). Both documents have been officially submitted to the UNFCCC in November 2016,[114] with reviewed and updated NDCs submitted in July and September 2021 ahead of the 26th Meeting of the Conference of the Parties to the UNFCCC.

Sri Lanka's NAP comprises nine sectors for climate change adaptation and several cross-cutting national needs, including disaster risk management and climate information management. Climate-induced displacement due to floods, droughts, landslides, cyclones, high winds, saline intrusion, and inundation is listed as an impact under the human settlements and infrastructure sector, including both sudden- and slow-onset disasters. Beyond that, there is no explicit reference to migration or displacement, but underlying drivers caused by the impacts of climate change are addressed

Table 11.4 Climate change governance in Sri Lanka

Relevant government entities	National Climate Change Commission (to be instituted) Ministry of Environment and Wildlife Resources Climate Change Secretariat National Experts Committee on Climate Change Adaptation National Council for Sustainable Development
Key domestic policies and laws	National Climate Change Adaptation Strategy 2011–2016 National Climate Change Policy of Sri Lanka (2012) Sri Lanka National Migration Health Policy (2013) National Action Programme for Combating Land Degradation of Sri Lanka (2014) Nationally Determined Contributions (2016/2021) National Adaptation Plan for Climate Change in Sri Lanka 2016–2025 Sustainable Development Act No. 19 of 2017 National Policy and Strategy for Sustainable Development (Draft)
International processes	UNFCCC/Paris Agreement Sustainable Development Goals (especially SDG1, SDG2, SDG3, and indicators 10.7.2 and 17.18.1) Global Compact for Safe, Orderly, and Regular Migration (especially objectives 2, 5, 21, and 23)

Sources: Prepared by the authors.

across all sectors with a range of adaptation options and actions (SLYCAN Trust, 2019c).[115]

The original 2016 NDC submission does not explicitly refer to migration or displacement but addresses risk reduction, risk management, and climate-resilient development in several of its adaptation sectors. Food security, water and irrigation, and loss and damage all focus on protecting agricultural livelihoods and reduce vulnerabilities to climate change through resistant crop varieties and livestock breeds, water and land management, integrated pest management, identifying adaptive measures and innovative technologies, meteorological forecasting and early warning, and the introduction of risk transfer instruments.[116] The updated 2021 NDCs explicitly reference migration, displacement, and planned relocation as forms of climate-induced population movement and acknowledge the interlinkages between human mobility and climate-related vulnerabilities. This connection is included in greater detail than in the original NDC submission, and further study as well as enhanced availability and analysis of data and information are identified as key needs to address the nexus of climate change and human mobility.[117]

The NDC sector on loss and damage also includes the establishment of a local mechanism under the Warsaw International Mechanism (WIM), which is based on the international WIM which has a dedicated action area on migration, displacement, and mobility.[118] The WIM under the UNFCCC has also set up a Task Force on Displacement with the objective to "develop recommendations for integrated approaches to avert, minimize, and address displacement related to the adverse impacts of climate change,"[119] which has published a report in 2018 with information on the technical work it has undertaken since its establishment.[120]

There is considerable potential to further integrate human mobility in the context of climate change into national adaptation planning and future revisions of the NDCs and NAP, for example by considering data collection and baseline assessments, local and sectoral planning processes, and monitoring, evaluation, and impact assessments.[121]

Furthermore, the facilitation of "orderly, safe, regular and responsible migration and mobility of people" is included as one of the targets under Sustainable Development Goal (SDG)10 (Reduced Inequalities), and progress toward the other SDGs, including SDG 13 (Climate Action), will be crucial to reduce out-migration from rural areas.[122] In addition, the Global Compact for Safe, Orderly and Regular Migration, an intergovernmental agreement formally endorsed by the United Nations General Assembly in 2018, establishes connections between climate change, disasters, and human mobility under several of its objectives.

Vulnerable Households and Gender-Specific Impacts

In the nexus of climate change and migration, minorities and vulnerable groups are not always represented due to a lack of gender-disaggregated data. However, it is clear that climate migration in Sri Lanka is a problem with highly differential impacts based on gender and age inequities.[123]

As family members migrate out of rural areas, their spouses, children, and elderly relatives stay behind. Due to the high gender disparity in relation to internal and international migration, the duty of childcare usually falls on women or members of the extended family.[124] In 2019, out of the entire economically inactive population of Sri Lanka – approximately 8.6 million people – 26.8% were male and 73.2% female, while the unemployment rate stood at 6.9% for women as opposed to 3.2% for men.[125] Furthermore, most unpaid family workers are women.[126]

The challenges of women "trapped" in the rural areas of Sri Lanka are varied and include a triple burden of household and childcare duties, agricultural responsibilities, and additional income and food generation, for example, through home gardening.[127] While migrating family members are vulnerable to exploitation, unsafe work conditions, injuries, illness, and other adverse impacts on their health, women staying behind to face the brunt of climate impacts together with children, the elderly, and people with disabilities or special needs.

Increased levels of poverty and more frequent sudden-onset disasters disrupt the lives of children and put their development, wellbeing, and security at risk.[128] The absence of one parent has a negative effect on the overall health and development of children, rendering them vulnerable to violations of their basic rights to quality education, welfare, and freedom from child labour.[129] They are also vulnerable to mistreatment, abuse, neglect, or dropping out of school, and the special attention of the healthcare systems to these families is of great importance.[130]

Another threat that disproportionately affects children is food insecurity at the household level, which can lead to insufficient intake of nutrition and impede the growth and the physical and cognitive development of children. Studies have shown that 25% of children in households with a migrant worker are underweight and can develop deficiencies in their skill development and coping abilities.[131] The prevalence of stunting (being too short for one's age) has increased from 13.1% in 2012 to 17.1% in 2016, while the prevalence of wasting (being too thin for one's height) among children under five has reached 15%. Pregnant women and nursing mothers are likewise at heightened danger from a lack of adequate nutrition.[132]

In addition to these impacts on children, the disruption of the family structure also affects the mental and physical health of adults left behind, leading to a higher prevalence of alcohol abuse among these family members.[133] Elderly caregivers (mostly parents of the migrating family member or their spouse) are even more likely to have their overall health significantly affected by the absence of the migrating family member and the added duties.[134]

Male out-migration also reduces the efficiency of traditional risk-sharing mechanisms when women have to assume traditional male responsibilities in agriculture and the village social ecosystem without having equal or direct access to technical, financial, and social resources. As key actors for maintaining the social cohesion of families, raising children, and keeping the household running, climate-induced migration imparts additional responsibilities on them without giving them additional rights, for example, in the context of land and property rights.[135]

There are large gender disparities in access to and control over resources, access to markets, and access to skills training. Women own only 16% of all privately owned land in Sri Lanka, but land ownership is a prerequisite to accessing irrigation organizations and thereby government-provided water.[136] Due to their responsibilities, women are also limited in their ability to seek paid employment and are particularly vulnerable to economic and social risks.[137]

To alleviate these impacts, there is a need to collect gender-disaggregated data and evaluate the socio-economic characteristics of vulnerable households in Sri Lanka, their existing protection systems, gender-specific impacts, the impacts on youth and children, and aspects of equity and social justice. Promoting women's education, health, agricultural knowledge, and rights could reduce the impact of climate change on women and increase the overall resilience of rural communities.[138]

Challenges and Opportunities

In a survey conducted by McNamara et al. in 2017, a total of 262 experts working on people moving in the context of environmental change (PMEC) identified risk reduction, rural development planning, and preventing environmental push factors as the three most relevant response options, followed by increased adaptation financing and alternative livelihood training.[139]

Sri Lanka is already taking action to increase agricultural investment, boost rural development, enhance food security, and reduce poverty.[140] Water from the Mahaweli river basin originating in the Southern wet zone is being diverted to feed dry zone tanks and reservoirs and increase agricultural production, food security, and household incomes as well as to provide safe and reliable drinking water.[141] Financial assistance is given to farmer families affected by drought, and families are being relocated from areas that are highly prone to landslides.[142]

In its "Vision 2025" development document and the 2019 National Policy Framework "Vistas of Prosperity and Splendour," the respective Government of Sri Lanka has committed to undertake agricultural reforms, develop underserved districts, and enhance environmental protection and disaster risk management in the face of climate change.[143] The "Vistas of Prosperity and Splendour" additionally commit to "provide houses from housing schemes for displaced persons" as a direct reference to disaster-related mobility. Technical best practices including climate-smart agriculture, integrated land, water, and pest management, adaptive strategies, disaster risk reduction, risk transfer, and risk management mechanisms are promoted and developed, and a framework of institutions, laws, policies, plans, and strategies has been established.[144]

Turning the agriculture sector into a driver of rural development and reducing climate-related and economic reasons for migration while keeping it inclusive of women left behind and disenfranchised youth in rural areas is a considerable challenge.[145] Strong multi-stakeholder partnerships between central and local government, civil society organizations, farming and fishing societies, and the private sector (such as insurance companies) can enhance the resilience of the rural sector,[146] combined with renewed availability of resources and work, expanded social safety nets and rehabilitation mechanisms, increased awareness and knowledge,[147] and coupling risk assessments with immediate risk reduction investments.[148]

Conclusion

As discussed in this chapter, climate-induced migration in Sri Lanka is mostly caused by the erosion of livelihoods and ecosystem services in the rural sector and threatens the income, food security, health, and wellbeing of both the migrants and their family members staying behind. The major types of migration – permanent internal migration, temporary disaster displacement, departures for foreign employment, and cyclical economic migration – have complex linkages and interdependencies with climate risks and vulnerabilities. These connections are hard to track and to measure, and there are gaps regarding data availability, understanding, awareness, and institutional capacities when it comes to addressing climate mobility in Sri Lanka.

Over the past decades, rural and agriculture development have helped millions of people globally to escape poverty by addressing some of the root causes of migration, including rural poverty, food insecurity, inequality, unemployment, and natural resource depletion due to environmental degradation and climate change.[149] Finding a way to reduce involuntary climate-induced migration or turning it into an adaptation response will be critical for achieving the SDGs and facilitating sustainable rural development in Sri Lanka.[150]

Connecting Sri Lanka's experiences to the global processes related to climate migration could create synergies between the national and global level and allow the country to further benefit from ongoing processes such as NDC review and the WIM activities to enhance climate action related to migration and displacement. Addressing climate risks and vulnerabilities to increase the resilience of the affected populations while simultaneously developing and diversifying the rural economy in a sustainable manner could reduce the existing drivers of migration and stop forced displacement and involuntary migration.

Notes

1 Asian Development Bank. (2018). *Addressing climate change and migration in Asia and the Pacific*. Author.
2 Perera, E. L. (2014). Internal migration patterns and issues in Sri Lanka. In *Research symposium 2014: Emerging population issues and challenges*. University of Ruhuna.
3 Anderson, T., Shamsuddoha, M., & Dixit, A. (2016). *Climate change knows no borders. An analysis of climate induced migration, protection gaps and need for*

solidarity in South Asia. Climate Action Network – South Asia/Bread for the World/ActionAid.

4 Ranathunga, S. P. (2011). *Impact of rural to urban labour migration and the remittances on sending household welfare: A Sri Lankan case study*. Department of Economics, University of Waikato.

5 Anderson et al., *Climate change knows no borders*.

6 GEF Small Grants Programme. (2016). Coping with climate change and variability: Lessons from Sri Lankan communities. In *Proceedings of the national workshop on community based adaptation, July 16–18, 2013*. UNDP Global Environment Facility/Small Grants Programme (UNDP, GEF/SGP).

7 Anderson et al., *Climate change knows no borders*.

8 Stapleton, S. O., Nadin, R., Watson, C., & Kellett, J. (2017). *Climate change, migration and displacement: The need for a risk-informed and coherent approach*. Overseas Development Institute and United Nations Development Programme.

9 International Organization for Migration. (2008). *Migration and climate change: IOM migration research series, No. 31*. Author.

10 Central Bank of Sri Lanka. (2019). *Economic and social statistics of Sri Lanka 2019*. Central Bank of Sri Lanka.

11 Ibid.

12 The World Bank. (2020). *World Bank open data*. Retrieved from https://datahelpdesk.worldbank.org/knowledgebase/articles/906519-world-bankcountry-and-lending-groups.

13 Ibid.

14 United Nations Development Programme. (2019). *Human development report 2019*. Author.

15 World Health Organization. (2019). *World malaria report 2019*. World Health Organization.

16 UNDP/OPHI. (2020). *Global multidimensional poverty index 2020. Charting pathways out of multidimensional poverty: Achieving the SDGs*. United Nations Development Programme and Oxford Poverty and Human Development Initiative.

17 United Nations Development Programme, *Human development report 2019*.

18 Department of Census and Statistics. (2019). *Global multidimensional poverty for Sri Lanka*. Ministry of Economic Reforms and Public Distribution.

19 Ibid.

20 Ministry of Mahaweli Development and Environment. (2015). *National adaptation plan for climate change impacts in Sri Lanka: 2016–2025*. Ministry of Environment of Sri Lanka; Abeywardana, N., Schütt, B., Wagalawatta, T., & Bebermeier, W. (2019). Indigenous agricultural systems in the dry zone of Sri Lanka: Management transformation assessment and sustainability. *Sustainability, 11*. https://doi.org/10.3390/su11030910.

21 IPCC. (2014). *Climate change 2014: Synthesis report. Contribution of working groups I, II and III to the fifth assessment report of the intergovernmental panel on climate change*. Intergovernmental Panel on Climate Change.

22 Mani, M., Bandyopadhyay, S., Chonabayashi, S., Markandya, A., & Mosier, T. (2017). *South Asia's hotspots: Impacts of temperature and precipitation changes on living standards. South Asia development matters*. The World Bank.

23 Niranjan, F., Uddika, N. P., Bantilan, M. C., & Singh, N. P. (2015). Assessing agricultural vulnerability to climate change in Sri Lanka. *Sri Lanka Journal of Food and Agriculture*, 85–92; Nianthi, K. R., & Shaw, R. (2015). Climate change and its impact on coastal economy of Sri Lanka. In R. Krishnamurthy (Ed.), *The*

global challenge. Research Publishing; Asian Development Bank. (2017a). *A region at risk: The human dimensions of climate change in Asia and the Pacific*. Author; Anderson et al., *Climate change knows no borders*; World Meteorological Organization. (2016, April 24). Climate and health experts in South Asia act on heatwaves. *World Meteorological Organization*. Retrieved from https://public.wmo.int/en/media/news/climate-and-health-experts-south-asiaact-heatwaves.
24 Ministry of Mahaweli Development and Environment, *National adaptation plan for climate change impacts in Sri Lanka*.
25 United Nations Office for Disaster Risk Reduction. (2019). *Disaster risk reduction in Sri Lanka. Status report 2019*. United Nations Office for Disaster Risk Reduction, Regional Office for Asia and the Pacific.
26 Ibid.
27 Department of Census and Statistics. (2020a). *National accounts estimates of Sri Lanka. Provisional estimates for the year 2019*. Ministry of Finance, Economy and Policy Development.
28 Department of Census and Statistics. (2020b). *Quarterly report of the Sri Lanka labour force survey. Quarterly report 2019, fourth quarter*. Ministry of Finance, Economy and Policy Development.
29 Department of Census and Statistics. (2020c). *Statistical data sheet 2019*. Ministry of Finance, Economy and Policy Development.
30 Agriculture Division. (2019). *Agriculture sector modernization project*. Ministry of Mahaweli, Agriculture, Irrigation and Rural Development. Retrieved from www.agrimin.gov.lk/web/index.php/home-1/12-project/841-agriculture-sectormodernization-project.
31 Department of Census and Statistics. (2012). *Census of population and housing 2012*. Author.
32 Government of Sri Lanka. (2018). *State of Sri Lankan cities*. UN-Habitat.
33 Agriculture Division, *Agriculture sector modernization project*.
34 IPCC. (2018). *Global warming of 1.5°C. An IPCC special report on the impacts of global warming of 1.5°C above pre-industrial levels and related global greenhouse gas emission pathways*. Intergovernmental Panel on Climate Change.
35 Asian Development Bank, *Addressing climate change and migration in Asia and the Pacific*.
36 United Nations Office for Disaster Risk Reduction, *Disaster risk reduction in Sri Lanka*.
37 National Drought Mitigation Center, University of Nebraska. (2020, June 27). Types of drought. *National Drought Mitigation Center*. Retrieved from https://drought.unl.edu/Education/DroughtIn-depth/TypesofDrought.aspx.
38 Basnayake, B. M., Weddagala, W. M., Mahaliyanaarachchi, R. P., Sivasankar, P., & Elapata, M. S. (2017). Awareness of paddy farmers on climate change and its impact on crop production: A study in Kalthota irrigation scheme. *International Forestry and Environment Symposium*, 20. https://doi.org/10.31357/fesympo.v22i0.3336.
39 Panabokke, C. R. (2009). *Small village tank systems of Sri Lanka: Their evolution, setting, distribution and essential functions*. Hector Kobbekaduwa Agrarian Research and Training Institute.
40 International Union for Conservation of Nature. (2015). *Project implementation plan. IUCN programme on restoring traditional cascading tank systems Technical Note #1*. IUCN, Sri Lanka Country Office.
41 Krishnamurthy, K., Turano, E., Nanayakkara, L., & Kumarasiri, R. H. (2014). *Sri Lanka. Consolidated livelihood exercise for analysing resilience*. World Food Programme/Ministry of Economic Development.

42 Ibid.
43 International Organization for Migration. (2018b). *Migration governance snapshot: The democratic socialist Republic of Sri Lanka*. International Organization for Migration; Stapleton et al., *Climate change, migration and displacement*.
44 International Organization for Migration. (2014). *Migration, environment and climate change: Evidence for policy (MECLEP). Glossary*. International Organization for Migration.
45 Fundamental Rights chapter, Article 14 (1) (h)
46 Department of Census and Statistics. (2016). *Household income and expenditure survey 2016. HIES final report 2016*. Ministry of National Policies and Economic Affairs.
47 Epidemiology Unit, Ministry of Health, Nutrition & Indigenous Medicine. (2017a). *Weekly epidemiological report 28th–3rd February 2017. Migrant health (Part I)* (Vol. 44). Ministry of Health, Nutrition & Indigenous Medicine; Epidemiology Unit, Ministry of Health, Nutrition & Indigenous Medicine. (2017b). *Weekly epidemiological report 4th–10th February 2017. Migrant health (Part II)* (Vol. 44). Ministry of Health, Nutrition & Indigenous Medicine.
48 Perera, Internal migration patterns and issues in Sri Lanka
49 Department of Census and Statistics, *Census of population and housing 2012*.
50 Perera, A. (2017). Climate change-fueled drought drives Sri Lanka's farmers to cities. *Reuters*. Retrieved from www.reuters.com/article/sri-lanka-migration drought/feature-climate-change-fueled-drought-drives-sri-lankas-farmers-to-cities-idUSL8N1N54BV.
51 Ranathunga, *Impact of rural to urban labour migration and the remittances on sending household welfare*.
52 Samaratunga, P. A., Jayaweera, R., & Perera, N. (2012). *Impact of migration and remittances on investment in agriculture and food security in Sri Lanka. Research studies: Agricultural economic policy series no. 8*. Institute of Policy Studies of Sri Lanka.
53 Department of Census and Statistics, *Census of population and housing 2012*.
54 Weeraratne, B. (2016). *Re-defining urban areas in Sri Lanka. Working paper series no. 23*. Institute of Policy Studies of Sri Lanka.
55 Government of Sri Lanka, *State of Sri Lankan cities*.
56 Internal Displacement Monitoring Centre. (2015). *The risk of disaster-induced displacement in South Asia*. IDMC.
57 Krishnamurthy et al., *Sri Lanka. Consolidated livelihood exercise for analysing resilience*.
58 Institute of Policy Studies of Sri Lanka. (2018). *Policy insights: Linkages in climate change, migration and remittances in Sri Lanka*. Author.
59 Internal Displacement Monitoring Centre. (2020). *GRID 2020. Global report on internal displacement*. Author.
60 Anderson et al., *Climate change knows no borders*.
61 Epidemiology Unit, Ministry of Health, Nutrition & Indigenous Medicine, *Weekly epidemiological report 28th–3rd February 2017*; Epidemiology Unit, Ministry of Health, Nutrition & Indigenous Medicine, *Weekly epidemiological report 4th–10th February 2017*.
62 United Nations Office for Disaster Risk Reduction, *Disaster risk reduction in Sri Lanka*.
63 Department of Census and Statistics, *Quarterly report of the Sri Lanka labour force survey*.
64 Sri Lanka Bureau of Foreign Employment. (2018). *Different perspectives of departure details*. Author.

65 International Labour Organization. (2018b). *Sri Lankan female migrant workers and the family background report*. ILO Country Office for Sri Lanka and the Maldives.
66 Sri Lanka Bureau of Foreign Employment, *Different perspectives of departure details*.
67 International Labour Organization, *Sri Lankan female migrant workers and the family background report*; United Nations Sri Lanka, 2015.
68 Asian Development Bank/OECD/International Labour Organization. (2018). *Labor migration in Asia. Increasing the development impact of migration through finance and technology*. Author.
69 Institute of Policy Studies of Sri Lanka, *Policy insights*.
70 International Labour Organization, Labour Migration Branch. (2019). *Review of law, policy and practice of recruitment of migrant workers in Sri Lanka*. International Labour Organization.
71 Sri Lanka Bureau of Foreign Employment, *Different perspectives of departure details*.
72 Ministry of Environment. (2011). *Sri Lanka's second national communication on climate change*. Ministry of Environment of Sri Lanka.
73 Ongoing research conducted by SLYCAN Trust, a Sri Lankan civil society think tank.
74 Damayanthi, M. K., & Gamage, D. (2011). *Transformation of smallholder agriculture sector in Sri Lanka: An annotated compendium of statistics*. Hector Kobbekaduwa Agrarian Research and Training Institute; Ministry of Mahaweli Development and Environment, *National adaptation plan for climate change impacts in Sri Lanka*.
75 Food and Agriculture Organization. (2018). *Country gender assessment of agriculture and the rural sector in Sri Lanka*. Food and Agriculture Organization of the United Nations.
76 Perera, Climate change-fueled drought drives Sri Lanka's farmers to cities.
77 Anderson et al., *Climate change knows no borders*.
78 SLYCAN Trust, 2019.
79 International Labour Organization, *Sri Lankan female migrant workers and the family background report*.
80 SLYCAN Trust, 2019.
81 Risath, A. L., Sivatharsan, S., & Thishanth, P. (2017). Perception of construction workers on work motivation towards safe practices at building construction site: A case study in oluvil. *SEUSL Journal of Marketing*, *2*(1).
82 Sevanatha. (2003). *Understanding slums: Case studies for the global report on human settlements. The case of Colombo, Sri Lanka*. Urban Resource Centre.
83 Government of Sri Lanka, *State of Sri Lankan cities*.
84 SLYCAN Trust, 2019.
85 Ministry of Mahaweli Development and Environment. (2016). *Nationally determined contributions*. Ministry of Mahaweli Development and Environment of Sri Lanka.
86 Rigaud, K. K., De Sherbinin, A., Jones, B., Bergmann, J., Clement, V., Ober, K., . . . Midgley, A. (2018). *Groundswell. Preparing for internal climate migration*. World Bank Group.
87 Boas, I., Farbotko, C., Adams, H., Sterly, H., Bush, S., Van der Geest, K., . . . Hulme, M. (2019, November 26). Climate migration myths. *Nature Climate Change*, 898–903. https://doi.org/10.1038/s41558-019-0633-3.
88 Asian Development Bank. (2017a). *A region at risk*; Asian Development Bank. (2017b). *Ending water scarcity in Sri Lanka's dry zone*. Author.

89 De Alwis, D., & Noy, I. (2019). The cost of being under the weather: Droughts, floods, and health-care costs in Sri Lanka. *Asian Development Review*, *36*(2), 185–214. https://doi.org/10.1162/adev_a_00136.
90 International Organization for Migration. (2016). *Assessing the climate change environmental degradation and migration nexus in South Asia*. IOM.
91 GEF Small Grants Programme, Coping with climate change and variability.
92 Ibid.
93 SLYCAN Trust, 2019.
94 International Organization for Migration. (2018a). *IOM Sri Lanka country strategy 2018–2020*. Author; International Organization for Migration, *Migration governance snapshot*.
95 Boas et al., Climate migration myths.
96 Ibid.
97 International Organization for Migration, *Migration and climate change*.
98 Prabhakar, S. V., Shaw, R., Rüttinger, L., & Mori, H. (2017). *Climate-fragility risks in Asia: The development nexus*. Adelphi/Institute for Global Environmental Strategies.
99 SLYCAN Trust, 2019.
100 Asian Development Bank et al., *Labor migration in Asia*.
101 Ministry of Sustainable Development, Wildlife and Regional Development. (2018). *Sri Lanka voluntary national review on the status of implementing sustainable development goals*. Author.
102 Government of Sri Lanka. (2017). *Vision 2025. A country enriched*. Government of Sri Lanka; (Amarathunga, 2019)
103 Ministry of Health. (2013). *Sri Lanka national migration health policy*. Ministry of Health of Sri Lanka.
104 Ibid.
105 International Organization for Migration, *Migration governance snapshot*.
106 Ministry for Foreign Employment Promotion and Welfare. (2008). *National labour migration policy for Sri Lanka*. Ministry for Foreign Employment Promotion and Welfare.
107 Ministry of Health, *Sri Lanka national migration health policy*.
108 United Nations Office for Disaster Risk Reduction, *Disaster risk reduction in Sri Lanka*.
109 Dazé, A. (2019). *Alignment to advance climate-resilient development. Country case study: Sri Lanka*. NAP Global Network.
110 United Nations Office for Disaster Risk Reduction, *Disaster risk reduction in Sri Lanka*.
111 Ibid.
112 Government of Sri Lanka, *Vision 2025*.
113 SLYCAN Trust, 2019; SLYCAN Trust. (2021). *Discussion brief: Climate risk management and finance in Sri Lanka*. Author.
114 UNFCCC. (2020). *Interim NDC registry*. Retrieved from https://www4.unfccc.int/sites/ndcstaging/Pages/Home.aspx.
115 Ministry of Mahaweli Development and Environment, *National adaptation plan for climate change impacts in Sri Lanka*.
116 Ministry of Mahaweli Development and Environment, *Nationally determined contributions*.
117 Ministry of Environment. (2021). *Nationally determined contributions (updated submission)*. Ministry of Environment of Sri Lanka.
118 United Nations Framework Convention on Climate Change. (2019). *Warsaw international mechanism for loss and damage*. Retrieved from https://unfccc.int/topics/adaptation-and-resilience/workstreams/loss-and-damage-ld/warsaw-international-mechanism-for-loss-and-damage.

119 United Nations Framework Convention on Climate Change. (2020, June 28). *United Nations climate change*. Retrieved from https://unfccc.int/wim-excom/sub-groups/TFD#eq-1.
120 Task Force on Displacement. (2018). *Report of the task force on displacement*. UNFCCC Secretariat, Task Force on Displacement.
121 SLYCAN Trust. (2022). *Scoping paper: Integrating climate-related human mobility into nationally determined contributions and national adaptation plans. Human mobility in the context of climate change #5*. Author.
122 Ministry of Sustainable Development, Wildlife and Regional Development, *Sri Lanka voluntary national review on the status of implementing sustainable development goals*.
123 Brown, S., Budimir, M. U., Crawford, S., Clements, R., & Sneddon, A. (2019). *Gender and age inequality of disaster risk: Research paper*. UNICEF and UN Women.
124 Siriwardhana, C., Wickramage, K., Jayaweera, K., Adikari, A., Weerawarna, S., Van Bortel, T., . . . Sumathipala, A. (2013). Impact of economic labour migration: A qualitative exploration of left-behind family member perspectives in Sri Lanka. *Journal of Immigrant and Minority Health*, *17*(3), 885–894. https://doi.org/10.1007/s10903-013-9951-0.
125 Department of Census and Statistics, *Quarterly report of the Sri Lanka labour force survey*.
126 Asian Development Bank, 2016.
127 Cortes, G. (2016). Women and migrations: Those who stay. *EchoGéo*, *37*. https://doi.org/10.4000/echogeo.14892.
128 International Labour Organization. (2018a). *Assessment of the effects of annual drought and floods on child labour (hazardous and non-hazardous) and child welfare in Sri Lanka*. ILO Country Office for Sri Lanka and the Maldives.
129 Save the Children. (2013). *Sri Lanka's missing mothers. Working paper on the effects of maternal migration on children*. Save the Children.
130 Epidemiology Unit, Ministry of Health, Nutrition & Indigenous Medicine, *Weekly epidemiological report 28th–3rd February 2017*; Epidemiology Unit, Ministry of Health, Nutrition & Indigenous Medicine, *Weekly epidemiological report 4th–10th February 2017*.
131 Ibid.
132 Food and Agriculture Organization. (2020, June 28). Making migration a choice: Investing in food security and rural development. *FAO in Sri Lanka*. Retrieved from www.fao.org/srilanka/news/detail-events/en/c/1072652/.
133 Epidemiology Unit, Ministry of Health, Nutrition & Indigenous Medicine, *Weekly epidemiological report 28th–3rd February 2017*; Epidemiology Unit, Ministry of Health, Nutrition & Indigenous Medicine, *Weekly epidemiological report 4th–10th February 2017*.
134 Siriwardhana et al., Impact of economic labour migration.
135 Ibid.
136 Food and Agriculture Organization, *Country gender assessment of agriculture and the rural sector in Sri Lanka*.
137 GenderCC – Women for Climate Justice. (2020, June 28). Migration, gender and climate change. *GenderCC – Women for Climate Justice*. Retrieved from www.gendercc.net/gender-climate/migration.html.
138 Chindarkar, N. (2012). Gender and climate change-induced migration: Proposing a framework for analysis. *Environmental Research Letters*, 7(2). https://doi.org/10.1088/1748-9326/7/2/025601.
139 McNamara, K., Farbotko, C., Thornton, F., Dun, O., Ransan-Cooper, H., Chevalier, E., & Lkhagvasuren, P. (2017). Environment and migration experts: Who are they, and what are their views? *Migration, Environment and Climate Change: Policy Brief Series*, *3*(2).

140 Samaratunga et al., *Impact of migration and remittances on investment in agriculture and food security in Sri Lanka.*
141 Asian Development Bank, *Ending water scarcity in Sri Lanka's dry zone.*
142 Disaster Management Centre. (2017). *Annual report 2017.* Disaster Management of Centre of Sri Lanka.
143 Government of Sri Lanka, *Vision 2025.*
144 GEF Small Grants Programme, Coping with climate change and variability.
145 Steiner, A., Aguilar, G., Bomba, K., Bonilla, J. P., Campbell, A., Echeverria, R., Gandhi, R., Hedegaard, C., Holdorf, D., Ishii, N., Quinn, K., Ruter, B., Sunga, I., Sukhdev, P., Verghese, S., Voegele, J., Winters, P., Campbell, B., Dinesh, D., Huyer, S., Jarvis, A., Loboguerrero Rodriguez, A. M., Millan, A., Thornton, P., Wollenberg, L., & Zebiak, S. (2020). *Actions to transform food systems under climate change.* CGIAR Research Program on Climate Change, Agriculture and Food Security.
146 GEF Small Grants Programme, Coping with climate change and variability.
147 CGIAR Research Program on Climate Change, Agriculture and Food Security. (2015). *Putting farmers at the Centre of Climate Information Services.* CGIAR.
148 Global Facility for Disaster Reduction and Recovery. (2015). *Stories of impact. Addressing climate risks in Sri Lanka.* World Bank Group.
149 Food and Agriculture Organization, Making migration a choice.
150 Jobbins, G., Langdown, I., & Bernard, G. (2018). *Water and sanitation, migration and the 2030 agenda for sustainable development.* Overseas Development Institute.

Appendix

Table A.1 Human development indicators for South Asia

Country	*HDI*	*GDI*	*CHI*	*MPI*	*Life*	*Schooling*	*GNI/C*	*Literacy*	*E/W/S*
Afghanistan	0.496	0.723	N/A	0.272	64.5	10.1/3.9	1,746	43.02%	97/67/43
Bangladesh	0.614	0.895	23.6	0.198	72.3	11.2/6.1	4,057	73.91%	81/97/48
Bhutan	0.617	0.893	26.3	0.175	71.5	12.1/3.1	8,609	66.56%	97/97/69
India	0.647	0.892	25.7	0.123	69.4	12.3 6.5	6,829	74.37%	89/93/60
Maldives	0.719	0.939	20.4	0.003	78.6	12.1/6.8	12,549	97.74%	100/99/99
Nepal	0.579	0.897	24.9	0.148	70.5	12.2/4.9	2,748	67.91%	95/89/62
Pakistan	0.560	0.747	30.2	0.198	67.1	8.5/5.2	5,190	59.13%	54/91/60
Sri Lanka	0.780	0.938	11.8	0.009	76.8	14.0/11.1	11,611	91.71%	97/89/96

Source: Data for the South Asian region taken from (United Nations Development Programme, 2019), (The World Bank, 2020), and (Department of Census and Statistics, 2019). Covers the human development index (HDI), the gender development index (GDI), the coefficient of human inequality (CHI), the multidimensional poverty index (MPI), life expectancy at birth, expected/mean years of schooling, estimated gross national income per capita (in USD), total adult literacy, and rural population with access to electricity/basic drinking water sources/basic sanitation facilities (E/W/S).

Index

For Product Safety Concerns and Information please contact our EU
representative GPSR@taylorandfrancis.com
Taylor & Francis Verlag GmbH, Kaufingerstraße 24, 80331 München, Germany

www.ingramcontent.com/pod-product-compliance
Ingram Content Group UK Ltd.
Pitfield, Milton Keynes, MK11 3LW, UK
UKHW020142200926
475702UK00005B/871

* 9 7 8 1 0 3 2 3 4 4 2 8 7 *